0112
#48.00

The Gender of Constitutional Jurisprudence

To explain how constitutions shape and are shaped by women's lives, the contributors to this volume examine constitutional cases pertaining to women in twelve countries. Analyzing jurisprudence about reproductive, sexual, familial, socioeconomic, and democratic rights, they focus constructively on women's claims to equality, asking who makes these claims, what constitutional rights inform them, how they have evolved, what arguments work in defending them, and how they relate to other national issues. Their findings reveal significant similarities in outcomes and in reasoning about women's constitutional rights in these twelve countries, challenging the tradition of distinguishing constitutional jurisprudence depending on whether the country has a written or unwritten constitution, subscribes to civil or common law, is a federal or unitary state, limits constitutional adjudication to the public rather than also including the private domain, accords international norms binding or subject to incorporation force, or relies on a specialized or general court to adjudicate constitutional matters.

Beverley Baines is Associate Professor in the Faculty of Law at Queen's University, Kingston, Ontario, Canada, where she originated the Law Gender Equality and Feminist Jurisprudence courses. Her research interests include issues in constitutional law, feminist legal theory, anti-discrimination law, multiculturalism, and equality rights. She has contributed chapters to *Conversation among Friends – Entre Amies: Women and Constitutional Reform*, *Changing Patterns: Women in Canada*, and *Women and the Constitution*, and she has written articles for major Canadian and international journals.

Ruth Rubio-Marin is Associate Professor of Constitutional Law at the University of Seville, Spain. She is author *of Immigration as a Democratic Challenge: Citizenship and Inclusion in Germany and the United States* and of articles on language rights, nationality, immigration, and gender in law. She has taught at several North American academic institutions, including Princeton University and Columbia Law School, and is currently a member of the Hauser Global Law School Program at New York University.

The Gender of Constitutional Jurisprudence

Edited by

BEVERLEY BAINES
Queen's University

RUTH RUBIO-MARIN
Universidad de Sevilla

CAMBRIDGE
UNIVERSITY PRESS

K
3243
.G46
2005

PUBLISHED BY THE PRESS SYNDICATE OF THE UNIVERSITY OF CAMBRIDGE
The Pitt Building, Trumpington Street, Cambridge, United Kingdom

CAMBRIDGE UNIVERSITY PRESS
The Edinburgh Building, Cambridge CB2 2RU, UK
40 West 20th Street, New York, NY 10011-4211, USA
477 Williamstown Road, Port Melbourne, VIC 3207, Australia
Ruiz de Alarcón 13, 28014 Madrid, Spain
Dock House, The Waterfront, Cape Town 8001, South Africa

http://www.cambridge.org

© Cambridge University Press 2005

First published 2005

Printed in the United States of America

Typeface Sabon 10/12 pt.   *System* LATEX 2$_\varepsilon$ [TB]

A catalog record for this book is available from the British Library.

Library of Congress Cataloging in Publication Data
The gender of constitutional jurisprudence / edited by
Beverley Baines, Ruth Rubio-Marin.
   p. cm.
Includes bibliographical references and index.
ISBN 0-521-82336-6 – ISBN 0-521-53027-X (pb.)
1. Women's rights. 2. Constitutional law. I. Baines, Beverley, 1941–
II. Rubio-Marin, Ruth.
K3243.C66   2004
342.08′78–dc22   2004045100

ISBN 0 521 82336 6 hardback
ISBN 0 521 53027 X paperback

Contents

List of Contributors

Beverley Baines, B.A. (McGill), LL.B. (Queen's), is Associate Professor in the Faculty of Law at Queen's University, Kingston, Ontario, Canada, where she originated the Women and the Law (now Law Gender Equality) and Feminist Jurisprudence courses. Currently she teaches Public Law, Constitutional Law, and Equality Rights under the Charter in the Faculty of Law, as well as Law and Public Policy in the School of Public Policy. She is cross-appointed to the Department of Women's Studies where she was Co-ordinator, 1991–3. Her research interests include issues in constitutional law, feminist legal theory, antidiscrimination law, multiculturalism, and equality rights. She has published articles in Canadian and international journals, as well as contributing chapters on women and constitutional law to *Conversations among Friends – Entre Amies: Women and Constitutional Reform*, *Changing Patterns: Women in Canada*, and *Women and the Constitution*.

Hilal Elver is Distinguished Visiting Professor at the UCSB Global and International Studies Program. She was adjunct Professor of Comparative Law at Rutgers University School of Law, Newark, NJ. She earned her bachelor degree in Law and her Ph.D. in Law from the University of Ankara, School of Law in Turkey, where she taught Roman Law, Comparative Law, International Environmental Law, and Legal Status of Women until 1993. In the 1990s, the Turkish government appointed her as the Legal Advisor to the Ministry of Environment, then as the Legal Advisor and the General Director of Women's Status under the auspices of the Prime Ministry. In 1994–6, she taught environmental diplomacy as the UNEP Chair at the Mediterranean Academy of Diplomatic Studies in Malta. She was a Fulbright Scholar at the University of Michigan School of Law in 1993 and Visiting Fellow at the Center of International Studies at Princeton University in 1997. She has published several articles on environmental law and women's issues in Turkey. Recently, she published a book entitled *Peaceful Uses of International Rivers: The Case of Euphrates and Tigris Rivers* (Transnational Publishers).

Alda Facio is a jurist, writer, and international expert on gender and women's human rights. She has been a visiting professor on women's human rights in several universities in Spain and Latin America. In 1997, she co-founded the Women's Caucus for Gender Justice in the International Criminal Court and became its first director. In 1996, she received the first Women's Human Rights Award from Women, Law and Development International. Since 1990, she has been the Director of the Women, Justice, and Gender Program at the Latin American United Nations Institute for Crime Prevention (ILANUD). She designed a methodology for analyzing the law and legal traditions from a gender-sensitive perspective, which is in its fifth edition. She also has been a judge in the District Court of Guadalupe in Costa Rica, the Founder and General Director of the Costa Rican National Dance Company, a professor of Roman Law at the Law Faculty of the University of Costa Rica, and for six years she was the Costa Rican Alternate Delegate to the United Nations Offices in Geneva.

Ran Hirschl is an assistant professor of political science at the University of Toronto. His primary areas of interest are comparative public law, constitutional rights, and judicial politics. He holds bachelor's, master's, and LL.B. degrees from Tel-Aviv University, as well as a master of arts, master of philosophy, and a Ph.D. from Yale University. He has published extensively on comparative constitutional law and politics in journals such as *Law & Social Inquiry*, *Comparative Politics*, *Human Rights Quarterly*, *American Journal of Comparative Law*, *University of Richmond Law Review*, *Stanford Journal of International Law*, and *Canadian Journal of Law and Jurisprudence*, as well as in several acclaimed edited volumes. He is the author of *Towards Juristocracy: A Comparative Inquiry into the Origins and Consequences of the New Constitutionalism* (Harvard University Press, 2003).

Saras Jagwanth is a senior lecturer in the Department of Public Law at the University of Cape Town, where she teaches Constitutional and Administrative Law. She has a special interest in equality law. She has published in this area and is the coeditor of a volume on *Women and the Law* (HSRC Press).

Rodrigo Jiménez Sandoval is a Costa Rican lawyer and consultant specializing in the rights of people with disabilities and women's rights. He studied Law at the University of Costa Rica and since 1984 has been Professor of the International Law course at the Autonomous Central American University (UACA). He also has a degree in Education, and a Master's in Business. For more than ten years he has worked as legal advisor for many Costa Rican NGOs, including the Helen Keller Association, the Down Syndrome Association, and the Costa Rican Association of Handicapped People. He has also been a board member of the National Rehabilitation Council and of the National Rehabilitation Patronate. For eight years he served as an international consultant for the Inter-American Institute of Human Rights

(IIHR). He has also worked for the United Nations Development Program (UNDP), the World Bank, and the Fundación Arias para la Paz y el Progreso Humano. Since 1995, he has been Sub-Director of the Women, Justice, and Gender Program of ILANUD. He has written various books and many magazine articles on persons with disabilities and women's rights.

Isabel Karpin, B.A./LL.B. (Sydney), LLM. (Harvard), JS.D. (Columbia), is a senior lecturer at the University of Sydney, Faculty of Law. She specializes in the areas of feminist legal theory, constitutional law, law and culture, and health law. Her doctoral work at Columbia University, entitled *Embodying Justice: Legal Responses to the Transgressive Body*, examined the regulation of marginalized bodies, with a particular focus on the pregnant woman. With Professor Martha Fineman of Cornell Law School she coedited *Mothers in Law*, as well as publishing several book chapters and articles in both international and Australian journals. She is currently involved in two major research projects in the areas of new media and regulation of emergent genetic technologies.

Eric Millard is Professor of Legal Theory and Public Law at the University of Paris-Sud. His interests include legal epistemology, theory of the state, human rights, social politics, and gender and law. He is the author of *Famille et droit public* (Librairie générale de droit et jurisprudence, Paris, 1995) and co-author of several books, including *La Parité, enjeux et mise en oeuvre* (Presses universitaires du Mirail, 1998). He has written articles dealing with family law, constitutional law, social law, and legal theory. A graduate of Toulouse University, he holds a Ph.D. in public law from Lyon University (1994). He has been a professor at the Universities of Saint-Etienne, Toulouse, and Perpignan and a member of the Institut Universitaire de France. He gave lectures or courses at the Universities of Helsinki, Oslo, Copenhagen, Tallinn, Bologna, Casablanca, Baltimore, Montréal, and Queen's, as well as at many French universities.

Martha I. Morgan is the Robert S. Vance Professor of Law at the University of Alabama School of Law, teaching courses in constitutional law, civil rights legislation, comparative constitutional law, and gender and sexuality law. She received a B.S. from the University of Alabama and a J.D. from the George Washington University National Law Center. She has carried out research on women and constitution-making in Colombia and Nicaragua, as well as examining other law reform efforts by women in Costa Rica, Guatemala, and Nicaragua. Recently, her research has focused on the emerging gender jurisprudence in Latin America and on the domestic incorporation of gender rights contained in international human rights law. She serves as a consultant to the Women, Justice, and Gender Program of the United Nations Latin American Institute for the Prevention of Crime and Treatment of Delinquency in San José, Costa Rica, and to the Tigray Women's Law

Project of the Mekelle University Faculty of Law in Mekelle, Ethiopia. She also serves on the boards of directors of the Equal Justice Initiative of Alabama and the American Civil Liberties Union of Alabama.

Christina Murray is Professor of Constitutional and Human Rights Law at the University of Cape Town and Deputy Dean of the Law Faculty. Between 1994 and 1996, she served on a panel of seven experts advising the South African Constitutional Assembly in drafting the "final" Constitution. She has taught and written on the law of contract, human rights law (and particularly issues relating to gender equality and African customary law), international law, and constitutional law. She is the director of the Law, Race, and Gender Research Unit at the University of Cape Town. The Unit is concerned with judges' education on matters relating to race, gender, and cultural diversity.

Martha C. Nussbaum is Ernst Freund Distinguished Service Professor of Law and Ethics at the University of Chicago, appointed in the Philosophy Department, Law School, and Divinity School. She is an Associate in the Classics Department, a member of the Board of the Human Rights Program, and an Affiliate of the Committee on Southern Asian Studies. She is the founder and Coordinator of the new Center for Comparative Constitutionalism. Her most recent books are *Upheavals of Thought: The Intelligence of Emotions* (2001) and *Women and Human Development: The Capabilities Approach* (2000).

Karen O'Connell is a human rights lawyer with degrees in law and humanities from the University of Sydney. She is a doctoral candidate at Columbia University School of Law and currently holds an Audrey Harrison Commemorative Fellowship from the Australian Federation of University Women. Her research interests include feminist theory, technology, and human rights.

Ruth Rubio-Marin is Associate Professor of Constitutional Law at the University of Seville, Spain. She is author of *Immigration as a Democratic Challenge: Citizenship and Inclusion in Germany and the United States* (Cambridge University Press, 2000) and coauthor of *Mujer e Igualdad: la norma y su aplicación* (*Women and Equality: The Norm and Its Application*) (Instituto Andaluz de la Mujer, 1999) and of several articles on language rights, nationality, immigration, and gender in the law. She has taught at different North American academic institutions, including Princeton University and Columbia Law School, and she is currently part of the Hauser Global Law School Program at New York University.

Blanca Rodríguez Ruiz is a lecturer in constitutional law at the University of Seville, Spain. She received her Ph.D. in law from the European University Institute (Florence, Italy) and enjoyed a long postdoctoral research stay in Frankfurt am Main (Germany). Her work takes a discourse-theoretical approach to constitutional rights and gender equality issues. Her publications include "Discourse Theory and the Addressees of Basic Rights," in *Rechts-theorie*, vol. 32 (2001), pp. 87–133; "Familia e igualdad entre los sexos en el Estado Constitucional: una mirada crítica al Estado alemán," *Revista de la Facultad de Derecho de la Universidad de Granada*, vol. 4 (2001), pp. 311–40; "The Right to Privacy: A Discourse-Theoretical Approach," *Ratio Juris*, vol. 11 (1998), pp. 155–67; and *Privacy in Telecommunications: A European and an American Approach* (The Hague: Kluwer Law International, 1997). She recently visited at the Gender Institute in the London School of Economics.

Ute Sacksofsky is a Full Professor of Public Law and Comparative Public Law at the University Frankfurt a.M., Germany, since 1999, serving also as codirector of the Cornelia-Goethe-Center for Gender Studies. She served as law clerk to Justice Böckenförde at the Federal Constitutional Court (*Bundesverfassungsgericht*) from 1991 to 1995, having received her doctorate in law from the University of Freiburg in 1990, her Master of Public Administration from Harvard University in 1986, and her law degree from the University of Freiburg in 1983. Awarded various prizes and scholarships, she has been a legal expert in various hearings before Parliament and she has written extensively on gender and law (especially with respect to the constitutional guarantee of equality).

Ayelet Shachar is an assistant professor of law at the Faculty of Law University of Toronto. She has written extensively on group rights, gender equality, citizenship theory, and immigration law. She is the author of the award-winning book *Multicultural Jurisdictions: Cultural Differences and Women's Rights* (Cambridge University Press, 2001). Her recent publications appear in the *Cardozo Law Review*, *Georgetown Immigration Law Journal*, *Harvard Civil Rights–Civil Liberties Law Review*, *Journal of Political Philosophy*, *NOMOS*, and *Political Theory*, as well as several acclaimed edited volumes. Professor Shachar holds bachelor's degrees in law and political science and master's and doctoral degrees in law from Yale University. She served as law clerk to Deputy Chief Justice Aharon Barak of the Supreme Court of Israel. She is a past member of the Institute for Advanced Study at Princeton, and a current Fellow of the Institute for Women's Studies and Gender Studies at the University of Toronto.

Reva B. Siegel is Nicholas deB. Katzenbach Professor of Law at the Yale Law School. A graduate of the Yale Law School, Professor Siegel began her teaching career at the University of California at Berkeley and has been a member of the Yale faculty since 1994. She teaches constitutional law, antidiscrimination law, and legal history. Professor Siegel draws on legal history to explore contemporary questions of civil rights, and she has written on topics including the regulation of abortion, domestic labor, domestic violence, sexual harassment, and a variety of questions concerning the law of race discrimination. Much of this work situates law in a sociohistorical account of status inequality – demonstrating how the understandings and practices that sustain social stratification vary by group and evolve as contested over time. Professor Siegel is now working on a series of projects concerning popular constitutionalism and legislative enforcement of constitutional rights that challenge the new federalism restrictions the Court is imposing on Congress's power to enact civil rights legislation.

Acknowledgments

Like most of its kind, this project is the result of many joint efforts. It initially was conceived in a series of informal meetings held between the coeditors during Ruth Rubio-Marin's research stay at Queen's University in Kingston, Ontario. That stay was made possible by a Fellowship from the Canadian Embassy in Madrid, Spain. The idea was to hold a small conference and a series of workshops and internal sessions to discuss the themes and the structure that a gender focused book on comparative constitutional jurisprudence ought to have. This gathering took place in June 2000, and for their funding contribution we thank the Law Foundation of Ontario, the Office of Research Services at Queen's University, the Department of Constitutional Law in the University of Seville, and, above all, the Spanish Ministry for Social Affairs and the Foundation "El Monte." Finally, for their contributions in bringing the volume to fruition, we are pleased to recognize the insightful comments of Cambridge University Press's readers, the editorial support of Lewis Bateman at the Press, and Nigel McCready and Sharron Sluiter for their technical assistance at Queen's.

Beverley Baines, Kingston, Ontario
Ruth Rubio-Marin, Sevilla
October 2003

The Gender of Constitutional Jurisprudence

Introduction

Toward a Feminist Constitutional Agenda

Beverley Baines and Ruth Rubio-Marin

Women around the world increasingly resort to constitutional litigation to resolve controversies involving gender issues. This litigation has involved claims for political participation, freedom from discrimination and violence, sexual and reproductive rights, employment and civic rights, matrimonial and familial autonomy, as well as other social and economic rights. For the most part, constitutional law scholars have analyzed this jurisprudence doctrinally, confining their research mainly to individual flashpoint issues such as abortion or affirmative action. Such studies are usually framed by national boundaries; and, when comparative, their reach is often limited to a small number of countries sharing the same legal tradition. This explains the need for a feminist analysis of constitutional jurisprudence in which gender becomes the focal point and for a broader comparative constitutional law approach that encompasses both of the world's major legal traditions. Those are the focal points of this book.

Not long ago a feminist constitutional law scholar asked: "Can constitutions be for women too"?[1] Cognizant of the dangers of overgeneralizing about women's experiences and concerns, she was cautious about responding affirmatively. Nevertheless, her message was clear. Although women may be un-, or under-, represented among the ranks of those who draft domestic constitutions, we are not entirely without constitutional agency. Whether constitutional language adverts or not to women, we still advance claims for constitutional rights. And, despite legal theory's conventional assumptions about defining constitutionalism as "the relationship among a constitution's authority, its identity, and possible methodologies of interpretation,"[2]

---

[1] Donna Greschner, "Can Constitutions Be for Women Too?," in Dawn Currie and B. MacLean, eds., *The Administration of Justice* (Saskatoon: University of Saskatchewan Social Research Unit, 1986) 20.

[2] Larry Alexander, ed., *Constitutionalism: Philosophical Foundations* (Cambridge: Cambridge University Press, 1998) 1.

feminist theorists have not hesitated to conceptualize it more contextually, as illustrated by the feminist philosopher who concluded "the constitution we have depends upon the constitution we make and do and are."[3] Thus women activists, lawyers, judges, and scholars appear to agree that what is at stake no longer is whether constitutions can be for women but, rather, when and how to ensure that they recognize and promote women's rights.

The "when" question is easy to answer. Now. It is timely to assert, litigate, protect, and promote the constitutional rights of women because of the confluence of two twentieth-century developments. One is scholarly and the other juridical. In the first place, feminist scholarship has begun to embrace the study of legal phenomena. Of course, analyzing law from the perspective of gender is by no means new. In the eighteenth century, Mary Wollstonecraft issued her *Vindication of the Rights of Women*, a publication that clearly entailed commentary on legal rules that impacted on women's lives.[4] By the closing decades of the twentieth century, a number of scholars from various countries had published treatises on feminist legal theory, including therein works by the Norwegian scholar Tove Stang Dahl, British scholars such as Katherine O'Donovan and Carol Smart, the American scholar Catharine MacKinnon, and the Australian scholar Carole Pateman.[5] Moreover, some contemporary feminist legal scholarship is comparatively but not consistently constitutionally oriented.[6] The burgeoning literature on comparative constitutional law covers a wide range of topics, such as constitutionalism, rights, judicial review, federalism, governance, and economic development, while being virtually devoid of research that pertains to women's rights. In other words, there is a huge gap – a gender gap – in contemporary comparative constitutional analysis.[7] The same cannot be said

---

[3] Hanna Fenichel Pitkin, "The Idea of a Constitution" (1987) 37 *J. Legal Educ.* 167 at 168, continuing: "Except insofar as we *do*, what we think we *have* is powerless and will soon disappear. Except insofar as, in doing, we respect what we *are* – both our actuality and the genuine potential within us – our doing will be a disaster" (emphasis in original).

[4] Mary Wollstonecraft, *A Vindication of the Rights of Women, with Strictures on Political and Moral Subjects* (London: John Johnson, 1794).

[5] Tove Stang Dahl, *Women's Law: An Introduction to Feminist Jurisprudence* (Oslo: Norwegian University Press, 1987); Katherine O'Donovan, *Sexual Divisions in Law* (London: Weidenfeld and Nicholson, 1985); Carol Smart, *Feminism and the Power of Law* (London: Routledge, 1989); Catharine A. MacKinnon, *Feminism Unmodified: Discourses on Life and Law* (Cambridge, MA: Harvard University Press, 1987); Carole Pateman, *The Sexual Contract* (Stanford: Stanford University Press, 1988).

[6] Susan Bazilli, ed., *Putting Women on the Agenda* (Johannesburg: Ravan Press, 1991); Fiona Beveridge, Sue Nott and Kylie Stephen, eds., *Making Women Count: Integrating Gender into Law and Policy-making* (Aldershot: Ashgate Publishing Ltd., 2000).

[7] A striking exception is the recent publication of Fiona Beveridge, Sue Nott and Kylie Stephen, eds., *Making Women Count: Integrating Gender into Law and Policy-making* (Aldershot: Ashgate Publishing Ltd., 2000).

of comparative law scholarship in general.[8] Nor does it extend to the study of historically disadvantaged groups other than women. Recently, for instance, comparative constitutional law scholars not only examined contemporary ethnic group conflicts[9] but also studied the legal claims of religious communities.[10]

In the second place, and coincidentally with this spate of feminist legal theorizing, have appeared constitutional doctrines that impact or have the potential to impact on women's issues. The same was not true for women who entered the twentieth century. The constitutional rights of women received little or no juridical recognition until well into the twentieth century. Moreover, this holds true irrespective of whether a country is relatively new to the world's stage or whether its roots go back for centuries. It should come as no surprise, therefore, that much still remains to be done in the twenty-first century to promote the process of "constituting" (or recognizing, sustaining and promoting) women's rights.

This brings us to the "how" question, which is more a challenge than a question. Writ large, the immediate question is how to use constitution making processes and, more than anything, the existing constitutional judicial processes to achieve gender equality for women. The challenge is complex because feminists and judges emphasize different material facts, rely on different terminology, reason quite distinctively, and do not necessarily share the same goals when they examine the issue of gender equality. Most feminists believe gender equality will not be achieved until the subordination of women is overcome. In contrast, some jurists deny that women's subordination is real,[11] whereas others question the value of relying on constitutional strategies for redress.[12] To give yet a further example, although legal reasoning

---

[8] See, for all, V. Jackson and M. Tushnet, *Comparative Constitutional Law*, University Casebook Series (New York, New York Foundation Press, 1999); and N. Dorsen, M. Rosenfeld, A. Sajó and S. Baer, *Comparative Constitutionalism: Cases and Materials*, American Casebook Series (St. Paul, MN: Thomson/West, 2003).

[9] E.g., Yash Ghai, ed., *Autonomy and Ethnicity: Negotiating Competing Claims in Multi-ethnic States* (Cambridge: Cambridge University Press, 2000).

[10] Peter W. Edge and Graham Harvey, eds., *Law and Religion in Contemporary Society: Communities, Individualism, and the State* (Burlington, VI: Ashgate Publishing Co., 2000).

[11] E.g., *Gould v. Yukon Order of Pioneers* (1991), 14 C.H.R.R. D/176 (Wachowich J.) at D/190, discussing why the sex equality provision in the Canadian Constitution might not be "available to combat allegedly discriminatory behaviour against all women. In my view women, as a group, are not what is commonly understood to be a 'minority' in Canadian society. The intervener stated that a recent Yukon census showed that 53.1 percent of the population was male, while 46.9 percent was female. Whether this constitutes a minority that can be discriminated against is in doubt."

[12] E.g., Robert H. Bork, *The Tempting of America: The Political Seduction of the Law* (New York: Simon & Schuster Inc., 1990) 330: "I had taken the position that, except for this rational basis test, the equal protection clause [in the American Constitution] should be restricted to race and ethnicity. . . . There is unlikely to be much work for the equal protection clause to do with respect to governmental distinctions between the sexes because legislators are hardly

is invariably deductive, feminists are as likely, if not more likely, to reason inductively. Under these circumstances, common sense suggests developing the relationship between feminist theorizing and constitutional reasoning in several stages, rather than thrusting them together and holding our breath as we wait to see if the marriage will endure.

More specifically, we advocate developing a feminist constitutional agenda, which like any good ordering device should admit of some degree of flexibility. At a minimum, however, this feminist constitutional agenda should address the position of women with respect to: (i) constitutional agency; (ii) constitutional rights; (iii) constitutionally structured diversity; (iv) constitutional equality; and give special attention to (v) women's reproductive rights and sexual autonomy; (vi) women's rights within the family; (vii) women's socioeconomic development and democratic rights.

This listing is lengthy. However, it would be even longer were it to contain all the context- and fact-driven issues that could constitute an agenda structured solely along feminist lines. Indeed, its length offers no consolation to women who are lesbian, bisexual, or transgendered, women with disabilities, and/or elder women who do not see their rights reflected on it. They will assume their claims lie buried within the listed categories. Moreover, this listing is also vulnerable to the criticism that some issues might overlap more than one theme. These shortcomings notwithstanding, the virtue of making our proposed feminist constitutional agenda as extensive as it is, lies in the fact that it is significantly more detailed than most of the agendas that are designed from a purportedly "gender neutral" constitutional law perspective. Such scholarship tends to address issues as if they pertain either to federalism and separation of powers, or to constitutional rights. Typically, the latter research will be further bifurcated into studies focusing on one of two main strategies for dealing with rights conflicts. The more popular strategy is autonomy, which encompasses claims that range from privacy claims to the collective claim of self-determination.[13] Thus, when perceived in terms of self-determination, autonomy is the rallying cry of many indigenous, racial, ethnic, and linguistic groups. On occasion, most of these rights-seeking groups also turn to the other major strategy for managing rights conflicts, which is equality. Although these three major constitutional law categories – federalism, autonomy, and equality – might capture women's claims, they also might distort and/or impoverish them, viz. should claims of democratic underrepresentation be subsumed under autonomy or equality, or are they *sui generis*? Also, with only three categories at their disposal,

likely to impose invidious discriminations upon a group that comprises a slight majority of the electorate."

[13] Yash Ghai, ed., *Autonomy and Ethnicity: Negotiating Competing Claims in Multi-ethnic States* (Cambridge: Cambridge University Press, 2000) at 1: "One of the most sought after, and resisted, devices for conflict management is autonomy."

scholars might be tempted to portray the relationships among them as adversarial, viz. treating pornography as a contest between the pornographers' autonomy and the equality rights of women and girls, which would neglect entirely the entitlement of the latter to self-determination or autonomy.

Thus, we propose to design a feminist constitutional agenda as a middle course between the extensive and reality-driven delineation of issues that feminist scholars advance and the more rigidly bounded, often threefold, doctrinal categorization found in constitutional law scholarship. The main purpose of this introduction is to raise some of the major questions that should be addressed under each of the headings described in the hope that, when approaching the different national experiences that are described in this book, the reader will be able to identify the span of possible answers and assess their practical impact. The reader will realize that the themes are in fact drawn from the national chapters that follow. Not every theme is found in every chapter, and some chapters may contain other themes that have not been explicitly added to this agenda. Knowing that some themes overlap, and that some themes should be but are not self-evident in our listing, we invite feminist constitutional law scholars to continue what we have begun by de- and reconstructing our agenda themes as part of our larger project of encouraging judicial recognition of the constitutional structures and rights necessary to overcome the subordination of women. Our primary goal is, in short, to identify, sustain and promote the constitutional norms and strategies that will achieve gender equality for women. To this end, we invite feminist, legal, and other interested scholars to think about constitutions in a gendered way.

The contributors to this volume have done precisely that. This book is designed to explore these themes as they are manifested in the constitutions and constitutional jurisprudence issued by the national courts in twelve countries: Australia, Canada, Colombia, Costa Rica, France, Germany, India, Israel, South Africa, Spain, Turkey, and the United States. These countries span several continents, cover diverse legal traditions and collectively represent constitutional regimes that were adopted over a period of almost three centuries. Although the overall scope of this coverage matters, there was no magic in the number of countries chosen. Rather inclusion was based on balancing a number of structural features, including representation of the major legal traditions (civil law and common law), governance structures (monarchy and republic), legislative regimes (parliamentary and presidential), adjudicative mechanisms (constitutional courts and general courts), and jurisdictional structures (federal unions and unitary states). Other factors that distinguish these countries include their racial, religious, linguistic, and cultural demographics. As well, these particular countries derive their constitutional rights from a wide range of sources including entrenched bills of rights, unwritten principles, ordinary statutes, and international human rights treaties. Arguably the more extensive the structural, social, and legal diversity of these countries, the more compelling the similarities, if any, that crystallize from analyzing their jurisprudence.

Even though each national contribution should be perceived as part of the larger enterprise of conceptualizing the themes on a feminist constitutional agenda, each also stands alone as a chapter describing that country's constitutional jurisprudence as it pertains to women. Crucial to the selection process was, therefore, the willingness of country contributors to examine the role of women as constitutional agents, analyzing their engagement in constitutional litigation and adjudication, as well as in constitution making and amending processes. We also encouraged contributors to highlight the most progressive element(s) of the constitutions and of the constitutional jurisprudence that national courts have adjudicated on behalf of women's claims in the hope of encouraging strategical extrapolation.

More specifically, we asked them to discuss who makes constitutional claims, what kinds of rights inform these claims, how these claims have evolved over time, what kinds of arguments work in defense of these claims, and how these claims relate to the larger social, economic and political issues that contemporary countries are facing. We urged them to provide a comprehensive reference to the most important case law and relevant constitutional provisions, as well as a brief bibliography that could serve as a guide for further research. The contributors, all of whom are academics and/or advocates on behalf of women's rights, remained true to their training as lawyers, responding both critically and constructively. Their chapters illuminate their constructive critiques partly by addressing selected common themes and partly by developing the most original themes that each national experience offers in terms of constitutional gender jurisprudence.

Three caveats should be borne in mind. First, our feminist constitutional agenda is just that, an agenda and not a recipe. We propose themes to open this field for further examination and not to foreclose alternative approaches. While trying to identify some of the factors that are to be taken into account in a gender-sensitive constitutional analysis and inviting the contributors to reflect upon them in the context of their national experiences, aware of the richness and intricacies of each constitutional system, we have purposefully avoided drawing direct causal-effect conclusions that might have been rightfully criticized as oversimplifications. Second, although we asked the country contributors to emphasize constitutional doctrine and jurisprudence, we do not intend to suggest that constitutional progress is synonymous with social progress. In some instances, law may be more often an aspiration than a set of binding norms; judiciary systems may be more or less reliable when it comes to applying doctrine; and in some countries the doctrines relevant to women's rights are too new and/or fragmentary to be coherently systematized. Third, even as a study of this kind invites extrapolation from one country to another, we recognize the need for carefully keeping in mind the deep differences that exist between and among countries not only culturally but also in terms of their legal traditions. Legal traditions vary according to the significance they attach to constitutional law, to competing sources of law including religious authorities, indigenous traditions, and international law, as well as to judicial review.

WOMEN AND CONSTITUTIONAL AGENCY

For centuries, states openly barred women from participating in civic life, whether as voters or legislators, lawyers or jurists. Men also monopolized constitutional activities. Not surprisingly, women's initial forays into the realm of constitution-making focused primarily on voting, although their strategies differed. On the one hand, white women in two Australian colonies were not only the first to receive the franchise, but also in 1901 they became the first women to vote on a constitution. On the other hand, following decades of lobbying, in 1920 Americans became the first to secure a constitutional amendment guaranteeing women the right to vote. Although these initial strategies were important, however, it is curious that they did not lead to any further formal constitutional changes for women in either country.

The embrace of formal equality and the explicit commitment to sex equality only became a general trend in postwar constitutionalism. Women's role in promoting those provisions is unclear. Given pervasive underrepresentation in legislative and constituent assemblies, it would not be surprising to find that their activities were limited. However, during the 1980s and 1990s, women began to engage actively in processes of general constitutional renewal. For instance, not only did Canadian women lobby to strengthen the sex equality guarantees newly entrenched in the Charter of Rights and Freedoms (1982), but also women in Colombia successfully advocated for gender equality and gender-related provisions in their new Constitution (1991), and South African women actively participated in the process of drafting their new Constitution (1996). Finally, by procuring an amendment (1999) that requires gender parity in selected electoral contests, French feminists may have portended a new era, one in which women could seek specific gender-related constitutional amendments as needed rather than only during times of general constitutional change.

The foregoing suggests women who are active in feminist movements have begun to identify constitutions and constitutional change as relevant to our lives. With more comparative analysis, we may better understand when to initiate constitutional change on behalf of women, whether to intervene in changes already underway, what strategies are appropriate to each context, and how best to connect the international with the national fora, how to engage other women in these processes, and what results are most likely to undermine the prevailing patterns of political, social, and economic subordination of women. Thus, politically speaking, there is much to learn from the roles women have already played in the constitution making and amending processes and initiatives.

The process of litigation offers women ways of developing and changing the meaning of constitutional norms. The country chapters in this volume exemplify this process at work, tantalizing us with questions of measurement (how active have women been in litigating?) and quality (what claims do women litigate and with what consequences?). More specifically with respect to the level of women's litigious activity, what institutional mechanisms are most likely to overcome conventional barriers to accessibility by helping women as a group to avail themselves of constitutional tools? The possibilities include the design of standing rules and class action rules, as well as the provision of funding for litigation, of officials who institute actions such as *ombudpersons*, or of organizations that specifically protect women's rights in constitutional litigation such as the Women's Legal Education and Action Fund (LEAF) in Canada or the more controversial Commission for Gender Equality in South Africa.

Understanding women's constitutional agency requires an understanding of the types of claims that women bring, and the constitutional strategies on which they rely. There is no question that, although the strongest emphasis has been on equality provisions, gender-related litigation has proceeded under most of the other rights-based provisions as well as under some federalism provisions. In this context, it is worth considering whether specific groups of women are more litigious than others and if so, how this impacts on the way in which doctrine is shaped. It also is interesting to observe to what extent men's agency has had an impact on women's. Moreover, gender-related doctrine may be affected in cases in which women are defendants or not even parties, as for example in most sexual assault prosecutions. Finally, any assessment of the quality of women's constitutional litigious agency would not be complete without an assessment of the difference, if any, that is made by having women on the final appellate courts that decide constitutional matters.

In sum, women's constitutional agency involves lobbying, legislating, litigating, and adjudicating. Although all of these roles are open to women, as the different chapters show, our entry is not commensurate with our numbers, suggesting invisible but real public constraints, perhaps not unlike the proverbial glass ceiling in the private workplace. Nor should women mistake bestowals of nice-sounding principles for the efforts of agency. As the Turkish experience shows, men can use women's equality for their own purpose. In other words, progress and agency need not go hand-in-hand.

WOMEN AND CONSTITUTIONAL RIGHTS

Constitutional rights provide women and other rights seekers with the tools to challenge state activity in the courts. They offer more protection than statutory and other nonconstitutional rights which may not constrain legislation. Also controversies involving statutory and other nonconstitutional rights are not necessarily resolved by courts; often they are designed to be heard at least initially, if not finally, by administrative tribunals or government officials.

Nevertheless, arguably there is one important respect in which statutory and other nonconstitutional rights might be perceived as offering better protection to rights seekers, especially rights seekers who are unaccustomed to the methodology of legal reasoning. Put simply, while constitutional provisions tend to have a greater visibility and seem to permeate more easily the general legal culture than statutory rights do, statutory rights are often detailed, making their meanings more transparent and accessible to rights seekers. In contrast, constitutional rights are usually expressed in terms of abstract generalities so that their meanings are dependent on the interpretations judges have ascribed to them. Thus, understanding constitutional rights involves understanding the claims litigants have raised and judges have adjudicated. In fact, this may make less relevant the varying degrees in which rights can be constitutionally framed, which, as the national cases addressed here show, range from extremely detailed formulations to very limited or even nonexistent.

In any event, the country chapters reveal that women's constitutional rights claims have encompassed a wide array of grounds. Some of these grounds have been unique to women from individual countries. For instance, women have constitutionally reacted against the desecration of sacred land in Australia, police failure to warn about a serial rapist in Canada, forcing contraceptives on female prisoners as a condition of conjugal visits in Colombia, gendered prayer rights in Israel, the restitution of conjugal rights in India, the order of family names in Germany, or male preference rules in the inheritance of nobility titles in Spain. But many other grounds have been raised more generally. For example, women have often used constitutional instruments to fight against pregnancy and employment discrimination, domestic violence, political underrepresentation, sexual harassment, military service discrimination, sex crimes and/or their accompanying procedures, or unfair marriage, divorce, and succession rules.

Given their breadth, it is striking that few if any of these grounds are expressly prohibited in contemporary constitutions. This lacuna forces women to figure out constitutional strategies to react against the liabilities involved, ground by ground, and country by country. Having to contend on a case-by-case basis for subsuming specific prohibitions within the more abstractly worded provisions found in most constitutions is resource intensive and energy depleting. Moreover, many women simply cannot afford to undertake such an approach. Thus, the insights of comparative analysis suggest feminist and other legal scholars should reassess the current practice of refracting constitutional rights through a myriad of grounds. The flexibility of expressing constitutional rights abstractly may or may not assist women. One of the dangers in silence is that it forces women to rely on the more generic equality provision, but doing so forces women to phrase their claims always in comparative terms. Because the parameters for the comparison are provided by men's experience, presumably, this strategy has inherent limitations.

However, constitutional rights are no panacea. Constitutional rights espouse, and are expected to espouse, the fundamental values of a nation and this has both good and bad consequences for women because courts are prepared not only to uphold but also to limit women's claims in the name of these fundamental values. For instance, as we will see, this has worked to women's disadvantage when restrictive abortion laws were challenged in countries where the courts responded by upholding restrictions, or even by strengthening them, in the name of the foetus and the value of life. In other words, the antithetical consequences that ensue when constitutional rights also serve as constitutional limits should be factored into any consideration of the feasibility of adopting more explicit or grounded expressions of women's constitutional rights. Also, freedom of speech has traditionally been asserted against attempts to limit the harm women suffer because of pornography.

No analysis of women's constitutional rights would be complete without referring to the sphere of application of constitutional rights. Some countries, virtually all of the common law countries analyzed here, restrict the application of women's challenges to state (or public) activity, whereas others, mostly of the civil law tradition, allow women to rely on constitutional rights to challenge injustice and discrimination in the private sector, including the family, schools, workplace, or the media. This distinction between countries that require state action and those recognizing the "horizontal" effect or *Drittwirkung* of constitutional rights is especially relevant to women. It evokes the public/private controversy that fuels much of feminist theory. Often the most serious forms of discrimination are those that women encounter in the private sphere. Nevertheless, those countries that strictly adhere to the constitutional state action doctrine often have general antidiscrimination legislation addressing systematically the various forms of discrimination that women encounter in civil society so that, in practical terms, the difference might not be so dramatic.

Finally, some consideration should be granted to constitutional hermeneutics as well. Have different methods of constitutional interpretation a gender impact? Time may make a difference here. Presumably, if the constitution is an old document written at a time when women's subordinate status was accepted as the natural order of things, and if the courts prefer an originalist or textual approach rather than a "living tree" or teleological approach, this may have a negative impact on women's constitutional position. Also, the different relevance constitutions attach to international human rights instruments and supranational law can have a clear impact on women's constitutional status. Here again, the evidence drawn from our chapters seems to suggest such relevance is accorded more significance in civil law than in common law countries and that in those constitutional regimes that have accorded a special place for international norms in the constitutional order, this has indeed made a significant impact on the gender sympathies of the constitutional bench.[14] As we will see, some constitutions expressly incorporate international law as domestic law. Costa Rica even grants it superior legal force to that of the constitution. More common, however, is the recognition of the need to interpret constitutional rights in the light of relevant international or supranational law. CEDAW is, for instance, often invoked and European Law is sometimes very relevant to constitutional interpretation in EU Member States, like France, Germany, or Spain. How does this impact the constitutional status of women? When specific judicial bodies have the competence to interpret the international or supranational law at stake (such as the European Court of Human Rights or the European Court of Justice) and to bind national constitutional courts to receive such interpretations and to incorporate them to their own interpretation of the national constitutions, interesting questions arise concerning which becomes the final authority to which women can turn.

WOMEN AND CONSTITUTIONALLY STRUCTURED DIVERSITY

Although women have participated in revolutionary activities gender conflict has never caused a national revolution. Indeed, there is little evidence that gender conflict has influenced the design of the constitutional structures that promote national unity and postpone revolution. Instead, economic, cultural, and religious conflicts have dictated the choices of constitution makers in selecting their country's form of governance (whether monarchy or republic), territorial principle (whether federation or unitary state), and jurisdictional approach (whether to recognize customary or religious laws). Accordingly, feminist scholars are constrained to examining the impact on women of these various constitutional structures and the diversities that underlie them.

For instance, the choice between monarchical and republican forms of governance seems gendered because the vast majority of the world's monarchs have been and are men. Nevertheless, that is not always the case and also the rule of primogeniture, or male preference succession that prevails in many monarchies is indistinguishable from similar male preference leadership rules or choices to which various republics adhere. Seldom have

---

[14] On the topic, see R. Rubio-Marín and M. Morgan, "Constitutional Domestication of International Gender Norms: Categorizations, Illustrations, and Reflections from the Nearside of the Bridge," in K. Knopp, ed., *Gender and Human Rights* (Oxford: Oxford University Press) [2004].

republican leaders been female. In sum, the real question is what constitutional objective is served when male preference rules directly or indirectly structure institutions of governance, and will the gender neutrality of the most recently adopted constitutions make any difference?

When nations choose federation over unitary status as their territorial principle, usually it is for economic reasons, often attached to geographical considerations although sometimes ethnocultural conflict also plays a role, as happens in Canada or India. From the perspective of women, however, the major consequence of this choice is often to allocate "private" matters to the regional entities rather than to the national level. For instance, it is common to find that family law becomes a matter for regional concern, and frequently employment law follows suit. Criminal law is, in contrast, sometimes a national and sometimes primarily of regional concern. These and other territorial distributions of legislative power suggest the importance of examining their impact on women, particularly from the standpoint of feminist theorizing about the public/private split.

Without doubt the structural choice about which feminists have been most vocal is the decision to recognize customary or religious jurisdiction over certain relationships, often including those which are the most intimate and intense, such as marriage, divorce, custody, property, and succession. Nevertheless, feminist responses to these jurisdictional choices have not been monolithic; rather, they have been context specific. For instance, as we will see, many Australian and Canadian feminists have supported the recognition of legal rights for indigenous peoples, particularly the efforts indigenous women have made to identify and assert their customary rights. However, the recognition of personal religious laws in India, of religious laws in Israel, and of customary and religious laws in South Africa is more controversial. In these countries, feminists have not hesitated to identify some disadvantages women experience under these religious and customary jurisdictions, and to argue for the necessity of greater harmonization with women's constitutional rights. Finally, in a country such as Turkey, which has adopted a policy of secularism in spite of its overwhelmingly Muslim population, the ban on women wearing religious headscarves in universities has caused feminists to differ. Comparative constitutional analysis signals thus the necessity for examining the impact on women of governmental or judicial decisions to recognize or assimilate religious and/or customary laws.

WOMEN AND CONSTITUTIONAL EQUALITY DOCTRINE

Most constitutions, especially if they have been recently drafted, explicitly prohibit sex or gender discrimination, and/or guarantee equality rights to men and women or to male and female persons. Pragmatically speaking, the promise of these provisions is clear. Because the oppression of women remains a worldwide phenomenon despite some national variations, these provisions are available to support women's equality claims (in fact, many constitutions also explicitly approve of positive discrimination in cases where historic discrimination is being remedied). Although the equality provisions do not preclude men from claiming their protection, effectively they were drafted to protect women. The idea is so widely spread that even in countries without generic sex equality provisions in their constitutions such as Australia, Israel, or the United States, there is jurisprudence pertaining to women's constitutional right to equality. All are, in other words, past the moral and philosophic preliminaries of whether and why to identify women's equality as a constitutional matter. What remains are the more pragmatic issues of the what, when, and how of the constitutional adjudication of sex equality claims: What does sex equality mean? When can women claim infringement of their constitutional right to sex equality? How should courts remedy sex inequalities?

Quite independently, the contributors to this volume approach these questions from the same discursive starting point. They analyze the national constitutional jurisprudence as if sex equality had more than one meaning. Two doctrines prevail, although jurists do not always employ the same terminology as scholars. One is formal equality; the other, separate but equal. Both doctrines rely on the Aristotelian notions of treating alikes alike, and unalikes unalike. Accordingly both focus on identifying the relevant differences and similarities, whether biologically or socially determined, between men and women as groups. Where they differ is in their emancipatory strategies. Formal equality assumes the sex of a person reveals nothing about individual worth or autonomy; its main objective is to create a gender neutral legal order, which turns out to be one in which women are treated just like men. In contrast, its nomenclature suggests separate but equal doctrine emphasizes respect for and the value of women's differences, while promising to ensure they do not result in worse treatment.

Whatever the doctrine formally embraced, the same kinds of issues arise. Thus formal equality courts have struggled to accommodate pregnancy discrimination and affirmative action by treating them as limited exceptions, while separate but equal courts have found it difficult to distinguish legislative stereotyping or paternalism from the less debilitating manifestations of protective or symbolic legislation. Taken collectively, these doctrines portray sex as an abstract conceptual category that is vulnerable to the excesses of judicial discretion; and more important, both focus on open and direct differentiation between the sexes, thereby failing to identify discrimination that is embedded in gender neutral or gender specific legislation. Each of these critiques is exemplified, where pertinent, in the country chapters.

However, the country contributors also constructively advert to the existence of a third sex equality doctrine. Most contributors use the term "substantive equality" to denote this third doctrine. Unlike the other two equality doctrines, it is not obsessed with identifying similarities and differences between men and women (to build upon them the "similarly situated test"), nor with trying to classify them as biological or socially constructed. Substantive equality tries to identify patterns of oppression and subordination of women as a group by men as a group on the understanding that most sex discrimination originates with the long history of women's inequality in almost every area of life rather than inhering in sex as a conceptual category. Ultimately, therefore, the goal of substantive equality is to transform social patterns of discrimination, partly by uncovering the inequalities embedded in gender neutral laws and partly by challenging schemes that differentiate women by offering us only paternalistic benefits. Unfortunately, even under this doctrine there is hardly any way of getting around the objection that some of the "benefits" or "advantages" that the doctrine tries to extend to women rely on traditionally male definitions of the good life. At the same time, some of the goods at stake are so basic (think of life, physical integrity, shelter, and food) that they can be assumed to be a part of anybody's conception of the good life.

Although some national courts have never adverted to substantive equality, it is possible that some of these national differences are semantic. In other words, there may be other ways of referring to the third meaning of equality in constitutional litigation. Be that as it may, the delineation of these three doctrines not only has timing and remedial consequences but also poses issues about limits. What follows is, therefore, a brief delineation of some of the questions raised by adopting the different doctrines of equality.

With respect to timing, the country jurisprudence confirms a pattern in which reliance on the separate but equal and formal equality doctrines often precedes the invocation of substantive equality doctrine. Can we indeed identify general trends in this regard? Does this mean that the earlier doctrines have historically limited functions? If so, can these limitations be attributed mainly to their focus, which is on direct or intentional discrimination rather than on discrimination that is indirect or effects based? What happens when substantive equality appears in the national jurisprudence? Can the three doctrines coexist? What are the tensions that come about? What happens if the tensions are not faced or resolved?

What remedial implications attach to the different equality doctrines? Remedying discrimination and inequality is undoubtedly complex. In exercising judicial review, national courts may choose among various options including: striking down legislation and denying the benefits or privileges to everyone; expanding legislative benefits or privileges to the excluded group; or denouncing the discriminatory legislation while deferring to the legislature to make changes. Comparative constitutional analysis permits us not only to ask about the remedial strategies that national courts have adopted in cases where women (or men) allege sex discrimination, but also to compare these remedial responses cross-nationally. Within the parameters of substantive equality jurisprudence alone, this approach encourages us to ask: Does gender matter? Does context matter? Does the nature or scope of the benefits or privileges matter?

What does the national jurisprudence reveal about the limits of the different equality doctrines? As we will see, the country chapters suggest that three contexts are most apposite to examining these limits: affirmative action, protective legislation, and men's discrimination. With respect to affirmative action, what explains different national responses to it, in itself and as applied to specific realms? What national standards control the validity of affirmative action? What limits, if any, are imposed to exclude measures that benefit individual women while negatively impacting on women as a group because they are paternalistic and have stigmatizing effects or because they sanction sexist stereotypes? Are affirmative action measures accepted when, whatever their long term effects, they compensate the present generation of women for actual disadvantages they currently face? How is the necessity for affirmative action justified – by the rhetoric of equal opportunity or that of equality of results? What is the connection between substantive equality and affirmative action? Does a commitment to substantive equality, as opposed to formal equality, mean conceptualizing affirmative action more as a fulfillment of equality rather than as an exception to it?

Protective legislation has become a pariah in countries that subscribe only to formal equality. However, this does not obviate its existence; nor does it necessarily evoke the same constraints in countries imbued with the substantive equality approach. Moreover, protective legislation poses a particularly poignant problem for women in countries which are in transition to a new constitutional order. Although we rely on substantive equality doctrine to identify and abolish paternalistic and stigmatizing legislation, nevertheless some laws provide women with benefits or privileges that are hard to relinquish. Because this issue is most sensitive in countries in transition from regimes that were oppressive toward women, it is appropriate to ask whether the courts have made allowances for relevant exceptions. For instance, who should pay the costs when the generation claiming the retention of those double-edged benefits is the generation caught in the middle of a democratic transition? Might the older generation not be doubly punished, first in living under an oppressive regime and then by the subsequent emancipatory laws that deprive them of the compensation and protection that they had legitimately come to expect? What role does and should the doctrine of substantive equality play to resolve these questions?

How are the different equality doctrines equipped to remedy men's discrimination? How often and in what contexts do men raise constitutional claims based on gender discrimination? Related to that, how are men helping to shape the meaning of sex discrimination? The different doctrines provide different answers. For instance, formal equality identifies any differential treatment that benefits women as discriminatory against men, whereas substantive equality might characterize the identical situation as nondiscriminatory if its effect were to remedy disadvantages that women face. Or, again, measures that privilege women and not men may meet the separate but equal test while failing the substantive test for women's equality because they provide women with paternalistic benefits. Irrespective of whether the suspect measures are scrutinized to ensure they do not backfire against women, the question remains as to whether men should avail themselves of equality doctrine to access those benefits. Are there genuine cases of male sex discrimination wherein men are denied equal material or nonmaterial advantages because of gender roles that disadvantage them? What have the various national practices been? Has formal equality served this purpose, as for example when men have claimed their right to experience the benefits and burdens of paternity as fully as women experience the benefits and burdens of maternity? Have the courts made relevant distinctions between the different claims presented by men?

Finally, irrespective of which doctrine judges apply, they must relate it to the prevailing concept of discrimination and, on occasion, to other constitutional rights and freedoms. These relationships give rise to various issues, as the following questions illustrate. Must discrimination affect all women equally in order to qualify as such and, if so, with what consequences? Do national courts recognize intersectional discrimination, that is discrimination based on more than one prohibited ground, or must women choose only one ground (think of sex vs. aboriginal status, race, caste, or religious identity)? What are the consequences for sex equality of relying on a concept of discrimination that was shaped on grounds other than sex? Do the traditional liberal rights and freedoms – such as freedom of expression, freedom of religion, privacy, due process, the right to a fair trial, and other procedural guarantees in criminal law – limit the constitutional right to sex equality? Are these tensions recognized? How are they resolved?

CONSTITUTIONALIZING WOMEN'S REPRODUCTIVE RIGHTS AND SEXUAL AUTONOMY

Very few constitutions advert to reproductive rights even though they are vital to women as individuals and as a group. However, in most countries with constitutional justice there are a number of cases involving reproductive issues that are not specifically denominated, such as abortion, in vitro fertilization, contraception, and sterilization. Because these processes were (and some still are) criminalized or otherwise regulated, litigants have resorted to more generalized rights to challenge their constitutionality. Comparative analysis of this jurisprudence will reveal whether distortions have resulted from reclassifying these reproductive claims.

The abortion jurisprudence is particularly apposite to illustrate the complexities induced by having to argue reproductive rights claims from a default position. Many countries have criminalized abortion subject to one or more exceptions (e.g. therapeutic, rape survivors, medicalized procedures). In the absence of abortion rights, litigants are forced to turn to a broad and diverse range of rights to sustain women's entitlement to control their own bodies, including security of the person, liberty, equality, privacy, free development of one's personality, physical integrity, human dignity, physical and moral integrity, and freedom of thought and belief. Comparative constitutional law scholars should examine how these alternative rights were conceptualized, whether they differ, where they overlap, how easy or difficult they made it to argue abortion claims, what distortions they posed for such arguments, and what consequences they had for women's reproductive rights.

Irrespective of which rights were argued on behalf of women, however, invariably a claim is made, usually by the state, for constitutional protection of the right to life of the fetus. Indeed, this claim can be and has been advanced in IVF cases. Such fetal right to life claims raise four issues. First, do all constitutions explicitly protect the right to life and when they do, how is this right conceptualized? Second, are fetal claims always subsumed under this right and when they are, how is this argument sustained? Third, what is the relevance of arguing about fetal rights in cases where women's reproductive rights claims are the basis for challenging the constitutionality of a law? That is, do judges rule that women have reproductive rights before deciding whether these rights are trumped by the right to life, or do they ignore reproductive rights issues and focus only on fetal claims? Fourth, do judicial resolutions of the foregoing issues – interpretation of the right to life, analysis of fetal claims and approaches to women's reproductive rights – correlate with the outcomes in the cases, given they range from decriminalization albeit subject to regulation in some countries to continuing criminalization in the others?

Future comparative law studies may explore the constitutionality of regulating specific features of the abortion process, including counselling, funding, parental or spousal notification, and sex selection, as well as considering whether states might have a duty to provide abortion facilities. Moreover, the reproductive jurisprudence involving contraception, sterilization, and IVF merits examination partly for intrinsic reasons and partly because it may be instructive for abortion claims. For example, the constitutionality of regulating access to IVF as in Costa Rica, or of denying it to lesbians as in Australia or divorcees as in Israel, not only impacts on women's autonomy as a group but also has consequences for our equality rights since much of this litigation was conducted under this constitutional rubric. As many of our country contributors recognize, it is increasingly important to acknowledge that equality analysis also is relevant to abortion issues. Thus comparative law scholars should analyze equality as well as autonomy and privacy when they examine the constitutional mandates that are most likely to inform women's reproductive rights jurisprudence.

Abortion is not the only issue in which constitutions have been more commonly used to obstruct than to facilitate women's emancipation. Sexual offences, too, represent a site of controversy about which comparative constitutional law scholars would be hard pressed to deny that the entrenchment of constitutional rights has detrimentally affected women. Whether criminalized or otherwise regulated, sexual offences – including rape, prostitution, pornography, adultery, honor killings, hate speech, sexist speech, and sexual harassment – have created a veritable industry of constitutional litigation for the criminal defense bar. Relying on traditional legal rights such as the presumption of innocence, the right to a fair trial, and the right not to be subject to cruel and unusual punishment, as well as on freedom of expression, equality rights, and the right to life, liberty, and security of the person, male defendants have not hesitated to challenge the constitutionality of various sexual offences and the evidentiary or procedural rules pertaining to them. To illustrate, not only have men challenged the criminalization of rape in countries such as India and statutory rape in countries such as Canada and the United States, they also have invoked constitutional rights to argue for liberal access to the sexual history of the rape survivor and to her therapeutic counseling records in Canada, as well as to justify more lenient penalties for marital rape in Colombia.

As the victim-survivors, women are all but invisible, enduring these constitutional challenges without having a litigation status from which to respond. Despite this disempowerment, women have demanded that we be accorded constitutional protection for our sexual autonomy. Sometimes victims' lawyers make these assertions in court; sometimes prosecutors can be encouraged to voice them, albeit usually with the objective of protecting the state's interest in the impugned legislation. Either way, the discourse has been framed in terms of various rights including equality, life with dignity, freedom of expression, and honor. Not only should this jurisprudence illuminate how national courts address tensions among constitutional rights, but also it should yield a picture of which rights they favor. In sum, when women claim the right to constitutional protection of sexual autonomy, can national courts hear our voices?

WOMEN'S RIGHTS AND THE CONSTITUTIONAL DEFINITION
OF THE FAMILY

The family is often the object of explicit constitutional protection. However, as the following chapters show, the presence of constitutional provisions referring to the family does not determine whether countries have constitutional jurisprudence pertaining to it. Rather, such jurisprudence pervades all of the country chapters. In other words, the family has acquired a constitutional veneer, whether by political and/or judicial decree. Thus it is important to examine how this constitutionalization of the family has affected women's rights. The idea that constitutions should (implying can) stay out of the home is indeed a myth.

From a comparative law perspective such studies raise a number of issues. Writ large, we need to understand how constitutions and constitutional doctrines shape and are shaped by national conceptions of the family. For instance, is curial discourse restricted to recognizing only formally married, sequentially monogamous, heterosexual couples or have the national courts been asked to accord matrimonial status or at least some family benefits (e.g., survivors' pensions, protection of children born out of wedlock, succession, and property rights) to common law or de facto families, to single-parent families, to polygamous unions, or to gay men and lesbians? Can constitutions really be neutral about family arrangements? In rendering these decisions, moreover, have courts acknowledged their specific impact on women's well-being?

More specifically, how do judges decide cases in which they are asked to treat wives or mothers differently from husbands or fathers? Collectively speaking, there are many such cases and they cover a wide range of subject matters, including family or children's surnames, income tax deductions and attributions, disposition of matrimonial property, survivors' pensions, inheritance, divorce, alimony, custody and support of children, restoration of conjugal rights, adultery, adoption, and domestic violence. This jurisprudence should enable scholars to identify the constitutional justifications that convince national courts to sanction the division of family roles on the basis of gender.

There also are other issues that merit attention. For example, when constitutions make families the object of collective rights protection (typically, by sanctioning the right to family privacy), does that impair the rights of women as individuals? How do courts balance the interests of children versus those of the father and/or the mother? Does the embrace of the doctrine of the horizontal effects of constitutional rights open a path for fighting against unfairness and oppression inside of the home? Is domestic violence a constitutional offense? How, if at all, do constitutions conceptualize women's domestic labor? What is the constitutional debate surrounding the impact of personal, religious, and customary family law on women's rights? What role, if any, does federalism play in the constitutionalization of the family? Ultimately, feminist scholars should also ask: Does constitutional doctrine sustain the fiction of the split between the private and public?

WOMEN'S SOCIOECONOMIC DEVELOPMENT AND DEMOCRATIC RIGHTS IN THE CONSTITUTION

There is considerable overlap between socioeconomic issues and those to which family relationships give rise. Questions such as whether or not women's domestic labor is valued, who is expected to bear the responsibility of child raising, whether or not women heads of family are protected, whether marriage gives husbands control over women's property, and rules on alimony and child support have the greatest impact on women's socioeconomic well-being. However, it is worth asking some additional questions.

Given that virtually in no country are women men's socioeconomic equals, the first obvious question is whether constitutions specifically address women's socioeconomic needs and whether the kinds of protections constitutions contain can backfire against women, especially within market economies. For instance, the Spanish Constitution prohibits sex discrimination in employment but some other constitutions, like the Colombian, the Costa Rican, and the Turkish explicitly provide for special protection for women workers, which, as the case law discussed in those countries' chapters shows, raises the question as to whether such clauses end up being freedom restricting or enhancing.

Moreover, it would seem that the horizontal application of fundamental rights would have a clear impact on women's socioeconomic well-being as, together with the family, the workplace, and educational institutions are two of the most frequent scenarios for discrimination against women in civil society. It is thus important to ask whether sex discrimination at work by private employers is a constitutional offence. In relation to that is discrimination on the basis of pregnancy, or sexual harassment, conceptualized as a constitutional offence?

Any feminist constitutional agenda that looks at results, and not just at intentions and formalities, should also address the constitutional status of socioeconomic rights in general, as opposed to first- and second-generation rights. Even when phrased in gender neutral terms, the rights to housing, education, health care, social security, and food, recognized by some constitutions, like the South African, have a gender impact, and will do so, as long as poverty has the face of a woman; for example, consider debates such as the one currently taking place in India, as to whether to make education a fundamental right by amending their Constitution are gendered.

Needless to say, women's political status is crucial to the overcoming of their social and economic subordination. Most women can vote and serve as elected political representatives, although few constitutions advert to these democratic rights. There are some exceptions. The United States Constitution is exceptional insofar as it guarantees both sexes equal voting rights; similarly the South African Constitution is unique in describing the composition of the National Assembly in terms of both genders. In addition, several countries have taken positive steps to ensure that women's democratic rights are recognized as possessing a participatory, as well as a formal legal, dimension. They have constitutional provisions and/or jurisprudence permitting or requiring quotas aimed at increasing women's political representation and participation in the public realm. In some countries, like in

France, these have only come about after a highly disputed constitutional amendment process.

Constitutional law scholars should compare these participatory provisions and analyze the jurisprudence pertaining to them to identify their underlying conceptions. Although some may be perceived as temporary measures necessary to facilitate women's incorporation into the political and other public domains, others may be intended to redefine democratic representation more permanently according to a mirror representation approach. In addition, we need to examine the effect of context on adjudication. That is, have national courts reacted differently to quota, reserved seat, or parity legislation depending on whether it applies to political party candidacies, electoral lists, the judiciary, or public sector employment? Does it matter whether the quotas are specified, how they are derived, if they are mandatory, whether they also apply on grounds other than sex, or whether they contain explicit or implicit exonerations or sanctions?

Citizenship is also more broadly defined by the civic entitlements – both rights and duties – that the full members of any society can exercise. In terms of rights, we need to ask whether constitutions protect women's equal right to enjoy and to pass on membership status, given cases in which states have treated women unequally with respect to aboriginal, religious, citizenship, or residential status. In terms of duties, and related dignitary benefits, one of the major issues revolves around the constitutionality of exempting, excluding or limiting women's military, public, and jury service. Finally, no study of civic duties would be complete without addressing the issue of whether constitutions and constitutional doctrines treat women's reproductive capacity and unpaid domestic labour as social assets.

CONSTITUTING WOMEN: THE GENDER OF
CONSTITUTIONAL JURISPRUDENCE

In what follows, the country contributors take very seriously the task of responding on a selective national basis to the questions raised by our feminist agenda. Not only do their answers enrich our understanding of the position of women in constitutional jurisprudence but also they fill a huge gap in the literature on comparative constitutionalism, the gender gap. Individually and collectively they challenge our acceptance of particular constitutional arrangements forcing us to question what may have seemed simply inevitable or obvious. "Broadening our perspective," as a feminist comparative constitutional law scholar recently argued, "may enable us to ask better questions and to better understand the answers that we find."[15]

---

[15] Kim Lane Schepple, "The Agendas of Comparative Constitutionalism" (2003) 13 (2) *Law & Courts: Newsletter of the Law and Courts Section of the American Political Science Association* 5 at 22 online: Law and Courts Newsletter Web site <http://www.law.nyu.edu/lawcourts/pubs/newsletter/spring03.pdf> (date accessed: 11/11/03).

I

Speaking into a Silence

Embedded Constitutionalism, the Australian Constitution, and the Rights of Women

Isabel Karpin and Karen O'Connell

The Australian Constitution is a document that is mostly silent about rights. It has no comprehensive set of enumerated rights in the form of a *bill of rights*. Instead, it sets up a federal system and the basic framework of a representative democracy, with a few specific rights scattered throughout. Federal and state legislation provide the express means of protection of equality. Yet, the Constitution is a crucial part of the framework for understanding women's rights in Australia. Not only does it provide the source of federal legislative power with respect to equality but also, in recent years, a minority view on the High Court has asserted that equality is the underlying principle upon which the Constitution is founded.[1]

In this chapter, we explore the way that the Australian Constitution, without an explicit set of enumerated rights, can and should be used to establish and protect women's rights in practice. We consider how women have shaped the Australian Constitution both in its creation and throughout its development to the present day and argue that the federal system reinforces the traditional division of public and private life to the detriment of women. Looking at the formal mechanisms that exist for pursuing equality and antidiscrimination claims in Australia with reference to international covenants, domestic, federal, and state legislation, we show that Australian constitutional rights are embedded into a larger institutional, bureaucratic, and cultural framework. We examine the Constitution then, not as the locus of rights but as a framework for the articulation of the rights of women and other minority groups.

We conclude with an examination of the material rights of women in instances of constitutional claims for protection. We ask how women's claims have fared and what their outcomes offer for the future.

---

[1] *Leeth v. Commonwealth* (1992), 174 CLR 455.

EMBEDDED CONSTITUTIONALISM

The Australian constitutional *system* derives its full meaning only when read in the context of the constitutional conventions and the common law.[2] These in turn derive their full meaning from the domestic social and political arena and international norms and treaties. Any discussion of rights under the Australian Constitution then must start from the premise that the Constitution is both constitutive of and constituted by the legal, political, and cultural system in which it operates. Although this might seem a postmodern approach to constitutional jurisprudence, in Australia it is also a doctrinal truth. In 1965, Sir Owen Dixon, Chief Justice of the High Court between 1952 and 1964, expressed the Australian brand of constitutionalism as follows:

In Australia we have paid but little attention to the distinction, which appears to me to be fundamental between American Constitutional theory and our own. It concerns the existence of an anterior law providing the sources of juristic authority for our institutions when they came into being.... To me the lesson of all this appears to be that constitutional questions should be considered and resolved in the context of the whole law, of which the common law, including in that expression the doctrine of equity forms not the least essential part.[3]

The idea that the operation of the Constitution is determined not simply by its textual form but by systems of laws and values that give rise to it appears to be a fairly uncontroversial point. Tony Blackshield has described the Australian Constitution as "a skeleton and the flesh that goes on the bones [is]... filled out by practice, convention, habit and tradition."[4] Trevor Allan has similarly argued that the Australian Constitution becomes meaningful only once we accept that the principles of equality and individual liberty found in the common law give it form.[5]

Although scholars such as Blackshield and Allan recognize that the "skeleton" of the Constitution needs persistent fleshing out, it is not always the case that the material context is acknowledged. To the contrary, the acceptance of

---

[2] Conventions are an unwritten set of rules governing the role of the Queen (exercised through her representative in Australia – the Governor-General), the selection of the Prime Minister, and the membership of the cabinet among other things. For a fuller discussion, see C. Hughes, "Conventions: Dicey Revisited," in P. Weller and D. Janesch, eds., *Responsible Government in Australia* (Richmond, Victoria: Drummond for the Australasian Political Studies Association, 1980).

[3] Sir Owen Dixon, *Jesting Pilate* (Melbourne: Law Book Co., 1965) at 203, as quoted in G. Winterton et al., *Australian Federal Constitutional Law: Commentary and Materials* (Sydney: Law Book Co., 1999) at 848.

[4] Jane Innes, *Millenium Dilemma* (Wollongong: Wollongong University, 1998).

[5] T. R. S. Allan, "The Common Law as Constitution: Fundamental Rights and First Principles," in Cheryl Saunders, ed., *Courts of Final Jurisdiction: The Mason Court in Australia* (Sydney: Federation Press, 1996) at 147.

the Constitution as an abstract outline often results in an unacceptable decontextualization of constitutional claims, rights, and obligations. That is why in this chapter we attempt to untangle the Australian constitutional framework of equality with reference to the material context in which women's rights are actualized. It is only by doing this that we can explore how the Australian Constitution furthers or hinders the progress toward equality of the diverse group of Australian women. Before we turn to the embedded nature of the constitutional system, we need to outline the framework that forms the skeleton of the Australian Constitution.

THE STRUCTURE OF THE CONSTITUTION

The *Commonwealth of Australia Constitution Act* was passed by the British Parliament in 1900, setting up a Western-style democracy in the form of a constitutional monarchy based on the English system of government.[6] It is a document that emphasizes democratic structures rather than individual rights.

It has three overarching structural frameworks. The first of these, federalism and the second, the separation of powers doctrine, relate to the distribution of power among the different component parts of the Australian federation. The third, responsible and representative government, relates to the system of government. Each of these structural characteristics is significant to the recognition of women's rights.

Federalism

The primary aim of the Constitution when it was passed in 1901 was to unite the various Australian colonies as states under one federal compact. The Queen was to remain the sovereign and was to be represented in Australia by the Governor-General. Although today the Queen remains the formal head of state, her role is notional and symbolic.[7] Each of the states continues to claim sovereignty over their own domain but the Constitution allocates specific powers to the federal government. Those powers are primarily enumerated

---

[6] Despite the existence of the new Constitution, it took Australia many years to gain legislative independence from Britain. Under the *Colonial Laws Validity Act* 1865 (Imp) laws of the British Parliament could be extended to the colonies and override local legislation. The enactment of the *Statute of Westminster* 1931 (Imp) freed the colonies from British legislation except by consent. However, in Australia it applied only to Federal Parliament, as state Parliaments wished to retain dependence on British law. It was only with the *Australia Acts* of 1986 that British legislation was deemed not to apply to the States and Territories of Australia, as well as the Commonwealth.

[7] In 1975, there was a constitutional crisis when the Queen's representative, the Governor-General, sacked the elected Prime Minister. The implications of this event are too broad to explore in this paper.

in Section 51 of the Constitution. Unless the Commonwealth has specifically been given the power to legislate in a particular area, it may not do so. Where the Commonwealth does have such power, the states may continue to legislate in the area so long as they do not do so in a manner inconsistent with Commonwealth legislation.[8]

Separation of Powers

In theory a strict separation of powers exists in the Australian Constitution between the judiciary, the executive, and the legislature based on the structure of the Constitution.[9] Each arm occupies a separate chapter in the Constitution and the High Court has held this to require that the domains of each be kept separate from the other.[10] The aim of this separation is to cordon the judiciary from the polluting influences of politics. Although in practice there are many exceptions to this doctrine, the High Court has remained steady in its opposition to judges exercising powers that appear too political.

The constitution creates the High Court in Chapter III. The High Court is the highest appeal court in the land and has original jurisdiction to consider federal constitutional matters. All matters of constitutional interpretation therefore rest with the High Court. The seven judges on the High Court are selected by the Prime Minister and are appointed until age seventy. Currently all are men. Justice Gaudron, who served for fifteen years on the High Court, was the first and only female member of the High Court and provided a significant articulation of a rights jurisprudence. Justice Gaudron recently retired from the bench despite not having reached retirement age, citing personal reasons. Hopes that Justice Gaudron might be replaced by another woman were dashed with the appointment of conservative judge Dyson Heydon. The Prime Minister, John Howard, countered criticism of the appointment by saying that it was made on merit and that it was unrealistic for critics to expect gender to be a consideration in the decision.

Responsible and Representative Government. The system of responsible government stems from the Westminster system of government in England and refers to the requirement that the Queen and her representatives act on the advice of the ministers. It also covers the notion of parliamentary responsibility, in other words, that members of the executive are accountable directly to the people. Some suggest that it is because of this commitment to a

---

[8] *Australian Constitution* (brought into existence as the *Commonwealth of Australia Constitution Act* 1900 ([Imp.]) Section 109.

[9] *Boilermakers's Case* (1956), 94 CLR 254.

[10] *Boilermaker's Case*, ibid.

responsible government that the original drafters of the Constitution decided not to include a bill of rights.[11]

Responsible government, derived from the Westminster system, is coupled in the Australian Constitution with representative government. Representative government is provided for in those provisions of the Constitution that set out how the members of the House of Representatives and the Senate are to be elected to office and how the votes of the people are to be counted.[12]

WOMEN IN THE MAKING OF THE AUSTRALIAN CONSTITUTION

The Prehistory

The manner in which the Australian nation came into being is unusual in its commitment to democratic principles. The Constitution was not the result of a revolutionary war but was drafted over the course of several years in the context of a series of Federal Conventions. Delegates from most colonies attended these conventions and in many cases those delegates had been selected by popular election. After the draft was finalized, it was put to the vote and adopted in referenda that took place in each of the colonies.[13]

No women were delegates to these conventions. Women did, however, influence and shape the Constitution through indirect political means. According to Helen Irving, the 1890s saw the emergence of women as political actors. It is possible that this was a direct consequence of the debate around the Constitution and the opportunity it offered to have their needs and concerns addressed. The Constitution is, then, partly responsible for the genesis of political activism among women in Australia. Irving recounts the formation of different National Councils of Women in several colonies affiliated with the International Council of Women. All the colonies except Tasmania by the mid-1890s had suffrage leagues and several women's journals went into production.[14] However, not all women embraced the Constitution and what it offered. The feminist Rose Scott, for instance, who was an activist at the time of federation, saw the creation of a centralised federal government – the main reason for the Constitution – as a threat to women and democracy

---

[11] See Blackshield and Williams, eds., *Australian Constitutional Law and Theory: Commentary and Material*, 2nd ed. (Sydney: Federation Press, 1998).

[12] Sections 7 and 24 are the primary sections dealing with membership of the Senate and House of Representatives respectively.

[13] See Helen Irving, *To Constitute a Nation* (Cambridge: Cambridge University Press, 1999) at 1–6.

[14] "Interview with Helen Irving," in Innes, *Millennium Dilemma*, *supra* note 4 at 105–14; also see generally Irving, *To Constitute a Nation*, ibid., particularly Chapter 10.

because it would move decision making away from mothers to "a faraway federal parliament."[15]

Who Is a Citizen?

Given this genesis, Australia's Constitution has some basis in popular acceptance. However, those entitled to vote in state elections and therefore on the Constitution did not represent the people in their entirety. Australia enfranchised its women long before most other Western democracies, but only women from South Australia and Western Australia were enfranchised in time to vote on the Constitution.[16] In the case of Western Australia, only white women were enfranchised, with indigenous men and women of Australia, Asia, and Africa specifically excluded. In New South Wales, Tasmania, and Victoria, some Aboriginal men were eligible to vote while all women (indigenous and nonindigenous) were not.[17]

White women obtained voting rights and appeared to be accepted as citizens soon after federation. The Commonwealth made election to office a formal right along with the right to vote in 1902 but the first woman was not elected to the Federal parliament until 1943.[18] Margaret Thornton outlines this disjunction between voting rights and more general citizenship rights for women:

In classic definitional terms, citizenship is the status determining membership of a legally cognisable political community, although it involves more than a passive belonging. First, it includes abstract rights that are legally recognised and that apply equally to all citizens, at least in a formal sense. Second, the concept includes a more

[15] Marilyn Lake, "The Republic, The Federation and the Intrusion of the Political" in Jeanette Hoorn and David Goodman, eds., *Vox Re/Publicae: Feminism and the Republic* (special edition [1995–1996] 46–50 *Journal of Australian Studies*) at 12.

[16] South Australia extended the vote to women in 1894 and Western Australia did so in 1899. New South Wales gave women the right to vote in 1902, Tasmania 1903, Queensland 1905, and Victoria 1908. White women were given the vote at the federal level in 1902. Section 41 of the newly enacted Constitution extended voting rights at the federal level to all enfranchised citizens of the states.

[17] "In Queensland, Aborigines other than freeholders were excluded from the franchise by a proviso to s6 of the Elections Act 1885 (QLD) ("No aboriginal native of Australia, India, China, or the South Sea Islands..."). In Western Australia, a similar disqualification was imposed by a proviso to Section 12 of the Constitution Amendment Act 1893 ("No aboriginal native of Australia, Asia or Africa...") New South Wales, South Australia, Tasmania, and Victoria imposed no such disqualification, and accordingly Aborigines in those States were entitled to vote for the first federal Parliament in 1901." See Blackshield and Williams, eds., *Australian Constitutional Law*, supra note 11, at 160. Note that only in South Australia would that have included aboriginal women.

[18] Dame Enid Lyons was the first woman elected to the Commonwealth Parliament. She later became the first woman in federal Cabinet. The right to be elected to office was not available in most states for another fifteen to twenty years.

subtle layer of meaning that operates to qualify the first, relating to the degree of participation within the community of citizens.[19]

Women's formal rights, then, did not correlate to full participation as citizens. In Australia, it was seen as problematic even to have abstract citizenship rights entrenched in the Constitution. There is no constitutional provision defining citizenship or indeed referring to it.[20] Either Australians were British subjects by being born "within the King's allegiance" or they were naturalized under one of the State's *Naturalisation Acts*. In the latter case, subject status was not inalienable but could be lost when the individual moved on to another colony or nation. Citizenship was not included in the Constitution because it contained an inherent claim to certain rights and freedoms that would preclude racial discrimination.[21] Instead, the words "people" and "subject" were used. Furthermore, the fact that women were not expected (and for some time not able) to be active in public affairs suggests that citizenship was also gendered male.

Writing in Indigenous Women. The history of the inclusion (or exclusion) of indigenous women in the making of the Constitution and the system of government it set up is tied to the inclusion of indigenous people generally. Aboriginal peoples of Australia are not afforded special protection under the Constitution. The Races power in Section 51 (xxvi) that enabled the Commonwealth to make laws with respect to "[t]he people of any race, other than the aboriginal race in any State, for whom it is deemed necessary to make special laws" was intended to enable the government to discriminate against races other than the Aboriginal race. The first Australian Prime Minister, Edmund Barton, described the Races power, as it then was as necessary to enable "[t]he Commonwealth to regulate the affairs of the people of coloured or inferior races who are in the Commonwealth."[22] Aborigines were excepted from the Races power until 1967, not because the government wanted to protect them but because Aborigines were seen as a state matter and a dying race.[23] In 1967, the original Races power quoted earlier was amended to omit the words "other than the aboriginal race in any State." An overwhelming majority, over 90 percent of the population, passed the

[19] Margaret Thornton, "Embodying the Citizen," in *Public/Private* (Oxford: Oxford University Press, 1995) at 200.

[20] Helen Irving has documented the debates that occurred over the word citizen in the framing of the Constitution. See generally Irving, *To Constitute a Nation, supra* note 13, ch. 9.

[21] Irving, *To Constitute a Nation*, ibid., at 158–9. Irving quotes Sir John Forrest's concern "[t]hat coloured persons who have become British subjects might in this definition be considered citizens." He goes on: "A concept of citizenship should not be allowed to rule out discriminatory legislation against, in particular, the Chinese."

[22] As quoted in Blackshield and Williams, eds., *Australian Constitutional Law, supra* note 11 at 165.

[23] Patrick Wolfe, "Nation and Miscegenation," in (1994) *Social Analysis* at 101.

referendum, a unique event in Australia, where referendums usually fail. Over time it had become clear that the only way that positive legislation would be passed to assist indigenous Australia was if the Commonwealth had the power to make it. In an interesting historical twist, then, the one power included in the Constitution to enable overt discriminatory practices was, in 1967, touted as the one section that might offer the possibility of some redress for discriminatory practices.

Over the next twenty years, the Commonwealth passed a series of Acts that by increasing degrees set up an infrastructure to assist indigenous Australians, the most recent being largely under the control of Aboriginal and Torres Strait Islanders.[24] There has, however, been ongoing debate about whether the amended section can be used to allow discriminatory laws or only laws for the benefit of a race. Interestingly, for our purposes, the primary and most recent case on this question involved aboriginal women and the recognition of an historical connection between Aboriginal women and their land. Because this case highlights the intersecting effects of a Constitution framed around both a racist and sexist ideology, it also illustrates the importance of examining gender inequality in the context of its intersection with other kinds of systemic inequality, in this case racism. We will return to discuss this case later in this chapter.[25]

Federalism and the Public and Private Divide

The Constitution was drafted with the view that states' rights should be protected and centralized federal powers constrained. The Constitution therefore sets out specific areas of Commonwealth Government power. These include legislative powers, set out in Section 51, and executive powers, set out in Section 61. State powers are determined by state constitutions and are plenary and far-reaching. States generally have the power to make laws on any subject so long as the relevant law does not conflict with a specified area of Commonwealth coverage.[26] The Commonwealth's limited legislative powers were originally mostly over matters that are commonly thought of as public, economic, or financial as opposed to private or personal subject matters. However, as the years have passed, the Commonwealth's powers have expanded in line with its international obligations with respect to human rights. Nevertheless, some feminists have argued that the division of powers between the Commonwealth and the states parallels the artificial division between matters that relate to the public domain and matters that relate to the private domain respectively.

It is important then to any analysis of the Constitution as protector of women's rights, to consider the view that the Commonwealth Constitution

---

[24] The Aboriginal and Torres Strait Islander Commission (ATSIC) was established in 1990.
[25] *Kartinyeri v. The Commonwealth* (1998), 152 ALR 540.
[26] *Australian Constitution, supra* note 8, Section 109.

gave rise to a national polis set apart from the domestic or private concerns
of the States. Helen Irving notes that until 1946, a broad range of social
and welfare powers were excluded from Commonwealth jurisdiction.[27] She
goes on: "Maternity, widows', unemployment and family allowances, among
others, which are the very areas of greatest concern for women, were left in
the hands of the States."[28]

In 1946, the Constitution was amended so that the Commonwealth was
given power over these areas as well as sickness and hospital benefits and
medical and dental services. By contrast, the Federal Constitution did give
power over marriage and divorce to the Commonwealth at its inception.
Marriage was put under federal control because Australians sought to avoid
what they saw as the "culture of scandal and domestic distress resulting from
differing State divorce laws" in America.[29]

Rose Scott opposed the centralized power of federalism and its derogation
of power away from local and community politics and, therefore, in her view,
the mother. Scott argued that "National life is built upon noble family life. It
is the mother who makes the nation."[30] She viewed the moving of decision
making to a centralized and distant government as the end of democracy,
making it impossible for mothers to participate in government. Scott says:
"For Heaven's sake, dear friends, let us divert ourselves from the ridiculous
old fashioned idea that a great nation is made out of huge national debts,
standing armies, expensive buildings, much territory, artificial sentiment, fat
billets for some people while others starve."[31]

Similarly, the feminist legal theorist Margaret Thornton describes constitutionalization today as "typically involv[ing] the treatment of issues at a
very high level of abstraction so that distinctive private or subjective features
are sloughed off."[32] This leaves us with the question of whether in fact it is
better for Australian women to have matters that relate to the so-called domestic or private sphere included in our Federal Constitutional framework
or whether Scott is correct and this creates abstract rights in place of material
claims.[33]

---

[27] Helen Irving, "A Gendered Constitution? Women, Federation and Heads of Power," in Helen
Irving, ed., *A Woman's Constitution* (Sydney: Hale and Iremonger, 1996) at 102.
[28] Irving, "A Gendered Constitution?," ibid., at 102.
[29] See Irving, *To Constitute a Nation, supra* note 13, and *Australian Constitution, supra* note 8,
Section 51(xx), 51(xxi).
[30] As quoted in Lake, "The Republic," *supra* note 15.
[31] Lake, "The Republic," ibid.
[32] Margaret Thornton, "Towards Embodied Justice: Wrestling with Legal Ethics in the Age of
the New Corporatism," in (1999) 23 *Melbourne University Law Review* 754–72 at 754.
[33] According to Helen Irving, there were equally as many women arguing the opposite to Scott.
Irving, "Thinking of England: Women, Politics and the Queen," in Jeanette Hoorn and David
Goodman, eds., *Vox Re/Publicae: Feminism and the Republic* (special edition [1995–1996]
46–50 *Journal of Australian Studies*) 33–41.

Contemporary Developments

The Constitution as a text has remained relatively intact in its 1901 form one hundred years later. Given the sexist and racist origins that we have begun to document earlier, it is a rather startling fact that there have been only eight amendments to the text in its one-hundred-year history. Of those amendments, the most significant were those already discussed, the deletion of Section 127 excluding the reckoning of Aboriginal natives in the numbers of people, and the reduction in the tenure of High Court judges from appointment for life to retirement at age seventy in 1977.

At the most recent referendum in 1999, Australians were asked to vote to change our constitutional system from a constitutional monarchy to a republic. At the outset, the Republican movement failed to garner support from women. One commentator attributed this to the movement's "assertions of manly independence."[34] Marilyn Lake says: "[I]ts most confident exponents are men.... Conversely, monarchists in Australia are often discredited for being unable to separate from the mother or for being, literally, old women."[35]

In 1998, a People's Convention[36] was held to debate the question of the Republic. The Convention was made up of government appointees and elected representatives and women occupied approximately 35 percent of those positions. A Women's Constitutional Convention initiated by women from several nongovernment women's organizations was held prior to the People's Convention. It had no official link to the government backed People's Convention, but the outcomes of the Women's Convention were presented to the Chair of the Government's Constitutional Convention, and were raised on the Convention floor during the proceedings.[37] The Women's Constitutional Convention supported a republic, a Bill of Rights, and recognition for local government in the Constitution. However, support for a republic was qualified by concern that any future model of government supported equality in decision-making processes and recognised indigenous Australians. The Women's Convention also called for greater civic education in preparation for the vote on the Republic. In the end, the referendum was structured in terms that did not reflect the outcomes of either of the Conventions and, when put to the people, failed.

---

[34] Marilyn Lake, "The Republic," *supra* note 15.
[35] Marilyn Lake, "The Republic," ibid. Lake cites opinion polls leading up to the referendum on the question that demonstrates a marked division along gender lines.
[36] This is not to be confused with the constitutional conventions discussed earlier referring to certain unwritten but well-accepted rules.
[37] See Dr. Jennifer Curtin, "The 1998 Women's Constitutional Convention," Research Note 21 (1997–98), online: Parliament of Australia, Department of the Parliamentary Library <www.aph.gov.au/library/pubs/rn/1997-98/98rn21.htm> (date accessed: 18 April 2001).

At that same referendum, Australians were asked to vote on a new preamble to the Constitution written by the current Prime Minister, John Howard, and a highly regarded conservative poet, Les Murray. Two main groups were outraged by the Prime Minister's preamble. The first comprised indigenous Australians and the second women.

Howard's Preamble, far from enshrining the equality of men and women, attempted to capture the spirit of the Australian through the concept of "mateship."[38] "Mateship" is a fantasy form of *bon amie* between men purged of homoeroticism. It is an intensely masculine worldview that has its origins in the deprivations of the Australian bush and allegiances formed on the battlefield in World War I. A fervent debate followed in the media with some women arguing that this was inherently masculinist and resulted in half the population not being included in the fundamental conceptual apparatus for recognition of Australian identity. Indigenous Australians, too, felt excluded by the reference. The only indigenous Member of Parliament, Senator Aden Ridgeway, indicated the term was one that stemmed from Australia's colonial heritage and was a language used most comfortably by white Anglo-Australian men. The word *mateship* did not make it into the final draft of the preamble put to the Australian people and this may be because a significant number of women occupy positions in both the major parties and the largest independent party.

It also should be noted that the preamble was put to the people as a document of no legal significance whatsoever. We argue, however, that the Australian Constitution is particularly susceptible to symbolic and cultural power because of its open textured nature. The recent referendum and debate over the preamble was valuable in that it placed the question of Australian identity on the agenda. It raised the question of who is included automatically in that definition, who has to fight for inclusion, and who is inevitably left out.

EQUALITY RIGHTS IN AUSTRALIA

Is There a Right to Equality?

There is no comprehensive bill of rights in the Australian Constitution. There are, however, a few express freedoms and prohibitions limiting state power scattered throughout the Constitution and the High Court has recently found some rights implicit in the Constitution because of the system of government it establishes. In particular, the High Court has found a limited right to freedom of political communication to be implied from the system of

---

[38] The preamble read in part: "Australians are free to be proud of their country and heritage, free to realise themselves as individuals, and free to pursue their hopes and ideals. We value excellence as well as fairness, independence as dearly as mateship."

representative government that the Constitution sets up.[39] Australian High Court opinions are seriatim, which makes analysis of decisions a complex and sometimes uncertain business.

Perhaps the most significant decision in recent years on the question of the protection of equality in the Australian constitution is, however, the minority decision of Deane and Toohey JJ in the 1992 case of *Leeth v. Commonwealth*.[40] Deane and Toohey argued, with reference to the preamble to the Constitution, that: "[the] conceptual basis of the Constitution ... was the free agreement of 'the people' – all the people – of the federating colonies to unite in the Commonwealth under the Constitution. Implicit in that free agreement was the notion of the inherent equality of the people as parties to that compact."[41]

In other words, according to Deane and Toohey JJ, it is the conceptual basis of the Constitution and not the Constitution itself that ensures the right of each individual to be treated equally. Although Justice Deane and Justice Toohey were in the minority, two of the other five justices, Gaudron and Brennan, left the question open.[42]

Justice Gaudron relied on the separation of powers doctrine as a means to import values and principles of equality into the Constitution. In *Leeth*, Gaudron J expanded the separation of powers doctrine to include not just the delineation of powers the judiciary can exercise but also the manner of their exercise. She determined that the standard of justice that was required to constitute the judicial power of the Commonwealth encompassed a concept of equality. She said: "All are equal before the law. And the concept of equal justice – a concept which requires the like treatment of like persons in like circumstances, but also requires that genuine differences be treated as such – is fundamental to the judicial process."[43]

If a general right of equality was found in the Constitution either in its own right or through the separation of powers doctrine, there would be scope for making claims to equal rights for women in the text of the Constitution itself. However, this remains a minority position. This position was revisited in the case of *Kruger v. Commonwealth* (1997) 146 ALR 126, in which Gaudron J

---

[39] *Australian Capital Television Pty Ltd v. Commonwealth* (1992); 177 CLR 106; *Levy v. Victoria* (1997), 146 ALR 248; and *Lange v. Australian Broadcasting Corporation* (1997), 145 ALR 96.
[40] *Leeth* involved a prisoner who was convicted of a federal crime but housed in a state prison. In order to ensure that federal and state criminal offenders incarcerated in the same gaol would be treated equally the parole period was determined by the state rule. In other words, persons convicted of the same federal crime but housed in prisons in different states would be subject to potentially different parole periods. The argument put by Leeth was that there was a broad underlying requirement in the Constitution of equal treatment which was being denied to him because of this state-based rule.
[41] *Leeth v. Commonwealth* (1992), 174 CLR 455 at 486.
[42] The Australian High Court has seven judges including the Chief Justice.
[43] *Leeth, supra* note 41, at 502.

reaffirmed her view that equal treatment was implicit in judicial process but was not a general right. Justice Dawson and Justice McHugh gave limited support to Gaudron J's position but Dawson J and Gummow J rejected the approach of Deane and Toohey JJ. Justice Toohey held to his earlier position but together the views of Dawson, Gummow, Gaudron, and McHugh JJ result in the rejection of the doctrine of legal equality suggested by Deane and Toohey JJ. Justice Gaudron's more limited guarantee however, remains. Thus, whereas *Kruger* has probably put an end to the Deane and Toohey JJ line, it has left scope for the further development of the Gaudron J line. Interestingly, the concept of equal justice itself is imported into the Constitution rather than being derived from it. Its most likely derivation is the common law.

Women's Rights – an External Affair?

Instead of having direct Constitutional protection, equality rights in Australia are protected by Federal and State legislation. Each state of Australia has enacted antidiscrimination legislation enforcing equal treatment, regardless of sex, in a range of public fora such as employment, education, and the provision of goods and services.[44] In addition, the federal government has passed a series of acts aimed at ensuring equal treatment on the grounds of race, sex, and disability.[45] The federal government does not have the explicit power to make "equality rights" legislation. There is nothing in the Constitution directly giving it that power. Instead, to pass its antidiscrimination laws, the government had to rely on the existence of international treaties and its "external affairs power" in Section 51 of the Constitution. Although the Constitution does not give direction on the role of international agreements in domestic law, the High Court has found that where a law is needed to implement an international agreement, the federal government may rely on its power to make laws with respect to external affairs to enact domestic legislation in that area. Each of the federal antidiscrimination acts thus corresponds to an international treaty. For example, Australia has signed and ratified the *Convention on the Elimination of All Forms of Discrimination against Women* (CEDAW), and this international agreement effectively makes nondiscrimination against women an "external affair," giving the federal government the power to pass domestic legislation, the *Sex Discrimination Act* 1984 (Cth.), to enforce nondiscrimination. The federal

---

[44] *Anti-Discrimination Act*, 1977 (NSW); *Equal Opportunity Act*, 1995 (Vic); *Equal Opportunity Act*, 1984 (SA); *Equal Opportunity Act*, 1984 (WA): *Discrimination Act*, 1991 (ACT); *Anti-Discrimination Act*, 1991 (Qld); *Anti-Discrimination Act*, 1992 (NT); *Anti-Discrimination Act*, 1998 (Tas).

[45] *Racial Discrimination Act*, 1975 (Cth); *Sex Discrimination Act*, 1984 (Cth); and *Disability Discrimination Act*., 1992 (Cth).

Sex Discrimination Act is explicitly directed at equality of treatment between the sexes, and protects against discrimination on the grounds of sex, marital status, pregnancy, and potential pregnancy, sexual harassment, and dismissal from employment on the grounds of family responsibilities.

The Australian system of sex equality rights follows closely the international human rights conception of nondiscrimination based on sex. The *Sex Discrimination Act* protects against direct and indirect discrimination, although indirect discrimination is subject to a reasonableness test.[46] The Act is based on a formal equality model, and as such, has sometimes been used by male complainants to oppose benefits for women.[47] However, the *Sex Discrimination Act* acknowledges substantive equality in a limited way by allowing "special measures" to be taken to achieve substantive equality. Australia has no affirmative action legislation that allows or requires quota systems. For some years, Australia has had an *Affirmative Action Act*, currently, and in amended form, termed the *Equal Opportunity for Women in the Workplace Act*, that encouraged equality in employment practices.[48] However, this Act was named misleadingly, because, rather than enforcing substantive equality, it was based on the primacy of the merit principle.

The importance of international agreements in Australian constitutional law, and in equality rights, is illustrated by the constitutional challenge made against the sexual harassment provisions of the *Sex Discrimination Act* in *Aldridge v. Booth.*[49] In that case, the complainant, Ms. Aldridge, was an employee of Mr. Booth, and claimed that throughout her employment he subjected her to repeated acts of sexual harassment. The respondent argued that the sexual harassment provisions of the *Sex Discrimination Act* were unconstitutional because they went beyond the scope of the treaty, CEDAW, on which they were based. The Federal Court found that the sexual harassment provisions were valid, based on the broad antidiscrimination and equality principles underlying CEDAW, and the federal external affairs power. The former Sex Discrimination Commissioner, Quentin Bryce, describes the practical importance of Australia's acceptance of CEDAW in that case:

[*Aldridge v Booth*] decided that the provisions under Section 28 of the *Sex Discrimination Act* relating to sexual harassment were valid. They were being challenged. The [] Court had to consider the signing and the ratification of the *Convention on the Elimination of all forms of Discrimination Against Women* (CEDAW) by Australia. We had to run out during the hearing to get evidence of ratification. Evidence of depositing the documents in New York.[50]

---

[46] See *Sex Discrimination Act*, ibid., Section 5(2),7B(1),(2).
[47] See, for example, *Proudfoot v. ACT Board of Health*, [1992] HREOC (17 March 1992).
[48] *Affirmative Action (Equal Opportunity for Women) Act*, 1986 (Cth); *Equal Opportunity for Women in the Workplace Act*, 1999 (Cth).
[49] *Aldridge v. Booth* (1988), 80 ALR 1.
[50] Quentin Bryce, as quoted in Innes, *Millenium Dilemma, supra* note 4 at 17.

The Constitution also protects rights indirectly through the application of Section 109. Under Section 109 of the Constitution, if a state law is inconsistent with a federal law, the state law will be invalid to the extent of the inconsistency. This gives federal laws on antidiscrimination principles primacy over state laws. The external affairs power and Section 109 work as conduits of power, between local (state) and central (federal) and between national and international protection of rights.

The international human rights system, then, is extremely important to Australia's domestic protection of women's rights. International agreements give the Australian federal government the power to protect rights that it otherwise would not have. This means that it is impossible to understand the existence of women's rights in legislated form without looking at the Constitution, but the Constitution alone does almost nothing. It also raises as an issue the impact of the absence of express constitutional protections on women's *material* rights.

SPEAKING INTO A SILENCE: THE NEED FOR ARTICULATED RIGHTS?

In examining women's material rights under the Australian Constitution, it is clear that these can only be understood in the context of a complex framework of legal, political, and cultural constraints. We suggest it would be difficult otherwise to explain how it is that the racist and sexist origins of the text are not more enduring in terms of the everyday conditions in which we live. For instance, we have universal suffrage for all adults over eighteen and comprehensive antidiscrimination laws at the state and federal level, making both racial and sexual discrimination the subject of prohibition and penalty. All this is so despite the fact that the Constitution does not guarantee these. Although there continue to be serious inequalities, Australia compares favorably with many of the countries that have expressly enumerated equality protections in their Constitutions. Despite the existence of comprehensive equality legislation, there are drawbacks to a lack of entrenched protection of women's rights, namely, the lack of protection against parliamentary incursion into human rights. A temporary safeguard was achieved when in *Minister for Immigration and Ethnic Affairs v. Teoh*,[51] the High Court found that even if an international treaty has not been the subject of domestic implementing legislation, the mere fact of a government entering into the treaty created a legitimate expectation that governmental decision makers would act consistently with the terms of the treaty. Where they did not, procedural fairness required that the person affected by the decision be given adequate opportunity to respond. The Federal Government responded to the *Teoh* case by proposing legislation, the *Administrative Decisions (Effect of International Instruments) Bill* 1999, to "undo" this important judicial

[51] (1995), 128 ALR 353.

finding concerning the status of international treaties in Australian law. The purpose of the *Administrative Decisions Bill* is to make it clear that when the government enters into a treaty, no expectations are to arise from that act alone, in the absence of any legislation. The Bill has since lapsed and its future is uncertain.

In Australia, debate continues about how best to protect women's rights with many arguing that a statutory Bill of Rights might be better, as it would articulate a basic system of rights without entrenching the idiosyncrasies of the government of the day. Dame Roma Mitchell, the former Justice of the Supreme Court of South Australia has said: "I would still like us to have a bill of rights but not one that is entrenched. If one thinks back to the time when our Constitution came into being, what rights would have been included? None of the 'founding fathers' would have been in favour of declaring discrimination on the grounds of race illegal."[52]

One of the questions that has arisen for us in writing this is whether the existence of constitutional equality rights would in fact provide guarantees that would be meaningful for women. This is partly because of the way in which rights are arguably only ever an abstracted universalizing form that can never speak to the manifold differences that exist between those who might utilize them.[53] By contrast, the utility of rights is precisely their capacity to infiltrate the language and rhetoric of the lawmakers.

The absence of a Bill of Rights means that both the role of the judiciary and the parliament is crucial in protecting those rights that do exist or which may be implied. With respect to the judiciary, the High Court's willingness to "read" human rights into the common law is essential.

In practice, freedom of speech and other personal freedoms are as much judge-made law in, for example, the United States as they are in Britain and Australia, in the sense that any Bill of Rights will be subject to judicial interpretation. A system of normative fundamental rights can be useful to set limits on both the interpretive scope of the judges and the legislative power of parliament. However, if those limits turn out to be a matter of legalistic hair splitting, then their effectiveness will still ultimately depend on the politics of the court and the parliament. If, for instance, one must choose between race and gender equality when framing a claim and one is an Aboriginal woman, the effects will be unjust and distorted.

We are inclined to agree with a statutory Bill of Rights approach although at times like the present where the government is regressive and conservative it is hard to resist the desire for entrenched equality rights. Nevertheless,

---

[52] Jane Innes, "Interview Dame Roma Mitchell," (recorded 1999), online: University of Wollongong <www.uow.edu.au/law.civics/updates/roma_mitchell.html> (date accessed: 18 April 2001).

[53] Margaret Thornton, "Historicising Citizenship" (1996) 20 *Melbourne University Law Review* 1076.

in Australia we have had a lot of progress developing women's rights and constitutionally guaranteed rights can vanish where they are filtered through institutions that fail to acknowledge their significance.

EMBEDDING CONSTITUTIONAL RIGHTS

It should be clear from the preceding discussion that we see the process of examining the Constitutions of each of our countries from the perspective of women's rights as intimately connected to a broader feminist theorizing of the State. In recent feminist theories of the state, the Constitution is viewed as *one* of the discursive arenas in which power is organized and enacted rather than as the *grundnorm* or foundational and basic legal instrument of the nation determining all power relationships. Pringle and Watson put it like this:

Rethinking the State, we conclude, requires a shift away from seeing the state as a coherent, if contradictory, unity. Instead, we see it as a diverse set of discursive arenas that play a crucial role in organizing relations of power.... Women's interests and thereby feminist politics are constructed in the process of interaction with specific institutions and sites.[54]

Recognizing Constitutions as one site of power should not detract from the importance of finding feminist ways to engage with them. On the contrary, precisely because Constitutions "self-consciously and explicitly deal with fundamental questions relating to the organization of social and political life,"[55] it is crucial to find feminist strategies for engaging with and utilizing these forms. We have not only to recognize the importance of finding a way to, as Adrian Howe puts it, "break out of the constraints imposed by masculinist law scholars on current constitutional conversations,"[56] but we also have to find a contextual and strategic approach to those conversations.

We suggest that the Australian case offers a particularly clear illustration of the location of a Constitution within a larger bureaucratized system of power. Women's rights are embedded in many legal and nonlegal institutions including privatized and deregulated systems of powers such as the marketplace. As we noted earlier, Constitutions are often spoken of as the bones on which the flesh of civil society is hung, and yet this lifeless image of the body politic does not tell us *whose* body is represented, nor *where* the body is located. We are concerned with how women's rights are realized

---

[54] Rosemary Pringle and Sophie Watson, "Women's Interests and the Post-Structuralist State" in Michele Barrett and Anne Phillips, eds., *Destabilizing Theory: Contemporary Feminist Debates* (Stanford, CA: Stanford University Press, 1992) 53–73 at 70.

[55] Patrick Macklem, "Constitutional Ideologies" (1988) 20 *Ottawa Law Review* 117 at 118.

[56] Adrian Howe, "The Constitutional Centenary, Citizenship, The Republic and All That – Absent Feminist Conversationalists" (1995) 20 *Melbourne University Law Review* 218 at 226.

and what such rights look like when viewed in material form. In particular, we are interested in the role of the Constitution in forming and protecting the concrete rights of women. By examining how women's rights are created or undermined in practice, we can *locate* the Constitution in a material and political context.

REPRODUCTIVE RIGHTS AND WOMEN'S BUSINESS

The preceding discussion raises the question of how women's rights are protected in Australia if Constitutional rights are only one of the many legal and institutional factors to be considered. For example, in Australia, there is no constitutional guarantee of privacy or reproductive freedom and yet we have much the same reproductive freedoms and privacy as our U.S. and Canadian counterparts. The point here is that the legal system is only one regulatory mechanism by which women's freedoms are constrained.

We now turn to the way that various forms of regulatory and bureaucratic power constitute, transform, or deny women's freedoms by examining appeals to rights in recent Australian politics: the right of all women to access IVF programs and the right of indigenous women to control their sacred lands.

IVF and Women's Rights

Under the *Sex Discrimination Act* women have a right to equal treatment in the provision of goods and services, regardless of their marital status. "Services" includes medical services, such as IVF. Despite this, the Victorian State government passed legislation in 1995 restricting IVF services to married women. In 1997, they amended this legislation so that de facto (heterosexual) couples could access the services.[57] Only single and lesbian women were excluded by the legislation. If women in this category wanted to have a child using assisted reproductive technologies (ART) or IVF, they had to travel to another state for every treatment, or, in the case of ART, resort to unsafe methods of falling pregnant.

As discussed earlier, under Section 109 of the Constitution, if a state law is inconsistent with a federal law, the state law will be invalid to the extent of the inconsistency. However, it takes a court to declare the relevant sections of the legislation invalid on the grounds of inconsistency. The *Victorian Act* effectively denied IVF to single and lesbian women until a Victorian gynecologist, Dr. John McBain, challenged the legislation.[58] McBain was consulted

---

[57] *Fertility Treatment Act*, 1995 (Vic), Section 8(1) provided: "A woman who undergoes a treatment procedure must – be married and living with her husband on a genuine domestic basis; or be living with a man in a de facto relationship."

[58] *McBain v. State of Victoria*, [2000] FCA 1009 (28 July 2000).

by a woman wishing to access fertilization procedures, and was unable to provide the treatment to her because she was single. McBain applied to the Federal Court for a declaration that Section 8(1) of the State legislation restricting IVF on the basis of marital status was inconsistent with Section 22 of the *Sex Discrimination Act*, which prevents discrimination in the provision of services. The Catholic Church, represented by the Catholic Bishops Conference and the Australian Episcopal Conference of the Roman Catholic Church, appeared as amicus curiae in the case, arguing that the legislation was not inconsistent with the *Sex Discrimination Act*. The Federal Court found that the legislation was inconsistent, and was invalid to that extent.

The Catholic Bishops then applied to the High Court for relief in the form of administrative writs effectively setting aside the decision of the Federal Court. This was an extraordinary step, given that they were not a party in the original case. The Catholic Bishops argued that IVF services are services that can only be provided to a woman, and because the *Sex Discrimination Act* does not cover services that, by their nature, are only capable of being provided to one sex,[59] there is no inconsistency with the state legislation. They also argued that CEDAW does not apply to IVF services or to marital status discrimination and so there is no appropriate international treaty on which the Commonwealth could pass the relevant sections of the *Sex Discrimination Act*. A further extraordinary step was taken by the federal government, in the form of the Attorney General, who granted the Catholic Church a fiat to bring proceedings in its name. The fiat was limited in scope to allow the Catholic Bishops power to litigate the issues surrounding the inconsistency of legislation but not constitutional issues. This, in effect, meant that the federal government could support the discriminatory state legislation without having to put itself in the slightly ridiculous position of arguing against the constitutionality of its own federal legislation.

The High Court handed down its decision in McBain, finding that the Catholic Bishops lacked standing to bring their application.[60] The seven judges of the full court unanimously dismissed both applications, finding that there was no justiciable matter to be heard between the Catholic Bishops or the Attorney General and the respondents. The court did not address the substantive issues of sex discrimination and women's right to access IVF services, potentially leaving these issues open to future challenge.

The IVF example is a good illustration of the indirect impact of the Constitution on women's rights. Although there is no constitutional right to equal access to goods and services, the external affairs power given to the Commonwealth under Section 51(xxix) of the Constitution provided a "backdoor" for such rights by allowing the *Sex Discrimination Act*, based on CEDAW, to be passed as an "external affair." Of course, this assumes that

59 *Sex Discrimination Act*, *supra* note 45, Section 32.
60 *Re McBain; Ex parte Australian Catholic Bishops Conference*, [2002] HCA 16 (18 April 2002).

the federal government wants to protect such rights. In the case of IVF, the federal government has decided that it wants state governments to have the power to discriminate against single and lesbian women in the provision of IVF services. An amendment Bill proposing changes to the "goods and services" sections of the *Sex Discrimination Act* to allow state legislation to discriminate in the regulation of IVF services is currently before Federal Parliament.[61]

The developments around IVF and access to services demonstrates the complexity of the federal-state relationship, the Constitution, international agreements, and domestic legislation in formulating, or undermining, women's equality rights. Equal access to IVF is protected in the federal *Sex Discrimination Act*, which relies for its existence on the implementation of CEDAW through the external affairs power. However, the protection of women's rights in the *Sex Discrimination Act* relies on political and legal will. This illustrates the importance of other forms of institutional power in the concrete realization of expressed rights, for instance, the significance of the role of medical and religious institutions, and their perception of mothering or reproduction, in protecting or opposing women's rights. The discriminatory Victorian legislation was declared invalid because of the actions of an individual doctor concerned about the legal rights of his patients. Other doctors, such as this IVF specialist, testifying before a Senate Committee inquiring into the *Sex Discrimination Amendment Bill*, are not so protective of their patient's rights:

Another case [of mine] was of a woman who had had her tubes ligated, and had had children previously but, during the course of the interview, it transpired that the reason she did not have any children was that the children's services department had taken them into care for abuse and she wanted to replace those children using infertility services. I personally felt it was inappropriate and so I declined to assist, even though I suspect I may have been committing an act of discrimination.[62]

This makes it clear that women's rights will not be upheld as long as there are individuals with institutional power to oppose those rights. We think medical power is one of the sources of control over women that is underestimated and cannot necessarily be remedied by a bill of rights. Religious institutions also exert extralegal power. The Catholic Bishops have been the major driving force in the litigation to remove women's equal access to IVF services.

Although this example demonstrates the web of interests and power affecting women's rights and determining whether those rights are realized

---

[61] *Sex Discrimination Amendment Bill 2002.*

[62] Dr. David Molloy, *Transcript of evidence* (13 February 2001) at 13, as cited in Senate Legal and Constitutional Committee, *Inquiry into the Provisions of the Sex Discrimination Amendment Bill (No. 1) 2000* (Canberra: Commonwealth of Australia, 2001) (Dissenting Report of Senator Hogg and Senator Collins) at 72.

or undermined, this does not mean that the Constitution is irrelevant. This example also shows the importance of the Constitution as a conduit of rights through the external affairs power and Section 109. Of course, the protection that can derive from Section 109 is contingent on the fact that the federal statute be more progressive than state legislation and there is no constitutional obligation that this be the case. However, in practice federal legislation implementing international treaties is more progressive as it imports aspirational standards from the international human rights system.

Aboriginal Women's Rights

Another recent case stands out as a moment when the judiciary could have developed the constitutional jurisprudence of Australia to strengthen the rights of women and indigenous Australians. However, whereas the example of access to medical services, specifically IVF, demonstrates the potential weakness of a legislated system of equality rights, *Kartinyeri v. Commonwealth*[63] demonstrates that constitutional provisions are also vulnerable to alternate interpretations. Written, as they must be, in broad and general terms, they are incapable of expressing the particularity amongst the members of the group to which they refer. In this case, the races power refers only to the power to make laws for "the people of any race." The power is not given to consider the differing needs of women of the relevant race compared with men. Before going further, it must be stated that the Races power is just that, a power to make laws not a guarantee in the form of an absolute right individual or otherwise. Nevertheless, the 1967 amendment to the Races power discussed earlier was both intended and understood at the time to allow the federal government to assist and benefit the indigenous population and to stop the conservative states from both neglecting and discriminating against Aborigines.[64] Instead, in *Kartinyeri*, indigenous women lost because the Constitution was interpreted in a way that was conservative and legalistic. There was, of course, scope for a different interpretation of the Constitution.

---

[63] (1998), 72 ALJR 722.

[64] The official case for supporting the 1967 amendment to the Races power stated:

> "The purposes of these amendments to the Commonwealth Constitution are to remove any ground for the belief that, as at present worded, the Constitution discriminates in some ways against people of the Aboriginal race, and, at the same time, to make it possible for the Commonwealth Parliament to make special laws for the people of the Aboriginal race, wherever they may live, if the Commonwealth Parliament considers this desirable or necessary."

> *Justice and Equity: Resources on the Reconciliation Process and Social Justice for Indigenous Australians* (Sydney: Human Rights and Equal Opportunity Commission, 1995), CD-ROM.

Kartinyeri concerned the question of whether the Commonwealth government could pass laws to remove the rights of a group of indigenous women who claimed that the site of a proposed development was a sacred site for Aboriginal women. The case had a protracted history. It originated in a proposal to build tourist facilities on Hindmarsh Island in South Australia, including a bridge to the mainland to allow access to the new facilities. An organization representing a group of indigenous women opposed the development and bridge, on the grounds that it would damage or desecrate a significant area in the traditions of the Ngarrindjeri people. In fact, in the words of the original applicants, the construction of the bridge would "undermine cosmological and human reproduction and cause Ngarrindjeri society and its traditions to ultimately disappear."[65] Women of the Ngarrindjeri people knew of the sacred nature of the area and its significance, but their knowledge was secret according to Ngarrindjeri law. It was privileged knowledge that only women were allowed to access according to their traditions. As such, it could not be told to men. In addition it could not be told to women who were not authorized to have access to the knowledge. There was immediate dispute over the veracity of the claims, compounded by the fact that some Ngarrindjeri women were quoted as saying they knew nothing about the sacredness of the site. Because many of the women had been taken from their traditional community as children and brought up in a mission, it is not surprising that the claim was virtually impossible to verify. The competing claims of the Ngarrindjeri women along with the voice of the female developer became the subject of a story in *Who Weekly*, an Australian women's magazine. The magazine gave each woman a chance to speak freely in representing their position. McKee and Hartley write of how the article enabled the "truth value of each of the positions offered . . . [to be attested] . . . by personal reminiscence and experience."[66] In contrast, the legal presentation filtered out the voices of women and their concerns in favor of increasingly legalistic abstracted language.

The filtering out of women's voices has always been part of the relationship between white and Aboriginal Australia. Early attempts to recognize indigenous rights in Australia were mostly conducted by white men through negotiations with Aboriginal men. The assumption was that men were the leaders of their communities and not the women. The Sex Discrimination Commissioner's submission on Aboriginal Customary Law puts it like this: "This historical bias laid the foundation for an ongoing emphasis on the role of men, and a "feedback loop" in which male views are recognised and

---

[65] As cited by Gaudron J in *Wilson v. The Minister for Aboriginal and Torres Strait Islander Affairs* (1996), 189 CLR 1 at para. 7.

[66] Alan McKee and John Hartley, "Truth Integrity and a Little Gossip," In *Australia Alternative Law Journal* Vol. 21, No. 1 Feb. 1996, 17.

reflected back to communities by mainstream institutions while women's views are marginalised."[67]

The significance of the desecration of their sacred site for the Ngarrindjeri women was lost in the proliferating legal and political documentation.[68] There is a notable absence in the *Hindmarsh Island* cases of discussion of the consequences for Ngarrindjeri society and its female knowledge holders if desecration of their sacred site occurred. The absence is particularly striking given the assertion by the Ngarrindjeri women that their society would ultimately end if the building went ahead, and is evidence of the abstracting effect of constitutional language.

While the case was still being tried, a new federal government was elected to power. In order to put an end to the dispute, the new government passed the *Hindmarsh Island Bridge Act* 1997 (Cth.). The Act terminated the rights of Aboriginal people under the Heritage Protection Act to seek to restrain development of the Hindmarsh Island Bridge, regardless of whether the development would desecrate Aboriginal sacred sites.

The plaintiffs argued before the High Court that the *Hindmarsh Island Bridge Act* was invalid. A central plank of their argument was that the Races power of the Constitution only empowered laws for the *benefit or advancement* of people of any race. They contended that the Races power could not be relied on to pass racially discriminatory laws, if not for all races, then at least not for Aboriginal people, given the history of the power. Another argument raised on behalf of the plaintiffs was that the Races power was ambiguously expressed, and should be construed as far as possible in accordance with international human rights norms of nondiscrimination. What was not and could not be argued was that Aboriginal women were uniquely disadvantaged by this new law and that in so being there was not only racial discrimination present but also sex discrimination.

Despite the perception that the Races power was amended in 1967 to benefit Aborigines, the court looked both at the express terms of the Constitution and the original intention of the drafters and did not find that the power only authorized beneficial laws because in its terms it did not express such an intent. This is despite the fact that the amendment was passed on a

---

[67] Human Rights and Equal Opportunity Commission, *Submission to the Northern Territory Law Reform Committee Inquiry into Aboriginal Customary Law in Northern Territory* (HREOC, May 2003), available online at <http://www.humanrights.gov.au/sex_discrimination/customary_law/submission.html>.

[68] A separate but related issue here is the widespread speculation at the time that the women involved in asserting the "secret women's business" were wrong or misleading in their assertions. A Royal Commission held into what became known as the Hindmarsh Island Affair failed to support the assertions. However, a recent federal court case found to the contrary. In *Chapman v. Luminis Pty Ltd (No 5)*, [2001] FCA 1106 (21 August 2001), the court did not accept that the women's secret knowledge was fabricated or that it was not part of genuine Aboriginal tradition.

wave of support for the introduction of measures to assist Aborigines. Justice Gaudron rejected the argument that the amendment disclosed a constitutional intention that thereafter the power should extend only to beneficial laws.

However, she did go on to elaborate the meaning of the phrase "the people of any race for whom it is deemed necessary to make special laws." Gaudron J accepted that the Races power does not authorize special laws affecting rights and obligations in areas in which there is no relevant difference between the people of the race to whom the law is directed and the people of other races. Second, the law must be reasonably capable of being viewed as appropriate and adapted to the difference that is claimed where there is a relevant difference. So although the power is wide enough to authorise both advantageous and disadvantageous laws, she argued, it is difficult to conceive of circumstances in relation to Aboriginal Australians where a disadvantageous law would be valid, because it could not reasonably be viewed as appropriate and adapted to their different circumstances. These "different" circumstances Justice Gaudron described as serious disadvantage, including disadvantaged material circumstances and the vulnerability of indigenous culture. In other words, the term "special" laws required attention to the contemporary circumstances of the group in question and given the current state of disadvantage in Aboriginal populations, a special law could only be beneficial.

Nevertheless, Gaudron J accepted that the *Bridge Act* merely amended the *Heritage Protection Act* and that the *Heritage Protection Act* continued to be a valid act under the Races power because it continued to protect and preserve areas and objects of significance to Aborigines. Her argument is, we believe, ultimately undermined by her acceptance of the *Bridge Act* amendment and had the result of disadvantaging a group of Aboriginal women.

Several of the other judges also were persuaded by the view that the *Hindmarsh Island Bridge Act* was only in effect reducing the *Heritage Protection Act* and so repealed in part the *Heritage Protection Act* rather than being a whole new Act.[69] A repealing Act was, they considered, supported by the head of power that supports the law – in this case the Races power.

The only judge to hold the Act invalid was Justice Kirby who, in doing so, argued that the Constitution was not intended to violate human rights.[70]

The Court in *Kartinyeri* demonstrates that constitutional changes do not necessarily provide a stable base for a reliable system of rights. Nor does ordinary human rights legislation protect women's rights against a government with a social agenda at odds with principles of equality. It is difficult,

---

[69] Gummow and Hayne JJ held that special laws were quite likely to disadvantage one race even as they advantaged another, and that a restrictive interpretation could not be put on the Races power and therefore both beneficial and nonbeneficial legislation would be permitted.

[70] Justice Kirby in *Kartinyeri, supra* note 63 at 765.

therefore, to see how an entrenched right to equality in the Constitution would have offered a different outcome in *Kartinyeri* and the cases that follow it. What the case does then, is remind us that the Constitution – any Constitution – is limited by the forms of power in which it is embedded. Although we might view the Court as wrong-headed in this instance, it is clear that even entrenched rights offer no guarantees of redressing material harm.

CONCLUSION

The Australian Constitution was never intended to describe or protect the kinds of equality rights that we expect for women today. Fixed in a racist and sexist ideology, anything it might have had to say about women's rights would not have been something that we would have wanted entrenched for all time.

Despite this, it is clear from the Australian experience that the development of a sense of women's rights over the past one hundred years has built a web of interpretation around and within the document of the Constitution that does protect women's rights. Nevertheless, where there is a failure of legal imagination or a lack of political will, women's rights founder. The Constitution is a mere skeleton, not only embedded in the living body of the State but also in a political and social context that changes in its commitment to women's rights. That skeleton gives us a basic democratic structure but alone is lifeless and gives us little else.

Our approach to the Australian Constitution, then, is necessarily somewhat postmodern. The interests of women are not unitary but diverse so that the interests of indigenous women will not necessarily coalesce with the interests of white middle-class women. In addition, the interests that oppose women's rights are similarly diverse. The Constitution both actively constitutes and is constituted by those interests. We reject the view of the Constitution as a kind of monolithic and impervious instrument of power but, rather, see it as a text that is imbricated within existing webs of power, developing, responding, and actively resisting, at different moments, the various forces within which it is operating.

For feminists, then, to engage with the discursive power of Constitutions, it is strategically imperative to identify both the external local and global forces that make up the whole of the discursive frame. We agree with Tony Blackshield that the Constitution "is a piece of paper; pieces of paper don't do very much. It is what you do with them that counts."[71] We argue for an embedded approach to constitutional rights, one that acknowledges all of the diverse ways in which rights are filtered, translated, upheld, or undermined.

---

[71] Tony Blackshield, as cited in Jane Innes, *Millenium Dilemma, supra* note 4 at 1.

Suggested Further Readings Not Included in the Footnotes

Sandra S. Berns, "Law, Citizenship and the Politics of Identity: Sketching the Limits of Citizenship" (1998) 7 *Griffith Law Review* 1–29.

Greta Bird and Loretta Kelly, "Women Speak Out: Critical Perspectives on the Proposed Preamble to the Constitution" (2000) 6 *Australian Journal of Human Rights* 265–79.

Linda Burney, "The Constitutional Guarantees that Aboriginal People Want" in Jane Gardiner ed., *Here We Come, Ready or Not!* (Sydney: Women Into Politics Inc., 1998) 74–77.

Deborah Cass and Kim Rubenstein, "Representations of Women in the Australian Constitutional System" (1995) 17 *Adelaide Law Review* 3–47.

Adrian Howe, "The Constitutional Centenary, Citizenship, The Republic and All That – Absent Feminist Conversationalists" (1995) 20 *Melbourne University Law Review* 218.

Helen Irving, "Thinking of England: Women, Politics and the Queen" in Jeanette Hoorn and David Goodman, eds., *Vox Re(publicae): Feminism and the Republic* (special edition (1995–1996)) 46–50 *Journal of Australian Studies* (Melbourne: La Trobe University Press, 1996) 33–41.

Helen Irving, "With Other Men and Other Means: Women and the Constitution" (1994) 3 *Constitutional Centenary* 11–12.

Marilyn Lake, "Personality, Individuality, Nationality: Feminist Conceptions of Citizenship 1902–1940" (1994) *Australian Feminist Studies* 25–38.

Marilyn Lake, "The Meanings of the 'Self' in Claims for Self Government: Reclaiming Citizenship for Women and Indigenous People in Australia" (1996) 14 *Law in Context* 9–23.

Marilyn Lake, "The Republic, The Federation and the Intrusion of the Political" in Jeanette Hoorn and David Goodman, eds., *Vox Re(publicae): Feminism and the Republic* (special edition (1995–1996)) 46–50 *Journal of Australian Studies* (Melbourne: La Trobe University Press, 1996) 5–15.

Vicky Marquis, "A Feminist Republic? A Feminist Constitution?" (1993) 65 *Australian Quarterly* 29–44.

Marian Sawer, "Engendering Constitutional Debate" (1998) 23 *Alternative Law Journal* 78–81.

Margaret Thornton, "Embodying the Citizen" in *Public/Private: Feminist Legal Debates* (Oxford: Oxford University Press, 1995) 198–220.

Margaret Thornton, "Historicising Citizenship: Remembering Broken Promises" (1997) 20 *Melbourne University Law Review* 1072–86.

Margaret Thornton, "Towards Embodied Justice: Wrestling with Legal Ethics in the Age of the New Corporatism" (1999) 23 *Melbourne University Law Review* 754–72.

2

Using the Canadian Charter of Rights and Freedoms to Constitute Women

Beverley Baines

In 1867, Britain gave its Canadian colonies a written Constitution that imposed a federal system of parliamentary government.[1] While making jurisdiction a constraint on law-making, this Constitution did not provide Canadians with human rights protections (although rights such as freedom of contract and private property received common law protection). The legislatures could pass laws denying women the right to vote, hold public office, serve on juries or in the armed forces, immigrate, perform certain jobs, have an independent domicile or continue to work after marriage, dispose of property, have an abortion, receive unemployment insurance after giving birth, retain aboriginal status on marrying a non-aboriginal, or retain Canadian citizenship on marrying a non-Canadian. Whenever litigants challenged these laws by invoking international, statutory, or unwritten human rights protections, most Canadian judges refused to recognize their claims. Thus, constitutional litigation was not a viable strategy for women.

This picture changed significantly when the existing Constitution was supplemented by new constitutional provisions in 1982.[2] Prominent among these changes was the *Charter*, which delineates seven major rights: political (religion, expression, assembly, and association), democratic, mobility, legal, equality, language (official and minority educational), and aboriginal rights.[3] Canadians may assert *Charter* rights against both levels of government, albeit not against private actors unless they are carrying out a governmental

---

[1] *Constitution Act, 1867* (U.K.), 30 & 31 Vict., c. 3, reprinted in R.S.C. 1985, App. II, No. 5.

[2] *Constitution Act, 1982*, being Schedule B to the *Canada Act 1982* (U.K.), 1982, c. 11.

[3] *Canadian Charter of Rights and Freedoms*, Part I of the *Constitution Act, 1982*, ibid., ss. 1–34. Aboriginal constitutional rights also are found outside of the *Charter* in the *Constitution Act, 1982*, ibid., s. 35.

function.[4] This rights protection regime transformed the system of government from parliamentary to constitutional supremacy by assigning the enforcement of *Charter* rights to the regular courts.[5]

Canada has a unified court system that encompasses all criminal, civil, and constitutional matters. With the exception of references,[6] cases originate at the trial level and may, with leave, be appealed to a provincial appellate court and finally to the Supreme Court of Canada. This Court is composed of nine judges appointed by the Prime Minister and entitled to sit until age seventy-five. Aside from adding *Charter* adjudication to its docket, the new constitutional provisions did not restructure the Court. Nevertheless an important *de facto* change occurred. Simultaneously with the adoption of the *Charter*, the first woman judge was appointed to the Court; currently three women sit, one of whom is the Chief Justice. However, no constitutional or statutory rule guarantees continued gender representation on the Court, even though one would not be entirely unprecedented, given that by law at least three judges must come from the Province of Quebec.[7]

What does *Charter* jurisprudence reveal about the impact on women of adopting a rights protection regime? To assess this jurisprudence, I adopt three criteria:[8] Does the *Charter* rights protection regime facilitate the feminist "project of naming, of exposing the world as manmade"? Do *Charter* rights enable feminists to litigate contextually by presenting "various women's realities in all their complexities"? Has *Charter* jurisprudence served as a force for societal transformation, or has it kept feminists focused "on a fairer redistribution of resources"? First, however, I examine the role of feminists in the development of *Charter* equality doctrine.

FEMINISTS ADVOCATE EQUALITY

The adoption of the *Charter* cast Canadian feminists into two major roles. As lobbyists, feminists advocated for sex equality and other *Charter* rights, recognizing their fate depended on whether governments could limit or abrogate rights. As litigators, feminists often acted collectively to import the doctrine of substantive equality into *Charter* cases.

---

[4] *Charter*, ibid., s. 32.

[5] *Charter*, ibid., s. 24(1).

[6] In reference cases, governments may apply to courts for advisory opinions on the constitutionality of legislation.

[7] *Supreme Court Act*, R.S.C. 1985, c. S-26, s. 6.

[8] The three criteria (and quotes) that follow derive from Sherene Razack, *Canadian Feminism and the Law: The Women's Legal Education and Action Fund and the Pursuit of Equality* (Toronto: Second Story Press, 1991) at 127–38.

As Lobbyists

Between 1980 and 1982, feminists lobbied both levels of governments for recognition of women's constitutional rights.[9] This process went through three stages. The first stage involved legally knowledgeable women who "stressed the requirement for ironclad entrenched equality between women and men as a non-negotiable demand."[10] During the next stage, this objective was pursued more widely by established women's groups working with the Ad Hoc Committee of Canadian Women on the Constitution, a women's lobby group that arose spontaneously after the male Cabinet Minister responsible for the status of women ordered the cancellation of a women's constitutional conference less than a month before it was to take place. The final stage reached far beyond activists to individual women, each of whom perceived equality rights were under attack after government leaders agreed some *Charter* rights, including sex equality rights, could be temporarily overridden by a legislative declaration.[11] In fact, the potential for violating *Charter* equality rights led the Province of Quebec to enact five sex equality override laws in 1986, 1991, 1996, and 2001 in order to allow some government pension plans to differentiate between women's eligibility for pension (age sixty) and men's (age sixty-five).[12]

Ultimately, two sex equality provisions were included in the *Charter*. The general equality provision (Section 15) prohibits discrimination on nine listed grounds including sex, as well as permitting ameliorative programs for disadvantaged individuals or groups. It provides:

15. (1) Every individual is equal before and under the law and has the right to the equal protection and equal benefit of the law without discrimination and, in particular, without discrimination based on race, national or ethnic origin, colour, religion, sex, age or mental or physical disability.

(2) Subsection (1) does not preclude any law, program or activity that has as its object the amelioration of conditions of disadvantaged individuals or groups including those that are disadvantaged because of race, national or ethnic origin, colour, religion, sex, age or mental or physical disability.[13]

---

[9] Alexandra Dobrowolsky, *The Politics of Pragmatism: Women, Representation, and Constitutionalism in Canada* (Toronto: Oxford University Press, 2000).

[10] Penny Kome, *The Taking of Twenty-Eight: Women Challenge the Constitution* (Toronto: Women's Educational Press, 1983) at 17–18.

[11] *Charter*, ibid, note 3, s. 33(1), known as the "override", states: "Parliament or the legislature of a province may expressly declare in an Act of Parliament or of the legislature, as the case may be, that the Act or a provision thereof shall operate notwithstanding a provision included in section 2 or sections 7 to 15 of this *Charter*...."

[12] Tsvi Kahana, "The notwithstanding mechanism and public discussion: Lessons from the ignored practice of section 33 of the Charter" (2001), 44 *Canadian Public Administration* 255, noting the protection of these gendered pension plans accounted for five of the seventeen pieces of legislation invoking the override provision across the country since its inception.

[13] *Charter*, *supra* note 3.

The effect of Section 15 was delayed for three years to give governments time to review their existing legislation for consistency with its terms. The second provision (Section 28) deals only with sex equality and provides:

28. Notwithstanding anything in this Charter, the rights and freedoms referred to in it are guaranteed equally to male and female persons.[14]

Section 28 has yet to receive definitive meaning. However, the Court has indicated it is an interpretive, rather than substantive rights-bearing, provision.[15] Thus, its exemption from the override provision is of questionable value, which is regrettable, given Section 15 is not exempted.

A third sex equality provision (Section 35[4]) was entrenched by constitutional amendment in 1983.[16] This section provides:

35. (4) Notwithstanding any other provision of this Act, the aboriginal and treaty rights referred to in subsection (1) are guaranteed equally to male and female persons.

Limited to aboriginal claimants and yet to be interpreted, Section 35(4) is exempt from the *Charter's* override provision because it falls outside the *Charter*.

Aside from Section 15(1), the only *Charter* right to benefit women thus far is security of the person.[17] However, the courts have resolved other *Charter* issues – jurisdiction, standing, interpretation, remedies, and limits – taking a liberal approach to all but the last. Thus, jurisdictional challenges may arise "in any proceedings, before courts of all levels, and even before administrative tribunals."[18] Standing is virtually a nonissue: defendants in criminal prosecutions may dispute the validity of the statutes under which they were charged; parties to civil actions may impugn the constitutionality of statutes that govern their litigation in an effort to avoid their effects; parties may challenge the validity of statutes governing administrative tribunal decisions; and opponents of legislation who are not themselves impacted by it may nonetheless seek to have it declared constitutionally invalid.[19] The interpretation of *Charter* rights must be purposive, that is, broad, large, liberal,

---

[14] *Charter*, ibid.

[15] *Native Women's Association of Canada v. Canada*, [1994] 3 S.C.R. 627.

[16] *Constitution Amendment Proclamation, 1983*, SI/84–102, now *Constitution Act, 1982, supra* note 2, s. 35(4).

[17] *Charter, supra* note 3, s. 7, which provides: "Everyone has the right to life, liberty and security of the person and the right not to be deprived thereof except in accordance with the principles of fundamental justice."

[18] Peter W. Hogg, *Constitutional Law of Canada* (Toronto: Carswell, 1997), 4d. (looseleaf), c. 56 at 56–1.

[19] Hogg, *Constitutional Law of Canada*, ibid. at 56–2 ("It is even possible to bring proceedings in which the only relief sought is a declaration that a statute is invalid. Liberal rules of standing have made declaratory proceedings available to individuals or groups who oppose a particular statute, but who cannot show that the statute has any special impact upon them.")

and generous.[20] And the Court set out six remedies – nullification, temporary validity, severance, reading in, reading down, and constitutional exemption – to enforce *Charter* rights.[21]

The interpretation of the *Charter's* express limitations clause remains controversial.[22] Initially, the party upholding the impugned law had to justify its legitimacy and proportionality.[23] However, the Court has become deferential when legislatures are balancing the claims of competing groups.[24] According to one commentator, this "revised deferential understanding of the limitation provision ... poses the danger of moving the *Charter* far from its text, original design and chosen models."[25] Her argument is reminiscent of the feminist critique of the expansiveness of the original draft of the limitations clause. Sadly, the judiciary seems inclined to resurrect what the 1982 constitution-makers discarded.

As Litigators

After Section 15 became effective, the lower courts were inundated with equality cases. Of 591 cases decided during the first three years, less than 10 percent were based on sex, thirty-five of which were brought by or on behalf of men and only nine by or on behalf of women.[26] Although this litigation focused mainly on formal equality, even that represented an improvement over pre-*Charter* decisions denying gendered intermarriage and pregnancy discrimination laws violating women's equality rights.[27] Fortunately, the Supreme Court of Canada decided equality should not be restricted to formal equality, recognizing "that every difference in treatment between individuals under the law will not necessarily result in inequality and, as well, that identical treatment may frequently produce serious inequality."[28] Thereafter, the Court affirmed that this decision had signaled

---

[20] *Hunter v. Southam*, [1984] 2 S.C.R. 145 at 155–7.

[21] *Schachter v. Canada*, [1992] 2 S.C.R. 679.

[22] *Charter*, *supra* note 3, s. 1, which provides: "The Canadian Charter of Rights and Freedoms guarantees the rights and freedoms set out in it subject only to such reasonable limits prescribed by law as can be demonstrably justified in a free and democratic society."

[23] *R. v. Oakes*, [1986] 1 S.C.R. 103.

[24] *A.G. Quebec v. Irwin Toy Limited*, [1989] 1 S.C.R. 927 at 993–4. For a critique of the deferential approach, see Sheilah Martin, "Balancing Individual Rights to Equality and Social Goals" (2001), 80 *Canadian Bar Review* 299.

[25] Lorraine E. Weinrib, "Canada's *Charter of Rights*: Paradigm Lost?" (2002), 6 *Review of Constitutional Studies* 119–78.

[26] Gwen Brodsky and Shelagh Day, *Canadian Charter Equality Rights for Women: One Step Forward or Two Steps Back?* (Ottawa: Canadian Advisory Council on the Status of Women, 1989) at 49.

[27] *A.G. Canada v. Lavell*, [1974] S.C.R. 1349; *Bliss v. A.G. Canada*, [1979] 1 S.C.R. 183.

[28] *Law Society of British Columbia v. Andrews*, [1989] 1 S.C.R. 143 at 164. See: Colleen Sheppard, "The 'I' in the 'It': Reflections on a Feminist Approach to Constitutional Theory" in Richard

its commitment to substantive equality, stating the purpose of Section 15 is "to prevent the violation of essential human dignity and freedom through the imposition of disadvantage, stereotyping, or political or social prejudice, and to promote a society in which all persons enjoy equality recognition at law as human beings or as members of Canadian society, equally capable and equally deserving of concern, respect and consideration."[29]

Much of the credit for persuading the Court to adopt substantive equality analysis belongs to the Women's Legal Education and Action Fund, better known as LEAF. Following a nationally funded research study that concluded "a legal action fund to concentrate on issues of sex-based discrimination is an essential component of an effective strategy to promote the interests of women in the Canadian legal system,"[30] LEAF was created as a national nonprofit organization with the dual mandates of participating in litigation that promotes equality for women and of educating the public about this litigation and its relationship to women's equality.[31] LEAF advocates substantive equality, although its original proactive vision of initiating litigation has succumbed to the necessity of responding to a plethora of equality rights challenges raised by others. Thus, LEAF often intervenes in equality litigation.[32]

Even its most conservative critics acknowledge LEAF "has gone on to become not only the most frequent but also the most successful nongovernmental intervener in cases before the Supreme Court," serving as a model for the formation of other national litigation and advocacy groups.[33] What galls these critics is that these organizations derive funding from governments, a major source being the Court Challenges Program. Originally created to fund language rights litigation, this Program was expanded to include equality rights claims. Unexpectedly cancelled in 1992, the Program was reinstated in 1995 by a new government. The modesty of its current budget ($5.9 million in 2000–1) relative to overall government spending suggests the critics' real objection may be to the legitimacy such funds confer on the legal reforms advocated by LEAF and other advocacy organizations.

F. Devlin, *Canadian Perspectives on Legal Theory* (Toronto: Emond Montgomery Publications Limited, 1991), 415–31.

[29] *Law v. Canada*, [1999] 1 S.C.R. 497 at para. 51.

[30] M. Elizabeth Atcheson, Mary Eberts, and Beth Symes, *Women and Legal Action* (Ottawa: Canadian Advisory Council on the Status of Women, 1984) at 163.

[31] Women's Legal Education and Action Fund, *Equality and the Charter: Ten Years of Feminist Advocacy before the Supreme Court of Canada* (Toronto: Emond Montgomery Publications Limited, 1996).

[32] Nonparties with an "interest" (i.e., upon showing they will in some material way be affected by a legal issue) may seek leave to intervene in litigation. Recently, the Court has begun to insist interveners contribute something new, and not simply reinforce arguments by parties.

[33] F. L. Morton and Rainer Knopff, *The Charter Revolution and the Court Party* (Peterborough, ON: Broadview Press, 2000) at 26, 68–9.

NAMING MALE PRIVILEGE

"The project that is feminism applied to law," a Canadian women's studies scholar argued, "is fundamentally a project of naming, of exposing the world as man-made."[34] Adopting and elaborating her thesis, a feminist legal scholar explained "male privilege" as follows:

Women's inequalities and the discrimination that is so interwoven into women's daily lives are largely unrecognizable and incomprehensible to those in dominant positions. It is the privilege of not knowing and the, often unconscious, resistance to finding out that are at stake here. Section 15 offers a place from which privilege can be challenged and for this reason alone, it is an important tool.[35]

In other words, *Charter* litigation provides a vehicle for women to name "objective" reality for what it is, a world organized consistently with male practices and beliefs. Jurisprudence in five areas of law – athletics, reproduction, crime, family, and employment – illustrates how *Charter* adjudication has served this function.

Athletics

Before the *Charter*, several girls challenged their exclusions from single-sex recreational sports teams; one was successful, while two others failed because the antidiscrimination statute in their province exempted single-sex recreational sports teams.[36] After the *Charter*, another girl challenged that exemption, arguing it violated her *Charter* right to sex equality.[37] She was successful. According to the judges, the exemption permitted the posting of a "no females allowed" sign by every athletic organization in the province. However, they stopped well short of transforming recreational sports, observing there could be other situations where distinctions based on sex might be reasonable. In effect, the most promising feature of this case appeared subsequent to the court decision when an antidiscrimination tribunal decided even though male hockey did not need to be protected from females, female hockey should continue to be protected from males. Stating protection of female hockey is necessary to open athletic activities to women, the tribunal did not allow the formal equality of the court decision to impede a substantively equal outcome.[38]

34 Sherene Razack, *Canadian Feminism and the Law, supra* note 8 at 137.
35 Diana Majury, "Women's (In)Equality before and after the Charter" in Radha Jappan, ed., *Women's Legal Strategies in Canada* (Toronto: University of Toronto Press, 2002), 101 at 118.
36 *La Commission des Droits de la Personne* c. *La Federation Québeçois de Hockey Sur Glace, Inc.,* [1978] C.S. 1076; *Re Cummings and Ontario Minor Hockey Association* (1978), 26 O.R. (2d) 7; *Re Ontario Human Rights Commission and Ontario Rural Softball Association* (1979), 26 O.R. (2d) 134.
37 *Re Blainey and Ontario Hockey Association* (1986), 54 O.R. (2d) 513.
38 *Blainey v. Ontario Hockey Association* (1988), 9 C.H.R.R. D/716.

Reproduction

Prosecuted for performing abortions, a doctor argued the prohibition infringed women's right to privacy and to make unfettered decisions about their lives.[39] The Court, which has the power to redefine issues upon granting leave to appeal, characterized his challenge as based upon the Section 7 right to life, liberty, and security of the person, leaving the question of whether Canadians have a constitutional right to privacy unresolved. Then, in a 5–2 decision, the Court ruled the prohibition on abortion infringed security of the person, confirming that right extends beyond physical to psychological integrity. The only woman judge, Madame Justice Bertha Wilson, held the abortion provision also deprived women of the right to liberty, which she defined in terms of personal autonomy over important decisions intimately affecting one's private life. Although liberty had previously been restricted to situations involving incarceration, her definition was affirmed more recently.[40] Thus, it is available for future litigation involving women's reproductive claims and other related issues.

Madame Justice Wilson also captured the male privilege inherent in regulating abortion when she wrote: "It is probably impossible for a man to respond, even imaginatively, to such a dilemma not just because it is outside the realm of his personal experience (although this is, of course, the case) but because he can relate to it only by objectifying it, thereby eliminating the subjective elements of the female psyche which are at the heart of the dilemma."[41] However, the Court's decision stopped well short of creating a constitutional right to an abortion when the judges upheld the legitimacy of balancing fetal interests against those of women. In other words, the government failed only because the therapeutic exception – which required the involvement of four doctors, hospitalization, and a diagnosis of danger to the woman's life or health – was too stringent to achieve an appropriate balance. Thus, the decision left open the possibility for further, albeit more narrowly conditioned, regulation.

In fact, the national government tried to enact a new abortion provision with somewhat less stringent therapeutic exception requirements less than three years later, carrying the vote in the popularly elected House of Commons but failing by one vote in the appointed Senate.[42] As a result, the Canadian Supreme Court has yet to rule on the issue of whether a fetus is entitled to a right to life under Section 7 of the *Charter*. In a pregnancy

---

[39] *R. v. Morgentaler*, [1988] 1 S.C.R. 30. This decision decriminalized abortion, leaving it subject only to provincial health laws that can regulate but not prohibit it.

[40] *R.B. v. Children's Aid Society of Metropolitan Toronto*, [1995] 1 S.C.R. 315.

[41] *Morgentaler, supra* note 39, at para. 240.

[42] Janine Brodie, "Choice and No Choice in the House," in Janine Brodie, Shelley A. M. Gavigan, and Jane Jenson, *The Politics of Abortion* (Toronto: Oxford University Press, 1992) at 115.

intervention case, however, the Court denied it had a common law *parens patriae* jurisdiction to protect a fetus by detaining the mother who was addicted to glue-sniffing. Not only did LEAF intervene on *Charter* liberty, security of the person, and equality grounds but also the woman judge who wrote the majority opinion referred to the pregnant woman's right to make a considerable range of choices for herself.[43] Despite favorable outcomes in this and the abortion decision, these cases do not guarantee women the constitutional right to control our own bodies; from this perspective, societal transformation is not yet a reality.[44]

Crime

Men who are accused of crimes frequently invoke their *Charter* rights – of sex equality, liberty, a fair trial, full answer and defense, or freedom of expression – to impugn the constitutionality of the laws under which they were charged. In particular, men accused of sexual assault have relentlessly targeted the substantive and procedural features of those laws. For example, the first sex equality case the Canadian Supreme Court decided was an appeal by two men who had been charged with statutory rape.[45] At that time, statutory rape was defined as a man having sexual intercourse with a girl under the age of fourteen, irrespective of whether he believed she was fourteen or older. All seven judges agreed that because it was defined as an absolute liability offense, statutory rape clearly violated the men's Section 7 right to liberty. Ruling the government had not justified this violation, a majority of judges also decided the obvious remedy was simply to strike out the absolute liability clause, thereby treating the offense as a *mens rea* crime.

However, the accused men also claimed the provision infringed their sex equality rights because it applied only to the accused of one sex and to victims of one sex. The majority judges denied any infringement, reasoning that because the criminal statute defined the offence in terms of intercourse and further defined intercourse as penetration, only males could commit the offense. Continuing, they reasoned that girls and boys are victims of two different biological acts, and the provision was not discriminatory simply because it addressed one of these acts and not the other. They accepted that

---

43 *Winnipeg Child and Family Services (Northwest Area)* v. D.F.G., [1997] 3 S.C.R. 925.
44 See also: Hester Lessard, "The Construction of Health Care and the Ideology of the Private in Canadian Constitutional Law" (1993), 2 *Annals of Health Law* 121; Martha Jackman, "Constitutional Jurisdiction over Health in Canada" (2000), 8 *Health Law Journal* 95; Sanda Rodgers, "The Legal Regulation of Women's Reproductive Capacity in Canada" in Jocelyn Downie, T. Caulfield, C. Flood, eds., *Canadian Health Law and Policy* (Markham: Butterworths, 2002) 2d., 331; Rebecca J. Cook and Bernard M. Dickens, "Human Rights Dynamics of Abortion Law Reform" (2003), 25 *Human Rights Quarterly* 1.
45 *R. v. Hess and Nguyen*, [1990] 2. S.C.R. 906.

some women on occasion seek to have sex with boys, but held this could not qualify as the physical act required by the offense of statutory rape as defined in the criminal statute. Of course, Parliament could create a new offence to punish females for the act they can commit. Thus, the majority was not prepared to require Parliament to treat the victims of two different biological acts in the same way in the same section.

In contrast, the three dissenting judges found the statutory rape provision burdened men, whereas it did not burden women. Two declared this infringement justifiable because only males can cause pregnancies; the third agreed with the majority that the primary objective of the impugned provision was to protect children from premature sexual intercourse. Although focusing on the male act of penetration differs from being concerned about girls' pregnancies, this distinction is less significant than the fact that all of the judges relied on "biological realities" to decide the case. This biological fixation did not bode well for proponents of substantive equality, nor did the fact that both the majority and one of the dissenting opinions were authored by two of the three women who heard this case.

The picture did not improve when men attacked the rules limiting the admissibility of evidence of a sexual assault victim's prior sexual history.[46] Although the Court upheld the exclusion of evidence of sexual reputation, observing the notion there is a link between the victim's sexual reputation and whether she is a truthful witness has been universally discredited, the majority opinion (by then Madame Justice, now Chief Justice, McLachlin) found the accused's right to a fair trial was infringed by the rule limiting the admissibility of evidence of a victim's prior sexual conduct with persons other than the accused. Even though the purposes of the limited admissibility rule – to promote reporting of crimes and to prevent invasions of privacy – were laudable, its effects were too categorical and overbroad. Because the rule excluded all evidence of the victim's sexual activity with any person other than the accused unless it (i) rebutted the prosecution's evidence, (ii) tended to establish the identity of the assailant, or (iii) took place on the same occasion and evidenced consent, some relevant evidence might be excluded. Thus, it had to be struck down.

The dissent (by Madame Justice Claire L'Heureux-Dubé) upheld the exclusion precisely because it was categorical. As such, it was less vulnerable to the mythically and stereotypically based relevancy determinations that had saturated judicial decisions in the past. Listing the types of evidence the provision excluded – similar fact or pattern evidence, evidence tendered to support a defence of consent, evidence of prior acts of prostitution or

---

[46] *R. v. Seaboyer*, [1991] 2 S.C.R. 577. See: Christine Boyle, "Post-*Charter* Omne Animal Triste?" in Denis N. Magnusson and Daniel A. Soberman, eds., *Canadian Constitutional Dilemmas Revisited* (Kingston: Queen's University Institute of Intergovernmental Relations, 1997) 103 at 106–7.

allegations of prostitution, evidence showing motive to fabricate or bias –
the dissent questioned their relevancy; only evidence of prior false allegations
of sexual assault might be relevant and would be admissible in any event because it did not involve the admission of prior sexual history. Moreover,
even if the limited admissibility rule did infringe the *Charter*, it was justified
because Parliament's goal was to eliminate sex discrimination in the trial of
sexual offences.

Effectively, the controversy concerned the degree of trust that each of the
women judges was prepared to repose in the judiciary. Both the majority and
the dissent accepted limitations on admissibility given women's vulnerabil-
ities, although the majority put more faith in judicial discretion. However,
even the majority was not prepared to revive the old common law principle
of liberal judicial discretion. In a novel move, the majority judgment set out
the "new" common law rules pertaining to the exercise of judicial discretion
with respect to evidence of the victim's consensual sexual conduct if it proved
another person was the assailant, if it proved bias or motive to fabricate, if
it was known to the accused and tended to prove his belief in consent, if it
was similar fact evidence not used to show consent or unreliability, and if
it tended to rebut the prosecution's case. Moreover, in an even more radical move, Parliament consulted not only with the defense bar but also with
women's groups before enacting new legislation more or less codifying the
guidelines the Court had indicated were acceptable alternatives – legislation
the Court upheld in a subsequent *Charter* challenge.[47]

The second evidentiary issue pursued by men charged with sexual assault
revolved around the disclosure of victims' medical, counseling, and school
records. Because disclosure orders are the result of judicial rather than legislative decision making, the question of constitutionality involved the design of processes rather than laws. More specifically, in deciding whether
disclosure is called for, the judges must balance the sexual assault victim's
Charter rights to privacy and equality with the accused's *Charter* rights to
a fair trial and to full answer and defense. To illustrate, the Court con-
doned an automatic disclosure rule when the personal records of a sexual
assault victim, even third-party records, were already in the possession of
the prosecutor, whereas if these medical and therapeutic records remained
in the hands of the third parties who had made them, production was required only when they met a standard of being "likely relevant" to the defense.[48] Again, in the face of a claim for a class privilege protecting the
confidentiality of the victim's personal records held by sexual assault crisis
centers, the Court refused such recognition, with the minority concurring
opinion observing that granting case-by-case privilege might be appropriate

[47] *R. v. Darrach*, [2000] 2 S.C.R. 443.
[48] *R. v. O'Connor*, [1995] 4 S.C.R. 411.

in some circumstances.[49] Again, Parliament acted, passing a law supplementing the Court's "likely relevant" standard with the further requirement that production of the personal records of the sexual assault victim be "necessary in the interests of the parties." When another male accused of sexual assault challenged the constitutionality of this new provision, the Court upheld it, emphasizing it was passed after considerable public consultation took into account not only the accused's right to fair trial and to a full answer and defense but also the complainant's rights to privacy and equality.[50]

Finally, men accused of sexual assault offences also relied on their legal rights under the *Charter* to challenge the defenses available to them. In one case, the Court rejected the common law rule that drunkenness is no defense to a general intent offense such as sexual assault, holding instead that it could be a defense, although rarely so because of the minimal nature of the mental element required for crimes of general intent.[51] In another case, the Court dealt with the issue of consent, ruling the provincial appellate court was in error "in holding that a victim is required to offer some minimal word or gesture of objection and that lack of resistance must be equated with consent."[52] Recently, the Court followed up the issue of consent by holding there is no defense of "implied consent" to sexual assault.[53] In this particular case, one of the opinions authored by a woman justice stated the case was less about consent than about the myths and stereotypes surrounding sexual assault, views that the *International Convention on the Elimination of All Forms of Discrimination against Women* and Sections 7 and 15 of the *Charter* should have obviated long ago. Stung, the trial judge publicly criticized her opinion in a letter to a newspaper; in turn, he was criticized but not dismissed by the Canadian Judicial Council, a national body composed almost entirely of judges to decide judicial misconduct complaints.

One last case involving sexual assault merits attention, although it was neither a criminal nor a Canadian Supreme Court decision. Nor was it initiated by a man. Rather, a sexual assault victim used the *Charter* innovatively to sue a municipal police force in tort for injuries suffered when the police failed to

---

[49] *A.(L.L.) v. Beharriell*, [1995] 4 S.C.R. 536; *R. v. Carosella*, [1997] 1 S.C.R. 80. See: Karen Busby, "Discriminatory Uses of Personal Records in Sexual Violence Cases" (1997) 9 *Canadian Journal of Women and the Law* 148.

[50] *R. v. Mills*, [1999] 3 S.C.R. 668.

[51] *R. v. Daviault*, [1994] 3 S.C.R. 63.

[52] *R. v. M.(M.L.)*, [1994] 2 S.C.R. 3. In a one paragraph decision that did not explain what would constitute consent, the Court restored the trial judge's conviction of the stepfather for sexually assaulting his sixteen-year-old stepdaughter, noting that "there was evidence upon which a jury, properly instructed and acting judicially, could reasonably convict" and that "[t]he trial judge was in the same position."

[53] *R. v. Ewanchuk*, [1999] 1 S.C.R. 330.

warn women they were investigating the activities of a serial rapist.[54] She argued the failure to warn women violated Section 7 security of the person and Section 15 equality rights and should be remediable under Section 24 of the *Charter*. The police spent almost a decade proceeding through at least three levels of court claiming, ultimately unsuccessfully, no cause of action. When the substantive issues were finally heard the trial judge, a woman, found the police failure to warn potential victims about the serial rapist violated Sections 7 and 15. She awarded damages of almost $225,000 plus $2,000/year for fifteen years in transportation costs to the sexual assault victim. This case not only named the male privilege exercised by the predominantly male police force but also has the potential to change the way police forces across Canada treat women.

Sexual assault is not the only crime to give rise to litigation by men asserting their *Charter* rights against women's interests. For instance, the *Criminal Code* prohibits the making, distribution, and possession of pornography. In 1992, following closely on the heels of cases in which the Court upheld *Criminal Code* provisions prohibiting soliciting for the purposes of prostitution and the dissemination of hate propaganda in the face of *Charter* challenges,[55] the judges had to decide whether the antipornography provision was constitutional.[56] They first defined pornography as explicit sex with violence or explicit sex without violence but that is degrading or dehumanizing, thereby rejecting the traditional common law definition of pornography as simply explicit sex. Next they declared the provision violated the *Charter* right to freedom of expression. However, that did not end the matter because they also held it was a justified limitation on freedom of expression. They reasoned the legislative objective was not one of moral disapprobation but, rather, one of avoiding harm to society, particularly given that pornographic materials that portray women as a class as objects for sexual exploitation and abuse have a negative impact on the sense of self-worth and acceptance of individual women. Furthermore, they found the prohibition was proportional to the objective, as there were exclusions for materials having scientific, artistic, or literary merit, as well as for private use. They denied placing restrictions on access to pornography is sufficient to address the harm it causes; and they held the existence of other measures to alleviate the problem of violence

---

[54] *Jane Doe v. Metropolitan Toronto (Municipality) Commissioners of Police*, (1998), 39 O.R. (3d) 487. See Jane Doe, *The Story of Jane Doe: A Book about Rape* (Toronto: Random House Canada, 2003).

[55] *Reference re ss. 193 & 195.1(1)(c) of the Criminal Code*, [1990] 1 S.C.R. 1123 (prostitution); *R. v. Keegstra*, [1990] 3 S.C.R. 697 (hate propaganda).

[56] *R. v. Butler*, [1992] 1 S.C.R. 452. *Little Sisters Book and Art Emporium v. Canada*, [2000] 2 S.C.R. 1120 upheld customs legislation prohibiting the importation of pornography, but also ruled customs officials wrongly delayed, confiscated, or prohibited materials imported by the gay and lesbian bookstore, violating their Section 15 right to import erotica from the United States.

against women did not force Parliament to choose between or among them.

Family

The *Charter* was not expected to have any particular impact on family law because it does not apply to private law relationships. However, this expectation ignored the extent to which contemporary family relationships are now governed by legislation, whether national or provincial.[57] Marriage and divorce are regulated by the national Parliament, while the provinces have enacted various family law statutes to deal with the distribution of matrimonial property on divorce or death, as well as with issues of custody, access, and support on separation or divorce. Today, in other words, family law has an indelibly "public aspect."[58] As such, it is vulnerable to *Charter* challenge; or, in the words of one family law scholar, "Canada is now going through a process of constitutionalizing family law."[59]

More specifically, *Charter* arguments persuaded the Canadian Supreme Court to extend "spousal" recognition not only to unmarried heterosexual relationships (also known as "common law" relationships),[60] but also to same-sex partners.[61] Although these decisions signaled the end of a long tradition of ascribing privileges only to formally recognized heterosexual unions, they were not grounded on claims of sex equality. Instead, the litigants successfully argued marital status and sexual orientation were new grounds that should be guaranteed protection from discrimination in the *Charter's* equality rights provision even though they were not mentioned in it. In legal parlance, this meant the equality-seekers claimed the protection of Section 15(1) should be extended to grounds "analogous" to the "enumerated" grounds. Because the Court had already adopted an "analogous" grounds approach to interpreting Section 15(1) in its first equality case (deciding citizenship was analogous),[62] this hurdle proved not to be insuperable. In addition to equality, *Charter* security of the person arguments have been used successfully to convince the Court to extend state funding (known as legal aid) to indigent parents (who frequently are single parent mothers)

---

[57] Mary Jane Mossman, "Conversations about Families in Canadian Courts and Legislatures: Are there 'lessons' for the United States?" (2003), 31 *Hofstra Law Review*.

[58] Alison Harvison Young, "The Changing Family, Rights Discourse and The Supreme Court of Canada" (2001), 80 *Canadian Bar Review* 749 at 251.

[59] Nicholas Bala, "The Charter of Rights and Family Law in Canada: A New Era" (2001) 18 *Canadian Family Law Quarterly* 373 at 427.

[60] *Miron v. Trudel*, [1995] 2 S.C.R. 418. But see *Nova Scotia* v. *Walsh*, 2002 S.C.C. 83, which held excluding unmarried cohabiting opposite sex couples from the definition of "spouse" in matrimonial property legislation did not violate Section 15.

[61] *M. v. H.*, [1999] 2 S.C.R. 3.

[62] *Andrews, supra* note 28.

requiring legal counsel to defend against state-initiated child protection proceedings.[63] Unfortunately, the same argument ultimately failed to protect
parents from warrantless apprehensions of their children by protection authorities because the statute complied with the principles of fundamental
justice by providing for postapprehension judicial review.[64]

On the whole, the foregoing cases bear out the conclusion "that judges
will be persuaded about *Charter* arguments about *how* decisions are made
and about *who* should be able to enjoy various [family law] rights."[65] Yet,
to the extent the "core" of family law relates to "*what* rights arise out of a
familial relationship," the Court may be less likely to use the *Charter* to bring
about change.[66] On the one hand, *Charter* equality values likely caused the
Court to move away from treating the objective of economic self-sufficiency
as the preeminent consideration in determining the duration of spousal support (a position consistent with formal equality)[67] to one of recognizing
the impact of the feminization of poverty, viz. the negative employment effects caused by the role adopted in the first marriage continuing to operate
even after entry into a new relationship (a position more consistent with
substantive equality).[68] On the other hand, *Charter* equality values did not
prevail when the Court held the custodial mother's desire to move reopened
the custody issue, the outcome of which would be governed by the best interests of the child, rather than accepting it should be within the custodial
parent's power to decide issues such as change of residence.[69] And *Charter*
values did not even come into play in a very different custody issue, one
involving a child of mixed race parentage, wherein the African-American
father argued his race was relevant to the Court's decision about whether
sole custody should be awarded to the child's single Caucasian Canadian
mother.[70]

Finally, two sex equality cases brought by men merit consideration. In the
earlier case, a man challenged the *Citizenship Act* provisions that treated children born abroad of Canadian mothers differently from those with Canadian

[63] *New Brunswick (Minister of Health and Community Services)* v. *G.(J.)*, [1999] 3 S.C.R. 46.
[64] *Winnipeg Child and Family Services (Central Area)* v. *W. (K.L.)*, [2000] 2 S.C.R. 519.
[65] Bala, "The Charter of Rights," *supra* note 59, at 428.
[66] Bala, "The Charter of Rights," ibid.
[67] *Pelech v. Pelech*, [1987] 1 S.C.R. 801; *Richardson* v. *Richardson*, [1987] 1 S.C.R. 857; and
    Caron v. *Caron*, [1987] 1 S.C.R. 892. Known as the "trilogy," these cases restricted the test
    for overriding support obligations established on divorce such that the applicant must prove a
    radical change of circumstance that is causally related to a pattern of economic dependency in
    the marriage, see Martha J. Bailey, "*Pelech, Caron,* and *Richardson*" (1989–1990), 3 *Canadian
    Journal of Women and the Law* 615.
[68] *Moge v. Moge*, [1992] 3 S.C.R. 831. The Court rejected the trilogy's elevation of economic
    self-sufficiency to the preeminent objective, preferring instead that support obligations on
    marriage breakdown reflect the diverse dynamics of many unique marital relationships.
[69] *Gordon v. Goertz*, [1996] 2 S.C.R. 27.
[70] *Van de Perre v. Edwards*, [2001] S.C.C. 60.

fathers.[71] The latter could claim citizenship upon registration of their birth; the former had to pass both criminal clearance and security checks. The man, born in the United States to a Canadian mother and an American father, failed the security check when it revealed he had been charged with several criminal offences, including murder. His criminal record notwithstanding, the Court ruled screening his application more rigorously suggested women were not equally capable of passing on whatever it takes to be a good Canadian citizen. Even assuming the objective of safeguarding the security of citizens, the government failed to show how that goal was advanced by a two-tiered application system. In short, Canada had not established that the children of Canadian mothers were more dangerous than those of Canadian fathers.

More recently, a man successfully invoked Section 15 sex equality rights to challenge legislation that protected a birth mother from being forced to acknowledge a biological father on the birth registration form and to include his surname in the child's surname.[72] The most recently appointed woman judge (Madame Justice Marie Deschamps) wrote the Court's unanimous decision, ruling this legislation discriminated against men because it denied their aspirations to affirm their biological ties and familial bonds across the generations. Not only did women become discriminators but also their aspirations were ignored, despite being voiced by the women judges on the provincial appellate court that had ruled against the man's claim. One appellate justice described "the many mothers and would-be mothers... who have deliberately chosen to be single mothers" as women who would experience this man's claim as "discrimination against them."[73] Clearly she evinced more concern about male privilege than her counterparts on the higher court.

Employment

In Canada, employment discrimination is proscribed on various grounds, including sex, in national and provincial antidiscrimination statutes. Early in the *Charter* era but without relying on it, the Canadian Supreme Court held discrimination "arises where an employer... adopts a rule or standard... which has a discriminatory effect upon a prohibited ground on one employee or group of employees in that it imposes, because of some special characteristic of the employee or group, obligations, penalties, or restrictive conditions not imposed on other members of the work force."[74] This effects-based definition of discrimination was adopted four years later in the Court's

[71] *Benner v. Canada*, [1997] 1 S.C.R. 358.
[72] *Trociuk v. British Columbia*, 2003 S.C.C. 34.
[73] *Trociuk v. British Columbia* (2001), 200 D.L.R. (4th) 685 at 741.
[74] *Ontario Human Rights Commission and O'Malley v. Simpsons-Sears Ltd.*, [1985] 2 S.C.R. 536.

first *Charter* equality rights decision.[75] In other words, the Court does not require a showing of intent to discriminate in either the statutory or the constitutional human rights regimes; it is sufficient to establish the impact of the discriminatory act upon the person affected. This is one of two important ways in which statutory antidiscrimination jurisprudence has informed *Charter* equality rights jurisprudence.

The second way is more diffuse, albeit more specifically directed to achieving women's equality. After the *Charter* was adopted, the Canadian Supreme Court consistently rendered non-*Charter*, antidiscrimination employment decisions that accord with substantive equality for women. Beginning in 1987, the Court refused to eviscerate a remedial employment equity program ordered by an administrative tribunal after a finding of systemic sex discrimination,[76] and also upheld a sexual harassment remedy awarded against the national government as the employer of the offender.[77] In 1989, the Court read sexual harassment into the prohibition on sex discrimination in an antidiscrimination statute, as well as ruling an employer could be held liable for acts of sexual harassment by one employee against another.[78] That same year, the Court reversed a pre-*Charter* decision deciding that denying pregnancy benefits does constitute sex discrimination.[79] More recently, an appellate court denied a challenge to national pay equity legislation;[80] and the Canadian Supreme Court held an employment fitness test based on men's physiology and experience was not neutral but discriminatory.[81] This last case was one of several in which LEAF successfully intervened; moreover, its significance increases as lower courts come to recognize its implications for a broad range of workplace standards that systematically limit or exclude women or other historically disadvantaged minorities from employment opportunities.

However, litigants and interveners have a mixed record of success using the *Charter* to challenge employment discrimination directly. In one case, two male inmates failed to persuade the Court cross-gender guarding violated their *Charter* right to sex equality.[82] The Court upheld the constitutionality of this employment practice, which allowed female guards to perform frisk searches and to observe inmates in their cells in a men's penitentiary but did not permit male guards to perform similar duties in the women's prison, reasoning "historical, biological and sociological differences between men and

---

75 *Andrews, supra* note 28.

76 *Action Travail des Femmes v. Canadian National Railway Company*, [1987] 1 S.C.R. 1114.

77 *Robichaud v. Canada (Treasury Board)*, [1987] 2 S.C.R. 84.

78 *Janzen v. Platy Enterprises Ltd.*, [1989] 1 S.C.R. 1252.

79 *Brooks v. Canada Safeway Ltd.*, [1989] 1 S.C.R. 1219, reversing *Bliss, supra* note 27.

80 *Public Service Alliance of Canada v. Canada (Treasury Board)*, [1999] F.C. J. No. 1531.

81 *British Columbia (Public Service Employee Relations Committee) v. BCGSEU*, [1999] 3 S.C.R. 3.

82 *Weatherall and Conway v. Canada*, [1993] 2 S.C.R. 872.

women" make it "clear that the effect of cross-gender searching is different and more threatening for women than for men."[83] Although this reasoning seemed consistent with a finding of substantive equality (as that concept was defined in the first *Charter* equality rights decision),[84] the fact the Court required the government to justify cross gender guarding implies the practice did violate inmates' sex equality rights. Moreover, the government's justifications – female guards humanize male prisoners and promote employment equity in the correctional system – did little to disrupt male privilege.

In a second *Charter* employment case, an alleged sexual harasser had persuaded a provincial appellate court to stay (or stop) the harassment complaint from proceeding on the ground that administrative delays in processing the complaint had violated his *Charter* right to liberty and security of the person.[85] LEAF intervened on behalf of the female complainants, invoking their rights to security of the person and to sex equality. The Court held that while the *Charter* could be applied to the acts of the administrative agency (the human rights commission with whom the complaint had been lodged), in this case there was no infringement of the rights of the sexual harasser. More specifically, although there was no bar to extending the Section 7 right to life, liberty, and security of the person beyond the sphere of criminal law, the alleged harasser's liberty interest had not been infringed because the delay had not prevented him from making any "fundamental personal choices." Nor was his security of the person violated because the psychological harm he suffered, while real, was not caused by delay in the harassment complaint process but, rather, by the fact he was a public figure, a provincial government cabinet minister who lost his job when the complaint was initiated.

Although the preceding cases may count as successes, and their outcomes suggest they should, there is one employment case in which the *Charter* abjectly failed women. It involved employment equity which in Canada may be the result of voluntary, remedial, or proactive decisions.[86] Although governments may mandate proactive employment equity programs, most have yet to pass enabling legislation. The case arose in the mid-1990s when a change in government resulted in the repeal of that jurisdiction's proactive employment equity statute. Activists challenged the constitutionality of the repealing law, arguing it violated women's sex equality rights.[87] They were not successful. The provincial appellate court held the *Charter* mandates neither the enactment nor, as in this case, the retention of positive measures to achieve economic equality for women. Regrettably, the judges did not

---

[83] *Weatherall*, ibid.

[84] *Andrews, supra* note 28.

[85] *Blencoe v. Andrea Willis and The British Columbia Human Rights Commission*, [2000] 2 S.C.R. 307.

[86] Beverley Baines, "Occupational Sex Segregation and Employment Equity: Lessons from Canada" (2000) 8 *Canadian Labour and Employment Law Journal* 291.

[87] *Ferrel et al. v. Attorney General of Ontario* (1999), O.R. (3d) 97.

name the male privilege they sustained; presumably the potential for societal transformation was too threatening.[88]

The downside to naming male privilege is that judges may decide no woman is oppressed unless all women are oppressed. However, just as male privilege does not necessarily privilege all males, so too may the effects of oppression be harsher for some women than for others. In other words, arguing only for the notion all women share a core of oppression constrains important claims based on women's contextualized experiences, or diversity. At minimum, diversity demands respect for the claims of aboriginal, racially identified, young/elderly, lesbian, differently abled, immigrant, poor, and religious women. They should not have to abandon their race or national origin or gender, and so on, at the courtroom door in order to seek *Charter* equality rights. The jurisprudence that follows illustrates how women fared when they turned to *Charter* adjudication to realize their contextualized claims for equality rights.

Aboriginal Women

Before the Charter was adopted, the *Indian Act* deprived aboriginal women of their aboriginal status upon marriage to a nonaboriginal man. Although intermarriage had no such consequences for aboriginal men, the Canadian Supreme Court denied the legislation infringed sex equality, reasoning married aboriginal women were treated no differently from married nonaboriginal women.[89] When another aboriginal woman sought relief under the *Optional Protocol* to the *International Covenant on Civil and Political Rights*, the United Nations Human Rights Committee found her loss of aboriginal status infringed her right to enjoy her own culture as a member of an ethnic minority (Article 27), but made no finding about her right to sex equality (Article 26).[90] Four years later, Canada amended the *Indian Act*, albeit only partially redressing the problem.[91] Subsequently, the constitutionality

---

[88] Introducing *Privatization, Law, and the Challenge to Feminism* (Toronto: University of Toronto Press, 2002) at 34, editors Judy Fudge and Brenda Cossman argue:

> Many of the advances made by the women's movement over the last two decades are being undone. In the area of labour, for instance, pay equity and employment equity legislation is being rolled back. The entire landscape of legal regulation is undergoing a profound change. Reprivatization, commodification, and familialization are reconfiguring the legal regulation of women in a broad range of substantive areas.

[89] *Lavell, supra* note 27.
[90] *Lovelace v. Canada* (No. 24/1977), U.N. Doc. CCPR/3/Add.1, vol. II, at 320.
[91] Wendy Moss, "The Canadian State and Indian Women: The Struggle for Sex Equality under the Indian Act," in Caroline Andrew and Sanda Rodgers, *Women and the Canadian State*

of that legislation was challenged, this time by the chiefs of several Indian bands who oppose the reinstatement of women to Indian status.[92]

With these cases as background, it is not difficult to picture the controversy generated within the aboriginal community (about one million strong) when the Native Women's Association of Canada (NWAC) challenged the constitutionality of the national government's decision not to recognize and fund their organization during the 1992 constitutional negotiations.[93] As the government had already recognized and funded four traditional, male-dominated, aboriginal organizations, NWAC contended their *Charter* rights to freedom of expression and sex equality were infringed by this exclusion. The Court did not agree, holding funding was not a prerequisite to expression and NWAC did not represent all aboriginal women, some of whom participated in the traditional organizations. Unfortunately, this reasoning misses the point, which is that NWAC represented aboriginal women unrepresented by the four male-dominated organizations. These women supported keeping *Charter* rights in place during any process of transition to aboriginal self-government, a position that was unique, as the four traditional associations wanted immediate relief from all nonaboriginal laws, whether constitutional or otherwise.

Racially Identified Women

A black single mother who was a public housing tenant on social assistance relied on *Charter* equality rights to challenge a provincial law giving public housing tenants significantly less security of tenure than private sector tenants.[94] Although the municipal Housing Authority admitted that women, blacks, and social assistance recipients formed a disproportionately large percentage of tenants in public housing and on the waiting list for public housing, it argued the legislation did not distinguish on those grounds but, rather, on the grounds of tenancy. That is, it distinguished between groups of tenants. However, the provincial appellate court disagreed with the Housing Authority, holding the legislation discriminated on the basis of race, sex, and income, and hence violated *Charter* equality rights. Proceeding, the court found the impugned provisions were not properly tailored to achieve the objective of administrative flexibility. The Housing Authority failed, in other words, to justify infringing the *Charter* right to equality. Thus, the impugned provisions were declared of no force and effect.

(Montreal & Kingston: McGill-Queen's University Press, 1997) 79–88; and Teressa Anne Nahanee, "Indian Women, Sex Equality, and the Charter" in Andrew and Rogers, ibid., at 89–103.

[92] *Sawridge Band v. Canada*, [1997] F.C.J. No. 794. This litigation is ongoing.

[93] *Native Women's Association of Canada*, *supra* note 15.

[94] *Dartmouth/Halifax County Regional Housing Authority v. Sparks*, [1993] N.S.J. No. 97.

Young/Elderly Women

In two separate cases, young women relied on the *Charter* right to age equality to challenge legislation. The first case involved a thirty-year-old widow
who challenged the national compulsory social insurance scheme providing
income benefits to survivors of contributors.[95] The scheme gave survivors
over the age of forty-five full benefits immediately, while survivors between
thirty-five and forty-five received gradually reduced benefits; but survivors
under the age of thirty-five receive nothing unless and until they reached age
sixty-five. That the age-based distinctions were obvious did not prevent the
Court from denying there was any discrimination. Rather, the judges used
the opportunity presented by this case to set out four contextual factors
that are supposed to assist in establishing whether discrimination exists.[96]
However, none of these factors assisted this widow because the judges (all of
whom were over the age of fifty) were convinced "the greater opportunities
of youth" (e.g., ease of finding employment and potential for remarriage)
precluded a finding of disadvantage or discrimination. Although they denied
this characterization constituted a stereotype, it seemed singularly inapposite
with respect to this young widow who had worked for eleven years beside
her twenty-year older husband in his highly successful private business – a
business that nevertheless failed once he was no longer available to run it.
Moreover, absent any need for the national government to justify its legislative objective and the proportionality of the means to the objective, the
costs, and the gender implications of extending these survivors' pensions to
younger women remain unknown.

The more recent case involved a single woman under the age of thirty
who received one third the welfare payment given to recipients over thirty.[97]
To receive full benefits, she was required by the provincial social assistance
scheme to participate in designated training, community work, or educational programs, requirements not imposed on recipients over thirty. Splitting 5–4, the Court held the age-differentiated welfare scheme did not violate
Section 15 age equality rights, reasoning that participation in the programs
would promote long-term self-sufficiency and hence human dignity. The four

---

[95] *Law v. Canada, supra* note 29.
[96] *Law*, ibid., at para. 88(9) summarizing these four contextual factors as:

 1. Preexisting disadvantage, stereotyping, prejudice, or vulnerability experienced by the in-
    dividual or group in issue.
 2. The correspondence, or lack thereof, between the ground or grounds on which the claim
    is based and the actual need, capacity, or circumstances of the claimant or others.
 3. The ameliorative purpose or effects of the impugned law upon a more disadvantaged
    person or group in society.
 4. The nature and scope of the interest affected by the impugned law.

[97] *Gosselin v. Quebec,* 2002 S.C.C. 84.

dissenting Justices, writing separately, noted among other reasons that the scheme violated age equality not only when jobs were scarce but also by imposing the risk of severe poverty (e.g., payments of $170/month) on young welfare recipients who did not or could not participate in the programs. Because the welfare regime excluded claimants from any real possibility of having their basic needs met, the two dissenting women Justices also concluded it violated the Section 7 right to security of the person.

Lesbian Women

After the Canadian Supreme Court decided sexual orientation is analogous to the enumerated grounds of discrimination in Section 15(1) of the *Charter*,[98] and should be read into the list of prohibited grounds contained in a provincial antidiscrimination statute,[99] a lesbian challenged the validity of the definition of "spouse" in a provincial family law statute.[100] This provision, which governed claims for financial support between the partners on the breakdown of a conjugal relationship, defined "spouse" as "a man and a woman." Arguing it failed to include claims for support by lesbians and gay males, she claimed this opposite-sex definition infringed her *Charter* right to equality on the grounds of sexual orientation. In an 8–1 decision, the Court agreed the provision infringed the rights of same-sex couples and could not be justified. Although the support regime was primarily designed to redress the likelihood of serious economic detriment that heterosexual women suffer on the breakdown of conjugal relationships, that objective offered no reason for excluding same-sex couples even though they do not generally share the imbalance in power characteristic of opposite-sex couples. Moreover, even if the primary purpose of the impugned definition was to recognize and promote the traditional family, there was no evidence that denying status and benefits to same-sex partners enhanced respect for traditional families, or that any *Charter* values would be achieved by their exclusion.

Ultimately, the Court ruled the opposite-sex provision was of no force and effect, albeit temporarily suspending the order for six months to give the provincial legislature time to pass new legislation. In so ruling, the judges rejected the provincial appellate court's approach of reading "a man and a woman" out of, and reading "two persons" into, the impugned provision because that remedy would address only this provision, leaving opposite-sex definitions intact in a number of other statutory provisions. This decision was very important for lesbian women (and gay men) because it forced the national and provincial governments to review all statutes pertaining to "spouses" for consistency with *Charter* sexual orientation equality rights.

[98] *Egan v. Canada*, [1985] 2 S.C.R. 513.
[99] *Vriend v. Alberta*, [1998] 1 S.C.R. 493.
[100] *M. v. H.*, *supra* note 61.

Also this decision had the further effect of causing each government to consider whether to subsume lesbian and gay relationships under the legal definition of "marriage," or whether to create new familial relationships such as "cohabitation" or "civil union" regimes.[101]

Differently Abled Women

Litigants, some of whom were immigrant women with physical disabilities, challenged a provincial health insurance scheme linking coverage to residency.[102] Under this scheme, people who had immigrated to Canada but were not entitled to become permanent residents faced delays in or denial of coverage for basic medical services such as prenatal care for pregnant women, pediatric visits for children, and treatment of ongoing disabilities such as cerebral palsy. LEAF, in coalition with DisAbled Women's Network Canada and the Ontario Council of Immigrants with Disabilities, intervened in this litigation to argue this scheme discriminated against persons on the basis of immigration status and disability. In particular, it discriminated against persons with disabilities because some of the litigants had been denied permanent resident status on account of their physical disability. The provincial appellate court disagreed, attributing the ineligibility of these physically disabled immigrants only to national immigration rules. Although the provincial health insurance scheme utilized the immigration status categories set out in these national rules to regulate coverage, it had no responsibility for creating them. According to the court, while the provincial scheme distinguished between permanent and nonpermanent residency, it did not draw distinctions based on national origin, gender, age, or physical disability. It did not, in short, violate *Charter* equality rights. Thus some immigrants in Ontario, including pregnant women and women with disabilities, will continue to lack basic medical care.

Immigrant Women

In addition to the foregoing case, as well as to cases in which immigrant mothers facing deportation invoked their *Charter* right to security of the person

---

[101] In July 2003, after three lower courts ruled the opposite-sex requirement for marriage was unconstitutional – *Hendricks v. Quebec*, [2002] J.Q. No. 3818 (Quebec Superior Court); *Barbeau v. British Columbia* (2003), B.C.C.A. 251; *Halpern v. Canada*, [2003] O.J. No. 2268 (Ontario Court of Appeal) – the national government asked the Canadian Supreme Court to rule on the constitutionality of a draft bill proposing to legally recognize the union of same-sex couples while recognizing the freedom of churches and religious organizations not to perform marriages against their beliefs: <http://canada.justice.gc.ca/en/news/nr/2003/doc_30946.html> (accessed 10/09/03).

[102] *Irshad (Litigation Guardian of) v. Ontario (Ministry of Health)* (2001) 55 O.R. (3d) 43.

to protect themselves and their dependent Canadian-born children,[103] two immigrant women relied on *Charter* equality rights to challenge a national public service employment preference for citizens.[104] This preference applies to open competitions for public service employment, not at the application stage but, rather, thereafter when the general agency responsible for staffing refers a list of eligible, qualified applicants to the departments seeking to hire people. In a decision fraught with judicial factionalism, the preference was upheld by the concurring opinions of two judges who denied there was any violation of equality rights because it did not implicate the essential dignity of noncitizens and by the opinion of four judges who decided the preference violated *Charter* rights on the analogous ground of citizenship but the violation was justifiable because the disadvantage to noncitizens relative to citizens did not appear significant. The remaining three judges (in an opinion authored by two of the three women on the bench) dissented, holding the preference marginalizes immigrants from the fabric of Canadian life. Nor could it be justified, they wrote, given citizenship is not enhanced by discriminating against a vulnerable minority (noncitizens), and there is no evidence public service employment serves as an incentive to naturalization.

Poor Women

LEAF has supported litigation in which poor and low-income women have challenged the constitutionality of provincial social assistance and rental housing legislation, as well as the national (un)employment insurance law. For instance, in what has become known as the "spouse in the house" case, four women on social assistance challenged the constitutionality of a provincial law that cut off benefits to single parents living with an adult of the opposite sex.[105] Because the law applied irrespective of whether there was any meaningful financial interdependency or whether they were cohabiting as spouses, the women successfully argued it violated *Charter* equality rights based on sex, marital, and social assistance status. According to the provincial appellate court, the law discriminated not only because it

---

[103] *Baker v. Minister of Citizenship and Immigration*, [1999] 2 S.C.R. 817 (the Court ordered a redetermination of the application on humanitarian and compassionate grounds by a woman with Canadian-born dependent children for exemption to the requirement that her application for immigration be made abroad); *Francis v. Minister of Citizenship and Immigration*, <www.Ontariocourts.on.ca/decisions/1999/October/francis.htm> (the provincial appellate court denied the Canadian-born children's application to stop the deportation of their mother, observing that post-*Baker* the mother could remain in the country while applying for immigration on humanitarian and compassionate grounds and the best interests of the children would be relevant to her application).

[104] *Lavoie v. Canada (Public Service Commission)*, 2002 S.C.C. 23.

[105] *Falkiner v. Ontario (Ministry of Community and Social Services, Income Maintenance Branch)*, [2002] O.J. No. 1771, online: QL (OJ), on appeal to the S.C.C.

overwhelmingly affected women but also because it reinforced the stereo-type that women living with men must be financially dependent on that relationship. In addition, its breadth of application was so wide it could not be justified.

Religious Women

In 1994, when several schools expelled Muslim girls for wearing the *hijab* (Islamic headscarves), one of these girls complained to the provincial an-tidiscrimination commission, which ruled that her right to religious freedom had been infringed.[106] Strictly speaking, this was not a constitutional deci-sion because this particular province (Quebec) had included a Charter of Rights, which guaranteed the right to freedom of religion, in its antidis-crimination statute. However, most provincial antidiscrimination legislation only prohibits discrimination. Had the *hijab* become an issue in one of these provinces, the guarantee of religious freedom would not have been avail-able without invoking the *Charter*. In sum, girls who are Muslim or who subscribe to other religious faiths may seek to attack the constitutionality of school dress codes that prohibit them from wearing religious attire (e.g., where religious cover-up rules pertaining to women conflict with the more abbreviated clothing usually worn during physical education activities).

TRANSFORMING SOCIETY

Charter litigation can serve women by transforming societal relationships or it can constrain our sights so we focus primarily on achieving a fairer redistribution of resources. Although all of the *Charter* jurisprudence per-taining to women might be classified according to these alternatives, income tax jurisprudence presents a particularly apposite site for this evaluation. Not only have three major cases reached the Canadian Supreme Court since the *Charter* was adopted but also they are significant in the sense that they promote a "follow the money" philosophy.

Income Tax

According to a feminist legal expert on tax law and policy, "Canadian women had been aware since the early 1970s that the Income Tax Act had been constructed around fundamentally masculinist and hierarchical visions of women."[107] Such awareness should be attributed to the women who brought

---

[106] Sarah V. Wayland, "Religious expression in public schools: *kirpans* in Canada, *hijab* in France" (1997) 20 *Ethnic and Racial Studies* 545 at 558–60.

[107] Kathleen A. Lahey, "The Impact of the Canadian Charter of Rights and Freedoms on Income Tax Law and Policy" in David Schneiderman & Kate Sutherland, eds., *Charting*

the three *Charter* equality rights challenges to this Act. One, a lawyer, took issue with treating the personal deduction for childcare expenses as sufficient to meet all women's needs.[108] She argued her sex equality rights were violated when, as a businesswoman, she was denied the option of deducting childcare costs at the higher business expense rate. Another woman, a divorced custodial mother of two children, challenged the income-splitting provisions.[109] She claimed requiring her to add the child support payments from her ex-husband to her taxable income, while letting him treat them as deductions, infringed her *Charter* right to marital status and sex equality. The third case was initiated by an association of immigrant and visible minority women that had been denied registration as a charitable organization with tax exempt status.[110] The association failed to qualify for registration because some of its activities (e.g., creating a job skills directory and establishing support groups for professionals) did not meet the common law definition of "charitable." Three women's groups intervened, arguing that requiring all purposes to be charitable discriminates against immigrant and visible minority women on the basis of the analogous ground of immigrant status as well as the enumerated grounds of race, gender, and national or ethnic origin.

The Court denied the equality claims in all three cases. To the businesswoman, the majority judges said the attribution of childcare costs was a family matter, not a matter of law or public policy.[111] To the custodial mother, they emphasized income-splitting was not harmful but beneficial to the "postdivorce 'family unit'."[112] And the immigrant and visible minority association was told its "inability to bring itself within established guidelines of uniform application" was the problem.[113] In none of the three cases, in other words, did the *Charter* equality rights challenges disrupt the fundamental values reflected in income tax law and policy. Judicial deference to Parliament and male privilege prevailed, not *Charter* rights or the inclusion of women's values.

CONCLUSION

Charter jurisprudence has been relatively successful in naming male privilege and/or leading to legislative changes that benefit women in the areas

---

the Consequences: The Impact of Charter of Rights on Canadian Law and Politics (Toronto: University of Toronto Press, 1997) 109–68.

[108] *Symes v. Canada*, [1993] 4 S.C.R. 695.

[109] *Thibaudeau v. Canada*, [1995] 2 S.C.R. 513.

[110] *Vancouver Society of Immigrant and Visible Minority Women v. Minister of National Revenue*, [1999] 1 S.C.R. 10.

[111] *Symes, supra* note 108.

[112] *Thibaudeau, supra* note 109.

[113] *Vancouver Society of Immigrant and Visible Minority Women, supra* note 110.

of athletics, reproduction, crime, family, and employment. It has been mod-
estly successful in contextualizing women, recognizing some needs – those of
some lesbian, racially identified, and poor women – while failing to recognize
the needs of others, particularly aboriginal, young, immigrant, and religious
women. One problem is that many of these women require positive action
by the state, action the Canadian Supreme Court seems reluctant to read into
the new *Charter* rights protection regime. Regrettably, the *Charter* is unlikely
to fulfill the promise that led feminist lobbyists and litigators to support its
adoption unless judges take responsibility for identifying its transformative
potential in areas such as taxation.

Suggested Readings

Ellen Anderson, *Judging Bertha Wilson: Law as Large as Life* (Toronto: University of
   Toronto Press, 2001).
Beverley Baines, "Formatting Equality" (2000) 11 *Constitutional Forum* 65
Anne F. Bayefsky and Mary Eberts, eds., *Equality Rights and the Canadian Charter of
   Rights and Freedoms* (Toronto: Carswell, 1985).
Susan B. Boyd, *Child Custody, Law, and Women's Work* (Don Mills, ON: Oxford
   University Press Canada, 2003).
Canadian Journal of Women and the Law (1985) Volume I and following.
Audrey Macklin, "Symes v. M.N.R.: Where Sex Meets Class" (1992) 5 *Canadian
   Journal of Women and the Law* 498.
Melanie Randall, "Accountability of Public Authorities, Sex Discrimination and the
   Public/Private Divide in Tort Law: An Analysis of *Doe v. Metropolitan Toronto
   (Municipality) Commissioners of Police*" (2001) 26 *Queen's Law Journal* 451.
Julian V. Roberts and Renate M. Mohr, eds., *Confronting Sexual Assault: A Decade of
   Legal and Social Change* (Toronto: University of Toronto Press, 1994).
Lynn Smith and Eleanor Wachtel, *A Feminist Guide to the Canadian Constitution*
   (Ottawa: Canadian Advisory Council on the Status of Women, 1992).

3

Emancipatory Equality

Gender Jurisprudence under the Colombian Constitution

Martha I. Morgan

After decades of extreme violence, many Colombians eagerly embraced the 1991 Colombian Constitution, some hailing it as a peace treaty.[1] It was drafted and adopted by a specially elected constituent assembly approved in response to a student campaign that rallied support for constitutional reform under the slogan, "We can still save Colombia." Admittedly, the new Constitution has fallen far short of the bold expectations of those who envisioned it as a "peace treaty" for a country that is still marked by seemingly unfathomable levels of violence. But the 1991 constitutional assembly presented an opportunity for a broad spectrum of the diverse society to unite around a new "social contract," replacing the country's 1886 Constitution (then Latin America's oldest) with a modern document.

Despite the broadly proclaimed representativeness of the 1991 constituent assembly, women were vastly underrepresented – only four of the seventy-four members were women. But women and organizations advocating their causes were active outside the assembly as well. They participated in the official worktables organized, regionally and by sector, to collect citizen proposals for constitutional change. As a result of advocacy and lobbying activities, they obtained support for much of their agenda from both men and women within the assembly. In contrast to the 1886 Constitution, which did not even include an express equality provision, the 1991 Constitution includes broad tri-generational civil and political, social, and collective rights, including not

---

[1] For a more thorough discussion and citations concerning many of the topics covered in this chapter, see Martha I. Morgan, "Taking Machismo to Court" (1999) 30 *University of Miami Inter-American Law Review* 253, upon which much of it is based. Also see, Martha I. Morgan and Mónica Alzate Buitrago, "Founding Mothers in Contemporary Latin American Constitutions: Colombian Women, Constitution Making, and the New Constitutional Court" in Adrien Katherine Wing, ed., *Global Critical Race Feminism: An International Reader* (New York: New York University Press, 2000) 204; Martha I. Morgan and Mónica Alzate Buitrago, "Constitution-Making in a Time of Cholera: Women and the 1991 Colombian Constitution" (1992) 4 *Yale Journal of Law and Feminism* 353.

only provisions specifically addressing gender equality but also several other gender-related protections.

The Constitution proclaims that Colombia is a social state of law, a concept representing a middle ground between liberal and socialist notions of the state. The Charter also expressly recognizes and protects the cultural and ethnic diversity of the nation as well as a broad panoply of rights. To ensure that these broad new protections did not remain merely "paper guarantees," the new constitution created a Constitutional Court charged with safeguarding the supremacy of the new Charter. The Court's broad powers of judicial review include prior constitutional review of legislation implementing specified constitutional matters (including fundamental rights and duties and the procedures for their protection) and of international treaties and legislation approving them; review of ordinary legislation that the government objects to as unconstitutional; review of public actions that may be brought by any citizen to challenge the constitutionality of laws or decrees; and discretionary review of lower court decisions in *tutela* actions.[2] The last two of these streamlined mechanisms of review have been particularly critical to the success of the pioneering efforts at social change through litigation under the new Constitution.

Colombia's *tutela* allows any person to seek immediate judicial protection of their fundamental constitutional rights. Article 86 of the Constitution provides that this action may be filed before judges, at all times and places, and must be ruled on within ten days. Orders granting *tutelas* may be appealed to higher courts and are subject to discretionary review by the Constitutional Court, which generally sits in panels of three to hear such cases.[3]

Article 40(6)'s public action of unconstitutionality provides that any citizen, regardless of whether one has any personal injury or stake in the controversy, can "[i]nterpose public actions in defense of the Constitution and the law."[4] And among the functions Article 241 entrusts to the Constitutional Court is "to decide on petitions of unconstitutionality that citizens present against laws, both for their substantive content and for procedural errors in their formation," a power previously exercised by the Supreme Court.

The Constitutional Court is composed of nine members who are selected by the Senate from lists of three candidates submitted by the President, the Supreme Court, or the Council of State, depending upon the seat to be filled. After initial interim one-year appointments beginning in 1992, the members serve eight-year terms and may not be reappointed. During its first decade all members of the court were males; the first woman to hold a permanent position did not begin her term until March 1, 2001.

[2] *Constitución Política de Colombia de 1991, actualizada hasta Reforma de 2001*, art. 241 (hereinafter "*Const. Pol. Col.*").
[3] *Const. Pol. Col.*, ibid., art. 86.
[4] *Const. Pol. Col.*, ibid., art. 40(6).

There have been repeated proposals to limit the power of the new court; the most recent was introduced in July 2003. Critics of the Court's aggressive use of the Constitution's new writ of *tutela* to protect fundamental rights complain that the country is suffering from an epidemic of *tutelitis*. But others welcome the Court's initial activism on behalf of the beneficiaries of the newly framed constitutional rights, viewing it as a rare optimistic indicator in a country that otherwise shows signs of being on its deathbed.

Indeed, the Court's activist role is directly linked to trying to provide solutions to the reality of the violence that has permeated Colombian society by confronting prejudices, inequalities, and marginalization that have been factors in generating societal violence. In its gender jurisprudence, this is most obvious in cases involving domestic violence in which the Court has noted that "respect for the life and physical integrity of others, in a broad moral and legal sense, cannot be reduced to just police protection or criminal punishment of the aggressor; it includes the duty neither to abuse, nor offend, nor torture, nor threaten people, especially, one with whom one shares a domestic union of procreation and development of children and the family, and the promise of mutual material and spiritual fostering."[5]

This chapter describes some of the substantive guarantees that have figured prominently in early gender litigation under the new constitution and chronicles how broad substantive guarantees, supplemented and reinforced by the Constitution's incorporation of international human rights conventions, have become more than just "paper rights" in the hands of an avowedly "activist" Constitutional Court.

PRINCIPAL GENDER-RELATED SUBSTANTIVE PROVISIONS

In the 1970s and 1980s, women's movements throughout Latin America adopted much of the law reform-laden agenda of the period's international women's movement. Accepting the notion that law had helped shape attitudes and beliefs about gender and could be a useful tool in the struggle to change them, activists successfully pursued ratification of the Convention on the Elimination of All Forms of Discrimination Against Women (CEDAW) and began to use it to press for changes in their countries' often antiquated codes.

CEDAW contains four provisions that have been particularly important as a catalyst for legal reforms. The first two are definitional – Article 1's broad definition of discrimination against women[6] and Article 4's approval of

[5] Sentencia No. T-529/92.
[6] *CEDAW*, 18 December 1979, 1249 U.N.T.S. 14, art. 1:

> For the purposes of the present Convention, the term "discrimination against women" shall mean any distinction, exclusion or restriction made on the basis of sex which has the effect or purpose of impairing or nullifying the recognition, enjoyment or exercise by women, irrespective of their marital status, on a basis of equality of men and women, of human rights and fundamental freedoms in the political, economic, social, cultural, civil or any other field.

positive discrimination or affirmative action by providing that temporary special measures to accelerate de facto equality of opportunities and treatment shall not be considered discrimination as defined by the convention. Article 3 expressly charges party states to pursue all appropriate steps, including legislative measures, to ensure women's full development and progress. And during the past decade, Article 7, which obligates states to take all appropriate measures to eliminate discrimination against women in political and public life, has been a stimulus to the passage of laws providing quotas for women's participation in electoral contests or appointed public positions in at least twelve Latin American countries.

The Colombian Congress ratified CEDAW in 1981,[7] but little had been done to implement it prior to the adoption of the new Constitution a decade later. One of the fundamental demands made by women's rights activists was that the principles of CEDAW be incorporated into the new Constitution.[8]

As a result of the efforts of these advocates for women's rights, and of the parallel efforts of supportive men and women within the constitutional assembly, the Constitution contains several explicit guarantees related to women's rights. First, it expressly reflects CEDAW's dual strategy of prohibition of discrimination against women and approval of special positive measures as a means of assuring substantive rather than merely formal equality. Article 13 of the new Constitution incorporates these twin principles of equality in the following terms:

All persons are born free and equal before the law, shall receive the same protection and treatment from the authorities, and shall enjoy the same rights, liberties and opportunities without any discrimination for reasons of sex, race, national or family origin, language, religion, or political or philosophical opinion.

The State shall promote conditions so that equality will be real and effective and adopt measures in favor of groups discriminated against or marginalized.

The State shall specially protect those persons who because of their economic, physical or mental condition find themselves in circumstances of manifest weakness and punish abuses and mistreatment that are committed against them.[9]

---

[7] Ley 51 de 1981. The ratification was received by the United Nations on January 19, 1982, and CEDAW entered into effect in Colombia on February 18, 1982. The definition of discrimination had been further developed in a 1990 decree:

Discrimination can be direct or indirect.

Direct discrimination exists when a person receives a treatment less favorable than another because one belongs to one or the other sex.

Indirect discrimination means the application of conditions of employment that although equal in a formal sense, in practice favor one sex over the other.

Decreto 1398 de 1990.

[8] See *Propuestas de Mujeres a La Asamblea Nacional Constituyente* (Bogotá: January 1991).

[9] *Const. Pol. Col., supra* note 2, art. 13.

The Constitutional Court's decisions under Article 13 have used both principles of reasonableness and proportionality developed by the European Court of Human Rights and the concept of levels of scrutiny from the United States Supreme Court's opinions. Unlike the U.S. Supreme Court, which has applied a "heightened" review but not "strict scrutiny"[10] to gender classifications, the Colombian Court has applied "strict scrutiny" and has placed a heavy burden of proof on the defender of the challenged action when faced with discrimination based on sex (and, more recently, sexual orientation) as well as when dealing with infringements upon fundamental rights.[11]

In addition to Article 13's general equality provisions, Article 40 provides that "the authorities will guarantee the adequate and effective participation of women in the decision-making levels of Public Administration,"[12] Article 42 recognizes equal rights and responsibilities between spouses[13] and Article 43 prohibits discrimination against women and declares equal rights and opportunities between women and men.[14] Finally, Article 53 includes equality of opportunity and special protection for women, maternity, and minors among the fundamental principles to be considered by Congress in enacting a labor law.[15]

One of the most controversial features of the new Constitution was its extension of civil divorce to religious marriages. According to Article 42, "The civil effects of all marriages will be terminated by divorce according to the civil law."[16] Article 42 also recognizes that a family can be formed by "natural or judicial bonds, by the free decision of a man and a woman to contract marriage or by the responsible will to form it,"[17] and, as mentioned above, guarantees equality of rights among couples. It further provides: "Any form of violence within the family is considered destructive of its harmony and unity, and will be punished according to the law."[18]

Although Article 42 also recognizes the right of couples "to freely and responsibly decide the number of their children,"[19] the constitutional assembly rejected demands of women's groups that free choice about motherhood,

---

[10] As commonly formulated, the "strict scrutiny" test requires government to prove that its action is justified as a "necessary" or "narrowly tailored" means of achieving a "compelling" governmental purpose or end.

[11] See, e.g., Sentencia No. C-481/98: strict scrutiny is applicable to a law treating homosexuality as a ground of misconduct for teachers because, if sexual orientation is biologically determined, the law is equivalent to a sex classification and, if sexual preference involves personal choice, the law infringes on the right to the free development of one's personality.

[12] *Const. Pol. Col., supra* note 2, art. 40.

[13] *Const. Pol. Col.,* ibid., art. 42.

[14] *Const. Pol. Col.,* ibid., art. 43.

[15] *Const. Pol. Col.,* ibid., art. 53.

[16] *Const. Pol. Col.,* ibid., art. 42.

[17] *Const. Pol. Col.,* ibid.

[18] *Const. Pol. Col.,* ibid.

[19] *Const. Pol. Col.,* ibid.

including the right to legalized abortion, be explicitly guaranteed. By contrast, Article 43 guarantees special state assistance and protection to women during pregnancy and after childbirth, including "support benefits from it if they then become unemployed or abandoned."[20] It further provides that the "State will provide help in a special manner to women heads of family."[21] And, as mentioned earlier, protection for maternity is among the fundamental principles that Article 53 directs lawmakers to consider in enacting a labor law.[22]

Although its effects are not limited to women's rights, Article 93's incorporation of international human rights law has been significant in shaping early gender jurisprudence:

Article 93. International treaties and conventions ratified by the Congress that recognize human rights and that prohibit their limitation in states of emergency have prevalence[23] in the internal order.

The rights and duties consecrated in this Charter will be interpreted in accordance with international treaties on human rights ratified by Colombia.[24]

SURVEY OF SIGNIFICANT GENDER JURISPRUDENCE

Horizontal Effects within Traditionally "Private" Spheres

The framers of the 1991 Constitution expressly contemplated that its guarantees would not be limited to protections against state action but would have horizontal effects in at least some circumstances. The lengths to which the Constitutional Court has been willing to extend these horizontal effects – to cover not only such traditionally "private" spheres as private education and employment but to reach into the realm of family relations – has been one of the court's most important doctrinal developments.

The governing criterion for application of the horizontal effects doctrine is "a clear asymmetry in the relations of power between individuals that denies,

---

[20] *Const. Pol. Col.,* ibid., art. 43.

[21] *Const. Pol. Col.,* ibid.

[22] Other provisions that women have used in early gender litigation include Article 11's right to life; Article 15's guarantee to all persons of the "right to personal and family privacy and to their good name"; Article 16's recognition that "all persons have the right to the free development of their personality without limitations except those imposed by the rights of others and the legal order"; Article 18's guarantee of freedom of conscience; Article 21's right to dignity; Article 67's right to education; and Article 94's recognition of the existence of unenumerated human rights. *Const. Pol. Col.,* ibid.

[23] The Constitutional Court initially interpreted this to mean that international human rights laws had "supra-constitutional" status in the internal legal order but later revised its interpretation to accord this body of human rights law the same status as fundamental constitutional rights.

[24] *Const. Pol. Col., supra* note 2, art. 93.

restricts, or eliminates personal autonomy and justifies state intervention to avoid the *envilecimiento*, the absolute instrumentalization or degradation of a human being." Although constitutional protection of fundamental rights is generally not applicable in contractual or commercial relations, the Court has extended protection in the following realms: labor, pensions, medical care, information, sports, transportation, religious organizations, family violence, and social security.

The Home. Some of the new Constitutional Court's most noteworthy decisions are its early decisions reviewing cases in which women filed *tutelas* against husbands or companions who were subjecting them to domestic violence within the home.[25] Relying, on Title II, Chapter 1's fundamental rights to personal integrity (Article 12), health, and life (Article 11), and on Article 42's recognition that "[a]ny form of violence within the family is considered destructive of its harmony and unity, and will be sanctioned according to the law," women convinced the Court to reverse the lower courts' rejection of *tutelas*. In a series of cases, the Court granted women relief that at times included both direct orders to their abusers to abstain from further physical or moral violence against them and orders to local officials to provide appropriate protection. And, although orders in *tutela actions* generally are only injunctive in nature, fines and imprisonment may be imposed for violations of the orders.

Cognizant of the concerns of some that these *tutela* actions allowed judges to "penetrate the interior of the family" and that this was "a strictly private sphere," the Court explained the horizontal effects of the fundamental rights involved by pointing out that not solely private interests are jeopardized, but fundamental personal rights, likely including those of children whose rights are given constitutional priority over those of others. Indeed the public interest is affected at its most sensitive point because the institution threatened is constitutionally recognized as the basis of social organization.[26]

After the Colombian Congress, in 1996, enacted legislation providing a means of immediate judicial relief for victims of domestic violence (as opposed to the relief that previously was available only through penal or family court proceedings or administrative resort to the police), the Constitutional Court ruled that the prerequisites for *tutelas* were no longer present in domestic violence cases because this alternative judicial procedure for immediate relief was available.[27]

[25] See, e.g., Sentencia No. T-529/92; Sentencia No. T-382/94; Sentencia No. T-487/94; and Sentencia No. T-552/94.

[26] Sentencia No. T-552/94.

[27] Sentencia No. T-420/96. See *Ley de Violencia Intrafamiliar*, Ley 294/96. This law itself was challenged through a public action of unconstitutionality filed by Gloria Guzmán Duque. In Sentencia No. C-285/97, the Constitutional Court rejected her challenge to the law's provision of more lenient penalties for intrafamilial violence (1 to 4 years in prison) than for

Education. Another group of early gender cases in which the Court at times accorded horizontal effects to constitutional rights dealt with schools' treatment of pregnant students. In these cases, petitioners raised challenges both to expulsions from school based on pregnancy and to schools' refusals to readmit them following giving birth. The Constitutional Court granted *tutelas* in both types of cases and regardless of whether the schools were public or privately owned. It relied on the constitution's equality provisions as well as its protection of human dignity and the free development of the personality (Article 16), education (Articles 44 and 67) and maternity (Article 43).[28]

Pregnant teenagers and teenage mothers continue to confront negative cultural attitudes in schools. On September 21, 1998, the Court granted a *tutela* on behalf of pregnant students and students in *uniones de hecho*, or de facto marriages, who were forced to wear red aprons or pinafores.[29] The Court ruled that the school's practices violated rights of the family as the basic institution of society, the right to equal protection, and the right to the free development of one's personality. Similarly, on November 11, 1998, the Court granted a *tutela* against a school in Cali that refused to permit a pregnant sixteen-year-old to attend regularly scheduled classes, contending that she could 'contaminate' other students and lead them down a "bad path."[30]

In this line of cases, the Court has acknowledged the tension between private rights (even those of constitutional status themselves) and the rights it is according protection, defending its position:

> The protection that the Superior Statute [the Constitution] affords to maternity is of such intensity that not even those educational centers whose educational program is founded on a particular ethical or religious vision of the world – protected by liberty of conscience (Const. Article 18) – can use such vision to stigmatize, separate, or discriminate against a – pregnant student with respect to the benefits derived from the right to an education. In other words, as to the tension that can exist between the autonomy of private centers of education and the right of the future mother not to be discriminated against on the basis of her pregnancy, the latter, without doubt, prevails.[31]

Employment. The workplace is another area in which the Court's opinions have deemed certain constitutional protections applicable to both public and

---

other violent offences because the new law established additional new crimes and did not preclude conviction for other more serious crimes if their elements were proven. It upheld her challenge to the new law's unequal treatment of interspousal rape as a less serious offence than other forms of rape, however.

[28] Sentencia No. T-420/92; Sentencia No. T-292/94.
[29] Sentencia No. T-516/98. See Adriana Palacio Garcés, "Damaris ya no es la chica de rojo" *El Tiempo* (24 September 1998).
[30] Sentencia No. T-656/98.
[31] Sentencia No. T-656/98.

private relationships. Many of the Court's employment cases are challenges to provisions of the Labor Code or raise issues involving Article 53 of the Constitution, which requires Congress to embody certain fundamental principles within the Labor Code, thus presenting more traditional vertical challenges to governmental action, but other cases have granted *tutelas* directly against private employers.

For example, the Court has expanded protection to pregnant workers by developing a concept of *fuero de maternidad* (analogous to the longstanding concept of *fuero sindical* that protects the job security of union activists), which protects against loss of employment for reasons related to pregnancy.[32] Thus, in September 1997, the Court ruled that women workers cannot be dismissed from their jobs without cause during pregnancy or within the first three months after giving birth, and that employers who unlawfully terminate an employee during these periods are obligated to pay the employee sixty days' salary as provided in Article 239 of the Labor Code and also to reinstate all employment rights. Judge Alejandro Martínez Caballero's opinion relied on Articles 13 and 43 and on Article 53's recognition of special protection for women, maternity, and minor workers as fundamental principles that must be taken into account in labor legislation, to affirm Article 239's constitutionality, but only after supplementing it with a judicial gloss denying all effect to such unlawful terminations.[33] Although the *tutela* is generally not available to seek reinstatement because of the availability of other means of judicial relief under labor laws, an exception exists in cases of pregnant workers; the *tutela* may be used as a transitory mechanism to prevent irreparable injury when reinstatement is required to assure the minimum necessities of life (*el mínimo vital*) for a mother or her newborn.[34]

In an earlier case involving social security coverage, the Court ruled against Avianca Airlines in a *tutela* action brought by a copilot denied health care coverage for a miscarriage on the grounds that it was not an illness. The Court found violations of fundamental rights related to health, procreation, social security protections for maternity, and personal integrity. It characterized the decision to deny coverage as "a discrimination based on the woman's role in procreation and consequently, an undue enrichment."[35]

The Court has addressed employment-related gender issues in numerous other contexts. For example, its 1997 decision in an action presented by María del Pilar Leyva and Sandra Cadena Cortázar struck down a part of Article 242 of the Labor Code that prohibited women factory workers from

---

[32] Interview with Catalina Botero (Bogotá: 16 December 1998).

[33] Sentencia No. C-470/97. For other opinions dealing with pregnancy and maternity rights in the workplace and recognizing that the Constitution and international conventions guarantee special protection for pregnant and nursing employees, see, e.g., Sentencias No. T-568/96; and C-710/96.

[34] Sentencias Nos. T-606/95; T-311/96; T-373/98; and T-426/98.

[35] Sentencia No. T-341/94.

working at night.[36] The 1951 law provided that: "Women, regardless of age, cannot be employed during the night in any industrial company, except a company in which only members of the same family are employed." In a unanimous opinion written by Judge Hernando Herrera Vergara, the court held that the law violated the constitutional guarantee of equal rights and opportunities for women and men and added that the state has a constitutional obligation to promote women's participation in public and private administrative levels.

Another case from late 1997, although not directly involving claims of sex discrimination, bears mentioning here. In October, the Constitutional Court ruled that all employees whether public or private have a constitutional right to earn a salary that is proportional to the quantity and quality of the work they perform – "for equal work, equal pay."[37] The Court stated that salary differentials were permitted but must correspond to justified, real, proven reasons and not simply to the subjective preferences of the employer or the intent to impede or discourage union activity or other worker organizing. The concept endorsed seems to be one based on the principle of equal pay for equal work, however, not the broader concept of pay equity, or equal pay for work of equal value.

The Court has also addressed the rights of domestic workers (a category that is largely female), although again not through the lens of gender equality. In 1995, the Court itself raised the issue in a public action of unconstitutionality brought by the People's Defender against another provision of the labor code.[38] The Court invalidated portions of the Code that provided lesser *auxilio de cesantía* (unemployment benefits) for domestic workers, concluding that if domestic service is a luxury, those who enjoy it must pay for it in a manner similar to how other employees are paid. Limiting the benefits to domestic workers conflicted with raising their standard of living as the constitutional principle of social solidarity required. However, the opinion found certain differences in the Labor Code's treatment of domestic workers such as different maximum hours of work to be reasonable in light of the nature of their work. In July 1998, the Court upheld the Labor Code's broad definition of what constitutes "salary" for domestic workers.[39] But the opinion by Judge Fabio Morón also warned employers that domestic workers have the right to overtime pay for hours in excess of ten hours a day.

[36] Sentencia No. C-622/97; "Mujeres podrán trabajar de noche en las industrias" *El Tiempo* (28 November 1997).

[37] Sentencia No. SU 519/97.

[38] Sentencia No. C-051/95. The Court also invalidated the labor code's authorization of lesser social benefits for employees of nonprofit entities, which was challenged by the People's Defender.

[39] Sentencia No. C-372/98; "Sí al pago de horas extras para empleadas domésticas" *El Tiempo* (22 July 1998).

In 1994, the Court ruled on a *tutela* that challenged a social security agency's policy of providing medical benefits to the wives or permanent companions of male employee members but not to women employee members' husbands or companions. The action was filed by Amanda Cardona de los Ríos after the agency denied coverage to her husband, Octavio de los Ríos Uribe, a sixty-three-year-old butcher without any social insurance.[40] In an opinion by Judge Eduardo Cifuentes, the Court ruled that the agency's action violated Article 13's equality guarantees and ordered it to put an end to this sex discrimination by considering the application for benefits for the petitioner's spouse within forty-eight hours. In 1996, the Court ruled that an older law that terminated survivor benefits to a worker's widow if she remarried violated widows' constitutional rights of equality and the right to the free development of one's personality.[41] It announced that any woman denied benefits pursuant to this law after 1991 could obtain payments.

Other gender-related cases include several related to military training and service. In 1994, the court rejected arguments that not subjecting women to obligatory military service (but authorizing their voluntary service) was unconstitutional, referring among other things, to biological differences and differences in education (especially physical).[42] In April of 2003, the Minister of Defense proposed a law to require that, upon reaching eighteen years of age, Colombian women be subject to be called to obligatory military service (or to obligatory social service) when the circumstances of the country demand it. The proposal, which drew opposition from many groups including the Colombian Women for Peace Initiative and the Medellín Youth Network, was expected to be discussed in a Colombian Senate Commission in late 2003.

In 1995, Adriana Granados, a nineteen-year-old woman, filed a *tutela* claiming a right of admission to Colombia's navy.[43] Her success in that case paved the way for the enrollment of the first twenty-eight women cadets.[44] After *tutelas* in 1996 dealing with admission to the air force[45] and to the naval officer training school,[46] in 1997, thirty-four women joined the *Fuerza Aérea* as pilot trainees and twenty entered the naval officers' training school.[47] Military installations have been adapted to provide private lodging, separate bathrooms, pregnancy tests, and maternity uniforms.[48]

---

[40] Sentencia No. T-098/94.
[41] Sentencia No. C-309/96.
[42] Sentencia No. C-511/94.
[43] Sentencia No. T-624/95.
[44] Pamela Mercer, "Colombians Winning Quick Redress from Courts with Writs" *The New York Times* (29 November 1996) A19.
[45] Sentencia No. T-704/96.
[46] Sentencia No. T-463/96.
[47] "De Coronelas a Generalas" *Mujer/Fempress* (November 1998) 14.
[48] "De Coronelas," ibid.

In September 2001, three of the newly appointed justices granted a *tutela*
that provides a striking demonstration of their continuing adherence to the
doctrine of horizontal effects. The *tutela* was filed by Olinda María Calderón
Calderón, an indigenous woman who was employed as a caretaker by the
resident of an apartment on the twenty-second floor of The Conquistador
Building in Cartegena. The action was filed against the manager of the building who had issued a directive to the building's elevator operators stating
that domestic employees, and especially Senora Calderón, were not to be
permitted to use the building's main elevators and could only use the service
elevator. Despite her own sickness, the petitioner was forced to use the stairs
when the service elevator was not working. The directive also prohibited her
from receiving guests and warned that any employee violating the directive
would be fired. She sought judicial protection of her fundamental rights to
life, to equality, and to the free development of her personality. She alleged
discrimination based on the nature of her employment and on her indigenous origin. The *tutela* did not expressly allege gender discrimination but the
justices' opinion pointed out the indirect effects of the directive on women,
given that most of the affected domestic workers were generally women –
campesinas, indigenous, or of color: To differentiate among people with respect to the use of common goods based exclusively on personal factors like
their social condition, in this case that of domestic workers or employees, is
a discriminatory act that violates the right to equality and reinforces social
stereotypes and prejudices against those who perform domestic work.

Accordingly, the Constitutional Court not only agreed with the lower
court that the petitioner must be allowed to use the main elevators when the
service elevator was out of order but also ruled that "the fundamental right
to equality was violated by the simple act of prohibiting her from using any
of the elevators like any other human being of equal dignity."[49]

Substantive Equality

Although the Court's horizontal applications of fundamental gender rights
in the *tutela* decisions and other gender equality cases discussed above have
approached equality mostly from the perspective of *formal* equality and the
prohibition of invidious or negative gender discrimination, another key area
of doctrinal development has been with respect to Article 13's textual em-
bodiment of the concept of *substantive* equality. As Judge Eduardo Cifuentes
Muñoz notes, the Constitutional Court has accepted that women are among
the marginalized groups entitled to affirmative measures:

The general tendency of the Court's jurisprudence has been to recognize that historically women belong to a group that has been in conditions of manifest weakness

49 Sentencia No. T-1042/01.

before men and thus it is necessary that at all levels the state must take positive differential action. And at the same time, apart from this positive differentiation, the woman has equal rights with the man, independent of positive discrimination, within the bosom of the family, in social institutions like universities and schools, and in institutions like Social Security and the world of work.[50]

Early on, the Constitutional Court focused on the gender implications of Article 13's requirement that "[t]he state will promote conditions so that equality is real and effective and will adopt measures in favor of groups discriminated against or marginalized."[51] In late 1992, the Court invoked both the positive and negative aspects of Article 13's concept of equality in a challenge to a law granting single (*célibes*, celibate or never married) daughters of military officials special social welfare rights.[52] In an opinion by Judge José Gregorio Hernandez Galindo, the Court upheld the discrimination in favor of daughters over sons as a measure to make the principle of equality "real and effective," given women's frequent economic dependency on men in Colombian society. By contrast, it ruled that the discrimination between single and married daughters violated Article 13's protection against discrimination and the guarantee of the free development of one's personality, reasoning that "every person, in the exercise of their liberty, must be able to choose without coercion and in a manner free of stimulation established by the legislator, between contracting marriage or remaining single." Accordingly, the law was held valid, except for the terms "*célibes*" and "remains in a state of celibacy" which were held unenforceable. Although this decision demonstrates the Court's reliance on the "positive" aspect of Article 13 in the realm of gender classifications and the Court's sensitivity to contextualizing discrimination, its potential for perpetuating stereotypical views of women as economically dependent also suggests some of the tension in the Court's early gender jurisprudence.

In the context of women's employment-related rights, the Court also invoked the principle of positive discrimination in a case rejecting a challenge to a law setting differential retirement and pension eligibility ages for women and men. The 1993 law set retirement eligibility ages of fifty-five for women and sixty for men (subject to be increased to fifty-seven and sixty-two in 2014); employees could choose to continue working for five additional years.[53] The Court requested and considered statistical evidence and opinions by social scientists before concluding that this law's positive discrimination in regard to retirement and pension rights was a rational, reasonable, and proportional measure designed to compensate for women's continuing

---

[50] Interview with Eduardo Cifuentes Muñoz, Magistrate of the Colombian Constitutional Court (Bogotá: 5 July 1995).

[51] *Const. Pol. Col.*, *supra* note 2, art. 13.

[52] Sentencia No. C-588/92.

[53] Sentencia No. C-410/94.

inferior position in the labor force and for the physical and mental burdens placed upon them because of their double workload as members of the paid labor force and as those responsible for the society's unpaid domestic work. The opinion pointed to evidence placing the combined workload of women at ninety-six hours a week compared to forty-eight hours for men. The Court made it clear that the legislator could well "take positive measures directed to correcting *de facto* inequalities to compensate for the relegation suffered and to promote the real and effective equality of the woman in the economic and social orders."

By contrast, the Court rejected a municipality's attempt to rely on Article 13's acceptance of positive discrimination to denominate certain housekeeping and maintenance positions as exclusively for women. It established a strict test of necessity for any attempt to limit employment to persons of one sex and concluded that it was not indispensable that one be a woman to perform the essential tasks of these jobs. Men could perform the jobs as well as women, and excluding men meant "contributing to perpetuating prejudices disregarding the essential equality of all human beings."[54]

In its most extensive treatment of concepts of substantive equality, on March 29, 2000, the Constitutional Court announced its unanimous opinion in an automatic review of the constitutionality of a quota law passed by the Colombian Congress in June 1999.[55] Although earlier attempts had failed, both houses of Congress finally approved legislation designed to comply with Article 40's requirement that "the authorities will guarantee the adequate and effective participation of women in decision-making levels of Public Administration." Among other things, the law established a 30 percent quota for women in high level decision-making positions in the public sector. Before announcing its decision, the Court requested statistics on the representation of women in high public positions; sought the opinions of different persons and organizations, including those dedicated to studying gender; and held a public audience to hear further opinions on the law.

The Court's opinion noted that positive actions, including inverse discrimination, are expressly authorized by the Constitution, which guarantees not only the principle of nondiscrimination but also alludes to a substantive dimension of equality that has "a remedial, compensatory, emancipatory character, corrective and defensive of persons and groups situated in conditions of inferiority." Consequently, "authorities can appeal to race or sex, or other *suspect* category, not to marginalize certain persons or groups or to perpetuate inequalities, but to lessen the harmful effect of social practices that have placed these same people or groups in unfavorable positions."

The Court declared many, but not all, provisions of the law to be consistent with the Constitution's express commitment to ensuring women's adequate

[54] Sentencia No. T-026/96.
[55] Sentencia No. C-371/2000.

and effective participation in decision-making positions within the public sector (Article 40) and its explicit embrace of substantive equality in Article 13.

The Court rejected "Darwinian" arguments that all an egalitarian order must guarantee are equitable conditions at the starting point and thus affirmative actions can only be used to remove obstacles in conditions at the point of departure not to address inequalities in actual results at the point of arrival. Instead, it relied on verifiable empirical observations and corroborated by annexed statistics on women graduates establishing that, "the population qualified to occupy positions of high political responsibility has (for a good time) been equitably distributed between men and women, and the balance is inclining all the time more in favor of the latter." A review of the statistics on the low participation of women in the highest decision-making levels supported only one conclusion: "If in spite of the existence today of equality at the starting point, [results at] the arrival point continue being inequitable, it is because it is not the merits, or not only these, that determine that the majority of the most high responsibilities of the State are in the hands of men."

The opinion prefaced its analysis of the constitutionality of the separate articles of the law by emphasizing three guiding principles:

(1) The validity of these measures depends on the real operation of discriminatory circumstances.
(2) Not every use of inverse discrimination is constitutional. In each case there has to be an analysis of whether the difference in treatment is reasonable and proportional.
(3) Affirmative actions must be temporary, because once "real and effective" equality is realized, they lose their reason for being.

Applying these criteria, the Court upheld the 30 percent quotas for high level decision-making posts established in Article 4, so long as the quotas are understood to be temporary measures and are applied gradually, as new positions become vacant. The quotas were obligatory and "rigid," but the Court found they were justified under the proportionality framework it has used to determine whether a difference in treatment is constitutional. Under this framework the court examines each provision and considers:

(1) If it seeks a valid end in light of the Constitution,
(2) If the different treatment is "adequate" to achieve the desired end,
(3) If the means used is "necessary," in the sense that there exists no less burdensome one, in terms of the sacrifice of other constitutional principles, to reach the desired end, and
(4) If the different treatment is "proportional *stricto sensu*," meaning that it does not sacrifice values, principles, or rights (among which is equality) that have a greater weight than those that are intended to be satisfied through such treatment.

Examining the proportionality and reasonableness of Article 4's 30 percent quota, the Court had no doubt that it would significantly increase women's participation in the covered positions. Dismissing arguments against the law's failure to establish a quota of 50 percent, it noted that the law imposed a quota of "at least" 30 percent and did not close the doors to women's occupying a higher percentage of the positions. The percentage chosen was not gratuitous or unfounded but was the figure the United Nations considers a "critical mass" and was the percentage that Colombia accepted in the Beijing Action Platform and that several other countries (including Argentina, Bolivia, Brazil, Panama, and Venezuela) have adopted in legislation designed to stimulate women's participation in popular elections. The Court also rejected arguments that the law failed to address the causes of women's underrepresentation, noting its symbolic value in combating one of the causes: the long patriarchal tradition of considering women's role to be principally in the private sphere with the result that women capable and willing to participate in public life remain "invisible." Additionally, women's entry into these positions would open a space for them to propose and design policies favoring the entire feminine population. The measure was necessary, as less burdensome means such as education or simple promises to promote equality were important but insufficient.

Turning to the final consideration of whether this quota sacrificed rights and principles of greater weight, the Court rejected four arguments. Noting that the abolition of slavery could not be considered a prejudice to the "owners" of slaves, and that men still had the possibility of filling 70 percent of the covered positions, it concluded that the argument based on asserted violations of men's equality rights and right to work failed. Second, arguments that the quota discriminated against women by suggesting they are inferior or disabled and cannot obtain high positions on their own merits (which the court predicted inevitably would be voiced by someone) were belied by the fact that such measures are adopted, not as measures of state paternalism but precisely because women are equally capable and yet state intervention is necessary to remove obstacles that have historically impeded their access and to correct the social practices that generate inequitable conditions. Arguments that the quota threatened the nature of positions of free selection and the efficacy and efficiency of the public administration were also rejected.

The Court upheld the provision recognizing exceptions from Article 4's mandatory 30 percent quota for career positions, positions filled by popular elections (noting that imposing restrictions on the people's freedom to elect representatives would alter the principle of popular sovereignty), and positions filled by the system of *ternas* (involving selections from nominations of three candidates) and lists. By contrast, another provision applicable to positions filled from lists, which mandated that women be named until the 30 percent quota was met, was deemed neither necessary nor proportional.

Instead, it was found to be discriminatory and contrary to the principle of equality because individual men automatically would be excluded from a broad category of positions until this percentage was achieved. A provision governing career positions was approved insofar as it required that equal numbers of men and women be involved in the selection process (but only as limited to subjective aspects of the selection process), and a provision requiring that *ternas* include at least one woman was approved.

Finally, three portions of the opinion reveal the tension between the Constitution's commitment to collectivism and substantive equality and its embrace of liberalism's respect for individualism. In two instances, the Court resolved the tension in favor of individualism; in the other, it strove to accommodate both values but in the end, limited the force of substantive equality. First, the Court found that 30 percent quotas related to political parties and their electoral candidates violated various constitutional provisions related to the autonomy of political parties and organizations. In the second instance, it ruled that a provision in the law specifying requirements for a National Plan, which included a section calling for the elimination of school texts with discriminatory content was unconstitutional because it was inconsistent with academic freedom and freedom of expression and would be censorship. Provisions requiring education concerning the equality of the sexes and promotion of gender-sensitive values, including promoting the sharing of household chores and childcare by men and women were approved, however.

Finally, the opinion exposed what appears to be an erosion or weakening of the Court's horizontal effects doctrine. Although upholding quotas for high public positions, the Court was careful to limit its decision to the public sector. Article 9 of the law called upon public authorities to develop measures tending to promote the participation of women in the private sector. The Court upheld this provision and said that lawmakers could adopt indicative guidelines directed to promoting the participation of certain groups but warned that these could not be mandatory. The Court reaffirmed the horizontal effects of fundamental rights but cautioned that the force of equality principles differs in the private sector given that the Constitution also protects pluralism, freedom of association, and free development of the personality.

Following the Court's opinion on the draft law, in May 2000, Congress revised and approved a Quota Law that was subsequently approved by the president.[56]

Diverse Family Structures

Several of the Constitutional Court's decisions have dealt with the Constitution's recognition of Colombia's diverse family structures. As a result of

[56] Ley de Cuotas, Ley 581 de 2000.

factors such as war and other violence, poverty, and high rates of teenage pregnancy, over 25 percent of families are headed by single women. The number of such families in Bogotá reportedly increased from 25 percent in 1991 to 30 percent in 2001. Women become heads of families not because of changes in roles within the family as much as because of changes in the presence or status of men.[57] In addition, according to a study completed in July 1998, by the National Administrative Statistics Department (DANE), the number of Colombian families living in *uniones de hechos* (*de facto* unions) has increased from 10 percent in 1983 to 35 percent in 1998.[58] The study also revealed an increase in the number of widows, corresponding to an increase in deaths, especially of men between twenty and forty-four years old as a result of the intensification of the violence.

Article 43 of the Constitution states that "[t]he state shall support the woman head of family in a special manner."[59] Relying on this provision as well as on constitutional guarantees of the right to work and due process, the Court granted an early *tutela* prohibiting municipal authorities from closing a small business owned by a woman head of family.[60] The *tutela* was filed by Rosa Ana Orduz vda. (*viuda* or widow) de Briceño after the authorities revoked the permission they had granted her to run the family blacksmith shop following her husband's death. She and her oldest son were operating the shop out of the house she shared with her three young children and eight other members of her extended family. When the neighborhood grew and a residential complex was built next to her house, some of the new residents complained that the business disturbed them, and the authorities ordered the business closed. The opinion by Judge Carlos Gaviria Díaz found violations of due process and labor rights as well as of the obligation Article 43 imposes on the state to afford special protection for women heads of family.[61]

In an important case dealing with *uniones de hecho*, the Court protected the property rights of a woman upon the death of her companion in a de facto union. It ruled that disregarding the value of the woman's domestic work in acquiring and improving the home where the couple had lived in favor of inheritance rights of the man's sister and only heir violated the companion's rights of equality and due process.[62]

The action was filed by Esther Varela who had lived with Hernando Guerrero Trujillo for 24 years prior to his death. For the last twenty-one years they had shared possession of a house he bought in 1970. When he died in 1989, the courts in Cali rejected Varela's claim that, as his companion

[57] See "¿Por Que Llega A Ser Jefa de Familia?" *Mujer/Fempress* (November 1998) 14.
[58] Socorro Ramírez, "Revolución Silenciosa" *Mujer/Fempress* (October 1998), <http://www.fempress.cl/204/temas2.html> (date accessed: 17 June 2002).
[59] *Const. Pol. Col.*, *supra* note 2, art. 43.
[60] Sentencia No. T-414/93.
[61] Sentencia No. T-414/93.
[62] Sentencia No. T-494/92.

in a de facto marriage, the value of her domestic work should be considered in determining the rights to his property. Instead, the courts awarded the property to his sister.

Judge Ciro Angarita wrote the decision for the Constitutional Court finding for Varela and, lest there be any doubt about its views on the applicability of the ruling to other situations, announcing that the constitutional doctrine enunciated would have binding effect on authorities in similar cases involving domestic work in relations between men and women. He criticized the lower court's view that contributions to a de facto union must be money or things that have market value.

The Court also has relied upon Article 42's recognition that the family can be formed by legal or natural bonds and on its guarantee of equal rights and duties for all children whether born within marriage or not to invalidate numerous provisions of the Civil Code that discriminated against children born outside marriage.[63]

When faced with arguments that a 1989 law requiring that birth registries follow the Spanish tradition of using double *apellidos* (surnames) with that of the father listed before that of the mother violated Articles 13, 42, and 43 and international human rights laws, however, the Court upheld the law.[64] The majority did not see this as having anything to do with equality of rights and obligations. There had to be an order and the law provided one. Judges Cifuentes, Gaviria, and Martínez dissented, contending that the law was not innocuous but reflected a long-standing patriarchal tradition that relegates women to a secondary plane.[65] They pointed out that the need for uniformity would also be met by placing the mother's last name first but argued that the sensible solution, consistent with the constitutional principle of equality of rights, would be to allow couples to decide the order by mutual consent.

Reproductive Freedom and Control

Rights of Women Prisoners. In addition to the cases mentioned earlier regarding pregnant teenagers' use of *tutelas* to avoid expulsion or to regain admission to school, the Constitutional Court has also used the *tutela* to protect the reproductive rights of women prisoners. In 1993, the Court granted an order against the enforcement of prison regulations requiring female prisoners to be fitted with an IUD or take contraceptives as a condition of conjugal visits when male prisoners were not subjected to any similar requirements.[66]

---

[63] See, e.g., Sentencia No. C-105/94; and Sentencia No. SU 253/98.

[64] Sentencia No. C-152/94.

[65] Salvamento de voto a la Sentencia No. C-152/94.

[66] Sentencia No. T-273/93. The court had earlier concluded that incarcerated persons' right to conjugal visits was a limited fundamental right, dependent upon the capacity of the facility to accommodate such visits. Sentencia No. T-222/93. The court also charged the state to equip all detention facilities to permit conjugal visits.

This case also illustrates the importance that the Constitutional Court has attached to international human rights conventions, as expressly mandated in Article 93.

Attorney Blanca Amelia Medina Torres, who was a pretrial detainee in The Good Shepard Women's Detention Center in Bogotá, filed a *tutela* challenging regulations and practices requiring that women inmates who desired conjugal visits take sex education courses and either show they were incapable of conceiving or be fitted with an IUD or take contraceptives. The warden of the prison defended the regulations, arguing that Medina Torres would try to get pregnant to escape punishment. The court said that this assumption violated Article 83 of the Colombian Constitution that requires public authorities to presume the good faith of individuals in *all* actions that come before them. According to the Court, the unequal treatment of women prisoners constituted sex discrimination in violation of Article 13, violated reproductive and family rights provisions of articles 42 ("[t]he couple has the right to decide freely and responsibly the number of their children") and 43 ("[d]uring pregnancy and after birth, women will enjoy special assistance and protection of the state") of the Constitution as well as similar provisions in international human rights documents incorporated in the Constitution (including the U.N. Convention on the Elimination of All Forms of Discrimination against Women).[67]

Abortion. Not surprisingly in this overwhelmingly Catholic country, another reproductive freedom issue – that of abortion – met with less success in the Constitutional Court. In 1994, a majority of the Constitutional Court rejected a direct constitutional challenge to the country's strict criminal abortion law as it then existed.[68] This public action of unconstitutionality against Article 343 of the Penal Code was filed by a man, Alexander Sochandamandou.

Over objections of three dissenting judges, the Court upheld the law as a valid protection of the right to life as guaranteed by Article 11 of the Constitution.[69] Judge Antonio Barrera Carbonell wrote the Court's opinion,

[67] The opinion cited the text of the Convention's preamble to the effect that "women's role in procreation must not be a reason for discrimination," and Article 16, which embraces the same right as Article 43 of the Colombian Constitution. It also found violations of Article 11 of the American Convention on Human Rights (the San José Pact) ("No person shall be the object of arbitrary or abusive interferences in their private lives, in that of their family, in their home and correspondence, nor to illegal attacks on their honor or reputation") and the similar provision in Article 17 of the International Pact on Human Rights.

[68] Sentencia No. C-133/94. Article 343 of the penal code in effect at the time provided: "A woman who causes her abortion or permits another to cause it, will incur imprisonment for from one (1) to three (3) years." It recognized no exceptions for therapeutic abortions.

[69] *Const. Pol. Col.*, *supra* note 2, art. 11: "The right to life is inviolable. There shall be no death penalty."

rejecting arguments that Article 343 violated the Constitution's recognition of a couple's right to decide their number of children,[70] or the constitutional guarantees of women's rights to equal protection,[71] to personal and family privacy,[72] and to the free development of their personality.[73] In closing, the majority did suggest a role for the legislature in resolving possible conflicting rights of women and the unborn.[74]

Judge Eduardo Cifuentes Muñoz wrote a dissenting opinion joined by Judges Carlos Gaviria Díaz and Alejandro Martínez Caballero, which referred to the U.S. Supreme Court's decision in *Roe v. Wade*,[75] and echoed its reasoning in some respects.[76] The dissent objected to recognizing the legal personhood of a fetus and placed little weight on the constitutional assembly's rejection of proposals to guarantee a right to abortion. For the dissenters, the Penal Code's criminalization of all abortion violated the procreative autonomy that was part of the Constitution's protection of the right of parents to decide upon the number of their children (Article 42) and of the right to free development of one's personality (Article 16).[77]

In 1997, the Colombian Constitutional Court again addressed the abortion issue. The case was an action of unconstitutionality filed by José Euripides Parra challenging the provisions of the Penal Code that provided criminal penalties for abortions in cases of pregnancies resulting from rape or involuntary insemination.[78] Article 345 of the Penal Code provided that "A woman pregnant as a result of violent or abusive carnal access or nonconsensual artificial insemination who causes her own abortion or permits another to cause it, will incur *arresto* of from four (4) months to one (1) year."[79] The Court rejected the challenger's demand that it invalidate the Code's recognition of "lesser" penalties in these cases and instead declare the even harsher penalties provided for other abortions in Article 343 to be uniformly applicable. The majority upheld the legislative judgment about the appropriate severity of the penalty for abortions in such "attenuating circumstances." But the five justices joining the main opinion once again expressed their views

---

[70] *Const. Pol. Col.*, ibid., art. 42.

[71] *Const. Pol. Col.*, ibid., art. 13.

[72] *Const. Pol. Col.*, ibid., art. 15.

[73] *Const. Pol. Col.*, ibid., art. 16.

[74] Sentencia No. C-133/94.

[75] 410 U.S. 113 (1973). *Planned Parenthood v. Casey*, 112 S. Ct. 2791 (1992), affirmed the "essential holding" of *Roe* but rejected its trimester framework in favor of an "undue burdens" analysis.

[76] Salvamento de Voto, in Sentencia C-133/94: "The protection of the unborn, according to the different periods of its development and its relative weight in comparison with the rights of the persons involved, in particular the pregnant woman – a solution that is graduated or by periods – allows avoiding an 'all or nothing' decision, that disregards fundamental rights."

[77] Salvamento de voto, in Sentencia C-133/94.

[78] Sentencia No. C-013/97.

[79] *Cód. Pen.*, art. 345.

about abortion as an attack on human life, which they saw as beginning with conception. Their opinion even included parts of papal encyclicals by Pope Paul VI and Pope John Paul II.[80]

Four justices wrote separate opinions expressing their differing views on this matter. Judge Jorge Arango Mejía objected to the use of the papal encyclicals and made it clear that he believed that Congress could decriminalize abortion without running afoul of the new Constitution. Three judges went further, writing a joint opinion dissenting from the majority's handling of the matter altogether. Judges Eduardo Cifuentes Muñoz, Carlos Gaviria Días, and Alejandro Martínez Caballero rejected arguments that this was a matter for determination by the legislative processes.[81]

These three judges argued that it violated the Constitution to impose criminal penalties on abortions by women who are pregnant because of rape or involuntary artificial insemination. They accused the judges in the majority of imposing their own moral and religious prejudices and labeled their rhetoric "sexist and patriarchal."[82]

The curtain had not gone down on the Court's abortion jurisprudence, however. In June 2001, the Court rejected an attack on the new Penal Code's treatment of the issue. On December 15, 1998, the Colombian Congress rejected a proposed Penal Code revision that would have depenalized abortion in certain instances, including cases of rape. Article 122 of the new Penal Code as finally adopted continues to consider all abortions illegal and punishable by one to three year prison terms. But Article 124 "Circumstances Attenuating Punishment" does provide for reducing the penalty for abortion by three-fourths when the pregnancy is the result of carnal access or nonconsensual, abusive, sexual acts, or of nonconsensual artificial insemination or fertilization. It also provides that, in these circumstances, when the abortion occurs in extraordinary abnormal conditions of motivation, the judicial officer can dispense with the punishment when it is not necessary in the specific case. The Court's 2001 opinion upholds the legislative grant of carefully limited power to the judge to reduce or dispense with punishment in exceptional circumstances.[83]

CONCLUSION

At the close of the first decade under the 1991 Colombian Constitution, the Constitutional Court had taken real strides toward a model of gender equality, which is emancipatory. Some of the key doctrinal developments have been in its horizontal application of fundamental rights even within the sphere of

---

[80] Sentencia No. C-013/97.
[81] Sentencia No. C-013/97, ibid. (separate opinion of Cifuentes, J).
[82] Sentencia No. C-013/97, ibid. (separate opinion of Cifuentes, J).
[83] Sentencia No. C-647/2001.

family relationships and its commitment to both formal and substantive concepts of equality. The Constitution's incorporation of international human rights conventions also has had a positive influence on the Court's gender jurisprudence. Whereas treatment of abortion by the majority of the members of the Court has slighted both women's autonomy rights and their equality rights, the Court has generally ruled in favor of gay and lesbian rights.

However, tensions are evident in the Court's early gender doctrine. The vast number of cases that the Court has decided, and the Constitutional Court's practice of sitting in panels of three judges when reviewing most *tutelas*, has produced seemingly inconsistent results that sometimes vary according to the composition of the panel. Some of the tension simply mirrors that in the new Charter – the product of a constitutional assembly that, although mostly male, was the most diverse group to sit around a table of power in the country's history. The drafters broke new ground and tended to err on the side of inclusion. Thus, the tensions between individualism and social solidarity are evident in the text of the Constitution itself.

How these tensions will be addressed by new members of the Constitutional Court as well as what will be the fate of the early gender jurisprudence surveyed in this chapter are difficult to foretell. But, according to a popular saying in Latin America, "We make the road by walking." The path that the Constitutional Court has begun walking has given many Colombians at least one source of badly needed hope for the future of their violence-torn country.

Suggested Readings

Conference of Supreme Courts of the Americas, "Legal System of Colombia" (1996) 40 *Saint Louis University Law Journal* 1353–6.

Consejo Superior de la Judicatura, "Corte Constitucional: Sujetos de Especial Protección en La Constitución Política" (1992).

Judicial Branch of the Colombian State, online: <http://www.ramajudicial.gov.co>.

Martha I. Morgan and Mónica Alzate Buitrago, "Constitution-Making in a Time of Cholera: Women and the 1991 Colombian Constitution" (1992) 4 *Yale Journal of Law and Feminism* 353–413.

Martha I. Morgan and Mónica María Alzate Buitrago, "Founding Mothers in Contemporary Latin American Constitutions: Colombian Women, Constitution Making, and the New Constitutional Court" 204–18 in Katherine Wing Adrien, ed., *Global Critical Race Feminism: An International Reader* (New York: New York University Press, 2000).

Martha I. Morgan, "Taking *Machismo* to Court: The Gender Jurisprudence of the Colombian Constitutional Court," (1999) 30 *University of Miami Inter-American Law Review* 253–342.

Luz Estella Nagle, "Evolution of the Colombian Judiciary and the Constitutional Court" (1995) 6 *Indiana International and Comparative Law Review* 59–90.

Luz Estella Nagle, "The Cinderella of Government: Judicial Reform in Latin America" (2000) 30 *California Western International Law Journal* 345–79.

Observatorio legal de la mujer: El legado de la Constitución (Bogotá: Centro de Investigaciones Sociojurídicas, Universidad de los Andes, Facultad de Derecho, 1998).

Jenny Pearce, *Colombia: Inside the Labyrinth* (New York: Monthly Review Press, 1990).

R. Rodríguez, *Nueva estructura del poder público en Colombia*, 5th ed. (Bogotá: Editorial Temis, Libardo, 1994).

4

Gender Equality and International Human Rights in Costa Rican Constitutional Jurisprudence

Alda Facio, Rodrigo Jiménez Sandova, and Martha I. Morgan

On the farm "La Lucha" (The Struggle), in the central mountain range of Costa Rica, on March 12, 1948, José Figueres Ferrer took up arms against the government of Teodoro Picado. The Civil War had begun. This struggle shortly brought about dramatic changes in the constitutional order. On May 8, the victorious José Figueres, President of the Governing Junta, declared the Constitution of 1871 to be without force or effect (except for its chapters on social, national, and individual guarantees) and called a Constituent Assembly. Less than a year later, a new Constitution was approved, which made fundamental changes in the structure of government and the relationships between its inhabitants – changes that have had profound significance in the evolution of the country's long-standing constitutional acknowledgment of the equality of all Costa Ricans. This chapter will examine the 1949 Constitution, as amended, with respect to gender equality and Costa Rica's emerging constitutional gender jurisprudence, with particular emphasis on its incorporation of international human rights gender equality norms.

After gaining its independence from Spain in 1821, Costa Rica had seven prior Constitutions – adopted in 1821, 1844, 1847, 1848, 1859, 1869, and 1871.[1] The country's post-independence legal system is a civil law system with its roots in French and Spanish codes. Whereas the Constitution separates the powers of government into the traditional three official branches – legislative, executive, and judicial, it also recognizes an independent Supreme Electoral Tribunal that has jurisdiction over disputes involving electoral matters and functions as a fourth power with the same rank as the other powers.

At the head of the judicial branch is a Supreme Court, composed of twenty-two *magistrados(as)*, or justices, organized into four chambers, or *salas*: Sala I – Civil Agricultural, and Administrative Matters (five members);

---

[1] See, generally, Mario Alberto Jiménez Quesada, *Desarrollo constitucional de Costa Rica*, 4th ed. (San José: Juricentro, 1992).

Sala II – Family, Labor, and certain Civil Matters (five members), Sala III – Criminal Matters (five members); and Sala IV – Constitutional Matters (seven members). As of July 2003, five women were members of the Supreme Court – two served in each of Salas I and II and one in Sala IV. For the first time, the presiding justice in Sala I was a woman but no women served in Sala III, the Penal Chamber (where the first woman to serve on the high court had served). The justices are elected for eight-year terms by a two-thirds vote of the Legislative Assembly and may be reelected indefinitely unless two thirds of the assembly vote against their reelection. The Supreme Electoral Tribunal is composed of three members and, in July 2003, two members were women.

The Constitutional Chamber of the Supreme Court was created in 1989, replacing the prior decentralized system of constitutional review with a concentrated one.[2] The forms of constitutional control the Constitutional Chamber exercises include mechanisms of anticipatory review of legislative actions and methods of subsequent judicial review. The two forms of anticipatory review are the judicial review of executive vetoes of legislation based on unconstitutionality (the executive veto can be exercised at the president's discretion for either constitutional or political reasons) and prior legislative consultation in the Constitutional Chamber. The Legislative Assembly is required to seek prior constitutional consultation on the validity of constitutional amendments and treaties and any ten members of the legislature also may do so with respect to other legislative measures. Other specified officials also can request opinions on the constitutionality of pending legislation. The Chamber's opinions in cases of legislative consultation are binding as to procedural issues but only advisory in other aspects.

The three major methods of subsequent constitutional control are: (1) habeas corpus – challenges to deprivations of liberty and freedom of movement as protected in the Constitution and incorporated international human rights law; (2) *amparo* – challenges to deprivations of all other constitutionally secured rights (including those recognized in international human rights treaties that Costa Rica has duly ratified, which are considered as independent rights within the body of constitutional law) by acts or omissions[3] of public (and in some instance private) actors; and (3) actions of unconstitutionality – challenges against norms – laws, regulations, decrees, treaties – or omissions in such norms as inconsistent with the Constitution or the international human rights it incorporates and proclaims as superior

---

[2] For a historical review of the Costa Rican system of judicial review, see Robert S. Barker "Judicial Review in Costa Rica: Evolution and Recent Developments" (2000) VII *Southwestern Journal of Law and Trade in the Americas* 267–90.

[3] To bring an *amparo* action for an omission, one must establish a state duty to act and prove that the government has failed to take necessary actions, such as adopting the required regulations to implement a constitutional principle.

to other laws.[4] The Constitutional Chamber has the authority to reject actions that are not within its jurisdiction or that address issues very similar to those decided in previous cases. It also can convert a case filed as any one of these three forms of action to one of the other forms where appropriate. Decisions of the Constitutional Chamber in these actions are binding on all lower courts and may be reversed only by its own subsequent opinions or by constitutional amendment.

Any person who is directly affected by a challenged act, norm, or omission may file one of the above actions. The Defender of the People[5] is also authorized to file actions of unconstitutionality and any person who has knowledge of a deprivation of liberty or liberty of movement may file a habeas corpus action. In addition, those representing diffuse interests (e.g., those shared equally or identically by all members of a group such as women) or collective interests (e.g., such as collectives have when defending the rights of members or affected populations) are authorized to institute *amparo* actions and actions of unconstitutionality. This authorization of suits by those representing diffuse or collective interests has allowed women's organizations to challenge actions or laws that violate the constitutional rights of women without requiring proof of a specific injury to an identified woman.

With this brief overview of the Costa Rican legal system, we turn to a description of some of the principal features of the 1949 Constitution, as amended, with respect to gender. This is followed by an examination of several interrelated aspects of the gender jurisprudence that is developing under the Constitution and recent legislation implementing its equality guarantees and those of international conventions addressing gender discrimination it incorporates.

PRINCIPAL GENDER-RELATED FEATURES OF THE COSTA RICAN CONSTITUTIONAL ORDER

Since independence, Costa Rican Constitutions have recognized certain civil and political rights, but in early charters these were limited and discriminated based on gender, economic resources, and education. The movement toward universal recognition of these rights was gradual and it was not until the 1949 Constitution that franchise rights were extended to women, who exercised the right to vote for the first time in 1950. The 1949 Constitution also embraced economic, social, and cultural rights that had been introduced

---

[4] The Constitutional Chamber also has the authority to issue binding opinions, at the request of any judge, as to the constitutionality of any law, action, or inaction raised in a case pending before the judge.

[5] The Defender of the People, or Office of the Ombudsperson, is also one of the officials who may seek judicial opinions on whether pending legislation violates rights guaranteed by the Constitution or by human rights treaties or conventions effective in Costa Rica.

in the 1940s, and in the 1970s and 1980s, certain public rights, especially with respect to the environment, attained constitutional rank.

Three provisions of the Constitution have particular relevance to the gender issues we will discuss. First, the principal equality provision of the Costa Rican Constitution is Article 33, which until 1999 provided that "[e]very man is equal before the law and there shall not be any discrimination contrary to human dignity." Despite its reference to "every man," Article 33 was interpreted as guaranteeing gender equality,[6] and a 1999 amendment replaced the word "man" ("*hombre*") with "person" ("*persona*.").[7] Second, and of increasing importance in the struggle for constitutional protection of women's rights, is Article 7, providing that "[p]ublic treaties, international conventions and agreements, duly approved by the Legislative Assembly, shall have, from their promulgation or from the date that they designate, authority superior to the laws."[8] As we will describe, this article has been interpreted as incorporating international human rights law ratified by Costa Rica – including the Convention on the Elimination of All Forms of Discrimination against Women (CEDAW) as well as Inter-American conventions addressing gender equality and gender violence[9] – within the Constitution and as making such norms superior even to other provisions of the Constitution itself. Third, Article 95 includes among its list of principles that must be followed in the law governing the exercise of the right to vote: "Guarantees for the designation of authorities and candidates of political parties, according to democratic principles and without discrimination based on gender."[10]

The Constitution also includes several other gender-related provisions. Article 52 provides that marriage is based on the equality of rights between the partners, Article 53 recognizes the equality of rights between children that are born within a marriage and those born outside marriage, and Article 55 provides for special protection for mothers and children. Similarly,

---

[6] Indeed, in 1992, the Constitutional Chamber of the Supreme Court ruled that whenever legislation uses the terms "man" or "woman," the terms must be interpreted as synonymous with "person." Voto No. 3435-92. For further discussion and critique of this ruling, see the section on "Evolving Concepts of Gender Equality," infra.

[7] Law No. 7880 (27 May 1999), reforming both Articles 20 ("Every person is free...") and 33 in this respect. At the same time, Article 14(5) was reformed to extend eligibility criteria for naturalization to foreign persons of both sexes who marry Costa Ricans, as will be discussed further in the section on "Women's Participation in Decision-Making," infra.

[8] *Constitución Política de 7 de Noviembre de 1949 y sus Reformas*, art. 7 (hereinafter "*Const. Pol.*"), as reformed by Law No. 4123 (31 May 1968). Article 48 of the Costa Rican Constitution provides that all persons have right to file an *amparo* action in the Constitutional Chamber of the Supreme Court to maintain or reestablish the enjoyment of rights granted in the constitution, as well as those fundamental rights established in international human rights instruments applicable in the country.

[9] *Inter-American Convention to Prevent, Punish, or Eradicate Violence against Women*, Belen Do Para.

[10] *Const. Pol.*, *supra* note 8, art 95(8), as reformed by Law No. 7675 (2 July 1997).

Article 71 calls for special protection of women workers and Article 73 includes maternity among risks that must be covered by the social security system.

Based largely on the key constitutional provisions referenced above, a series of implementing laws have been enacted in recent years to promote the "real" or effective equality of women, as well as other traditionally marginalized groups such as persons with disabilities, indigenous peoples, and the elderly. With respect to gender equality, two of the most significant of these laws are the 1990 *Law for the Social Promotion of Women*,[11] which incorporates a broad range of statutory reforms, and subsequent changes to the *Electoral Code* in 1996, which require political parties to assure that 40 percent of their candidates for all levels of popular elections are women and that women hold 40 percent of other party positions.[12]

There are other aspects of Costa Rica's 1949 constitutional reform that marked important advances in the struggle for gender equality that are not featured in the discussion of gender jurisprudence that follows. Primary among these was the complete abolition of the country's armed forces, which has had many general positive influences such as promoting political stability, strengthening democracy, and increasing funds available for health, education, and development. From a gender perspective doing away with the military forces has additional significance. The military has been one of the pillars of patriarchal power. Not only has it been in the hands of men and used to repress and violate human rights (including those of women who have been victims of rape, murder, and other forms of wartime torture and violence), its very purpose of engaging in armed conflict contributes to a broader culture of violence against women. Costa Rica's abolition of its army, by express provision in its 1949 Constitution, marked an important step toward a culture of peace and respect for human rights, including women's rights.[13]

EVOLVING CONCEPTS OF GENDER EQUALITY

The General Importance of International Human Rights Documents

Apart from the previously mentioned creation, in 1989, of a Constitutional Chamber of the Supreme Court, which replaced the previous decentralized

---

[11] Law No. 7142 (2 March 1990).
[12] *Código Electoral*, art. 58(n), 60.
[13] Another important change was the nationalization of bank accounts and the creation of a Development Bank whose credit policies are guided by social criteria, thus promoting income redistribution and greater equality in access to financial resources. Reference to this change is not meant to suggest that it has resulted in women having real equality in access to financing but it does constitute a step toward financial democratization that has benefited Costa Rican women.

system of constitutional control with a single body responsible for the development of binding constitutional jurisprudence, perhaps the most significant advance with respect to gender jurisprudence has been the primacy given by that Chamber (and the Supreme Electoral Tribunal, within its respective electoral jurisdiction) to international human rights law. The constitutional judge has been transformed into one who also applies international human rights norms, opening new possibilities for the advancement of the rights of women (and other historically marginalized groups) through constitutional litigation as well as through legislative changes the resulting jurisprudence may help stimulate. The significance of this incorporation becomes clear when one considers that no country's constitution, standing alone, provides the breadth and specificity of gender provisions that CEDAW does or addresses violence against women as comprehensively as does the Belen Do Para Inter-American Convention to Prevent, Punish, and Eradicate Violence against Women. Of course, the practical effectiveness of these norms depends on their interpretation and application, which, as we will see, has been inconsistent thus far.

Understanding how this incorporation and prioritization of international human rights law works requires a closer look at how Article 7 of the Costa Rican Constitution has been interpreted. The Constitutional Chamber of the Supreme Court has interpreted Article 7 as incorporating and according supra-constitutional status to international human rights conventions ratified by Costa Rica and as making them self-executing, or of immediate application.[14] In a 1993 opinion, the Constitutional Chamber declared: "As the jurisprudence of this chamber has recognized, human rights instruments applicable in Costa Rica have not only a value similar to the Constitution, but to the extent that they grant greater rights or guarantees to the people, they prevail over the Constitution."[15]

This interpretation of Article 7 has opened the door to the recognition of broad concepts of gender equality under several important international documents that Costa Rica has ratified, including: the Inter-American Conventions on Civil Rights for Women and on the Political Rights of Women;[16] the Convention on the Political Rights of Women;[17] CEDAW;[18] and the Belen Do Para Inter-American Convention to Prevent, Punish, and Eradicate Violence against Women.[19]

---

[14] The Constitutional Chamber also accords interpretations of the relevant regional human rights documents by the Inter-American Court of Human Rights, whether in contested cases or consultative opinions, the same value as the norm interpreted. Voto No. 2313-95.

[15] Voto No. 5759-93.

[16] Ratified by Law No. 1273 of March 13, 1951.

[17] Ratified by Law No. 3877 of June 3, 1967.

[18] Ratified by Law No. 6969 of October 2, 1984.

[19] Ratified by Law No. 7499 of May 2, 1995.

Not only has Article 7 and its incorporation and elevation of these international gender norms paved the way for direct judicial application of those norms, it also has served as a stimulus to a wide range of complementary gender legislation designed to implement the obligations these human rights documents impose on ratifying states. In recent years, the Legislative Assembly has promulgated the *Law for the Social Promotion of Women*, the *Sexual Harassment Law*, the *Law against Intrafamilial Violence*, and the *Maternal Nursing Law*, as well as reforms to the penal, labor, and family codes.[20]

The potential impact of the Constitutional Chamber's use of human rights law as incorporated by Article 7 is enormous, particularly when coupled with the previously described rules authorizing constitutional challenges to actions and omissions of public and, in some instances, private actors. For example, while CEDAW does not expressly define equality, Article 1's broad definition of "discrimination against women" embraces practices that have either discriminatory *purposes or effects* by persons acting in both what have traditionally been considered *public and private* spheres. As the cases we will examine demonstrate, the full potential of the constitutionalization of these international documents has yet to be realized. Cases where the justices have misunderstood or failed to fully implement the progressive gender perspectives reflected in these documents exist along side cases realizing their transformative potential.[21] On the whole, however, the trend in recent decisions is positive.

Citizenship

In 1992, the Constitutional Chamber was presented with an *amparo* challenging an application of Article 14(5) of the Constitution, which provided that foreign women who have been married to a Costa Rican for two years and have resided in the country during this period may obtain Costa Rican citizenship by naturalization. The justices declared that this provision discriminated against the foreign man who had married a Costa Rican woman and was contrary to fundamental equality principles of constitutional and international human rights law. Although the opinion expressly relied upon international instruments including Articles 2 and 7 of the Universal Declaration of Rights, Article II of the International Covenant on Civil and Political Rights, and Articles 1 and 24 of the Inter-American Convention on

---

[20] See, for example, *Ley de Promoción Social de la Mujer*, Law No. 7142 (March 2, 1990); *Ley Contra el Hostigamiento Sexual en el Empeo y la Docencia*, Law No. 7476 (February 3, 1995) ; *Ley Contra la Violencia Doméstica*, Law No. 7586 (March 25,1996); *Ley de Paternidad Responsable*, Law No. 8101 (March 27, 2001).

[21] Although some have suggested that these doctrinal inconsistencies may reflect the relative degree to which particular rights are clearly delineated in international law or that they may reflect class biases, such simple explanations may not fully capture the complexity of the actual instances of inconsistency.

Human Rights, it completely ignored CEDAW. The justices apparently did not see Article 14(5) as discriminating against women. Never mentioning that the naturalization rule discriminated against Costa Rican women by not permitting them to grant eligibility for citizenship to their spouses, the opinion overlooked the obvious origin of the challenged rule in the patriarchal belief that women must follow their husbands wherever they chose to reside.

This is also the opinion noted earlier in which the Constitutional Chamber broadly declared that wherever legislation uses the terms "man" or "woman," the terms must be interpreted as synonymous with "person." The opinion concluded that this would eliminate every possible "legal" discrimination based on sex. However well-intended, this impulsive adoption of a formalist stance of gender neutrality fails to accommodate a vision of humanity that accepts difference and aims to ensure enjoyment of human rights by women and men. Rather, it reflects a formalist vision of equality that accepts the male as the norm and seeks merely to eliminate those barriers that prevent women from being "equal" to men. It fails to recognize that there may be instances where corrective measures expressly applicable to women may be legitimate and even mandated. Although this early opinion reflects a concept of formal equality based on a male paradigm and fails to contemplate the absurd consequences that could flow from eliminating all references to women or men in legal texts, at least some of the more recent opinions of the Constitutional Chamber have embraced the principle that in reality women and men are "equally different" in certain respects.[22]

In 1999, Article 14(5) was amended to extend eligibility for naturalization to persons of both sexes who marry Costa Ricans. It now provides: "Foreign persons who upon marrying a Costa Rican lose their nationality or who after having been married to a Costa Rican for two years and having resided in the country during this same period, manifest their desire to acquire Costa Rican citizenship."[23]

Women's Participation in Decision-Making

Costa Rica's 1949 Constitution, as amended, affords a three-part textual framework for analyzing measures to increase women's participation in positions of public decision-making. In addition to Article 33's general equality provision and Article 7's incorporation of protections afforded in regional

---

[22] Voto No. 716-98 ("Thus some writers speak of how men as well as women can be 'equally different,' and that all must be considered equally valuable, being able to develop themselves equally fully, taking account of their similarities and differences").

[23] Law No. 7879 (May 27, 1999). Although the effect of this change is to make the eligibility criteria gender-neutral, article 14(4) was not deleted. It still reads: "The foreign woman who upon contracting marriage with a Costa Rican loses her citizenship."

and international human rights documents, Article 95 includes the following language:

The law will regulate the exercise of suffrage according to the following principles: (8) Guarantees for the designation of authorities and candidates of the political parties, according to democratic principles and without discrimination based on gender.

Neither Article 33's general equality principle nor Article 95's suffrage principles expressly embrace substantive equality. But these provisions, along with Article 7's incorporation of international human rights law, have laid the groundwork for acceptance of compensatory measures in legislative and judicial realms.

Perhaps the area where Costa Rica's constitutionalization of international human rights law has had its most positive effects on women's rights is with regard to corrective measures – often also referred to as affirmative action or positive discrimination.[24] In particular, CEDAW's recognition of the concept of substantive equality in Articles 4 and 7 provided support for corrective measures in both the 1990 *Law for the Social Promotion of Women* and in the *Electoral Code*. The Constitutional Chamber of the Costa Rican Supreme Court, as well as the Supreme Electoral Tribunal, have since issued opinions supportive of such measures.

In 1998, the Constitutional Chamber of the Supreme Court ruled in favor of Legislative Assembly Deputy Marlene Gómez Calderón in an *amparo* against the President of the Republic and the President of the Legislative Assembly challenging their respective unconstitutional omissions[25] in proposing and accepting candidates for political appointment to the Board of Directors of the Public Services Regulatory Authority that did not include any women candidates.[26] In this opinion by Magistrada Ana Virginia Calzada Miranda, the Chamber accepted Deputy Gómez Calderón's assertion of

---

[24] The terms positive discrimination and affirmative action can create confusion. Speaking of affirmative action makes it seem as if such measures are being granted as a benefit when in reality these are compensatory measures with respect to the real inequality in which groups discriminated against are found. Positive discrimination is an even more incorrect term given that this makes it appear that we are accepting discrimination against one group in order to favor another. Corrective measures do not discriminate against any group; their purpose is to eliminate privileges that some groups are able to enjoy because of their sex, color, class, and so on.

[25] Costa Rica's Constitutional Jurisdiction Law expressly states that the Constitutional Chamber has jurisdiction over *amparos* against acts or *omissions*. Art. 29, Ley de la jurisdicin Constitucional, No. 7135 (October 11, 1989). In this case, the Court relied upon both national and international law as imposing express affirmative obligations with respect to women's participation.

[26] Voto No. 716-98. However, the opinion rejected the claims against the legislative branch, characterizing their action as "limited to the simple ratification of the nominations made by the [executive branch], without having any direct interference in the nominations made and, thus, in the discrimination claimed."

"diffuse interest" claims on behalf of all Costa Rican women, which were based on Article 33's principle of equality, on Articles 1, 2, 3, 6, and 7 of CEDAW, and on the 1990 *Law for the Promotion of the Social Equality of Women.* The decision ruled against the executive branch and required the state to pay costs but limited its effects to allow the members of the board to complete the terms for which they had been elected and begun to serve.

Justice Calzada Miranda explained the Chamber's reasoning, quoting Article 7 of CEDAW and Article 4 of the 1990 law, both requiring state authorities to take appropriate measures to eliminate discrimination and promote women's participation in public positions. The opinion character-ized the selection of only men for these positions as a "situation involving discrimination against women by an act of omission – the failure to propose or designate women to the position – contrary to the democratic principle of equality established in the Constitution."

The Constitutional Chamber emphasized that recognizing differences in women's appreciation of the reality of society was fundamental in part be-cause it "strengthens democracy," and deemed the failure to nominate and name women to the Board of Directors to be "contrary to the democratic principle of equality established in Article 33 of the Constitution."

Despite the strong language of this opinion, a case from the following year revealed jurisprudential discrepancies in the Constitutional Chamber's application of norms governing corrective measures. The opinion in the sec-ond case rejected *amparo* claims under Article 33 and CEDAW brought by women members of the Costa Rican Educational Workers Union when no woman was elected to the board of directors or executive committee of the Workers Assembly of the Popular Development Bank, a mixed public and private body.[27] Despite an earlier decision of the National Workers Assem-bly that 40 percent of delegates to all assemblies should be women, those who filed the *amparo* had been among only fifty women delegates to the 290 member Assembly. The Assembly decided to fill the positions by voting for one of two lists of candidates. Only the losing list contained any fe-male candidates (two) and thus no women were elected. The Constitutional Chamber rejected the *amparo*, declaring: "The challengers cannot pretend that this Chamber should annul the election of the members of the National Board of Directors and National Executive Committee, if this resulted from a previously established procedure and where all the delegates, be they men or women, had the same possibility to form lists and thus become elected." Prior decisions of the Costa Rican Supreme Court are supposed to have *erga omnes* effect unless changed by the Court itself. Factual differences exist be-tween these two cases but, inexplicably, this later decision seemed to ignore CEDAW's concepts of substantial equality and resort to an earlier, suppos-edly superceded, concept of formal equality. Although three of the justices

---

[27] Voto No. 2166-99.

(including two women justices) dissented, as the majority of the justices saw it women delegates had the same opportunity to be elected as men, thus there was no unconstitutional discrimination.

In its most recent decision in this line of cases, on May 30, 2003, the Constitutional Chamber issued a long-awaited but remarkable opinion in a suit brought by five members of the Legislative Assembly or congress (four women and one man) against the president of the Assembly. On May 31, 2002, these legislators had filed an action challenging the constitutionality of their president's omission or failure to name female and male legislators to 2002–2003 permanent committees on housing, agricultural, and social affairs in proportion to their membership in the Assembly as a whole. A record-breaking twenty of the fifty-seven members of the 2002 assembly (or 35 percent) were women yet the membership of these committees was as follows: Housing Affairs – eight men (73 percent) and three women (27 percent); Agricultural Affairs – eight men (89 percent) and one woman (11 percent); and Social Affairs – three men (35 percent) and six women (65 percent).

The challengers argued that failure to name proportional numbers of women and men to each of these committees meant that their respective perspectives on the reality of Costa Rican society were missing from decision-making. They recounted how women traditionally had been excluded from participation in the formation of economic and agricultural development policies vital to the reduction of poverty. Women, they stressed, see reality from inside the home where the concrete results of these policies are felt and this perspective could contribute to such policy making. Similarly, they argued that because the majority of the social affairs committee had been women, the masculine perspective and coresponsibility were missing from its policy making.

The Constitutional Chamber accepted the challenge, unanimously ruling that the president's omissions were inconsistent with Article 33 of the Constitution, as well as CEDAW and the Inter-American Convention on Human Rights. The opinion also quoted Article 7 of CEDAW and Articles 1 and 5 of the *Law For the Social Promotion of Women* and made reference to the gender-related provisions of the *Electoral Code*. The justices concluded that the president's failure to name women and men in proportionality, or to provide sufficient evidence that he had deliberately and adequately considered or paid attention to the demands for women's participation legally required by the governing legal norms, limited the challengers' advancement to proportional membership in the committees, and in a greater sense their participation in the formation of laws of national interest.

Electoral Quotas for Women Candidates

In Costa Rica, the jurisprudence relating to electoral quotas for women has come from the Supreme Electoral Tribunal rather than the Constitutional

Chamber of the Supreme Court.[28] The Supreme Electoral Tribunal has played an important role in advancing gender equality through its recent interpretation, development, and application of the electoral law provisions requiring corrective measures within the electoral sphere.

In two recent resolutions, this tribunal has clarified and strengthened the constitutional and statutory bases for Costa Rica's quotas for women's participation in political parties and as candidates in popular elections. The first opinion was issued in 1999 and resulted from a request from the President of the National Institute on the Condition of Women that the Tribunal revise, clarify, and extend its 1997 interpretation of the Costa Rican *Electoral Code's* 40 percent quota for women's participation on party lists of electoral candidates at all levels of popular elections.[29] The opinion was written by Magistrada Anabelle León Feoli, who was then on the Tribunal and since has been elected to the Supreme Court. Her opinion began by concluding that the Institute did not have legal standing to seek the opinion requested but nevertheless acknowledging the tribunal's authority to recognize, on its own, the need for further interpretation of the electoral order when its own prior dispositions are not clear or sufficient or when a literal reading of them leads to distortion of underlying principles or contradictions with constitutional mandates.

The opinion then quoted relevant provisions from the Costa Rican Constitution (including Article 33) and numerous international treaties (including CEDAW) as well as Costa Rican legislation implementing these fundamental norms (including the *Law for the Promotion of the Social Equality of Women* and the *Electoral Code*) that regulate in a specific manner the political participation of women. In particular, Articles 58(n) and 60 of the *Electoral Code* require that political parties include in their statutes mechanisms for assuring women's participation at a minimum quota of 40 percent in party structures, in popular elections, and in party assemblies at the district, county, and provincial levels. Following discussion of relevant legal norms, the opinion discussed prior cases of the Constitutional Chamber of the Supreme Court addressing women's participation in political spheres and concluding that failure to place women in public positions is contrary to constitutional principles of equality.

The Tribunal deemed it necessary to revise its own prior interpretation that allowed the names of women candidates to be listed in any order and instead established a requirement that the stipulated 40 percent participation of women candidates be listed in electable positions. The Tribunal reiterated

---

[28] Some of the inconsistencies in Costa Rican gender jurisprudence may be partly attributable to the fact that these two different bodies, each with their own internal biases or differences of opinion at times, have been involved in the interpretive processes.

[29] Resolution No. 1863-99. Costa Rica is a unitary state but is divided into electoral districts, counties, and provinces.

this position in a subsequent resolution in response to a request for further clarification.[30] This second opinion stressed that the 40 percent quota was a minimum that could be exceeded. It also provided guidance on compliance with the requirement that women candidates be in electable positions. Two of the suggested mechanisms were to alternate names of women and men on the lists or to use the history of previous elections to determine the number of positions with real possibilities of being elected.

Substantive Equality and Corrective Measures

As we will discuss more fully in the section on labor law, several of the Constitutional Chamber's gender decisions address issues in the employment realm. Here we begin by highlighting one of these opinions, noteworthy for its broad acceptance of CEDAW principles of substantive equality. In this 1999 opinion, the Chamber rejected a challenge brought by male employees of the National Bank of Costa Rica against the bank's regulations that established different retirement ages of fifty-five for women and fifty-seven for men.[31] The regulation also required thirty years of service for both men and women but allowed each year in excess of thirty to lower the otherwise applicable minimum age by one year. After setting out the text of CEDAW Articles 1, 2, 3, 4, 5, and 11.1 and of Article 1(a) of Convention No. 111 of the International Labor Organization, the Chamber upheld the validity of the challenged norm. The Chamber's discussion of the validity of the challenged norm stressed that its purpose was not to restrict the rights of men but to grant special or compensatory protection to women workers for their other often unrecognized and unrewarded parallel social roles.

Costa Rican jurisprudence has taken solid, if uneven, steps toward the reconceptualization of gender equality based on CEDAW's embrace of the principle of substantive equality. But looking at two earlier cases where the judges, to different degrees, missed the mark in their understanding of gender equality will help illustrate further the problems that have confronted Costa Rican women's human rights activists seeking to establish a consistent and coherent body of progressive gender jurisprudence.

A striking illustration of the lack of clarity and consistency in the Constitutional Chamber's gender jurisprudence is a 1993 *amparo* opinion which rejected a woman athlete's challenge to local authorities' practice of awarding

---

[30] Resolution 2837.

[31] Voto No. 6472-99. The opinion also made reference to economic finance studies showing that the regulation was not contrary to the principles of justice underlying social security.

Although concerns do exist about potential harmful effects of laws providing sex-based differences in retirement ages, including cutting short career lines and leaving women dependent on sometimes inadequate pensions for longer, because they tend to live longer on average, courts in some of the countries examined in other chapters of this book have reached similar results in cases challenging differential retirement ages.

separate and unequal monetary prizes in a municipal race.[32] The general first place prize (that had always been captured by male runners) was three times the amount of the first place award that was designated for "women" runners. The opinion stated:

There is, of course, a special prize for women with less value than that reserved for the "major" category. But this alone does not constitute discriminatory treatment because it only recognizes that if a woman does not obtain first place in this major category, she is guaranteed a special prize for having achieved the goal in the special category. On the other hand, though the possibility that the major category could be won by a woman remains open, the truth is that this precaution recognizes that the man has greater resistance for this type of competition and thus while there is not a prize dedicated exclusively to him, ordinarily he will win it.

Here the Chamber misunderstands the principle that all are equally different and for that reason none should have greater rights than others. It lends its approval to an absolutely discriminatory disposition – lesser prizes for women – viewing it as a "special" measure to aid women who cannot be expected to compete with men in these type of contests.

The following year, the Chamber again grappled with the concept of corrective measures. This time it struck down a measure that it acknowledged might have been intended as a corrective gender measure.[33] The case was an action of unconstitutionality filed by two men against Article 7 of the 1990 *Law for the Promotion of the Social Equality of Women*, which provided in relevant part, "[a]ll real property granted through social development programs must be registered in the name of both spouses in case of matrimony, in the name of the woman in case of a de facto union...." With respect to the men's claims of sex discrimination, the opinion acknowledged that this provision may have been intended to protect women in de facto unions who had traditionally been left unprotected in many situations and that such compensatory measures were sanctioned in international human rights law, if temporary. The opinion nonetheless viewed Article 7 as discriminating in favor of women in de facto unions as against women in formal marriages and thus contrary to the recognition of fundamental family rights in Articles 51 and 52 of the Constitution and in international human rights instruments. The Chamber's decision was authored by Magistrada Ana Virginia Calzada Miranda. It judicially excised the words "in the name of the woman" from Article 7, leaving it to require the property be registered in the names of both spouses in both formal marriages and de facto unions. For women in de facto unions, the Chamber's preservation of this excised version of Article 7 represented an advance over their previous legal situation, but the Chamber's failure to give closer attention

---

[32] Voto No. 4410-93.
[33] Voto No. 0346-94.

to whether this legislative attempt to provide special protection for these women should have been upheld as a corrective measure stands in contrast to its more favorable treatment of corrective measures in some of the more recent cases.

Other Applications of Gender Equality Principles in Costa Rican Labor Law

Costa Rican labor law jurisprudence increasingly bears the imprimatur of gender equality principles grounded in Article 33, in international human rights documents (via Article 7 of the Constitution), and in legislation designed to implement these fundamental guarantees. In particular, Article 11 of CEDAW and Articles 1 and 5 of Convention 111 of the International Labor Organization, which reaffirm principles of nondiscrimination in the labor sphere, reinforce Article 33 and complementary equality provisions in the Constitution's social guarantees with respect to labor rights (contained in Title IV).

The Chamber has been receptive to claims of gender discrimination when presented with challenges to practices such as access to training, cautioning that such discrimination is unconstitutional regardless of whether the discrimination was purposeful or not deliberate. In 1996, the Chamber considered an *amparo* initiated by two women police officers against the National Police School for excluding them from a training course and thus impeding their chances of advancement.[34] The director of the school contended that women were excluded because only two women had applied and a minimum of ten women was required to avoid problems with lodging. Despite an order from the Minister of Public Security that they be admitted, the director of the school gave orders that they be turned away when they appeared for the course.

The Chamber had little trouble accepting the women's claim that this discrimination violated the general equality clause of Article 33, despite the authorities' attempt to explain it as based on lack of material resources rather than on gender.

The Chamber also has accepted claims of gender discrimination in several cases presenting challenges to provisions governing employment-related benefits. For example, in 2000, the Chamber ruled that an eligibility provision of the social security system that treated women workers who requested maternity benefits differently from workers requesting benefits for other temporary health conditions was unconstitutional.[35] Workers who had not been employed for the period required to receive full health benefits were entitled to partial benefits for other temporary health conditions but women

[34] Voto No. 4666-96.
[35] Voto No. 2570-00.

workers were not entitled to any pregnancy benefits unless they had worked the minimum period required to receive full benefits.

Earlier the Chamber had considered an action of unconstitutionality against three aspects of Article 49 of the Costa Rican Bureau of Social Security's *Regulations on Invalids, Aged, and Death*, which governed pensions for surviving companions of workers in *unions de hecho*, or de facto marriages.[36] The Chamber's 1991 opinion declared that all three of the challenged discriminatory provisions lacked any rational basis and thus were unconstitutional under Article 33. The three provisions were: (1) a provision requiring a showing of economic dependency for surviving wives in de facto unions while no such showing was required of other widows; (2) a provision requiring that de facto unions have lasted five years if there are no offspring of the union; and (3) a provision that extended pension eligibility to women companions surviving the death of a worker in de facto union but not to male companions who survived the death of a female worker.

With respect to this final provision, however, the opinion seems to approach the problem as one of discrimination against the surviving male companion without recognizing that this type of provision also discriminates against women workers by not allowing them to earn and provide the same benefits for their surviving companions that male workers are able to provide. It is quite possible that the reason for this provision was not a desire to discriminate against men but, rather, the view that the woman worker does not contribute to the social security system to the same extent that men do given the discriminatory wages they receive and thus they should not be given equal pension rights to those of male workers.

The Constitutional Chamber addressed a similar issue in the field of social security in a 1994 opinion by Justice Ana Virginia Calzada Miranda that offered a clearer gender analysis of the problem. The case was an action of unconstitutionality against Article 57 of the Costa Rican Social Security *Bureau Regulations on Sickness and Maternity*.[37] Although filed by a man, the primary allegation of unconstitutionality was that "this norm is evidently discriminatory against the woman," because if the insured man wants to insure his wife all he has to do is prove the existence of the marriage whereas if the insured woman wants to insure her husband, she must comply with a series of additional requirements (e.g., proof that her spouse is sick, unable to work, a student, unemployed and economically dependent on her). He also alleged that the rule impeded the access of men, as spouses, to social security rights as an indirect beneficiary and as a member of the nuclear family.

[36] Voto No. 1569-91. According to a 1999 poll of households, forty percent of Costa Rican couples live in *uniones de hecho* rather than formal marriages.
[37] Voto No. 0629-94.

Both the Social Security Bureau and the Attorney General admitted that the rules were unconstitutional. The Bureau noted that prior reforms had liberalized the eligibility rules for husbands, and asserted that within the limits posed by the country's economic development, it was pushing for a reform that would achieve total equality. Justice Calzada's opinion traced the history of the regulation from its original 1942 version, which did not provide any possibility that an insured woman's spouse could be insured, through its amendments in 1967, 1975, and 1989, which gradually extended limited eligibility. Indeed, by the time the Chamber's opinion was released, it noted that a 1992 amendment had equalized the treatment of spouses, independent of sex. The opinion's findings of unconstitutionality of the prior versions of the rule relied on Article 33's general equality clause and upon the special protection for the family in Articles 51 and 52 of the Costa Rican Constitution and international instruments, as well as upon the equality provision of Article II of the Inter-American Declaration of Human Rights.

Examination of another 1994 opinion from the labor sphere provides a vivid illustration of the inadequacy of a vision of gender equality that is limited to concepts of formal equality and direct discrimination and of the negative results of the sporadic nature of the Chamber's application of CEDAW's broader visions of equality. In 1994, the Chamber rejected an action of unconstitutionality filed against Article 104 of the Labor Code, which establishes a twelve-hour working day with a half day of rest weekly for domestic workers.[38] The constitutional challenges were based on Article 33's equality clause; Articles 58 and 59 of the Constitution, which establish a work schedule of eight hours daily, forty-eight hours weekly, and require one day of rest after six consecutive days of work; and Convention 111 of the International Labor Organization.

The Chamber's majority opinion rejected all the challenges, reasoning that: "The norm questioned does not introduce an arbitrary distinction or an inequality contrary to human dignity, since as has been said, domestic service is an exceptional situation that as such cannot be equalized to other cases such as agriculture, industry, or other services...."

The majority of the justices failed to consider the horizontal discrimination that women face in the workplace.[39] But not all the justices

---

[38] Voto No. 3150-94.
[39] Gender discrimination and segregation in the workplace is manifested in two ways, which have a direct impact on women's salaries and thus on the amount of power they enjoy:

  1. Horizontal discrimination – The seclusion of women in the private sphere based on the construction of social roles and stereotypes that structure the gender division of work. (In this manner jobs are assigned based on the sex that has traditionally performed such roles; for example, teaching, nursing, domestic service to women; mechanics, medicine, engineering to men.)
  2. Vertical Discrimination – The placement of women in positions of subordination and submission with respect to men and disvaluing the responsibilities they are assigned.

demonstrated such blindness to the reality of the gendered workplace. A dissenting opinion argued strenuously that the Labor Code's treatment of domestic workers was unconstitutional under Articles 33, 58, and 59, as well as contrary to CEDAW because it discriminated against them both as workers and based on gender. A very high percentage of domestic workers are women and the legislation appeared to be based upon cultural perceptions of domestic work whether paid or not, as "women's work" and thus devalued.

The dissenting opinion distinguished the position of domestic workers from that of workers in other positions considered "exceptional" and thus not subject to the general labor schedule which, unlike domestic work, required overtime pay for work in excess of eight hours per day or 48 hours per week. The other exceptions involved persons in high positions who receive other benefits to compensate for their different work schedules and persons whose work is of such a nature they do not need the protection of the general work schedule. And in any event these other persons were limited to a twelve-hour maximum workday with a minimum rest period of one hour and a half, whereas the regular work schedule for domestic workers is a twelve-hour day with only an hour rest period. This difference in treatment did not correspond to any of the presuppositions underlying the Labor Code's exceptions. Rather than discrediting their work, lengthening their work day, and shortening their rest periods, legislators should support and protect domestic workers against discrimination, particularly given the nature of their work, their low pay, and the social tendency to devalue their work.

Equality Principles in the Sphere of Sexuality and Reproductive Choice

The final realm of gender jurisprudence we examine is that dealing with sexuality and reproductive choice. The issues these cases present are controversial in any traditionally Catholic society. Where Catholicism is constitutionally established as the state religion, as in Article 75 of the Costa Rican Constitution, the situation is even more highly charged. Indeed, in this sphere even resort to the constitutionalization of international human rights law may fail to provide express support for what we believe should be accepted as the full range of basic human rights. Not surprisingly then, Costa Rican women have encountered many obstacles to the enjoyment of reproductive rights. Nevertheless, the movement for women's human rights has consistently struggled to gain recognition of sexual and reproductive rights including in the arena of constitutional litigation. Again, the Chamber's record is mixed. It includes earlier cases, which resulted in opinions supportive of certain reproductive rights. The disturbing case here is the Chamber's recent opinion on in vitro fertilization which represents a major loss for human rights advocates.

In 1991, several members of the Costa Rican women's movement presented the newly established Constitutional Chamber with an *amparo* against the Human Reproduction Committee of the Costa Rican College of Physicians and Surgeons challenging their interpretation and application of Articles 5 and 12 of Executive Decree No. 18080-S governing sterilizations as requiring that married women have the consent of their spouses to obtain a therapeutic sterilization. The regulations did not expressly state that a married woman had to have her husband's consent but did provide that all requests for sterilizations be signed by "los interesados," which the challengers alleged was being used to require such consent.[40] With two dissenting justices, the majority of the Chamber issued a "conforming interpretation," ruling that while the regulation did not expressly require such consent, if it were interpreted as the petitioners claimed, it would be unconstitutional because contrary to the equality principles of Articles 33 and 52 of the Constitution and to the liberty guaranteed by Article 28,[41] as well as to CEDAW and several other of the international human rights documents that have been ratified by Costa Rica and thus are incorporated through Article 7. According to the opinion, requiring women but not men to have such consent would be contrary to the general equality provision of Article 33 and to the guarantee of equality between spouses of Article 52. But the justices pointed out that the constitutional principle most affected was that of liberty, which would be violated even if such a consent requirement were applied to men as well.

Whereas this opinion was an important victory in respect to women's reproductive health, the regulation requiring that sterilizations be authorized by the Human Reproduction Committee remained in effect. Formally, this was not discriminatory toward women but its discriminatory effects are obvious – women do not enjoy equal access to sterilization because for biological reasons, men can obtain sterilizations in a doctor's private office, whereas women must do so in a hospital. De facto, men do not need the authorization of the Committee while women do.

In 1999, an Executive Decree on health and reproductive rights was issued, which left to the individual the decision of whether or not to be sterilized, without the necessity of seeking the authorization of any public entity or authority designated by the state.[42] Not surprisingly, in a patriarchal

---

[40] Voto No. 2196-92. The Chamber's opinion noted that issues related to sterilization as a method of contraception and to the right of women to be sterilized for reasons other than to avoid pregnancies posing risks to their health were not questioned in this case and would not be analyzed.

[41] Article 28 provides, in relevant part: "No one can be bothered or persecuted for the manifestation of their opinions nor for any act that does not violate the law. Private actions that do not damage morality or the public order or harm a third person, are outside the reach of the law...."

[42] Executive Decree No. 27913-S (14 May 1999).

Catholic state such as Costa Rica, this recognition of equality and liberty in this sphere was challenged through an action of unconstitutionality against the new Decree. The allegations were that the decree's recognition of voluntary sterilization was unconstitutional because the inevitable destruction of some fertilized eggs was contrary to constitutional and international human rights to physical integrity and to protection of the family. In December 2000, the Constitutional Chamber rejected this challenge to the constitutionality of the new decree.[43] The opinion relied in part on a decision earlier that year in a case in which a man had filed an *amparo* action seeking to prevent his wife from being sterilized without his consent and alleging that his right to a family was threatened. In rejecting the action of unconstitutionality against the 1999 decree, the Chamber quoted from this earlier *amparo* opinion:

It is necessary to point out that although the Constitution establishes a special protection for the family, it also does so for individuals, which includes their liberty to control their own body, as long as this is not legitimately prohibited and does not threaten other fundamental rights, as would be those of the embryo or fetus of a pregnant woman. It follows that all persons, men as well as women, enjoy the right to be sterilized without the necessity of seeking the consent of their spouse or companion, given that the rights to reproduction and the control of one's own body in situations that do not collide with the equal rights of others or with the public order, are of individual and personal exercise, in the manner that no one, regardless of their condition or relationship with the one who exercises them, can impose their will upon the other.

Our discussion of reproductive rights ends with an examination of the Constitutional Chamber's alarming 2000 opinion. In 2000, an action of unconstitutionality was brought against Decree 24029-S, *In Vitro Fertilization and Transfer of Embryos*. This 1995 decree authorized and regulated these scientific reproductive techniques.[44] The challenger attacked this decree as contrary to the right of life, even though it authorized use of the in vitro technique only under very strict regulations. The decree included an absolute prohibition on fertilizing more than six ovum per period of treatment and a requirement that all fertilized ovum be transferred to the patient's uterus, with absolute prohibitions on discarding or preserving them for later use in either the same patient or other patients. The decree also absolutely prohibited any genetic manipulation, experimentation, or commercialization.

Taking a page from feminist litigation discussed earlier and its reliance on Article 7's incorporation of international human rights documents, the challenger in this case claimed that the decree violated Article 21 of the Constitution's guarantee that "human life is inviolable," as well as provisions of the Inter-American Human Rights Convention and the Convention on the Rights of the Child, because the technique regulated by this decree involved

[43] Voto No. 11015-00.
[44] Voto No. 2000-02306.

a high loss of embryos given that more embryos are injected into a woman's uterus than are either expected to, or likely to, survive. Thus, the question posed was: "When does human life begin?"

The majority of the Constitutional Chamber recognized that specialists disagreed on the answer to this question, but sided with those contending that life begins at the very moment of conception. They also acknowledged that the decree imposed much stricter limitations on the use of the technique than other countries, using text from Article 11 of Spain's *Law on the Techniques of Assisted Reproduction*[45] as an example of a more permissive approach. Nevertheless, they proceeded to declare the decree unconstitutional, relying primarily on Article 21 of the Constitution's recognition of the inviolability of life and on Article 4.1 of the Inter-American Human Rights Convention, which provides: "All persons have the right to have their life respected. This right will be protected by the law and, in general, from the moment of conception. No one can be deprived of life arbitrarily."[46]

The opinion rejected the argument that the technique did not differ from natural reproduction, where there are embryos that fail to become implanted in the uterus or that otherwise do not develop to birth. "In vitro fertilization involves a conscious, voluntary manipulation of the female and male reproductive cells for the purpose of obtaining a new life, which produces a situation where, beforehand, it is known that human life in a considerable percentage of the cases, does not have the possibility of continuing."

Two of the justices, including Justice Ana Virginia Calzada, dissented from this opinion, arguing that what was really contrary to the right to life was the majority's ruling:

The technology of in vitro fertilization, in the manner regulated by Executive Decree No. 24029-S is not incompatible with the right to life or with human dignity, rather to the contrary, it constitutes an instrument that science and technology have given to human beings to favor it, since infertility, in our opinion, must be seen as the consequence of a genuine state of infirmity, and thus must be treated in this context, with preventive, diagnostic, and therapeutic measures.

The majority's opinion in this case is contrary to women's right to control their own bodies and makes prospects for recognition of other reproductive rights such as the right to abortion, even in situations where the pregnancy results from rape, even dimmer.[47]

---

[45] Law No. 35 /1988.

[46] The opinion also found the decree was invalid because beyond the authority of the executive power to regulate through an executive decree.

[47] Costa Rica's Penal Code imposes a range of criminal penalties for most abortions under Section II of Title I on "Crimes against Life." *Código Penal*, Law No. 4573/1970. For example, Article 119 provides that a woman who causes her own abortion shall be punished with one to three years' imprisonment, with the penalty reduced to six months to two years if the fetus

CONCLUSION

The incorporation of international human rights laws into Costa Rican constitutional law as supra-constitutional norms has produced a generally positive, if uneven, body of jurisprudence that reconceptualizes and broadens principles of gender equality. These legal instruments have provided support for constitutional litigation that has led the judiciary to a more realistic and contextualized analysis of gender equality in diverse areas of Costa Rican society. Defenders of women's human rights in Costa Rica now generally have sufficient constitutional sources upon which to base future arguments for furthering a broad vision of gender equality. Perhaps the major deficiencies remaining with respect to legal sources to support real and effective gender equality are in the area of reproductive rights, where greater doctrinal development and legal recognition will be required.

In some cases, the advances in real equality in gender relations have been very important, as in the case of the approval and enforcement of quotas in the electoral-political sphere and in the cases imposing affirmative duties to nominate and appoint significant or proportional numbers of women to decision-making positions, which have opened the doors to a greater participation of women in the decision-making of the state. By contrast, the negative effects of some of the decisions of the Constitutional Chamber, such as the recent decision on in vitro fertilization, are also clear.

The relative weakness of international norms and the influence of religion may contribute to the Chamber's mixed results in reproductive rights cases. The newness of the Chamber and its role in the country's legal system may have played a role in the confused results in some of the early cases. But some of the jurisprudential inconsistencies encountered in Costa Rican gender jurisprudence, like that found in the work of other courts, likely result from the different views of the justices who author the opinions and their legal staff. In this respect it is worth noting, as we have earlier, that women judges have been the authors of some of the most advanced opinions thus far.

More than a decade has passed since the last fundamental reforms in Costa Rican constitutional law, which included the creation of the Constitutional Chamber of the Supreme Court. During this time, there have been both advances and backwards steps with respect to gender rights. Looking to the future, the challenge for the Constitutional Chamber is to continue the generally positive trend in its gender cases and to develop a coherent

---

was of less than six months' gestation. Article 118's corresponding penalties for performing an abortion with the consent of the woman are the same. Article 120 reduces the penalties for both the woman and the person performing the abortion to three months to two years if the abortion was performed "to hide the dishonor of the woman." And Article 93(4) and (5) allow for judicial pardons under certain circumstances for abortions "to save the woman's honor" and for the woman if the pregnancy results from rape. Finally, Article 123 classifies as "nonpunishable" medical abortions performed for the purpose of avoiding a risk to the life or health of the mother that could not be avoided by other means.

and consistent body of equality jurisprudence. The challenge for the movement for women's human rights, as well as entities responsible for promoting equality between women and men, is to refocus and reinforce their activities aimed at: promoting CEDAW's concept of equality and the understanding that as human beings we all are equally different; developing efforts directed towards helping women demand their constitutional rights through the judicial system; sensitizing and training the persons responsible for the administration of constitutional justice in the application of women's human rights; developing strategies for obtaining positions in offices of the administration of constitutional justice; promoting constitutional reforms that reinforce gender equality; designing curricular proposals for the study of constitutional law with a gender perspective in law schools, judicial training programs, and in any other educational facilities that teach constitutional law; popularizing Costa Rican constitutional law so that all people claim their rights and obligations and thus from this empowered status can change patriarchal attitudes and take the actions necessary to strengthen a democracy based in respect for the human rights of all – women and men. If these challenges are met, Costa Rica's developing gender jurisprudence, influenced as it is by international human rights norms, can provide a model for courts within the region and beyond.

Suggested Readings

Robert S. Barker, "Judicial Review in Costa Rica: Evolution and Recent Developments" (2000) VII *Southwestern Journal of Law and Trade in the Americas* 267–90.

Andrew Brynes, "El uso de las normas internacionales de derechos humanos en la interpretación constitucional para el adelanto de los derechos humanos de las mujeres" en *Género y Derecho* (Santiago: ILANUD, Ediciones Lom, 1999) 67.

"El Sistema Costarricense de Informacion Judicial," online: <www.poder-judicial. go.cr> (date accessed: June 17, 2002).

Mario Alberto Jiménez Quesada, *Desarrollo constitucional de Costa Rica*, 4th ed. (San José, Juricentro, 1992).

Ilse Abshagen Leitinger, ed. & trans., *The Costa Rican Women's Movement: A Reader* (Pittsburgh: University of Pittsburgh Press, 1997).

Zarela Villanueva Monge and Alexandra Bogantes Rodríguez, *Principio de Igualdad y Jurisprudencia Constitucional* (San José: Corte Suprema de Justicia Poder Judicial, 1996).

Alda Facio Montejo, *Cuando el Genero Suena Cambios Trae* (San José: ILANUD, 1999).

Manuel Rojas, *Lucha social y guerra civil en Costa Rica 1940–1948* (San José: Editorial Porvenir, 1982).

Michelle A. Saint-Germain and Martha I. Morgan, "Equality: Costa Rican Women Demand the Real Thing" (1991) 11 *Women and Politics* 23.

Rodrigo Jiménez Sandoval, *La Igualdad de Género en el Derecho Laboral Centroamericano* (San José: ILANUD-OIT, 2001).

Naomi Seizler, *Sterilization, Gender and the Law in Costa Rica* (San José: ILANUD, 2000).

5

Constituting Women

The French Ways

Eric Millard

The French situation might appear to be a paradox when studying women in constitutional law. On the one hand, the Constitution of 1958, as amended, has not fundamentally altered women's constitutional status. The prevailing principle of republican universalism, conceived during the French Revolution in 1789, remains the key notion in the constitutional debate and the inspiration of all legal provisions. On the other hand, a recent constitutional reform vested parliament with the power to organize a "parity" or strict gender equality, democracy. This power resulted in the enactment of a statute requiring that, under certain conditions, an equal number of male and female candidates must appear on the lists submitted to voters for most elections. From this point of view, the French experience could appear a very innovative one.

France has a civil law system, with a clear separation between civil and administrative law (the former is codified for most issues, the latter is closer to case law) and separate adjudicative bodies (namely, the Cour de cassation [civil] and the Conseil d'Etat [administrative]). Insofar as most matters pertaining to women's legal status are governed by written texts (the Constitution, regular statutes, and sometimes administrative rules), adjudicative bodies are generally limited to applying those texts to concrete cases without creating new law.

The current Constitution is known as the Constitution of the Vth Republic. Adopted in 1958, it established a system of government that is sometimes characterized as a "presidential" system and sometimes as a "unique parliamentary system."[1] The president is directly elected by the people and has

---

[1] Some controversy attaches to the characterization of the French system of government. On the one hand, when the Constitution was enacted, some analysts referred to it as "presidential" because it had some features normally found in presidential systems (e.g., a president with some personal powers). On the other hand, it also contained features normally found in parliamentary systems (e.g., responsible government, non-confidence votes), causing others

specific powers, including the enactment of some rules, even where the government has more competence. Since the 1970s, a member of the government has been in charge of women's issues,[2] and some specific programs have been created to inform women of their rights and to coordinate and promote actions on women's issues.

The Preamble to the 1958 Constitution expressly refers to two Declarations of Rights: the *Declaration of Man and Citizen Rights of 1789*; and the Preamble of the former 1946 Constitution. Both of these texts have been considered constitutionally binding since 1971.[3] The 1789 text enacted classical liberal rights (freedom, equality before law, equality before taxes [égalité devant l'impôt]) and the 1946 text supplemented it with economic and social rights (including the equality of men and women before the law). The Constitution recognizes relevant international law, including human rights treaties, when ratified, and gives them a legal force superior to that of statutes. This includes the European Union treaties and the Convention for the Protection of Human Rights and Fundamental Freedoms (also known as the European Convention on Human Rights [ECHR]).

The Constitution provides for a limited process of a priori review of the constitutionality of statutes only.[4] Concrete review of legislation and *amparo*-type actions for the protection of fundamental rights do not exist under the French constitutional system. Abstract and a priori review of legislation is performed by the Constitutional Council (Conseil Constitutionnel), the members of which are appointed by political authorities (the President of the Republic and the Presidents of the Houses of Parliament). Membership is for nine years and is nonrenewable. Appointment is unrestricted, except for

to refer to it as "parliamentary." This latter characterization is especially apposite to the periods of "cohabitation" wherein the prime minister and the president were political opponents (1986–8, 1993–5, and 1997–2002). During those periods, the source of the constitutional power of the government was Parliament; the powers of the president were not sufficient to allow him to act against the will of Parliament. Thus, the French system of government could be characterized as "presidential" when and only when the president and government are political allies, and from a political analysis perspective. French analysts now generally recognize their system of government is "parliamentary"; see, for example, Marie-Anne Cohendet, *La cohabitation* (Paris: P.U.F., 1993).

[2] Rank and title depend on government policy, although usually this member is a Secrétaire d'Etat (the lower rank).

[3] In 1971, for the first time (Conseil constitutionnel, 07/16/1971, Liberté d'association, 71–44 DC), the Constitutional Council reviewed the substance of a statute, and stated that some of the provisions limiting freedom of association were contrary to constitutional law (that is, contrary to a principle derived from a 1901 statute that is constitutionally binding because the 1946 Preamble refers to it). The Constitutional Council stated the underlying premises were that both the 1946 Preamble and the *Declaration of Man and Citizen Rights of 1789* are constitutionally binding.

[4] In France judicial review is a priori, that is before the statute adopted by Parliament is enforceable. Once the statute has the force of law (that is, it has been signed by the president and published in the *Journal Officiel*), no review is possible.

the requirement of French citizenship. At present, three of the nine members are women, the first having been appointed in 1992. There are debates as to whether or not this organ constitutes a "court" in the strict sense. On the one hand, it has the power to review the constitutionality of statutes referred to it by political authorities. On the other hand, citizens cannot seek judicial review of legislation that infringes their constitutional rights. Furthermore, the Constitutional Council is not competent to review judicial or administrative court statements.

France is an indivisible, secular, democratic, and social republic with a decentralized administration.[5] Rulings of the executive and of decentralized authorities are reviewed by the Conseil d'Etat.

The French experience of constituting women rests on the affirmation of the principle of universalism (Part 1), which at present has a new interpretation via the parity question (Part 2). The relationship between the French approach and international law is also a subject of debate (Part 3).

PART I: LEGAL UNIVERSALISM

The principle of universalism – or the principle of republican universalism – is a conceptualization stemming from several constitutional provisions, as well as from legal, political, and philosophical doctrine developed since 1789. The principle constitutes undoubtedly one of the most important heritages of the French Revolution. Thus, it is difficult to set it aside without appearing to move away from the founding principles of the Revolution and from the pillars of the Republic. This conceptualization is enforced by the courts in a broad sense, in particular by the Constitutional Council, which has existed since 1958 and has reviewed the constitutionality of laws both procedurally and substantively since 1971.[6] On the one hand, this conceptualization permits a kind of unity in the interpretation of constitutional provisions; on the other hand, it offers a hierarchical ordering of those provisions, preferring those that are founded on this principle over those that would alter it.

To understand the importance and role of these constitutional provisions the reasons and conditions for their appearance must be considered before explaining how they relate to and have endured through the principle of universalism. In this way, it will be easier to see how this principle, relied

---

[5] France is not a federal state, even though the Constitution guarantees the election and jurisdiction of local organs, because jurisdictional matters are controlled by Parliament and strictly limited.

[6] In 1958, the Constitutional Council was given a limited power to review statutes for consistency with the constitutional separation of powers between the Parliament and the executive. No one imagined substantive judicial review although Article 61 was vague enough to allow it. Before 1971, no statutes were referred; the cases addressed the competence of Parliament relative to the executive. In 1971, in response to a particular case the Constitutional Council decided it could review statutes substantively (*supra* note 3).

upon for two centuries as a model for valuing public policy and private behavior, has complicated gender issues that have, of course, gone through some evolution. In particular, the principle has given rise to debates over its real function; with views on its effect ranging from the reproduction of male domination to the promotion of gender equality.

Revolutionary Symbol

The politicians of the Revolution of 1789 gave no priority to questions concerning the situation of women. The oft-mentioned experience of Olympe de Gouge, who campaigned for the recognition of women's rights (1791) as a supplement to the *Declaration of Man and Citizen Rights of 1789*, remained an isolated case which, moreover, failed bitterly.

The Revolutionaries had other preoccupations. Yet the legal solutions they devised, because of their general nature, also applied to women and determined the way in which the constitutional and legal status of women was to be understood in the French system. This fact is clearly evidenced in two particular debates.

First, the Revolutionaries wanted to fight against the social structuring and the double standards of legal differentiation that characterized the *Ancien Régime*. The old society was divided into three orders (*les états*) corresponding to unequal prerogatives and legal statuses. Moreover, the law of the *Ancien Régime* was not the same in all territories.

The solution proposed by the Revolutionaries was to enforce the construction of a national legal equality, a uniformity of legal rules, and a formal equality of legal status. But this leveling was simply obtained by the suppression of restricting rules (i.e., guilds and social groups) and by the construction of equality among legal entities (yet not between real persons). This idea was established in the process of Napoleon's post-Revolutionary private law codification.[7]

Second, there was the question of sovereignty. For theoretical as well as contextual reasons, the Revolutionaries chose a constitutional theory that reconceptualized sovereignty. According to this theory, sovereignty was fictionally embodied in the entity of the nation. Persons exercising power, or appointing those who exercised power, were thus deprived of this sovereignty. This theory required a rethinking of the link between those who govern and those who are governed.[8] The "Representatives" (mainly Members of Parliament) did not represent something existing before their designation and legal action; they were organs expressing, or "embodying," sovereignty by this very designation and action. Two important consequences followed.

---

[7] The Civil Code was enacted in 1804, and the commercial code and the criminal code were enacted during the following years.

[8] Carré de Malberg, *Contribution à la Théorie générale de l'Etat* (Paris: Sirey, 1920).

First, all those contributing to this breakdown of sovereignty (Members of Parliament, but also the executive and voters)[9] could be considered as organs, and this authorized a functional organization of constitutional prerogatives. Voters and elected members fulfilled a function that permitted restrictions on the rights of voting and of elevation to certain worthy categories of people (see Part 2).

However, the legislative organ possessed sovereign power as an organ expressing the national will. In contrast, for historical reasons involving distrust of the courts of the *Ancien Regime*, the Revolutionaries limited the courts to the enforcement of statutes, strictly separating judicial powers from other powers. This lies at the root of the opposition in the French system to the establishment of a formal Constitution, at least insofar as it imposes a system of judicial review that allows an independent organ, usually a court, to invalidate or prevent the enforcement of legislation that is considered contrary to that Constitution. This is why the controversies involving women's issues mainly evoke questions of parliamentary law making. As sovereign, Parliament enforces the general declaration of rights and expresses the current national will (or what is the common good at a given moment). Consequently and in contrast both to common law systems (where there is a "cult" of the case instead of a "cult" of the general and abstract rule) and to more recently adopted civil law systems (where the cult of the general rule is less steeped in a history marked by the idea of formal equality), women's issues are not treated as matters of judicial review or conceived of as the expression of what is fair.

Legal Framework

The provisions combined in the principle of universalism are essentially the following.

First, there is the universality of inalienable and natural rights of human beings. This idea implies equality of rights among persons independent of other considerations, such as gender.[10]

Second, we have the unity and indivisibility of the Republic.[11] This provision significantly constricts the possibility of legally recognizing distinct social categories and in particular limits the recognition of social divisions, be they natural or constructed. Section 2 reinforces the principle of universality of Section 1 by ensuring the equality of all citizens before the law. However, it does not prohibit classifications unless they are based on origin,

---

[9] Carré de Malberg, a strong supporter of the sovereignty of parliament, did not go so far, but what I expose is the very logic of his system.
[10] *Declaration of Man and Citizen Rights of 1789*, art. 1.
[11] *Constitution of 1958*, 10/04, s.2.

race, or religion. It does not make reference to other distinctions, such as gender.

Finally, there is the principle of national sovereignty,[12] which gives all citizens of both genders equal rights to vote and to be elected.

What are the implications of this model, created at the time of the Revolution, for the constitutional situation of women? On the one hand, the formal equality of universalism entails the absence of formal gender considerations within constitutional provisions. On the other hand, it does not exclude (and even calls for) gender distinctions in legislation (insofar as there are socially perceived distinctions between men and women), which for a long time were treated as matters of parliamentary discretion, hence remaining more relevant to public debate than legal protection.

The Relevant Constitutional Provisions and Principles

Universalism – a thoroughly political principle – relies on legal provisions. The first, and most emblematic, provision is the *Declaration of Man and Citizen Rights of 1789*. Three of its seventeen articles contribute directly to this principle.

The Declaration is a political text above all, adopted at the beginning of the Revolution for rhetorical reasons. Article 1 of the Declaration provides: "Men are born and remain free and equal in rights." It is nevertheless immediately qualified by the following sentence: "Social distinctions may be based only on considerations of the common good."[13]

Article 6 states:

The Law is the expression of the general will. All citizens have the right to take part, personally or through their representatives, in its making. It must be the same for all, whether it protects or punishes. All citizens, being equal in its eyes, shall be equally eligible to all high offices, public positions and employments, according to their ability, and without other distinction than that of their virtues and talents.[14]

Finally, Article 16 indicates the terms of the Revolutionaries' constitutional theory: "Any society in which no provision is made for guaranteeing rights or for the separation of powers, has no Constitution."[15]

In practice, the *Declaration of Man and Citizen Rights* did not play any legal role before the end of World War II. In 1946, the constituent assembly adopted a text whose preamble directly referred to the Declaration, but no system of judicial review of legislation was established. This was changed by the present constitution of 1958. Its Preamble retained the

---

[12] Ibid., s.3.
[13] *Declaration of Man and Citizen Rights of 1789*, *supra* note 10.
[14] *Declaration of Man*, ibid., art. 6.
[15] *Declaration of Man*, ibid., art. 16.

constitutionalization of the Declaration: "The French people solemnly pro-
claim their attachment to the Rights of Man and the principles of national
sovereignty as defined by the Declaration of 1789, confirmed and complemented by the Preamble to the Constitution of 1946."[16] And Chapter VII
created the Constitutional Council, whose tasks included the judicial review
of legislation. In this way, the principle of universalism gained significant
constitutional force nearly two centuries after its birth.

The force of this principle is facilitated by the fact that there are no provisions contradicting it, and by the fact that the Constitution of 1958 is silent
on the gender issue. However, the 1946 Preamble, which also was made
part of the Constitution in 1958, proclaimed "as being especially necessary
to our times, the political, economic and social principles" that "The law
guarantees women equal rights to those of men in all spheres."[17] Was this
a simple reminder of the equality contained in the *Declaration of Man and
Citizen Rights of 1789* or a new principle? Answering this question entails
interpreting the principle of universalism and examining how this principle
is implemented.

The Complex Implementation of Gender Politics

The implementation of the principle of universalism depends on two
things: on the one hand, whether differences between men and women are
permissible; on the other, whether there are limits on such differentiation
and on the process to determine what those limits are.

As far as the second question is concerned, a significant change seems to
appear with the Constitution of the Vth Republic. The existence of an organ
with the power to review the constitutionality of laws shows that legislator is
no longer the sole judge of its own actions, as was the case before. However,
this change is qualified by several facts.

First, there is the procedure itself. As mentioned, the system of review of
laws in France is an a priori review, which means that it intervenes during
the process of the creation of law itself. Once enacted – once the text has
become law and has a binding force – then the statute cannot be challenged.
The ordinary courts (administrative and judicial) deciding the cases cannot
use arguments about possible inconsistencies between the statute involved
and the constitutional text (and the declarations of rights) to reject the application of the statute. Unless a statute is submitted to the Constitutional
Council, it cannot be opposed; it is enforceable unless later amended by its
author.

Furthermore, application to the Constitutional Council is open only to a
very restricted number of persons: the President of the Republic, the Prime

[16] *Constitution of 1958, supra* note 11, preamble.
[17] *Constitution of 1946*, preamble, ibid.

Minister, the Presidents of the Chambers, and a group of at least sixty members of one of the Assemblies. Again, citizens do not have the opportunity to invoke judicial review.

Then, the idea of review presupposes a legal norm that is challenged and a reference norm with which that legal norm must comply. Because the principle of universalism contained in the reference norm is broad and allows for competing interpretations it is difficult for the Constitutional Council to oppose a difference of status between men and women established in the law unless it is willing to impose its own political interpretation of the general interest over the voice of the elected of the nation. Nothing in law prevents the Court from doing so, but the fact that the legitimacy of the Constitutional Council is a controversial issue makes the possibility of this happening quite unlikely. This is all the more true, as the Constitutional Council is aware that a constitutional amendment could alter the norm of reference, specifying its meaning in a way that contradicts the prior interpretation given by the Constitutional Council.

Finally, the absence of cases must be noted. The Constitutional Council has not had a chance to deal with the question of gender as a whole (only in the area of political representation, as we shall see in Part 2). The reason is that the birth and growth of the Constitutional Council has coincided with a decline of legislation that sanctions formal inequalities or differences in status between men and women and, to a lesser extent, an increase in legislative affirmations of more substantive notions of equality. It is certain that all attempts by legislators to revert to historically unequal ways of treating women would be censured by the Constitutional Council.

By contrast, the fact remains that the Constitutional Council could easily decide to use the principle of universalism to oppose affirmative action measures. The question of what constitutes discrimination is currently under discussion, and there is no consensus in the political debates.[18]

The Realization of Competing Views of the Principle of Universalism. The principle of universalism is implemented by political authorities and this implementation might adapt itself to very different political understandings. As a constitutional question, we are mainly concerned with its implementation in legislation. However, it must not be forgotten that administrators, acting within in their spheres of jurisdiction, also implement the principle of universalism under the guidance of the Conseil d'Etat. In fact, there are

---

[18] In another context, the Constitutional Council has relied on a strong conception of the principle of universalism, rendered as the indivisibility of the national community, to oppose the symbolic recognition of the Corsican People within the national community. See Cons. constitutionnel, 9 May 1991, 91–290 DC, J.O., 14 May 1991, p. 6350. The nexus between rejecting the Corsican claim for recognition and a potential claim by women to the recognition of their difference has to do with a reading of universalism, which rejects any claims for differential treatment.

three possibilities for administrative implementation: first, when a matter falls within executive authority (under Section 37 of the Constitution) and given the absence of a statute, the administrative court reviews the constitutionality of the rule; second, when the executive authority takes measures to enforce the law; finally, when the executive authority imposes rules on the running of the administration (e.g., status of public agents). In its interpretation of the principle of universalism, the Conseil d'Etat has adhered to a principle of formal equality and has only accepted departures from it in three cases, all of which are consistent with the classical understanding of universalism: if these departures are contemplated by statutes (because of the impossibility of reviewing the statute itself); if the differences of status clearly pertain to objectively different situations (because of the so-called self-evidence of this ground);[19] or if general interest requires it (as a consequence of the *Declaration of Man and Citizen Rights*, stating that "Social distinctions may be based only on considerations of the common good"[20]). Using these criteria and after accepting administrative discrimination based on gender, mainly in the public service for a long time, the Conseil d'Etat now seems to find them suspect due to the influence of European Law (see Part 3).

As for the application of the principle of universalism to the legislative domain, two questions have to be addressed: first, the treatment of legislative recognition of certain specific rights for women; and, second, the evolution undergone in the realization and interpretation of the principle.

Many rights are simply statutory. They are not mentioned in the declarations of rights, nor in the text of the Constitution. They are statutory rights which may be subject to constitutional scrutiny; legislators might decide to change them. Most of these rights are granted to both men and women without distinction. However, two of them are rights that have been specifically recognized for women: the right to birth control, which has been authorized under medical control since 1967; and the right to abortion, which was enacted in 1975 and later confirmed by statute, most recently in 2001. In its treatment of those rights, the Constitutional Council has refused to scrutinize the law against constitutional provisions and hence, against the principle of universalism, focusing instead on the relationship between international and national law (see Part 3).

But in other instances the principle of universalism has been crucial, although not always realized in the same way. Indeed, the interpretation of the

---

[19] This ground has evoked previous conceptions of biologically based gender distinctions such as motherhood or pregnancy, but cannot be applied as a general criterion to distinguish between men and women. Nevertheless, until the 1970s, the nature of the administrative functions to be performed played a role, as an objective tool of discrimination, to exclude women from some important offices in administration.

[20] *Declaration of Man and Citizen Rights of 1789, supra* note 10.

principle of universalism and its realization in matters of gender has changed enormously since the Revolution. Initially, legislators clearly favored an unequal status for men and women. Political rights will be dealt with later (in Part 2). But in civil, criminal, and social matters gender was understood as something that justified legal distinctions in the name of social distinctions which served the common good. Napoleon's Code confirmed this vision of a bourgeois society based on family hierarchy. In her professional life as in the exercise of her personal prerogatives, the woman had to submit first to the power of the father, and then to the power of the husband. This discrimination was present in the public field, where some professions were reserved for men and where the penalties for criminal offences like adultery were unequal to the detriment of women. In the nineteenth century, the legislative interpretation of universalism, coded in notions of the common good and social utility, provided a legal notion of womanhood that discriminated against women. Thus, formal equality was not realized; instead, equality was applied differently to men than to women.

From the end of the nineteenth century, legislators began to question whether this construction any longer corresponded with the perception of the common good. Universalism had come to be understood as a refusal to distinguish by using categories. The professional ban slowly disappeared during the twentieth century remaining only in some domains, such as the military and the penitentiary.[21] At the same time, though, some differentiations remained in place under the guise of the protection of women and childbirth. Some jobs considered dangerous and tiring remained forbidden to women.[22] For example, there were limitations on night work until those provisions were abolished in 2000–1. The new conception of universalism in professional matters, as prohibiting distinctions between men and women, was also realized in the adoption of the principle of equal pay for jobs of equal value[23] and then by a general law in 1983[24] imposing professional equality between men and women. Unfortunately, this general law and more recent efforts, such as another general law in 2001, have not had any real impact. Women represent more than 45 percent of the active population (47.9 percent of women work), yet the wage difference between men and women is estimated to be about 25 percent, a difference that increases with the level of employment (from 8 percent for nonqualified employees to 30 percent for high wage professions). Women are more often the victims of unemployment

---

[21] For military matters, some rare and specific army and security corps are still reserved to men (in spite of a 1998 rule suppressing any gender discrimination for access to the army), and as for penitentiary matters, the sex segregation of jails has justified the use of sex as criterion for employment (such discrimination has been accepted by the European Communities Court).

[22] *Women's Labour Act*, 11 February 1892.

[23] *Equal Treatment in Labour Act*, J.O., 22 December 1972.

[24] *Equal treatment in Labour Act*, J.O., 13 July 1983, enacting the new s.L-140-2 of the Labor Code.

(13.6 percent as compared with 10.2 percent), more often work part-time (around 33 percent), and even if women represent 75 percent of employees, they make up only a meager one third of managerial staff and of elite intellectual professions.[25]

At the same time as this law was passed, gender discrimination in wages or in access to work or to careers became punishable by criminal law, although in practice the burden of proof limited the efficacy of this protection of women's rights.[26] Provisions were also passed to fight against sexual harassment.[27] Progress was slower in family matters but from the 1960s until the mid-1990s the legal model of marriage and cohabitation[28] was constructed in egalitarian terms, both in terms of the couple's relationship as well as in terms of relationships between the couple and third parties such as children. Some say that there is no longer any question of gender hierarchy in the family. Both members of the couple have the same rights between them as in their relations with their children, whether they are legally married or not.

There is a further question. To the extent that the suppression of discrimination and the embedding of formal equality in the Constitution have not been sufficient to correct the substantive inequalities between men and women (and this is especially obvious in the professional field), is it possible to call on the notion of the social utility of legal distinctions to promote policies in favor of women? In the current legal and constitutional context, social utility could be the sole relevant ground. There are indeed no other possibilities, as far as the affirmation of legal equality between men and women is understood,[29] because of the prevailing conception of universalism, as equality before the law (i.e., men and women having the same rights), and not as a substantive equality giving specific rights to women to achieve real equality. Thus, the only way to pass this kind of legislation it is to try to reinterpret the *Declaration of Man and Citizen Rights*: just as at one time referring to the social utility of certain distinctions was used against women, now it could be used in their favor.

To date, the Constitutional Council has not yet dealt with this question, so the answer can be only hypothetical. However, given the strength with which the Council has lately embraced the notion of formal equality in its reading of the principle of universalism, it seems that only a constitutional amendment could allow legislators to promote policies of affirmative action. By contrast, the Conseil d'Etat seems to have handled the situation differently

---

[25] Various Gallup Polls 1998, 1999, 2003, and 2004.

[26] Women have to prove that their gender is the sole reason for the failure to hire, pay, and promote them. This proof is difficult to find, unless the offender admits it. In practice, other real or fictional reasons are advanced (such as personal incapacity, etc.).

[27] *Act enacting the new Criminal Code*, J.O., 16 December 1992, 92-1336, s.222-33.

[28] *Pacte civil de solidarité*, J.O., 15 November 1999, 99–944. The Civil Solidarity Pact made it possible for two adults, whether heterosexuals or homosexuals, to gain a recognition of some of their rights (common property, common house renting, official together life, etc.).

[29] 1946 Preamble: "Law guarantees equality between men and women."

when considering the implementation of administrative policies. Thus, in a 1996 report,[30] the administrative court (in this report, not in a decision) gave a more dynamic view of the principle of equality, accepting the principle of affirmative action based on the notion of the general interest. It remains to be seen whether the competent authorities will take up this interpretation of the principle of universalism; it does not seem that the current political elite possesses a clearly defined position on this question.[31]

Universalism or Universalization of Male Gender? Finally, we must address a question of political interpretation. Because it rests on formal equality (which does not purport to correct real inequalities), the principle of universalism has been often criticized as a principle that reproduces social inequalities as a whole, and especially social relations of gender.

Generally speaking, this principle – especially in its modern interpretation, which rejects differentiation altogether – may certainly be construed as an instrument that reproduces male domination. Refusing to question the constitutional relevance of gender structures ensures the legal invisibility of women, and this contributes to a social imbalance in favor of men and does not allow for changes to correct the situation to the advantage of women. Moreover, because the legal and political forces that interpret the principle are "male," there is no space for a specifically female legal expression independent of the male, while there is no guarantee that the current legal expression is gender neutral.

This is why this debate on universalism has come to mark a clear and sharp frontier within French feminism between: (a) those attached to the idea of universalism and desiring to improve the real situation of women within that idea by using temporary affirmative action measures without questioning the principle itself (which is seen as at the basis of the social reconstruction of gender relations);[32] and (b) those endorsing a differentialist conception, challenging the very notion of universalism and claiming that only a permanent different and specific legal treatment will respond to the real expectations of women.[33]

PART 2: PARITY, A MODERN FORM OF UNIVERSALISM OR THE
GRADUAL ABANDONING OF THE UNIVERSALIST IDEAL?

The introduction of parity to the system of political representation in France reveals both the contradictions and the difficulties that are linked to

---

[30] "Rapport sur l'égalité" Documentation française, 1996.
[31] The present government has discussed a related question (immigration), but without including the gender issue.
[32] For instance, Françoise Collin, *Le differend des sexes* (Paris: Pleins Feux, 1999); Michèle Riot-Sarcey, *Histoire du féminisme* (Paris: La découverte, 2002).
[33] For instance, Antoinette Fouque, *Il y a deux sexes* (Paris: Gallimard, 1999).

134 — Eric Millard

constitutional universalism, as well as the potential of feminist legal thought. Launched by the feminist movement in the early nineties in response to the Constitutional Council's interpretation of universalism, the idea of parity came into general use in the political debate, resulting in positive law reform. Because its terms differ from the well-known quota method, with the idea of parity France is undertaking a new and unique experience.

The idea of parity has been conceptualized as a twofold solution: first, as an answer to the endemic underrepresentation of women within the French political and institutional arena; and second, as an answer that could be legally and politically compatible with the principle of universalism.

Correcting the Endemic Underrepresentation of Women within the Political Sphere

Traditionally in France, political offices have been occupied by men. Whereas women represented a little over 51 percent of the population, and 53 percent of the electorate, they made up barely 10 percent of the National Assembly, less than 6 percent of the Senate, less than 10 percent of departmental councils, and barely a quarter of regional council membership. Similarly, women constituted more than 20 percent of town councilors, but less than 10 percent of mayors were women.[34] Nevertheless, it is striking that 40 percent of French European deputies and one third of ministers are women. Reasons for this state of affairs are numerous and complex. Only those due to the legal aspect are being considered in this study.

Revolutionary universalism has experienced, in political matters as in other matters, two successive interpretations.

The traditional understanding of the principle of national sovereignty in France does not per se demand representativeness of elected organs, because what is sought is not to represent a real population, but, indeed, to provide organs for a mere fiction, the nation. This conception allows the focus to be placed on the capacity of the voting organ and the elected organ because it conceives voting and running for office more as a function (fulfilled by those who are judged competent for it according to the common good, and in a democracy, it is now people) than as a right (to vote or to be a candidate) given to everyone.[35] In fact, this functionalist logic allowed political power

[34] Data is for organs functioning on 1 January 2001 (before the enforcement of the parity reform).
[35] As far as we are looking for an organ, and not for the representation of people, what is stressed is not that some people have the right to vote and to be elected, but that those who vote or stand for offices are fulfilling the very function of providing an organ. On such a basis, stressing the idea of function before the idea of right, the universality of voters and candidates is not fundamental. It could be decided that only men are competent for such functions, or only rich people. Even if France is now a democracy, the idea of voting as a function is still prevailing (and justifies the exclusion of foreigners for instance). It is clear

to be reserved to men for a century and a half. Moreover, the so-called rights of eligibility and of suffrage were sometimes combined with an additional requirement of wealth.

When suffrage became universal during the Third Republic (1875–1940),[36] it remained conditional upon nationality, age, dignity, and sex. Women were still excluded. In spite of numerous claims, it was not until 1944 that women gained the right to vote and were granted its corollary, eligibility. This was the beginning of a shift toward the modern reading of universalism, a shift away from the necessity of distinguishing between men and women on the ground of social good to embracing the need for preventing differential treatment. Since that time, the electorate has been unified, and "all French citizens of either sex who have reached their majority and are in possession of their civil and political rights may vote as provided by statute."[37]

Nevertheless, in this area again, in spite of the removal of formal legal barriers women remain a small minority within political organs. In view of this, the idea of affirmative action as remedial began to take hold.

Learning from Failure

At first, the quota method was envisaged. In 1982, on the occasion of a reform of the ballot system for town council elections, an amendment to the new bill was voted on by Parliament, which held that "candidates' lists shall not comprise more than 75 per cent of people of the same sex."[38] A broad political consensus appeared to support this provision. Nevertheless, the entire statute was referred to the Constitutional Council by sixty members of the right-wing opposition party sitting in the National Assembly.

The Constitutional Council stated that the establishment of quotas was contrary to the Constitution.[39] The argument was simple and in accordance with the traditional principle of universalism. The court considered that the question had to be decided in the light of the principle of national sovereignty and of the universality of the right of suffrage. The Council recalled first that "No section of the people nor any individual may arrogate to itself, or to himself, the exercise [of national sovereignty]."[40] Then, it stated that "suffrage is equal" and that, according to the sixth Article of the *Declaration of Man and Citizen Rights of 1789*: "All citizens, being equal in the eyes of the law, shall be equally eligible to all high offices, public positions and

that it is not a mere popular sovereignty system but a national sovereignty system, which is now democratic because the national sovereignty is expressed through the people voting and running for office.

[36] Universal suffrage had been adopted before, during the Second Republic (1848–51).

[37] *Constitution of 1958*, *supra* note 11, art. 3.

[38] Article 4 of the text voted by the Parliament and invalidated by the Constitutional Council.

[39] Cons. constitutionnel, 18 November 1982, J.O., 19 November 1982, p. 3475, 82–146 DC.

[40] C.c., 18 November 1982, ibid.

employments, according to their ability, and without other distinction than that of their virtues and talents."[41] After that, it asserted that "the condition of being a citizen confers voting and eligibility rights equally on all those who are not excluded on the grounds of age, incapacity or nationality, or for a reason aiming at preserving the freedom of the voter, or the independence of the elected person" and that "any division or categorization of electorate, or of eligible persons, are against those Constitutional principles."[42]

This analysis deserves some attention. The argument links the right of suffrage to eligibility, yet the two questions may be grasped differently. For instance, because of their age, some voters, in some elections, cannot be elected. It is true that these restrictions are provided by organic statutes whereas it is the Constitution itself (in the 1946 Preamble), which ascribes to the legislative power the task of guaranteeing gender equality. The Constitution also provides in Article 3 that: "All French citizens of either sex who have reached their majority and are in possession of their civil and political rights may vote as provided by statute."[43] But this constitutional provision, which enables the legislative power, is not enough to allow Parliament to withdraw from universalism; as the enabling provision is interpreted in the light of the constitutional principle of universalism. In that sense, it was indeed the gender categorization that the Constitutional Council intended to refuse in the case.

At this point, there were two tenable interpretations, resting on two different theoretical analyses with different consequences for the determination of the procedure which could be used to introduce a quota-based system:

a) The Constitutional Council was building a barrier against any possibility of gender classifications, so that any affirmative action measure in the field would require that the Constitution be amended first. This was the interpretation that prevailed among legal scholars;

b) The Constitutional Council was refusing the new statute because it was founded on the quota method, which was in itself seen as contrary to the idea of equality. The classifications inferred by such a method were unequal because they divided men and women in accordance with an unequal criterion (75 percent vs. 25 percent), even if the statute did not specify which category (men or women) was or had to be disadvantaged, and even if the reference to such proportions did not prevent equality from being reached in fact (no more than 75 percent does not mean no less than 75 percent). It is from this second interpretation that the idea of parity was conceived and developed.

---

[41] C.c., 18 November 1982, ibid.
[42] C.c., 18 November 1982, ibid.
[43] *Constitution of 1958, supra* note 11, art. 3.

Rethinking the Idea of Affirmative Action

The failure of the 1982 reform resulted in a reassessment of the concept of quotas. Perhaps parity could represent the path to true equality, substantive equality. Instead of imposing a discriminating logic, it would simply realize the duality of humankind in those fora in which decisions were made that concerned the entire humankind. In that sense, parity would not contravene the principle of universalism. Conversely, concepts such as equity and quotas become suspect in the light of parity, the former because it is impossible to measure its meaning, the latter because it does not involve true equality, that is, the reality of women as representing half of humankind. In fact, quotas could amount to a low ceiling confirming women's underrepresentation. This result, it was proposed, could be avoided with parity.

The consistency and force of such a reading is debatable. From a strictly legal and constitutional point of view, it rests on a very weak position that confuses material with mathematical equality as the necessity of amending the Constitution to adopt the reform (and so of breaking the universalist frame) would show. However, its influence has been effective.

The initiative for this theorization, along with the political action which led to legal reforms, was because of the feminist movement. Doubtless, the ambiguity of the meaning of parity (see later) transcended the opposition between universalists and differentialists. But the theme of parity has given rise to a profound and fruitful reflection on the very idea of affirmative action, and to lobbying networks and activities, on a national level as well as on European and international levels.[44]

However, such activities would not have been effective if politicians had not joined in support. The reasons for political involvement were diverse, but a determining rationale was the fact that politicians found in this debate a way of addressing the current political crisis. Opinion polls showed that more than a majority of French people supported the idea of parity, generalized as follows: "Because women have been excluded, by principle and by the law of democracy, they must be restored by the law, for it is by the law that a society reveals itself."[45] It is nevertheless remarkable that the theme of parity has basically only been taken up and concretized by politicians in terms of political representation (in a broad sense, linked to elections), while in feminist theory it concerns all the places of decision and of representation, including elections and appointments in public and private spheres (associations, professions, administrations, etc.).

[44] Beijing Conference, 1995.
[45] "Manifesto of the 577 for democracy," as published in *Le Monde* 11/10/1993. 577 is a symbolic number, referring to the number of deputies in the National Assembly.

Legal and Constitutional Reforms

The goal of introducing a parity-based system in the French legal system without amending the constitutional text failed. The first private bill was written in 1994; others followed. One new statute concerned elections to the Corsican Assembly, providing that: "for each list of candidates there shall be parity between male and female candidates."[46] The Constitutional Council stated on 14 January 1999 that this provision was contrary to the Constitution.[47] It expressly referred to the 1982 decision that had rejected the quota method. This confirms that, according to the Constitutional Council in 1982, the very idea of gender classifications was invalid (and it confirms also that the legal starting point of the parity debate, combining gender considerations with universalism was doomed to fail). By specifying that this statement "is held in the present state of law,"[48] the Constitutional Council indicated that it did not intend to express a political opposition based on political principles but, rather, was relying on a procedural requirement, namely the amendment of the Constitution before enforcement of any quotas, even equal quotas as in parity.

The required constitutional amendment was adopted on 28 June 1999. It was a minor reform adopted by the two assemblies.[49] One of the possibilities was to embed parity in the constitutional text; the debate in such case would have focused on whether this requirement was to be limited in time in accordance with the affirmative action philosophy. But the text finally submitted to Congress simply removed the constitutional barrier, adding to Article 3 of the Constitution a provision whereby "statutes shall promote the equal access by women and men to elective offices and positions" and to the end of Article 4 a provision whereby "Political parties shall contribute to the implementation of the principle [of parity] as provided by statute."[50]

---

[46] Text voted by the Parliament and invalidated by the Constitutional Council.

[47] Cons. constitutionnel, J.O., 20 January 1999, p. 1028, 98–407 DC.

[48] C.c., 20 January 1999, ibid.

[49] The constitutional amendment process, as found in *constitution of 1958, supra* note 11, s.89, is as follows:

The President of the Republic, on a proposal by the Prime Minister, and Members of Parliament alike shall have the right to initiate an amendment of the *Constitution*. A constitutional amendment put forward by the government or by a member of parliament shall be passed by the two assemblies in identical terms. The amendment shall have effect after approval by referendum. However, a government bill to amend the *Constitution* shall not be submitted to referendum where the President of the Republic decides to submit it to Parliament convened in Congress; the government bill to amend the *Constitution* shall then be approved only if it is adopted by a three-fifths majority of the votes cast. The Bureau of the Congress shall be that of the National Assembly.

This reform was a president's bill, and the approval was submitted to Congress. The process was long enough, because of the lengthy resistance of the Senate.

[50] *Constitution of 1958, supra* note 11, art. 3, 4.

So, on the one hand, the legislature now had the power to make laws about parity, as a constitutional basis had been established for that power; on the other hand, these provisions restricted the amendment to the parity principle, without dealing with or reconsidering the practical repercussions that the principle entailed, such as what form ballots would take.

Indeed, and by definition, parity can only be realized in list systems for the following reason. As long as parity deals with the candidacies, and not directly with the elected organs, it can only apply to elections in which there are more than two candidates to be elected, at the same time, in the same district, and by the same voters. In other words, voters have to choose a list, and not single candidates, although this does not assume that parity is only possible within a proportional system. Thus, the concrete and practical question that the legislative power has to solve is not only how to impose parity when there are list-system ballots but also whether to extend the list-systems and how to imagine new systems inspired by the idea of parity for the numerous other elections that do not use the list-system (mainly for the legislative election for the National Assembly, which is an election on majority basis with single candidates).[51]

The 6 June 2000 Act dealing with "equal access by women and men to elective offices and positions" applied to all political elections with four exceptions. The Presidential election is excepted because that function is exercised by a single person. Elections for departmental councils are excepted because they are elections on a majority basis for a single member in each district. Elections to the Senate are excepted when they are elections on a majority basis.[52] And elections for town councils in small towns (less than thirty-five hundred inhabitants) are excepted because prior candidacy is not required and because the voters are not obliged to vote for the proposed lists (they can add a candidate, change the order, refuse a candidate, or mix candidates from different lists; this is called "*panachage*").

Thus, the statute applies to elections for town councils in towns with more than thirty-five hundred inhabitants (around twenty-six hundred towns – out of more than thirty-six thousand – which encompasses the great majority of the population), elections to regional councils, elections to Corsican Assembly, elections to the Senate when they are organized on the basis of proportional representation, and elections to the European Assembly. For all of those elections, each list must draw 50 percent of its candidates from each sex, more or less one unit. To avoid the bypassing of the parity requirement (mainly due to the risk that women might be systematically relegated to the

---

[51] The Vth republic system (except in 1986) imposed a majority-based ballot, similar to the Anglo-American system, but with two rounds.

[52] Ballot systems vary according to the size of the department, which is the district for the election to the Senate; for small departments (electing less than three senators), the election is organized on a majority basis.

end of lists, in position of non-eligibility), this requirement is checked on the one hand for the list taken as a whole, and on the other hand for each section of six candidates. For elections to the Senate and to the European Assembly, systematic alternation from the beginning to the end of the list in accordance with sex is required. Any list that does not respect these requirements would be deemed illegitimate and would not be presented to voters.

Although the ballot system for the National Assembly elections did not change, it was nevertheless felt that it was not possible or desirable to leave this organ unaffected by parity. Accordingly, political parties are invited to ensure the parity of candidacies. The requirement would be satisfied for each political party, if for each election they nominated 50 percent female candidates and 50 percent male candidates (allowing for 2 percent in either direction). Political parties that fail to act in this way can be punished by withholding state financial aid. Because this requirement does not address the results of balloting, there is the concern that female candidacies may be relegated by political parties to districts that are considered as lost in advance or difficult to win.

This parity law was referred to the Constitutional Council. The parliamentary opposition questioned it, arguing as follows. First, the constitutional amendment did not oblige the legislative power to guarantee parity; it only invited Parliament to "promote the equal access of women and men to elective offices and positions."[53] Constraining provisions would not be allowed, only incentives promoting the participation of women that would not limit voters' liberty of choice, as for instance the kind of rules adopted for the election to the National Assembly. It was alleged that the new measures should remain consistent with the principle of universalism, that the statute should only be a goal to be reached. Moreover, the new statute did not respect candidates' freedom to stand for election because it did not allow some men to compete again in the future elections, as they would be required to relinquish their place in the candidacy lists to women.

The Constitutional Council did not uphold the challenge. It asserted that the constituent power introduced, as it was empowered to do, new provisions that derogated from some constitutional rules or principles (i.e., principle of universalism); that the constituent power intended to allow legislators to institute any mechanism aiming to give effect to the equal access by women and men to elective offices and positions; that, to this end, it was now possible for legislators to pass provisions which could either encourage or compel equality; it was the responsibility of legislators to reconcile the new constitutional provisions with the other constitutional rules and principles from which the constituent power did not empower the legislators to derogate.[54]

---

[53] New Article 4 of the French Constitution, after the parity reform.
[54] Cons. constitutionnel, 30 May 2000, J.O., 7 June 2000, p. 8564, 2000–429 DC.

The Constitutional Council also held that in this case, the impugned provisions in the referred statute, mandating candidates of each sex in the lists of candidates for elections taking place on a proportional representation basis, were within the scope of measures allowed by the third article of the Constitution; and that such measures did not ignore any constitutional principles from which the constitutional amendment did not intend legislators to depart.[55]

It is too soon to appreciate the real impact of the new statute. From the point of view of parity supporters, it is obvious that the new provisions do not go as far as was claimed. Moreover, it must be noted that the real power centers in a modern democracy remain free from the requirement of parity (this is true for the majority of executive functions, on national or local levels) or are incompletely and imperfectly ruled by the parity requirement (i.e., elections for parliamentary chambers).

The first elections to be conducted under the new provisions were the elections for town councils in March 2001. Opinion polls confirmed the attachment of the population to the principle of parity and the new requirements forced the political parties to considerably renew their methods for selecting candidates. One of the problems that was often invoked, besides the obligation to leave out a number of male candidates (outgoing or beforehand candidates), was the difficulty to find and to form, in a short period of time, a sufficient number of female candidacies acceptable to the political parties. In other words, leaving aside the inevitable flaws of the system (for example, it is possible for a male candidate, once he is removed, to try and reserve his candidacy for his wife or daughter), the new system entails a renewal of the political class. Of course, some people express fears about the candidates' qualifications, not so much on the level of questioning women's position in politics, but on the more subtle level of selecting female candidates who lack experience or who are not experts in politics. These concerns, however, remain in the minority. They ignore the purpose of parity which is precisely to include women in the political sphere. To require women who have been excluded from political life to master it just as men have is inconsistent with the aim of parity itself. Needless to say, any change entails a period of adaptation. In some cases, there are clear risks. But risks are the price of the reform, and it is reasonable to conclude that they are not too high a price to pay, in comparison with the goals sought.

The results of the March 2001 elections confirmed that point. In the towns where the new law was in force, the town councils are now comprised of 47.5 percent women (compared to the previous 20 percent). Nevertheless, a great majority of the mayors (elected by the council) are men; women lead the executive in only 6.9 percent of the 181 towns affected by the parity

---

[55] C.c., 30 May 2000, ibid.

requirement. Interestingly, it seems that the political parties avoided, as far as they could, direct confrontations between men and women. Often, when a woman was heading a list (and thus implicitly destined for the mayor's office), the other main parties supported a woman on their own.[56] It is also interesting to compare the gender profiles of councilors. The main differences, which were expected, remain age and lack of political experience (because of the greater difficulty for working women to find time and freedom to participate in politics while they work and are much more involved in domestic and family life than men[57]), as well as lack of political affiliation (the necessity for political parties to find female candidates meant they had to look mainly outside of their affiliated members, which traditionally have been men).

The elections for department councils, for which there was no parity requirement, were held on the same day. The candidates were only 20.1 percent female, and only 9.8 percent of the elected councilors are women. Insofar as the claim for parity is for a greater presence of women in political spheres, it is obvious that it was necessary to adopt this reform (and that it should be extended to all the elections), and that the new reform is efficient. The elections held in March 2004 confirmed that.

In the elections for Senate in September 2001, political parties were obliged to respect the parity requirement, confirming this efficiency. Although some parties chose to present two lists instead of one in order to elect the two men who were their leaders, nevertheless twenty new women became senators. These elections involved one third of the seats; now 10 percent are held by women where previously women had only 5 percent. Thus, nine years after the introduction of the parity requirement, women should occupy around 50 percent of the Senate seats.[58]

However, the results of the elections for the National Assembly were more questionable. These elections did not impose a priori controls on candidacies. Rather, parties that refused to adhere to the parity requirement for their candidates merely faced financial sanctions, an option that appeared to appeal many, particularly the major parties. In June 2002, the first elections held under the new parity requirement (and the most recent) resulted in the election of 507 men and only 77 women. Thus, the National Assembly is far from achieving the goal of parity.

Moreover, it is hard to predict the future of the parity requirements. There are some proposals for reducing their impact in elections to the European Parliament and the Senate.

---

[56] For that reason, women, as mayors, are not limited to the smaller towns, and there are in fact more female mayors in the bigger towns than in smaller ones.

[57] All the studies show that there is no parity at all in that sphere.

[58] A recent reform (July 2003) changed the turnover of seats from one third to one half, but did not change the gender parity rules.

Parity: Representativeness within, or Contrary to, the Principle of Universalism?

The question of reconciling the principle of universalism with parity remains open. It is clear that the Constitutional Council regarded parity as a departure from universalism. In principle, though, parity is not necessarily incompatible with universalism even though in the political debate, parity has been interpreted as potentially nonuniversalistic. I want to suggest that we can interpret parity within the frame of universalism. To do that, we should keep in mind that in the universalistism paradigm, national sovereignty, under the Vth Republic, belongs to the people. Beyond this rhetorical argument (to which I will return), such words do not have any other legal meaning than the one that exists in the process of determining the electorate. The French theory of representation (theory of the organ) does not cast the issue in terms of representativeness. As long as what is to be represented is the nation, a fiction: after all there is no logical requirement for the decision making organ to be representative (even if, of course, in a democracy, there is the idea that this organ draws its legitimacy from the people).

Thus, the electorate does not have to reproduce the national society, but shall be constituted to permit the expression of the national will that is most consonant with the common good, according to the prevailing social conceptions. For a long time, this analysis justified laws excluding women from the political sphere. Consequently, if it is now judged socially consonant with the common good, there is no reason why the organs entrusted with the task of expressing the national will should not be constituted in a paritarian way (that is, by providing systems of designation which require a proportionate representation of men and women within these organs). It is true that in a democracy, the common good requires that the electorate shall be formed by the greatest number of people (universal suffrage), and that each of its members shall be entitled to an equal right of suffrage. The common good requires also the freedom of candidacy with the aim that everyone may have access to elective positions, and to the end that the voter might have an effective choice. But parity fulfils all of these requirements. This is particularly true because parity does not deal at all with the eligibility conditions, which can only be applied to each single candidate, but concerns only the composition of the candidates' lists (without adding new qualifications for the candidates of the list, or limiting the amount of lists themselves).

In that sense, embracing parity is part of the renewal of the logic of political life. It is promoting a new way of dealing with political questions. It amounts to breaking the masculinist logic in politics for the benefit of common good. And it is only in that sense that affirmative action can be reconciled with a universalistic framework. Thus, affirmative action is in the general interest, not only because it is in the interest of those who profit from it, but also because it is the political majority's choice (common good) and not a mere question of justice (that it could also be a question of justice, no one doubts). From the point of view of the strict consistency of the theory of national sovereignty, and more generally republican universalism, parity is absolutely admissible. But to this end, it must be admitted that it is not a question of representativeness, and that democracy within the national sovereignty frame is thought of in other terms than those of mere representativeness.

Now, the constitutional texts on this issue necessarily have a rhetorical force, beyond their purely legal qualifications. Saying that national sovereignty belongs to the people has obviously no legal meaning to the extent that the definition of the legal conditions under which someone is a member of the electorate are not specified. But politically, such texts have consequences. In a democracy, the national sovereign cannot politically cut itself off from a logic of representativeness. And here, indeed, parity departs from the logic of universalism. Let me explain. Whereas in the feminist debate people have debated the reasons underlying the parity model, this has not been the focus of the political debate. Rather, it has been assumed that the presence of women in politics is fair and legitimate, thus making representativeness an implicit criterion of justice.The legislators invoked parity to deal only with the presence of men and women within political organs, without tackling more global questions of the political process. By doing so, the legislators limited parity to the organization of a double presence, that is the presence at the same time of men and women equally, without dealing with the practical consequences that such a presence would be likely to generate. This limitation is intensified by the fact that the provisions introduced in the legal order are without time limits. The objective looks to be permanent, no longer a temporary correction but a principle. Thus, parity reasoning, from the perspective of the amendment, does not question the way politics is done, neither is it simply a mode of affirmative action. Rather, it has become a question of political justice: representing the parity of humankind.

There is also the question of whether the demand for representativeness should be limited to gender. This question can no longer be avoided if the reason for parity is not founded on a notion of the common good. If parity is put forward as an answer to the claim (based on justice) that sociological realities must be represented within the political organs in proportion to their presence within society, why should that representativeness be restricted to gender lines? What arguments allow parity to deal exclusively with the fundamental duality of mankind, and to ignore other criteria and claims such as those based on ethnicity, religion, and language?

PART 3: FRENCH UNIVERSALISM IN THE FACE
OF INTERNATIONAL LAW

Could international law restore a balance within French universalism, or even force France to renounce universalism and take a new way toward substantive equality and the affirmation of specific women's rights? The first temptation is to give a negative answer, at least considering the principles themselves. This forces us to move away from parity to focus more generally on other issues pertaining to the constitutional position of women.

The main legal reason for our hesitation is that the French constitutional conception of the relations between national law and international law is dualistic. International law does not have binding legal force unless it has achieved acceptance and integration into the national legal order. At the end of such a procedure, international norms are given a superior value to those of domestic statutes. Nevertheless, this value is not a constitutional value, nor a supra-constitutional value. A reviewing procedure exists for solving possible inconsistencies between international treaties and the constitution; but this procedure is optional. According to Article 54:

If the Constitutional Council, on a reference from the President of the Republic, from the Prime Minister, from the President of one or the other Assembly, or from sixty deputies or sixty senators, has declared that an international commitment contains a clause contrary to the Constitution, authorization to ratify or approve the international commitment in question may be given only after amendment of the Constitution.[59]

By contrast, the Constitutional Council refuses, when reviewing the constitutionality of statutes, to invalidate statutes based on their incompatibility with international law and (mainly) with international commitments. In particular, when the Constitutional Council had to rule on a statute allowing abortion under certain conditions,[60] the Council refused to declare that a statute could be judged contrary to the right to life as protected by the ECHR.[61] The Constitutional Council did not analyze whether, materially, there was an inconsistency between the right to abortion and the right to life; it merely refused to exercise control on the ground that the right to life was not protected by a national norm, but by an international norm, stating that a statute which could materially contradict an international commitment would not necessarily be contrary to the Constitution.[62] The argument

---

[59] *Constitution of 1958*, *supra* note 11, art. 54

[60] Cons. constitutionnel, 15 January 1975, J.O. 16 January 1975, p. 671, 74-54 DC.

[61] *European Convention on Human Rights*, 4 November 1950, art. 2: "Everyone's right to life shall be protected by law. No one shall be deprived of his life intentionally save in the execution of a sentence of a court following his conviction of a crime for which this penalty is provided by law."

[62] It must be said that the debate was not, legally or *constitutionally*, a debate expressed in terms such as "women's rights versus the rights of the fetus." The reasons are clearly that, on the one hand, no *constitutional* texts or national declaration of rights recognize any specific rights for women (recall that under universalism, it is the task of the legislator to provide those women's rights, and the question was whether it was possible to recognize them consistently with the European Convention); on the other hand, there are debates to decide if the fetus could be considered as a legal person at all (i.e., if it could have rights).

used by the Constitutional Council arises from the fact that Article 55 of the Constitution gives legal validity to a treaty within the French legal order only if the treaty is effectively put into operation by the other committed States (this is the condition of reciprocity). According to the Constitutional Council, such a condition could vary with circumstances, and must be factually examined in each specific case, taking the real context of the case into account. As the power of the Constitutional Council is limited to a priori statements (reviewing statutes before their enforcement), the judges considered that they were not in position to exercise their jurisdiction. It is because of this doctrine that when parity was discussed, the incorporation of the Convention on the Elimination of All Forms of Discrimination against Women (CEDAW, ratified in 1983) was not called upon to reinforce the law of parity.[63]

This reasoning is questionable. On the one hand, as the question concerns human rights and multilateral agreements, it seems difficult to require strict reciprocity.[64] How could it be possible, according to the philosophy of this Convention, to let one state use another state's human rights violations as a justification for its own violations? On the other hand, this Convention is closely linked to the European construction because, even if the ECHR is not adopted within the European union, it is considered by the members of the Union and by organs of the Union (such as the Luxembourg Court), as an element of the Union's law, carrying the idea of a constitutional declaration of rights. Because of this link, one can say that the Convention comes directly into force within the State members' legal order.

Nevertheless, the Constitutional Council's statement consequently vested the ordinary courts with the power to enforce international law within the French system (when ruling on ordinary cases). From this point of view, it should be noted that the courts do not have a unified doctrine when acting in this way. In principle, they are willing to examine whether there is an inconsistency between international law and the relevant texts or acts. But they do not necessarily accept that these international norms are applicable. In particular, the Conseil d'Etat considers that courts must decide in each case whether the relevant international agreements have created rights, or if they merely intend to provide directives for the committed state.

This is not true, of course, for European law (including the ECHR). The direct enforcement doctrine is adopted by all the ordinary courts, and here, international law prevails over contrary national provisions. Notably, when drawing conclusions from the relevant Constitutional Council doctrine, the Conseil d'Etat has examined the consistency between the right to abortion as protected by French statute and the European right to life. The Conseil

---

[63] 18 December 1979, 1249 U.N.T.S. 20378, recognizing the usefulness of affirmative action in achieving the goal of creating a better place for women in political life.

[64] If reciprocity was a qualification for a democratic state to be bound by a human rights agreement, it would mean that it could not benefit citizens of states that fail to respect human rights.

stated that there was no inconsistency because the right to abortion was conditioned and limited by the French statute (because of its time limits). Abortion is possible during the first ten weeks of pregnancy; this was recently extended to twelve weeks. The statute also requires a preliminary process to inform the woman and to question her intention. An abortion must be carried out by a physician in an hospital, and it must be justified by the woman's state of distress.[65]

Even if there is a connection between European law and French law when ordinary French courts state a case, does this mean that the French universalism will be relinquished? Again, the answer could be negative and the second reason could be found in the philosophy of the ECHR. This philosophy, in its current interpretation, is very close to the universalistic one. The Convention, as interpreted by the European Court, protects the traditional values of freedom and formal equality. The European Court of Human Rights is suspicious about affirmative action measures.

By contrast, the law of the European Union is full of even more contradictions, and as a consequence it has occasionally forced France to overcome some instances of legal discrimination against women. Although rare, such evolution did occur after France was condemned by the Luxembourg Court for discrimination.[66] It must be noted that what was at stake were formal inequalities unfavorable to women. For instance, one European Council Directive[67] obliged France to change some of its legal provisions (the so-called provisions for protecting woman and motherhood) that forbade women from working at night, and the French policy for access to civil service employment in France, which used gender as a determining condition for access to some positions, as mentioned earlier.

So the question now is to ascertain whether the European Union could legally influence France into a new interpretation of universalism, as yet to be established, which would allow some justified distinctions on the necessity "to promote equal opportunities for men and women."[68] With regard to this question, it must be said that this has not been done yet.[69] However,

---

[65] Conseil d'Etat, *Confédération nationale des associations familiales catholiques*, 21 December 1990. It should be noted that the French law does not deal with abortion as a right for women. Abortion in general is still a crime, except for therapeutic reasons. But within the first twelve weeks, claiming the state of distress, which can be claimed only by the mother and does not have to be justified, will be sufficient to procure an abortion.

[66] See *Commission* v. *France*, case no.312-86, 1988 O.J.L. page 03315. Some evolution, nevertheless, occurred without condemnation.

[67] *Council Directive 76/207 of 9 February 1976 on gender equality of access to employment, vocational training and promotion, and working conditions*, [1976] O.J.L. February 14 1976, p.0040.

[68] *Council Directive 76/207*, ibid., art. 2.

[69] It must be noted that this concerns ordinary international law as well as European law: French authorities have been very careful not to sign a treaty that would lead them to change the Constitution and relinquish the universalist principle (as stated earlier, a treaty must be consistent with the Constitution, or the Constitution has to be changed, art.54).

European law could lead France to a third stage in its conception of universalism, all the more so since the parity reform has seriously shaken the reference myth.

Suggested Readings

Paritary Rights, Ius Gentium, vol. 7, no. 1, Fall 2001, University of Baltimore.

Philippe Blacher, "Droit Constitutionnel et identité féminine" (1996) 49 *Revue administrative* 38.

Olivia Bui-Xuan, *Le droit public français entre universalisme et differentialisme* (Paris: Universite Paris II, 2003).

Gisèle Halimi, dir., *La parité dans la vie politique, Rapport de l'Observatoire de la parité entre les hommes et les femmes* (Paris: La documentation française, 1999).

Daniele Lochak, "Les hommes politiques, les sages (?)..., et les femmes" (1983) *Droit Social* 131.

Jaqueline Martin, dir., *La parité, enjeux et mise en œuvre* (Toulouse: Presses Universitaires du Mirail, 1998).

Eliane Vogel-Polsky, *La citoyenneté européenne et les femmes* (Louvain: Presses Universitaires de Louvain, 1994).

6

Gender in the German Constitution

Blanca Rodríguez Ruiz and Ute Sacksofsky

The German "Basic Law," as the Federal Constitution is called, dates from May 23, 1949. It was enacted in the western part of Germany, after Germany had lost World War II, and was strongly influenced by the experience of the Nazi Regime. The Basic Law, therefore, contains a strongly worded list of fundamental rights. Whereas the Basic Law was designed as a temporary constitution until Germany would be united again, unification did not occur in the manner expected. So, instead of designing an entirely new constitution, the Eastern Part adopted the Basic Law with the proviso that it should be amended in some respects (Article 5 of the Unification Treaty). This led to a Constitutional Amendment in 1994, which affected the Article dealing with gender equality (as will be explained later).

Sixteen states comprise the Federal Republic of Germany. Constitutions exist, therefore, on the state level as well as on the federal level. Not all state constitutions contain a fully-fledged fundamental rights catalogue. Many of those that do, however, include some form of gender equality clause.[1] In particular, the constitutions of the "neue Länder," the states reestablished on the territory of former East Germany, contain constitutional guarantees obliging the state to further real equality between men and women.[2] However, the state constitutions have not played an important role in this area so far. Although there are virtually no decisions of State Constitutional Courts pertaining to gender equality at this time, on the federal level a large body of jurisprudence has developed. The power of the Federal Constitutional Court (FCC) has been well established, and there is a full array of cases pertaining to the relationship between men and women.

---

[1] See, e.g., the Constitutions of Bavaria (Article 118.2); Bremen (Article 2.2); Hessen (Article 1); Rheinland-Pfalz (Article 17.3); Saarland (Article 12); Schleswig-Holstein (Article 6).

[2] See the Constitutions of Berlin (Article 6.2); Brandenburg (Article 12.3.2); Mecklenburg-Vorpommern (Article 13); Sachsen (Article 8); Sachsen-Anhalt (Article 34).

With the singular exception of abortion, the German FCC has dealt with gender issues from the lenses of Article 3 equality clauses. As originally drafted, these clauses read as follows:[3]

(1) All persons shall be equal before the law.
(2) Men and women shall have equal rights.
(3) No person shall be favored or disfavored because of his sex, parentage, race, language, homeland, and origin, faith or religious or political opinions.

The Amending Act of 27 October 1994 introduced the following second sentence in article 3.2:[4] "The State shall promote the actual implementation of equal rights for women and men and take steps to eliminate disadvantages that now exist."

In addition to Article 3, the provisions of article 6 dedicated to the protection of marriage, the family, parents, and illegitimate children need to be considered:

(1) Marriage and the family shall enjoy the specific protection of the State.
(2) The care and upbringing of children is the natural right of parents and a duty primarily incumbent upon them. The State shall watch over them in the performance of this duty.
(3) ...
(4) Every mother shall be entitled to the protection and care of the community.
(5) Children born outside of marriage shall be provided by legislation with the same opportunities for physical and moral development and for their position in society as are enjoyed by those born within marriage.

This is the constitutional framework within which gender issues are decided in Germany. We must now examine how it has been applied. We shall concentrate on the FCC's current perception of Article 3's equality clauses, preceded by an overview of the evolution of this perception over the time.[5] Affirmative action will be considered in the light of the most recent developments in the case law of the FCC on Article 3, as validated by Article 3.2.2. Next we will examine the relationship between Article 3 and the provisions

---

[3] *The Basic Law for the Federal Republic of Germany* (23 May 1949), trans. Christian Tomuschat and David P. Curry (Druck Verlag Kettler GmbH, Bönen/Westfalen, 1998) (hereinafter *Basic Law*). This translation will be followed throughout the text.

[4] It also introduced a second sentence in Paragraph 3, whereby "No person shall be disfavored because of disability."

[5] On this evolution, see Ute Sacksofsky, *Das Grundrecht auf Gleichberechtigung* (Baden-Baden: 2 Erweiterte Auflage, Nomos Verlagsgesellschaft, Baden-Baden, 1996), on which much of this chapter is based.

of Article 6 from the perspective of the impact of gender equality on the protection of family. Finally, we will look at the issue of abortion.

ARTICLE 3 AND THE RIGHT TO EQUALITY

From the earliest constitutional case law until the early 1990s, the FCC referred indifferently to Article 3.2, Article 3.3, or both, when dealing with sexual discrimination. It seemed to be assuming that insofar as the sexes are concerned, the recognition of their equality of rights and the ban on sexual discrimination were synonymous, that neither provision had anything to add to the other. Paragraphs 2 and 3 were regarded as specifications of the equality clause of Paragraph 1.[6] The effect of this specification was to subject public power to more stringent conditions for different treatment in the context of Paragraphs 2 and 3, than in the context of Paragraph 1.

With respect to the general equal protection clause, and according to the earlier decisions of the FCC, the Basic Law forbids arbitrary differentiation among individuals. It demands, in brief, that equals be treated equally and nonequals be treated according to their differences.[7] As a result, Article 3.1 was read[8] as imposing very few limits on the State's scope of action.

Articles 3.2 and 3.3 were thought to specify the general clause of Paragraph 1 by classifying certain grounds for different treatment as arbitrary and therefore discriminatory. This interpretation of Article 3 prevailed for four decades; however, the Court made one substantial exception from the general rule that different treatment on account of sex was constitutionally forbidden. Different treatment on account of sex could be justified if it was based on "objective biological or functional" differences between the sexes.[9] This seems somewhat of a paradox. What, if not "objective biological or functional differences" should constitute gender differences? Equality of rights and the ban on discrimination between the sexes were read, in other words, as demands that each sex be treated according to its own specific features. The Court's approach to sex discrimination thus seemed closer to its own understanding of Article 3.1 than it seemed to realize.

Although this rhetoric prevailed until the early 1990s, its zenith was during the 1950s and 1960s. Sexual *equality* was then interpreted as the respect due to the "objective biological or functional" sexual *differences*. These, to

---

[6] *BVerfGE* 3, 225 (18 December 1953). As is customary in Germany, we will refer to the official collection of Decisions of the German FCC (*Entscheidungen des Bundesverfassungsgerichts*, hereinafter *BVerfGE*) edited by this Court, indicating the volume and page where a decision can be found. For the sake of clarity, the first reference to a decision will specify the date when it was issued.

[7] *BVerfGE* 3, 58, at 135 (17 December 1953).

[8] Since 1980, the doctrine pertaining to Article 3.1 has changed. The Court now uses a sliding scale depending on what interests are at stake. In some sense it now also uses proportionality.

[9] *BVerfGE* 3, 225, *supra* note 6.

be sure, were not differences in worth. All individuals were regarded as equal in worth and thus so were men and women. Particularly strong emphasis was laid upon the equal worth of men and women's roles within the family, of the roles of fathers and mothers, of the breadwinner's and the house-wife's work. Here, equal worth (*Gleichwertigkeit*) translated into equal rank (*Gleichordnung*). The legal provision granting the father the last word where parents could not reach an agreement on decisions concerning their chil-dren's welfare was declared unconstitutional on these grounds.[10] Yet equal worth was not thought to undermine but, rather, to underlie the natural and social differences between the sexes.

The Court first resorted to men and women's biological differences to jus-tify the criminalization of male but not of female homosexuality. Biology was seen as the basis of women's (natural) tendency to be accepting and giving, and of men's (natural) aggressiveness and inclination to demand. Only the latter tendencies were thought to deserve criminal punishment.[11] Moreover, the "natural" differences between the sexes were interpreted in terms wide enough to embrace the social construction of gender. Thus, the Court stressed the division of labor between women as mothers and housekeepers and men as breadwinners. This "functional difference" between the sexes conditioned by the "nature" of their relation, justified on constitutional grounds why a man could be legally obliged financially to support his children if they were born out of wedlock, while these children would in turn be raised by their mother.[12] Similarly justified was the legal rule that granted a widower's pen-sion only if the deceased wife had been the main breadwinner, whereas a widow's pension would be granted regardless of similar considerations.[13]

Biological or functional differences were systematically invoked in the early cases, even when they were not considered relevant enough to justify a different treatment between men and women. Interestingly, the rhetoric of "equal worth but different natures and functions" was only employed in women's favor and, although invoked, it was not followed where it could disadvantage women. The Court's aim was to acknowledge what it regarded as women's differences, but to avoid turning those differences into impair-ment. Appeals to the equal worth of both sexes clearly served this purpose. Indicative of the spirit of the times is the fact that men's claims to equality on the basis of Article 3.2 were systematically turned down.

This spirit changed in the 1970s. Until now, the recognition of equal rights for both sexes depended on their biological or social differences. This came at the expense of formal equality. The 1970s reversed this approach. The point of reference for dealing with sexual equality now became the

[10] *BVerfGE* 10, 59 (29 July 1959).
[11] *BVerfGE* 6, 389 (10 May 1957).
[12] *BVerfGE* 11, 277 (21 July 1960).
[13] *BVerfGE* 17, 1 (24 July 1963).

prohibition of discrimination contained in Article 3.3. The rhetoric of different treatment but equal value was progressively abandoned, and although the Court continued to appeal to the respect due to biological and functional differences between the sexes, it now pursued formal equality. To this end, relevant biological and functional differences were narrowly defined. They were acknowledged to exist, but hardly ever considered to be of legal consequence, mostly because the Court explicitly rejected the social construction of gender. With a few qualified exceptions, different treatment between the sexes was systematically condemned as discriminatory.

Equality was recognized, above all, between husband and wife. In a marriage between a German and a foreigner, it was discriminatory to grant the children German citizenship only if the father was German.[14] Also declared discriminatory were Sections 1355 and 1616 of the Civil Code,[15] which required all family members to take the husband's family name. To keep their birth name, wives had to add it to their husband's, thus forming a double name. Such unequal treatment was unconstitutional.[16] Because formal equality works both ways, however, the equal protection guarantee also worked in favor of men. Thus, the provision that granted women working outside the house one paid "housework" holiday a month but denied the same advantage to single men was declared unconstitutional.[17] By contrast, but in the same spirit, the Court denied that the refusal to make the cost of childcare a tax deduction discriminated against women who carried out paid work. The Court reasoned that where both spouses shared the role of the breadwinner they presumably also shared childcare and housework. The Court thus saw no discrimination against working women.[18]

Nevertheless, there were some exceptions to this trend. Thus, for example, the Court upheld for the second time the legal rule making a widower's pension, but not a widow's, dependent on whether the deceased spouse had mostly supported the family. The Court reasoned that the rule merely mirrored a division of roles between the sexes that was predominant at the time it had been enacted. Nevertheless, the Court acknowledged an evolution in social mores tending to undermine that division of roles, and declared it to be the future task of lawmakers to translate such an evolution into law.[19]

Similarly in the context of foreign pensions, the Court upheld the law giving women's income a lower average value than men's. The law regulated the fate of people in the Federal Republic of Germany, many of whom were eastern immigrants, who held pension policies against foreign insurers, or

---

[14] *BVerfGE* 37, 217 (21 March 1974).
[15] *Bürgerliches Gesetzbuch*, 1957 version (hereinafter *BGB*).
[16] *BVerfGE* 48, 327 (31 May 1978).
[17] *BVerfGE* 52, 369 (13 November 1979).
[18] *BVerfGE* 47, 1 (11 October 1977).
[19] *BVerfGE* 39, 169 (12 March 1975).

insurers that had disappeared with the war. In randomizing women's income below men's, the Court argued that this law was simply reflecting the most common situation, assuming it was the standard case. The law was ultimately excused for not undertaking a richer and more precise categorization of the individual circumstances of policyholders, on the grounds that it was an exceptional measure aimed at solving an exceptional postwar problem.[20]

The 1980s changed the interpretation of Article 3, moving away from formal equality and toward the acknowledgment of sexual differences that has survived to the present day. This new shift in emphasis meant the Court again embraced different treatment between the sexes provided this would help to overcome past discrimination against women. Of course, equal treatment continued to be imposed where statutes explicitly favored men.[21] Nevertheless, characteristic of this phase is not so much the perpetuation of equal treatment as the defense of difference where it appears to favor women. This should not be read as a resurgence of the view of existing differences as "natural," as was typically the case in the 1950s and 1960s. For now, unlike previously, the Court looks not to the past but to the future, and justifies different treatment as a means toward prospective substantive equality.

Accordingly, the law giving women's income a lower average value than men's for the purpose of determining the amount of retirement pensions was deemed unconstitutional, even though this law admittedly mirrored reality. The Court held that the Basic Law makes it the lawmaker's duty not to confirm but to correct women's past de facto disadvantages. Turning its previous ruling on the matter on its head, the Court now argues that giving women's and men's income an equal average value, and thereby bringing women's income up to men's level for retirement purposes, would serve this purpose.[22]

The 1990s, on the basis of a double and complementary strategy, confirmed and intensified this approach of the 1980s. First of all, the FCC finally discarded the rhetoric of "biological and functional differences," which it had continued to use during the 1980s as a formal litany. In order to justify different treatment between the sexes, the Court adopted two new criteria. Article 3.3 allows for different treatment between the sexes if this appears necessary to solve problems that by their own nature can only arise in the context of women or of men.[23] Also, different treatment can also be required by other constitutional provisions. One such provision is the recognition of equal rights between the sexes of Article 3.2.[24] This implies, and

---

[20] *BVerfGE* 43, 213 (26 January 1977).
[21] For example: *BVerfGE* 78, 38 (8 March 1988), concerning the family name; *BVerfGE* 84, 9 (5 March 1991) and *BVerfGE* 92, 91 (24 January 1995), concerning conflict of laws.
[22] *BVerfGE* 57, 335 (16 June 1981).
[23] *BVerfGE* 85, 191 (28 January 1992), where the law forbidding women's night work was declared unconstitutional.
[24] *BVerfGE* 92, 91, *supra* note 21.

here is the second strategy referred to earlier, that the Court starts to treat Articles 3.2 and 3.3 as separate norms. Whereas the latter recognizes a prohibition of discrimination on several specified grounds, including sex, the former pursues the actual equality of rights between the sexes. Article 3.3 thus remains a specification of the general clause of Article 3.1 in that it lists some grounds for different treatment, including sex, that are considered particularly suspect. In this context, different treatment is subject to qualified scrutiny by courts, although it is not ruled out where it mirrors differences intrinsic in the elements of the comparison (e.g., the protection of pregnant and breast-feeding women at work). Article 3.2 adds something new. It adds an exception to the ban of different treatment of Articles 3.1 and 3.3, notably by allowing for a favorable treatment of women where this aims at compensating for past disadvantages.

This new reading of Article 3.2 amounts to a turning point in the understanding of gender equality. With it, the provision ceases to contemplate the relation between the sexes through the lenses of equal treatment viz. discrimination. This is the task of Article 3.3. Article 3.2 now looks at the sexes through the lenses of equal rights viz. domination. It approves of unequal treatment where this tends to bring about the equality of rights between women and men, notably when it helps to overcome men's traditional domination over women. Moreover, this new reading of Article 3.2 introduces a group approach to the relation between the sexes as a complement, one should say as a correction, to Article 3.3's approach, which focuses on the individual. For Article 3.3 forbids every instance of different treatment unless this is justified by actual differences in a particular case, whereas Article 3.2 allows for and even requires different treatment where it helps to do away with men's domination over women as a group. It legitimizes, in other words, women's positive discrimination on constitutional grounds.

It is in this new spirit that the FCC now approaches measures that on their face appear protective of women. It tries to figure out their indirect as well as their direct effects, and whether these effects confirm rather than overcome women's traditional subordination.

Let us look at some telling examples. The first one concerns a provision that prohibited women's night work. Although this provision allegedly had women's welfare at heart, the Court found the *prohibition* of women's night work paternalistic and condemned it for perpetuating an image of women both as mothers and as indefensible creatures, an image that serves women's subordination.[25]

In another case, a woman was not short-listed for a job as a mechanic, for which she had applied and possessed the required qualifications. As a

---

[25] *BVerfGE* 85, 191, *supra* note 23. This decision had very few practical consequences, because on 25 July 1991 the European Court of Justice had held a similar French employment law incompatible with Article 5. *Stoeckel*, C-345/89, Directive 76/207/EEC.

reason, her prospective boss told her in writing that this was not a job for a woman. In the ensuing case before the labor courts the employer argued that the woman's qualifications were not as good as those of the short-listed (male) candidates. The reason given to the woman by him and his assistant had only been meant to spare her feelings. The woman lost in the labor courts but won before the FCC.[26] To reach this decision the Court argued that the statutory provision in question (Section 611a BGB) was meant to fulfill the positive duty of the State to further real equality between men and women according to Article 3.2. According to the Court, a constitutional provision is violated if a statutory law that has been enacted to fulfill constitutional obligations is misconstrued in a way that grossly fails its aim.

A third example concerns a provision in force in the states of Baden-Württemberg and Bavaria that obliged men to pay a contribution to fire-fighting forces. The contribution was aimed at replacing men's physical duty to contribute to fire-fighting if necessary, a duty that exists in some German states yet has never been resorted to because of the existence of professional fire-fighting forces. Both this duty and its financial proxy were considered unconstitutional under Article 3.3. They were also unjustified under Article 3.2. For, although the measure might appear favorable to women, it rested on the traditional sexual stereotypes that portray men as protectors and women as needing protection, stereotypes that lie at the bottom of female subordination.[27]

AFFIRMATIVE ACTION

Factual substantive equality demands that the State take positive steps to remove the sources of subordination, including measures of affirmative action. In Germany, various affirmative action programmes are in effect. Since the 1980s, an increasing number of states have enacted statutes to further equality between the sexes in public service (*Gleichstellungsgesetze/ Frauenfördergesetze*).[28] One of the most important goals of these statutes has been to promote the number of women in higher positions. In 1994, the federal level followed with the *Bundesgleichstellungsgesetz*. Most of the statutes contain a variety of measures. Such measures include, for instance, the requirement to develop affirmative action plans and monitor their implementation, the institution of a new position whose occupant must take part in all decisions that could potentially influence the position of women (*Gleichstellungsbeauftragte*), and additional procedural steps to increase the

---

[26] *BVerfGE* 89, 276 (16 November 1993).
[27] *BVerfGE* 92, 91, *supra* note 21.
[28] See D. Schiek et al., *Frauengleichstellungsgesetze des Bundes und der Länder* (Köln: Bund-Verlag, 1996).

chances of hiring women.[29] Some of the statutes also try to further gender equality in private business. When bidding for public commissions, enterprises that fulfill certain requirements with regard to hiring and promoting women have a better chance to be awarded the contract.

Most of these statutes also foresee some form of quotas for women in the public sector. These quotas have given rise to heated debates concerning their constitutionality as a means of furthering gender equality.[30] Three types of quotas have been contemplated by law in order to promote women's access to the public sector, and are accordingly mostly discussed in legal literature. These are the so-called decision quotas, fixed quotas, and goal quotas.

Decision quotas require that where a male and a female candidate to a position are equally qualified, preference should be given to the woman in sectors where women are underrepresented. In most cases, such a quota is complemented by the proviso that the preference will hold unless the male candidate exhibits outweighing grounds to the contrary. Fixed quotas, by contrast, guarantee a certain number of positions to women. This type of quota has been enacted in practice only for training jobs (*Ausbildungsplätze*). Finally, goal quotas are based on an affirmative action plan for women that has been developed by the institution that is hiring. If an office doesn't fulfill the goals set forth in that plan, the employment or promotion of a man requires the permission of the superior authority. Goal quotas are less legally binding as an individual woman candidate cannot file suit to enforce an affirmative action plan.

Most common and most debated are the decision quotas. Aside from the equality clauses of Article 3 of the Federal Constitution, one other constitutional provision plays an important role in this discussion. Article 33.2 provides: "Every German shall be equally eligible for any public office according to his aptitude, qualifications, and professional achievements."

It has therefore been more or less agreed that the German Constitution forbids quotas that give preference to women who are not equally qualified with their competitors. Quotas that promote women "similarly" qualified would not stand a chance before the courts. All quotas in practice have therefore been phrased to require "equal qualification." In other words: only in cases in which – considering qualification – one also could use a lottery to determine who to hire, the decision quotas take effect. It is therefore not surprising that in practice they had little effect, if any.

Nevertheless, court proceedings before administrative courts and labor courts have been many. The results have varied. Some courts have held

---

[29] Provisions such as the requirement that when hiring at least the same number of women must be invited for personal interviews, or the requirement that an open position be advertised anew if no women applied; see, for instance, *Hessian Equal Rights Statute*, art. 8, 9.

[30] See for all Ute Sacksofsky, *Das Grundrecht auf Gleichberechtigung, supra* note 5, at 405ff (and the bibliography listed in footnote 117 therein).

decision quotas to be constitutional; some have held them to be unconstitutional.[31] The FCC has not yet ruled on this matter directly. Nevertheless, we have seen how the most recent case law is more open to the point of view of positive discrimination when dealing with gender equality. It thus seems likely that, were the Court to decide on the question at this point, it would uphold all three forms of quotas as they have been enacted in statutory law.

In the meantime, the European Court of Justice has decided four cases on various forms of quotas, three of them stemming from German Courts. The European Court of Justice had to rule on the conformity of quotas with European Law, in particular with the directive 76/207/EEC on the implementation of the principle of equal treatment between men and women as regards access to employment, vocational training and promotion, and working conditions. Article 2(4) of this directive provides for the possibility of recurring to "measures to promote equal opportunity for men and women, in particular by removing existing inequalities which affect women's opportunities in the areas referred to in article 1(1)." Let us briefly look at the relevant cases.

The first one, the *Kalanke* case,[32] concerned a provision of the State of Bremen according to which women had to be given priority over male candidates with equal qualifications in the event of promotion in a sector where women are underrepresented. The decision of the European Court of Justice held that a provision granting women absolute priority over men for employment or promotion is not covered by the purpose of equal opportunities embraced by the directive 76/207 EEC. The problem seemed to be that the law of the State of Bremen, unlike most similar German laws, did not leave the way open for exceptions in the face of a candidate's specific characteristics that could be relevant to the post.

The second case, the *Marshall* case,[33] concerned a provision of Nordrhein-Westfalen that was similar to the one at issue in the *Kalanke* case, yet included the saving clause that was missing in the law of Bremen. The clause accounted for "reasons specific to an individual [male] candidate [that may] tilt the balance in his favor." This time the Court upheld the Law and the decision taken on its basis. The equal treatment directive was not violated because the challenged Law did not prefer women to men absolutely and unconditionally. Whether the saving clause of the Law of Nordrhein-Westfalen had the significance that it was granted by the European Court of Justice is more than

---

[31] There has been a tendency in the administrative courts to find quotas to be in violation of the constitutional equal rights guarantee, whereas labor courts have tended to be more open to quotas. For an overview of the cases, see Laubinger, "Die 'Frauenquote' im öffentlichen Dienst" (1996) 87 *Verwaltungsarchiv* 305–27, 473–533.

[32] C-450-93 (17 October 1995).

[33] C-409/95 (11 November 1997).

doubtful. For what could those "reasons specific to a male candidate" be? Either they can be counted as qualifications, in which case the male candidate is simply better qualified than his female counterparts and should be preferred for the post, or else they are simply irrelevant. Indeed, if they are not *qualifications* strictly speaking, then they are most likely to belong to the "reasons" for employment and promotion of male candidates that positive discrimination and quotas are precisely trying to fight.

Thus, the saving clause either reiterates the establishment of a decision quota, merely stressing that qualifications really have to be equal *everything considered*, or it thwarts the purpose of positive discrimination at its core and its inclusion is self-defeating. But even under the former reading the clause is dubious because it epitomizes the bias implicit in the definition of relevant qualifications, and the likely danger that these qualifications be tailored to fit a man's background. Many of the state equality statutes have therefore tried to exclude bias from the evaluation of "qualification" by stating that more years of service do not necessarily lead to better qualification (a criterion often used) or that abilities acquired outside the job have to be recognised (if relevant). Be that as it may, most German provisions of decision quotas include such a saving clause that has saved, if nothing else, their conformity with European Law.

In the third case the European Court of Justice upheld goal quotas as well as fixed quotas for training jobs of the Hessian Statute.[34] It deemed that the goal quotas did not give absolute and unconditional preference to women, and therefore the case resembled the *Marshall* case rather than *Kalanke*. As far as the fixed quotas were concerned, the Court emphasized their limited scope, as they did not apply to real jobs but only to trainee positions.

In the fourth case the Court once again found a quota regime a violation of European Law.[35] In Sweden women were given preference for university hiring if they were (only) similarly qualified. This was deemed a violation of the employment directive. Also, the Court held that a member State is not allowed to set aside a certain number of positions only for women.

These four decisions of the European Court of Justice have taken some of the heat out of the debate about the constitutionality of quotas. First of all, even if all types of quotas were held to be constitutional by the FCC, the more restrictive EC limitations are binding for Germany. Second, considering the limited scope of quotas put into law in Germany in the first place, combined with the limitations imposed by the European Court of Justice upon those quotas, it seems that there is little at stake for the men who want to challenge them.

---

[34] *Badeck*, C-158/97 (28 March 2000).
[35] *Abrahamson et al.*, No. C-407/98 (7 July 2000).

EQUALITY, THE NUCLEAR FAMILY, AND THE ILLUSION OF NEUTRALITY

Marrying Equality and the Family

The protection that Article 6 grants marriage and the family (Paragraph 1), parents' care and upbringing of their children (Paragraph 2) and children born out of wedlock (Paragraph 5) has often complemented the equality clauses and has given them a specific content in the family context. In addition, Paragraph 4 makes the legal protection of mothers, including pregnant women, a constitutional obligation. Of particular importance is the protection of mothers in the labor context. Here labor laws, in particular the Law for the Protection of Mothers (*Mutterschutzgesetz*), have assumed this obligation to the extent that the FCC has received very few cases concerning the discrimination against mothers or pregnant women at work.[36]

Paragraphs 2, 4, and 5 of Article 6 appear to protect women's interests. By contrast, the right to gender equality appears to run against the protection that Article 6.1 grants marriage and the family, at least where the traditional housewife family model is concerned.

Nevertheless, the FCC has always tried to work out the compatibility between Articles 3 and 6.1. During the 1950s and 1960s, as the Court still embraced the traditional division of roles within the family, it worked out the congruity between Articles 3 and 6.1 by resorting to the rhetoric of the equal worth but biological and functional differences between the sexes. Where the division of roles could not be reconciled with equal worth, it could not justify any differential treatment. But during the 1950s and 1960s, recall, this was the case whenever women were seen at a disadvantage with respect to men, so that cases on gender discrimination were nearly always decided in women's favor.

Beyond this the Court has tried to avoid the direct confrontation of Article 6.1 and Articles 3.2 and/or 3.3. It has been prone to citing both provisions together when they appeared to point in the same direction and could be relied upon to reach the same result. Where their content seemed to conflict, by contrast, the Court theoretically allowed for family unity to restrict women's right to equality. Yet, it then invariably submitted that, upon close scrutiny, Article 6.1 was not at stake in the specific instance under examination, or else denied that in that instance gender equality needed to be restricted on family grounds.

---

[36] The FCC has corrected some deficiencies of the Law for the Protection of Mothers (see e.g., *BVerfGE* 52, 357 [13 November 1979]). More recently, a series of decisions have dealt with the reorganization of the civil service in former Eastern Germany after reunification and the regulation of layoffs. The Court declared that the reorganization was unconstitutional in that it did not provide special rules for pregnant women (see, for all, *BVerfGE* 84, 133 [24 April 1991] at 155ff).

Thus, in the context of fathers' last word on children's welfare, the Court reversed the question and argued that whenever parents disagree to the extent of making a reconciled solution impracticable, family unity was already de facto disrupted. Placing last decisions in the hands of a court dealing with matters related to guardianship instead of in one parent's hands would add nothing to the broken unity. Moreover, the Court reinforced mothers' right to equality with considerations on children's welfare under Article 6.2. In a tone characteristic of its early cases, the Court argued that "as experience shows" fathers are likely to neglect children's welfare as a side effect of marital instability, whereas implicitly presuming a community of interests between mother and children.

Similarly, the Court acknowledged family unity as a possible limit to gender equality when dealing with the regulation of the family name but immediately denied that this was an issue in the cases under consideration. The question whether or not family unity under Article 6.1 demands one common family name, although initially left open,[37] was soon given an unambiguous negative answer, in opposition to the dominant view among commentators and courts.[38] Nor was family unity found to require that both spouses share citizenship, or that children otherwise assume their father's citizenship instead of their mother's.[39] Rather, the law ruling out German citizenship for children of a German mother and a foreign father was found to violate the mother's rights under Article 6.2, in that it withheld from her children the benefits attached to German citizenship.

The Constitution and the Housewife Family Model

The German FCC had to face the question of which family model, if any, Article 6.1 specifically protects. It had to do so at an early date, when the legal scholarship overwhelmingly maintained that only the traditional nuclear family organized around a housewife and a breadwinner enjoyed the protection of Article 6.1. At that time, the FCC appeared tacitly to support this view, relying as it did on rhetoric that exalted the equal worth of both sexes while demanding respect for their objective natural and functional differences.

Explicitly, however, the FCC has always rejected claims that bound the constitutional protection of families together with wives' homemaking. Article 6.1 protects only the nuclear family,[40] yet it does so regardless of the internal organization that the family adopts. More precisely, Article 6.1 recognises

---

[37] *BVerfGE* 17, 169 (26 December 1963).

[38] *BVerfGE* 48, 327, *supra* note 16, at 335; see also *BVerfGE* 78, 38, *supra* note 21, at 84, 89).

[39] *BVerfGE* 37, 217, *supra* note 14.

[40] *BVerfGE* 48, 327, *supra* note 16, at 339. The nuclear family is formed by spouses and their natural children, by step, foster, and adoptive children (*BVerfGE* 18, 97 [30 June 1964] at 106; *BVerfGE* 68, 187 [17 October 1984]; and *BVerfGE* 79, 256 [31 January 1989] at 267).

nuclear families' right to a private sphere within which they must feel free to make internal decisions, such as those concerning whether one or both spouses will be income earners.[41] Article 6.1 grants the housewife-model of family neither exclusive nor preferential protection. Moreover, it makes it the State's constitutional duty to stay neutral with respect to the internal organization of families.[42]

Thus, the Court has recognized that relationships of paid work between spouses must be considered valid for tax purposes under Articles 3 and 6.1. Denying this would amount to imposing the housewife family model upon spouses tied by a working relationship; it would thereby disadvantage them with respect to nonmarried couples in a similar situation.[43]

Most revealing are the Court's decisions dealing with the so-called help for the unemployed (*Arbeitslosenhilfe*), foreseen in the Law for the Promotion of Work (*Arbeitsförderungsgesetz*, hereinafter *AFG*). This is the financial assistance granted to those unemployed workers who either do not meet the requirements for unemployment benefits, or have exhausted them without finding a new job. It aims at preventing people in such a situation from having to fall back onto public welfare. The amount of the assistance is made relative both to the income the beneficiary received prior to unemployment and to his or her actual financial needs. These factors are partly shaped by the needs of those he or she must legally support, as well as, in the case of married applicants, by the other spouse's income, unemployment benefits, or unemployment help.

Although the FCC has found this general idea unobjectionable, it has declared that some of the rules that give it specific content are unconstitutional under Articles 3.1 and 6.1 of the Basic Law. Thus, the Court condemned the rule that only allowed one spouse to receive unemployment help.[44] A similar fate awaited the rule that determined one spouse's unemployment help on the basis of the other's income, if this surpassed a minimum fixed amount.[45] This decision is particularly important. Overruling a previous decision,[46] the Court now introduced the idea that one spouse's income, although relevant in order to determine the other's need for unemployment help, should not be taken out of context. More specifically, the need for unemployment help must be measured on the basis of the family's global income. Taking sheer

---

It also embraces the relationship between a single mother and her children (*BVerfGE* 8, 210 [23 October 1958] at 215).

[41] *BVerfGE* 6, 55 [17 January 1957] at 58.

[42] *BVerfGE* 9, 237 (14 April 1959) at 242.

[43] *BVerfGE* 13, 290 (24 January 1962); *BVerfGE* 13, 318 (24 January 1962); and *BVerfGE* 13, 331 (24 January 1962); *BVerfGE* 16, 241 (8 July 1963); *BVerfGE* 16, 243 (8 July 1963); and *BVerfGE* 18, 257 (26 November 1964).

[44] *BVerfGE* 67, 186 (10 July 1984).

[45] *BVerfGE* 87, 234 (17 November 1992).

[46] *BVerfGE* 75, 382 (16 June 1987).

financial need as the only criterion, and identifying need with the perception of an income lower than a preestablished fixed amount, would disadvantage two-income marriages with respect to other living arrangements, thus violating Article 3.1 and the neutrality of Article 6.1 of the Basic Law. Moreover, it would go against Article 3.2, which seeks to promote women's actual equality by fighting men's traditional domination in most social spheres, including their prominent position in the labor world.

Taxing the Family

Article 6.1's neutrality with respect to families' internal organization is settled constitutional doctrine. Yet this doctrine has proved difficult to sustain in practice, in particular in the context of tax law. Tax norms play a crucial role in the definition of a social framework and trigger automatic consequences for internal familial structures and women's role within them. The FCC first referred to the neutrality of Article 6.1 in a case concerning precisely the taxation of married couples. After the war, Germany inherited a cumulative taxing system for married couples, which brought the income of both spouses together for taxation purposes. Because of the progressive character of the income tax, this system subjected marriages with double income to a greater financial burden than they would bear under separate taxation. The FCC found that thus conceived, the income tax discriminated against married couples or families where both spouses were income earners, while favoring nonmarried couples in the same situation and singles (Articles 3.1 and 6.1). Moreover, families where both spouses were income earners were penalized by comparison with families with only one breadwinner, usually the husband. Indeed, the explicit purpose of cumulative taxation, dating back to the times of National Socialism, was to discourage wives from entering the labor market. The rule aimed at having an "educational effect" on women, at leading them back to homemaking, an intent that the Court declared incompatible with Articles 3 and 6.1.[47]

After this constitutional ruling, income tax was reformed in terms that aimed at neutrality with respect to the internal earning structure of the family. Married couples now have a choice between being taxed separately or alternatively embracing what is known as the "splitting" system. According to this system the total earnings of a married couple are divided into two and they are taxed by doubling the amount of tax due on half their joint income. Given progressive taxation, the "splitting" system has the effect that a married couple pays less or at the most the same as an unmarried couple with the same internal distribution of income, except for very special and rare circumstances. Actually, again on account of progressive taxation, "splitting" makes more sense the higher the difference in income level

---

[47] *BVerfGE* 6, 55, *supra* note 41.

between the spouses, and thus benefits in particular marriages with only one breadwinner. It gives economic content to the notion of equal worth of men and women's contributions to the household where these contributions are tailored according to traditional gender roles. This has led the FCC to look favorably upon the "splitting" system as a means to benefit married couples according to the constitutional command of Article 6.1.[48]

However, the system's neutrality is illusory. If we look at it more closely, the choice between separate taxation and "splitting" makes it unprofitable for both spouses to stay in the labor market unless they have similarly high incomes. This is not the most common case and indeed it is not common for housewives who wish to go back to the labor market after being out of it for a certain length of time. Thus, in a two-income marriage where one of the spouses earns so much less than the other as to make separate taxation unattractive, "splitting" makes the additional lower earnings more expensive from a tax point of view than the higher ones alone were. It thus penalizes the lower income, usually the wife's. This has made it the target of feminist criticism.[49] Only separate taxation works in favor of women's presence in the labor market after their marriage. The problem is that just in the same measure as separate taxation supports working wives, it disfavors more traditional family arrangements, thereby infringing against the neutrality imposed by Article 6.1.

In the end, neutrality seems impossible to attain in this matter. In as much as neutrality is not itself a choice, Article 6.1 offers no guidance for solving this question. Article 3, by contrast, demands that wives be supported in their choice to stay in, enter, or reenter the labor market. Moreover, Article 3.2 imposes substantive equality and the elimination of men's group domination over women, while the housewife family model supports men's domination. All of these considerations point to the separate taxation of spouses as a constitutional command.

Another instance of the difficulty of devising tax laws that stay neutral with respect to internal family arrangements is the deduction of childcare costs. We have seen that when the FCC first contemplated this question in 1977, it denied that income-earning mothers had a right to a tax deduction for childcare costs.[50] At a time when formal gender equality was sought, the Court did not see a case of discrimination of women against men (Articles 3.2 and 3.3), as the rule was declared to affect them both on equal footing. Moreover, although the State must offer parents financial assistance, it must do so in the form it thinks most appropriate, which rules out a specific claim to tax advantages. And indeed, all parents were already granted a child

---

[48] *BVerfGE* 61, 319 (3 November 1982).

[49] See for all Ute Sacksofsky, "Steuerung der Familie durch Steuern" in: *Neue Juristische Wochenschrift*, 2000, at 1896ff.

[50] *BVerfGE* 47, 1, *supra* note 18.

allowance (*Kindergeld*). Most important, the Court declared that the State is obliged to offer equal financial support to *all* parents independently from their family's internal financial arrangements, on account of the neutrality of Article 6.1 on this point, and of the equal worth granted to housework and income earning.

Two subsequent constitutional decisions on the costs incurred by single mothers and fathers qualified the above ruling. The Court stated that, under Article 3.1 in conjunction with Article 6.1, single parents who are compelled to earn theirs and their children's subsistence must enjoy some compensatory tax advantage, as they cannot take advantage of the "splitting" system.[51]

The legislators readily provided for the possibility for single parents to deduct childcare costs if they had been incurred by necessity. This time, however, it was for married income-earning parents to question the constitutionality of their legal exclusion from similar benefits. On this occasion, the FCC[52] ruled that childcare costs must enjoy compensatory tax advantages under Article 6.1 and 6.2, even where both parents are income earners and childcare could not be considered to be strictly speaking compulsory under the circumstances. No reference is made to gender equality, yet the decision reveals an understanding of Article 3.2 as commanding that this equality be positively pursued, and that the structural disadvantages surrounding women's subordination to men be dismantled.

Yet the Court did not stop there. In a rhetorical *tour-de-force*, it continued to rule that *all* families with children must have a claim to tax advantages related to childcare, whether or not both parents are income earners and whether or not they actually incur childcare costs! Parents have a right to children's care and upbringing.[53] But exercising this right has costs. Children's upbringing and education impose heavy financial constraints on their parents that go well beyond the amount granted by the State as a child allowance. Those costs should be included in families' nontaxable subsistence minimum on account of Article 6.2. Whether or not both parents are income earners is to this purpose none of the State's concern. Nor is it for the State to decide whether parents cover their children's educational needs by resorting to childcare or in any other way. Relevant is only that such needs generate costs that the State should meet.

The result is that all parents are constitutionally entitled to a nontaxable minimum to cover their children's educational needs, regardless of their internal financial arrangements and whether or not they actually incur educational costs in the form of paid childcare. As in 1977, the Court thus opts for maintaining an appearance of neutrality by imposing the equal treatment of substantively different cases. On this occasion, however,

---

[51] *BVerfGE* 61, 319, *supra* note 48; *BVerfGE* 68, 143 (17 October 1984).
[52] *BVerfGE* 99, 216 (10 November 1998).
[53] *Basic Law, supra* note 3, art. 6.2.

the needs of working parents were not reduced to those of traditional families. Rather, the pursuit of factual equality between the sexes led the Court to raise the needs of traditional families up to those of working parents.

Although this seems to be a step forward, there are three reasons for criticizing it. First, after the decision, the amount of tax deduction for children had to be increased. In a progressive tax system, this helps rich more than poor families. Second, in combination with the "splitting" system, the decision is another big subsidy for traditional families. Finally, the one group completely forgotten by the Court are single parents. Because the possibility of a tax deduction for childcare originated as compensation for not being able to profit from the "splitting" system, after the decision, single parents, which in effect mostly mean single mothers, have to pay higher taxes than before.

The Man in the Family

The question of men's rights is implicit in any debate concerning the tension between formal and substantive gender equality, between an individual and a group conception of equality. Assuming equality must involve the elimination of women's subordination, it follows that the rights of individual men must yield, where necessary, to the rights of women as a group. The trouble is that the recognition of rights for women at the expense of men sometimes builds upon and reinforces traditional views of gender. Thus, if we take the goal of substantive equality between the sexes seriously, achieving it might sometimes require that the rights of individual men be protected over the rights of individual women.

The decisions concerning the rights of fathers over their natural children sustain that impression. In 1981, a number of fathers of children born out of wedlock raised claims at the FCC.[54] The existing legislation granted mothers exclusive custody over children born out of wedlock even where mother and father lived together and wished to share their children's custody. Moreover, the law granted mothers of such children the right to decide on and even against fathers' visiting rights. The claimants demanded a right to shared custody over their children and/or visiting rights even against the mother's will. They appealed to the protection of the family, to parents' right to the care and upbringing of their children, and to the rights of children born out of wedlock under Articles 6.1, 6.2 and 6.5, all in conjunction with gender equality. The Court turned down all of these claims appealing ultimately to the welfare of the child. Where a child's custody has to be decided from its birth, only the mother has developed a relation to the child and it is in

[54] *BVerfGE* 56, 363 (24 March 1981).

the child's interest that this be preserved.[55] Articles 6.1 and 6.2 only protect families as living communities and the relationship between fathers and their children in so far as they live together. This applies even where living apart is the mother's choice. In such cases, granting fathers shared custody or even visiting rights against the mother's will would raise disharmony that would in turn impair the children's welfare and their rights under Article 6.5.

Yet, the rights of fathers of children born out of marriage were denied even where father, mother, and children did form a living community. If father and mother were already living in harmony, the Court argued, there was no need for the father to claim a right that he could exercise against the mother. As soon as disharmony erupts then the above considerations on children's welfare apply. Should a father want to secure his rights under Article 6.2 in times of harmony, he should either marry his children's mother or adopt his children. When a father decides against these solutions he is assumed to be waiving his rights as a father. Similarly, a mother's decision against marriage or adoption amounts to a statement against the father's rights that should be respected for the sake of children's welfare. All these conclusions were found not to contradict Article 3.2.

The underlying assumption is that fatherhood does not have the same impact upon men as motherhood has upon women, that a fathers' attachment to his children builds only indirectly through their relationship with the children's mother, that men are mostly interested in relationships, while women give priority to caring for their offspring. Family and child-rearing were thus understood to be primarily a women's field, in which men only played a secondary role. In the end, we are facing a case in which biological and functional differences between the sexes do appear to play a role and impose an exception to gender equality, although the Court did not base its decision on such differences but upon children's welfare.

In 1991, the FCC qualified its previous ruling when it was asked to decide on the constitutionality of Section 1 738.1 of the *BGB*, which granted the exclusive custody of children born out of wedlock to their father upon his acknowledgement of paternity.[56] The Court had to decide whether single mothers could be completely excluded from custody in this event, even where both parents agreed to share custody of their common children. At issue was thus a case on women's rights to equality, an easy case in which women's claims were supported by the men they directly affected. Nevertheless, the Court took this chance to make some general remarks on the custody of children born outside of marriage, which partly revised its previous decision on the matter.

---

[55] When a child has bonded with both parents, the Court has declared it against both Article 3.2 and the child's welfare that the mother automatically be granted the child's custody (*BVerfGE* 55, 171 [5 November 1980]).
[56] *BVerfGE* 84, 168 (7 May 1991).

It confirmed that, as a general rule, single mothers must be granted the exclusive custody of their children. Yet, it submitted that joint custody between mother and father should be allowed where both mother and father wish to embrace this solution. To justify this decision, the Court recognized that fathers also have a right to the care and upbringing of their children under Article 6.2, at least when they live with them. Moreover, the Court argued that this solution was also indicated by the right of children born outside of marriage to enjoy the same opportunities for their physical, moral, and social development as children born within marriage, as recognized in Article 6.5. Behind this new line of argument lies a change in the vision of the social role of men. Men's role within the family is now given more relevance than in 1981. All of this bespeaks the pursuit of substantive equality between men and women from a group perspective. It confirms that in order to overcome men's domination over women, women and men's social roles must both be reshaped. Emphasizing man's presence in the family and the importance of his role as a father is crucial to this end.

ABORTION

Whereas in the areas of gender equality previously discussed, the FCC on the whole proved to be rather sensitive to the position of women (as compared to society at-large), it took a very harsh line against women on abortion. One reason may be that the Court has never recognized the equality issues involved in abortion. Even though the Court has recognized that the women involved might have some fundamental interest at stake, it has never really focused on the burden imposed on women by being denied the possibility of an abortion.

The Court has issued two major decisions on abortion,[57] in 1975 and in 1993, respectively. In both cases, the Court struck down rather liberal abortion laws as unconstitutional, because they did not sufficiently protect the fetus. Doctrinally, three factors rendered the cases unusual. First, contrary to nearly all constitutional decisions involving basic rights, no individual was alleging a violation of his or her constitutional rights. The abortion cases reached the Court on account of a rarely used proceeding called "abstract norm review" (*abstrakte Normenkontrolle*). Unlike in the context of constitutional complaints, in the context of abstract norm reviews the Court analizes the constitutionality of a norm without contemplating any specific case to which it has been applied. According to Article 93.1.2 of the Basic Law, such proceedings can be initiated by the Federal Government, state Governments or one third of the members of the Federal legislature (*Bundestag*).

---

[57] A third decision involved the compatibility of the *Bavarian Abortion Law* with federal Law, but was decided entirely on issues of federal versus state powers (*BVerfGE* 98, 265 [October 27, 1998]).

Both abortion cases were brought by the (conservative) opposition in the Bundestag, joined by the Government of Bavaria and (in the earlier case) other conservatively ruled state Governments.

Second, in these abortion cases there was no "person" whose rights could have been violated. Under German Civil Law, a human being is considered a "person," and a holder of rights, only after birth. Traditionally, the fetus itself was therefore not considered to have rights.

Third, no State action was involved. There was no statute allowing one person to invade another person's privacy, and no court that enforced such a legal rule. One needed an entirely new approach, and the Court invented it. The Court declared the State had an affirmative duty to protect the right to life and health against invasion from others. But let us look more closely at the two cases.

In its first decision on abortion,[58] the FCC was confronted with the partial decriminalization of abortion, introduced in the Criminal Code in 1974. According to the new provisions, abortion would not be prosecuted if carried out by a doctor with the pregnant woman's consent within the first twelve weeks after conception. Nor would it be prosecuted within the first twenty-two weeks after conception, if the fetus presented serious health deficiencies (eugenic indication) or at any time if the pregnancy irremediably posed serious threats to the mother's life or health (medical indication). In all cases, medical counseling was made a precondition for legal abortion. Confronted with the constitutionality of this new regulation, the Court did not approach it from the standpoint of women's rights. It focused instead on the State's duty toward the unborn life under Articles 1.1 and 2 of the Basic Law. These clauses read as follows:

Article 1.1: Human dignity shall be inviolable. To respect and protect it shall be the duty of all State authority.
Article 2: 1. Every person shall have the right to free development of his personality insofar as he does not violate the rights of others or offend against the constitutional order or the moral law.
2. Every person shall have the right to life and physical integrity. Freedom of the person shall be inviolable. These rights may be interfered with only pursuant to a law.

The State must not only respect the fundamental right to life by not interfering with its exercise; it must also actively protect it. Protection must be granted in every specific instance where life or physical integrity is at stake, including the case of the unborn life. This is so whether or not one claims that a fetus can be the holder of rights conceived as subjective claims. For fundamental rights have an objective dimension that imposes duties upon the State even where such rights have not been or cannot even be claimed by

---

[58] *BVerfGE* 39, 1 (25 February, 1975).

a specific right holder. Thus, the State is under the constitutional obligation to protect a fetus's life even against the fetus' mother and at every stage of development of the unborn life.

Criminal prosecution was not assumed to be the only way to ensure such protection. Preventive means of protection were particularly encouraged, as the Court recognized that a fetus is dependent on the mother. Yet the Court insisted that under Articles 1.1 and 2 of the Basic Law, any alternative to criminal prosecution must state clearly that it is the duty of the woman to carry her pregnancy to term.[59] The law must clearly show that it disapproves of abortion. Accordingly, the legalization of abortion during the first twelve weeks of pregnancy was declared unconstitutional.

The rights of a pregnant woman also were contemplated under Article 2 and an attempt was made to balance those rights against the State's duties toward the unborn life. The Court held that such a conflict of interest must generally be resolved in favor of the fetus. The fetus has its whole existence at stake, whereas the pregnant woman can still hope to reshape her life and develop her personality in a different existential framework. Nonetheless, there are occasions where preserving the fetus's life places an unreasonable burden on the pregnant woman, a burden – as the Court states – that goes beyond the burdens normally imposed by pregnancy. The medical and eugenic indications included in the law respond to such a test of unreasonableness. It is also unreasonable to impose upon a woman a pregnancy resulting from rape or one that would unduly burden her on account of her difficult social situation. The Court thus upheld the legal regulation of medical and eugenic abortion and declared it acceptable from a constitutional perspective that abortion also be allowed when carried out on criminal or social grounds.

That abortion also touches on gender equality could not have been further removed from the Court's imagination at that time. As it turned out, the Court's ruling missed its mark. In the last instance, the ruling that abortion cannot be prosecuted when practiced on social grounds left the door open for a much more liberal practice of abortion than the Court had intended to sanction, indeed in some German states nearly as liberal as the one the Court had intended to condemn. The law ensuing the Court's decision facilitated this result by setting the time limit of twelve weeks of pregnancy for legal abortions practised on social grounds. As a practical result, in some, especially the northern states, abortion was as good as free during these weeks. In the southern German states, however, it was still not easy to obtain a legal abortion. Also, there was the threat of criminal prosecution for women, as courts deemed it their task to review whether the social grounds on which an abortion was performed did indeed indicate such a burden on the woman that it outweighed the fetus's right to life.

[59] *BVerfGE* 39, 1, ibid., at 44.

During that period of time, abortion was paid for by (public) health insurance. This situation survived until the German reunification called for a new legal framework to harmonize the regulation of abortion in former Western and Eastern Germany. In East Germany, free abortion had been legal and subsidized for the first twelve weeks of pregnancy. The result was expressed in the *Law on Aid to Pregnant Women and Family* from 1992. It had been reached after extensive debates in Parliament and had been supported by members of different parties. This law was the subject of the second abortion decision of the FCC.[60]

This new law assumed a preventative rather than a punitive approach to abortion, and did so by resorting to counseling as a precondition for legal abortion. More precisely, the law legalized and subsidized abortions practiced during the first twelve weeks of pregnancy as long as the pregnant woman had gone through a prior counseling process. This new law brought an important change to the old abortion regime, leaving the final decision whether to abort to the woman alone. True, she had to go through a mandatory counseling process, but at least nobody had the right to review her decision.

The legislature tried to defend its law on the grounds that counseling is more effective than criminalization to prevent abortions. However, even though the FCC accepted counseling as an alternative to criminal punishment, it hardened its stance on the disapproval of abortion. It forcefully reiterated that the fetus, from the point of nidation (at the latest) on, develops "*as* a human being," not to *become* a human being. The right to life of the fetus does not depend on its acceptance by the woman, but is the fetus's own fundamental and inalienable right on account of its existence. The Court declared this to be the case independent of particular religious or philosophical convictions, realizing that the State has to be neutral in questions of religion and philosophy.

As in the earlier decision, the Court continued that the State has a duty to protect a fetus's life at every stage of development and even against the fetus's mother, and it gave preference to this duty over the mother's rights under Article 2. Also, the Court limited the range of possibilities left open to the legislature to fulfill this duty to protect. In other cases dealing with affirmative duties to protect life and health against the invasion by third parties – especially in the context of environmental law – the Court had always emphasized the broad scope for the legislature's value judgments and predictions. Constitutional review therefore was very limited. The FCC had established that it could find a violation of an affirmative duty to protect life and health only if the State had done nothing at all, or if the means of

---

[60] *BVerfGE* 88, 203 (28 May 1993).

protection the State had employed were obviously completely unsuitable or entirely insufficient to reach their goal.[61]

This level of review was tightened considerably in the second abortion decision. The Court now declares that the protection has to be "adequate," that is sufficient to be effective, and that it has to rely on a diligent appraisal of facts and reliable predictions.[62]

In spite of the strict standard of review, the Court left the final decision about abortion to the woman, holding that this decision did not have to be reviewed by State authority. Nevertheless, the Court tried to emphasize that abortion – except in very few circumstances – was fundamentally wrong. The State could *tolerate* abortion if this was a side effect of a policy tending toward the protection of the unborn life. Yet it could not *approve of* it on constitutional grounds. The legislators could thus decriminalise abortion and rule that it would not be prosecuted, but they could not make abortion legal, unless there were objective grounds to consider pregnancy an unreasonable burden for women. The normal burdens of pregnancy did not justify abortion. Only burdens that required an amount of self-sacrifice that could not be expected of a woman would suffice, such as the medical, the eugenic, the criminal, and the social grounds for abortion.[63] It was the State's duty to try to enlighten women, to open perspectives, and offer them help before letting them opt for abortion. The regulation of counseling was considered constitutionally deficient in that it did not adopt a pro-pregnancy attitude that was clear enough. Indeed, the Court's ruling included a detailed account of how counseling had to be legally drafted in order to fulfill the State's constitutional duty to protect the unborn life. The most important practical outcome of this is that decriminalized yet illegal abortion cannot be covered by State health insurance.

Whereas large portions of the decision are full of rhetoric that is appalling to women, there are also some passages that might prove useful in subsequent equal rights cases. For one, the Court pointed to the involvement of the (potential) father. Most important, the Court declared that the State has the duty to create the adequate structural conditions that would facilitate women's option for carrying the pregnancy to term. The State was obliged to enact legislation that made it easier to combine work and child-rearing. The State was, in other words, under the obligation to create a "children-friendly society."

CONCLUSION

With only the exception of abortion, the FCC has been quite helpful in furthering substantive equality between men and women in Germany.

---

[61] *BVerfGE* 79, 174 (11 November 1988) at 202.
[62] *BVerfGE* 88, 203, *supra* note 60, at 254.
[63] *BVerfGE* 88, 203, ibid., at 257.

Compared to society-at-large, the Court has been more open to claims of real gender equality. For a long time, the Court interpreted the guarantee of equal rights for men and women as a right to formal equality that forbade different treatment unless it was justified by objective biological or functional differences. The cases, therefore, turned on the question of what constituted such "objective or functional differences." During the 1950s and 1960s, the Court accepted the view that men and women had naturally different roles, while insisting that these differences might not disadvantage women. This spirit changed in the 1970s and early 1980s. During this period, the Court pursued formal equality. To this end, "biological and functional differences" were narrowly defined. The result was that different treatment between the sexes was systematically condemned as discriminatory. The 1980s brought a new move in the constitutional case law on Article 3. The Court began to acknowledge that formal equality was not sufficient to further the status of women. More and more, the Court emphasized the duty of the state to further (real) gender equality. In this respect, Germany still has a long way to go.

Suggested Readings

Susanne Baer, *Würde oder Gleichheit?* (Baden-Baden: Nomos, 1995).

Christine Fuchsloch, *Das Verbot der mittelbaren Geschlechtsdiskriminierung* (Baden-Baden: Nomos, 1995).

Werner Heun, "Artikel 3" in Horst Dreier, ed., *Grundgesetz. Kommentar*, vol. 1 (Tübingen: Mohr Siebeck, 1996) 228–93.

Jutta Limbach and Marion Eckertz-Höfer, eds., *Frauenrechte im Grundgesetz des geeinten Deutschland* (Baden-Baden: Nomos, 1993).

Lerke Osterloh, "Artikel 3" in Michael Sacks, ed., *Grundgesetz. Kommentar*, 2nd ed. (München: Beck, 1999) 208–79.

Heide Pfarr, *Quoten und Grundgesetz* (Baden-Baden: Nomos, 1988).

Michael Sachs, "Besondere Gleichheitsgarantien" in Josef Isensee and Paul Kirchhof, eds., *Handbuch des Staatsrechts der Bundesrepublik Deutschland*, vol. 2 (Tübingen: Mohr, 1992) 1017–83.

Ute Sacksofsky, *Das Grundrecht auf Gleichberechtigung*, 2nd ed. (Baden-Baden: Nomos, 1996).

Vera Slupik, *Die Entscheidung des Grundgesetzes für Parität im Geschlechterverhältnis* (Berlin: Duncker & Humblot, 1988).

Christian Starck, "Artikel 3" in Hermann von Mangoldt, Friedrich Klein, and Christian Starck, eds., *Das Bonner Grundgesetz. Kommentar*, 4th ed. (München: Verlag Franz Vahlen, 1999), 310–495.

7

India, Sex Equality, and Constitutional Law

Martha C. Nussbaum

> Whatever else Hindu society may adopt it will never give up its social structure – the enslavement of the Shudra and the enslavement of women. It is for this reason that law must come to the rescue in order that society may move on.
>
> — B. R. Ambedkar, *The Statesman*, September 21, 1951

> An increasing number of women on the Bench will hopefully change the perception of women from being passive recipients of rights and in need of protection to being fully autonomous in their decision-making and equal participants in public life. This millenium should belong to the woman. Let us hope this great institution will take the lead in ensuring that it does.
>
> — Indira Jaising, feminist legal scholar and Supreme Court Advocate, in a volume of essays celebrating the fiftieth anniversary of the Indian Supreme Court, 2000

India's Constitution is in some ways very attuned to issues of sex equality, which were prominently debated when the Constitution was adopted in 1950. The framers of the Constitution were very conscious of deeply entrenched inequalities, both those based on caste and those based on sex, and they made their removal one of their central goals. The text of the Constitution remains in many ways exemplary in its treatment of issues of gender and sex. Traditions of interpretation have been more uneven: sex equality has enjoyed some important victories, but discriminatory perceptions of women still exercise a reactionary influence.

I. THE BASIC STRUCTURE OF THE INDIAN DEMOCRACY

The Constitution establishes a liberal parliamentary democracy. Its parliament has two houses: the Lok Sabha (House of the People), the main legislative body, and the Rajya Sabha (Council of the States), a primarily deliberative body whose members are chosen by the legislative assemblies of the states (and in some cases by the president). The structure of government specified is federal, with many powers reserved to the states.

The Constitution provides for a Supreme Court, with a Chief Justice and (initially) no more than seven other Justices (now twenty-five others, who do not all sit simultaneously but are divided into panels), and also for High Courts (Appellate Courts, one in each state). The entire court structure is federal. Indian states do not have their own state court systems; all cases go to a single set of courts whether they raise state or federal issues. High courts often consider constitutional questions, but they are subject to review by the Supreme Court. The Supreme Court hears cases in panels, who often disagree with one another; there is no procedure for resolving these conflicts in Indian law. Moreover, justices typically write opinions seriatim, so that it can be very difficult to figure out what the Court as a whole thinks on any issue. These features lead to a certain unclarity in all areas of doctrine.

The Justices of the Supreme Court were initially appointed by the president, in consultation with the sitting justices and the justices of the various state High Courts. In 1992, the procedure was changed, when the Supreme Court ruled that the Court would play the central role in appointments.[1] A collegium of the most senior justices now plays the central role in the selection process. This change was originally designed to protect judicial independence, but feminists and other progressive legal thinkers have criticized the selections of the justices for their narrow and undemocratic character. The recent decision also holds that seniority among High Court judges is to be a central qualification for appointment to the Supreme Court, a procedure that strongly disadvantages women, in that at present few women have sufficient seniority to be considered.

The first woman was appointed to the Supreme Court only in 1990, and typically (as currently) there is but a single token woman on the Court. In 2000, a crucial sex equality case pertaining to the Muslim community (a petition challenging the constitutionality of the 1986 *Muslim Women (Protection of Rights on Divorce) Act*, discussed in Section IV) was heard by a bench consisting of five Judges, of which none was a woman and none belonged to any minority community (including the Muslim community). The recent decision about appointments made no reference to the importance of ensuring that the Court should represent the diversity of the nation. Elite women of the sort who might sit on the Supreme Court have not always represented well the interests of poor women, as the history of many developing nations shows; nonetheless, prominent women in Indian law do tend to be more aware of women's issues than their male counterparts.

The selection procedure is also under fire from another source: the current BJP (Hindu nationalist)–led Government has announced its intention to seek modification of the current selection procedure by amending the Constitution

[1] *Supreme Court Advocates-of-Record Association* v. *Union of India*, AIR 1993, 4 SCC 441.

to introduce a National Commission for the appointment of judges. The consequences of this proposal for women are unclear: much would depend on the composition of such a Commission.

The role of the Supreme Court has evolved over the years in the direction of greater authority and independence. Nehru, fearing that a conservative judiciary might frustrate progressive social goals, seems to have favored parliamentary sovereignty and a limited role for the Court. He was known to favor constitutional amendment by simple majority. In order to protect his policies of land reform against the *zamindars* (quasi-feudal landowners) from being blocked by the courts, he succeeded in amending the Constitution to exempt these property laws from judicial review. Nonetheless, he also accepted a system in which the Supreme Court is the ultimate interpreter of a group of fundamental rights that form Section III of the Constitution. These rights cannot be amended by a majority vote of Parliament. A struggle over the status of the fundamental rights has been waged on and off since Independence. The struggle has been complex. On the one hand, there has been a struggle over property rights, in which progressive legislators have tried to protect land reform from the Court: in this struggle the Court seems to play a conservative role. This struggle was finally settled when the Constitution was amended to eliminate the right of private property from the Constitution, at which point the Court became more progressive in property matters. On the other hand, there has been a struggle over the authority of the Executive and the majority party, in which the Court has typically intervened to defend liberal rights against an authoritarian state.

The primary focus of the struggle has been the amending power of Parliament. In 1976, in *Golak Nath*,[2] the Supreme Court held that fundamental rights can be amended only by a new constituent assembly (akin to a constitutional congress), not by vote of Parliament. Parliament soon responded by passing the Twenty-Fourth Amendment, which made fundamental rights amendable by Parliament. In 1973, in *Keshavananda Bharati*,[3] the Court upheld Parliament and reversed *Golak Nath*; nevertheless, the Court limited Parliament's amending authority and laid down a framework integrating the principle of judicial review with the authority of the socialist state. Amendments that attack the Constitution's "essential features" or "basic structure" (for example, the holding of fair and free elections) would be held unconstitutional. In certain specific areas of state action, however, pertaining to material redistribution, the Directive Principles of State Policy (which will be described shortly) might on occasion override fundamental rights *subject to judicial review*.

In 1976, during the Emergency, Indira Gandhi, after purging the Court to remove her opponents, tried to override *Keshavananda* by getting Parliament

[2] AIR 1967 SC 1643.
[3] AIR 1973 SC 1918.

to adopt the Forty-Second Amendment, a sweeping fifty-nine-clause constitutional revision that claimed unlimited sovereignty for Parliament, abolished judicial review, and completely subordinated the fundamental rights to parliamentary action. The amendment, tantamount to a new constitution, was accepted by a Parliament intimidated by arrests of leading members and censorship. After Mrs. Gandhi was repudiated at the polls in 1977, the new government restored the independence of the judiciary. In *Minerva Mills*,[4] the Court declared unconstitutional the portions of this amendment that collide with *Keshavananda*. Meanwhile, the fundamental right to property was removed by the Forty-Fourth Amendment in 1978. Subsequent Supreme Court decisions have held the *Keshavananda* idea of "basic features" to include the rule of law, secularism and federalism, free and fair elections, and judicial review itself.

Thus, the fundamental rights play a central role in constitutional jurisprudence, in conjunction with the crucial idea of "the basic features." These fundamental rights, although in many ways comparable to (and influenced by) the U.S. Bill of Rights, are both more numerous and explicit than those recognized in the U.S. Constitution. Their formulation is typically positive ("All citizens shall have the right...") rather than negative, in terms of what the state may not do. The account of each right includes a great deal of detail, designed to resolve controversy in advance – perhaps because of the framers' skepticism about judicial review. The list of explicit entitlements is correspondingly detailed, including matters, such as the freedom of travel and the right to form labor unions, that U.S. constitutional law has arrived at by judicial interpretation of more generally specified rights.

Article 13 of the Constitution explicitly invalidates all "laws in force" that are inconsistent with the list of fundamental rights – although, as we shall see, it remains disputed whether "laws in force" includes the personal laws.[5]

Section IV of the Constitution is a set of Directive Principles of State Policy: unenforceable aspirational guidelines that should be goals for governmental action. These include such general matters as the promotion of good nutrition, humane working conditions, and the economic interests of traditionally subordinated groups. But they also include some much more concrete matters, including one that later became particularly important to women (as we shall see in Section VI). Article 44 states that: "The state shall endeavour to secure for the citizens a uniform civil code throughout the territory of India." This provision came to be entered among the Directive

---

[4] AIR 1980 SC 1789.
[5] India is basically a common law country in the Anglo-American tradition. Sources of law include the Constitution, statutes, the common law tradition, and the personal laws – most of which were themselves codified by the British, often with a good deal of interposition of British material.

Principles because there was insufficient agreement to put it into an enforceable section of the Constitution.

An important feature, to be discussed in Section VI, is the right to petition the Supreme Court. The Court receives thousands of petitions and hears only a tiny fraction of them. Nonetheless, the right has been important to women.

II. EQUALITY AND NONDISCRIMINATION

The issue of sex equality was much discussed during the drafting of the Constitution, and the fundamental rights were drafted so as to reflect this emphasis. Article 14 says that the state shall not deny to any person "equality before the law or the equal protection of the laws." Article 15 prohibits state discrimination "on grounds only of religion, race, caste, sex, place of birth or any of them." Other rights that are highly relevant to sex equality include Article 13 (invalidating all laws inconsistent with the fundamental rights); Article 16 (equality of opportunity in public employment); Article 19 (protecting freedom of speech and expression, freedom of association, freedom of travel, freedom of residence, and freedom to form labor unions); Article 21 (stating that no citizen shall be deprived of life or liberty "except according to procedure established by law"); Article 23 (prohibition of traffic in human beings and forced labor); and Article 25 (freedom of conscience and religion). Section IV will further discuss the tensions between Articles 14 and 15 and the continuing presence of systems of personal law with entrenched sex inequality. Section V will discuss the evolution of an interpretative tradition of substantive due process out of Article 21 aimed at protecting women against some sex-specific abuses.

The understanding of equality in the Constitution is explicitly aimed at securing substantive equality for previously subordinated groups, and is designed to ward off merely formal understandings of equality that have, in the U.S. context, been used to oppose affirmative action. Substantive equality is not defined, but the Directive Principles give a great deal of attention to the advancement of economic equality, and the fundamental rights are themselves specified in a way that makes room for affirmative action programs designed to advance the material situation of women and the lower castes. The notion of formal equality that is carefully avoided is the notion that equality means treating everyone the same, and not using race or sex as a ground of any type of differential treatment – an understanding that has been used in the United States to subvert affirmative action. Thus, Article 15 states that "[n]othing in this article shall prevent the State from making any special provision for women and children," and that "[n]othing in this article . . . shall prevent the State from making any special provision for the advancement of any socially and educationally backward classes of citizens or for the Scheduled Castes and the Scheduled Tribes." Similar clauses appear in Article 16 (equality of opportunity in public employment) and in

Article 19 (various other rights and liberties). The Indian tradition (extending back to the early twentieth century) is strongly in favor of quotas and
other affirmative action measures for deprived groups. In short, the Framers
understood the goal of equality in terms of an end to systematic hierarchy
and discrimination, based on both caste and sex. Affirmative action is thus
endorsed in principle – although in practice specific affirmative action measures have often proved controversial.

The jurisprudence interpreting these articles however, has a more mixed
history.[6] The Supreme Court has interpreted Article 14 as a prohibition
against "unreasonable" classifications based on sex. The standard of reasonableness, set out in *Budhan Choudry v. State of Bihar*[7] requires that "(i) . . . the
classification must be founded on an intelligible differentiation which distinguishes persons or things that are grouped together from others left out
of the group" and "(ii) . . . that differentia must have a rational relation to
the object sought to be achieved by the statute in question." These criteria import a formal idea of equality: only those individuals who are similar
need be treated similarly; it turns away from what appears to have been the
original intent of the articles, to break down hierarchies founded upon caste
and sex. In keeping with this formal understanding of equality, the clauses
of Articles 15 and 16 pertaining to affirmative measures were initially interpreted by the Court as exceptions to the (allegedly formal) doctrine of equal
treatment articulated within the articles, rather than as part of the articles'
substantive doctrine of equality.[8]

The substantive approach to equality, present from the period of the
Founding in statements of Nehru's law minister B. R. Ambedkar (himself
a lower-caste man), and, arguably, plainly expressed in the Constitution's
text, has gradually prevailed in the jurisprudence, though not consistently.
Under this approach, the sections of Articles 15 and 16 pertaining to women
are not exceptions, but part of the articles' articulation of an anti-hierarchical
understanding of equality.[9] In *Kerala v. N. M. Thomas* (1976),[10] the Supreme
Court began to articulate this approach, stating: "Though complete identity of equality of opportunity is impossible in this world, measures compensatory in character and which are calculated to mitigate surmountable
obstacles to ensure equality of opportunity can never incur the wrath of
article 16(1)."

[6] See the excellent treatment of these questions in Ratna Kapur and Brenda Cossman, *Subversive Sites: Feminist Engagements with Law in India* (Delhi: Sage, 1996) Chapter 3, to which
my discussion in this section is indebted.
[7] AIR 1955 SC 191.
[8] For a typical statement of this approach, see *Anjali Roy v. State of W. B.*, AIR 1952 Cal. 825
at 830–831.
[9] For one early example of this approach at the State High Court level, see *Motiram More
Dattatrava v. State of Bombay*, AIR 1953 Bom 311 at 314.
[10] AIR 1976 SC 490.

Although some legal commentators enamored of formal equality continue to criticize this opinion, the approach has consistently prevailed in subsequent jurisprudence. In *Marri Chandra Shekhar Rao v. Dean Seth G. S. M* (1990)[11] and in *Indra Sawhney v. Union of India* (1993),[12] the Supreme Court insists that equality may require treating people differently in order to overcome disadvantages. The opinion appears to defend affirmative action measures on substantive equality grounds.

Two problems in the original framing of the relevant articles have caused difficulty for the promotion of substantive equality. Both Articles 14 and 15 are framed in narrow negative terms, as prohibitions against certain types of State action. Other rights in the Constitution typically are formulated more expansively: thus, Article 19 states that "All citizens shall have the right. . . . " Thus, inequalities in private employment and in the private sector generally appear to be beyond the reach of Articles 14 and 15 – although, in some instances, as we shall see, they have been addressed, and although the private sector is much smaller in India, even today, than in many other nations. Second, the word "only" in Article 15 has been understood in some instances to drive a wedge between sex and gender: if a form of discrimination is based upon aspects of women's situation that are not biological but social, it has in some instances been held (particularly in significant cases in 1981 and 1987) that this is not unconstitutional discrimination, because not on the basis "only" of sex.[13]

If we now turn to several specific areas of jurisprudence about sex equality, we see, again, a tension between formal and substantive understandings of equality, with a gradual trend in favor of the substantive conception. In areas involving challenges to traditional conceptions of marriage and the husband's authority within the conjugal home, it is perhaps not surprising that the traditional notions of the almost entirely all-male judiciary at times prevail over their abstract allegiance to substantive equality. Cases involving discrimination in employment seem to have been easier to bring into line with the substantive understanding.

Divorce

Provisions of divorce law that provide different conditions for divorce for husbands and wives have frequently been challenged on sex equality grounds. Thus, the *Indian Divorce Act* provides that a wife may only petition for divorce on the basis of her husband's adultery combined with desertion, cruelty, rape, incest, or bigamy, whereas the husband may petition on grounds

---

[11] 1990 3, SCC 130.
[12] AIR 1993 SC 477.
[13] *Air India v. Nargesh Meerza*, AIR 1981, 4 SCC 335; *Miss Lena Khan v. Union of India and Ors*, AIR 1987, 2 SCC 402.

of adultery alone. This asymmetry, although challenged, was defended by a State High Court, in an early case (1953), as securely grounded in biological differences between women and men: the woman's adultery may result in conception, whereas "[a] husband commits an adultery somewhere but he does not bear a child as a result of such adultery, and make it the legitimate child of his wife's to be maintained by the wife."[14] More recently, the constitutionality of the asymmetry was questioned by another state court, in a 1989 opinion suggesting that *Dwaraka's* approach (which appears to be the sort of formal equality approach feminists have often criticized, in which a biological difference is taken to license differential treatment, even when it perpetuates hierarchy), is mistaken because it perpetuates sex discrimination; but the case was decided without a clear resolution of these issues.[15]

Similar tensions have arisen in considering the section of the Indian Penal Code that makes only male adultery an offence, and the section of the Code of Criminal Procedure that allows only a husband of an adulterous woman to prosecute the man with whom she commits adultery but does not permit the wife of an adulterous man to prosecute the man. The former asymmetry has been challenged by men on sex equality grounds, but the challenge was rejected in 1954 with reference to the Constitution's general approach of providing special benefits for women and children.[16] Although this approach appears to endorse a substantive model of equality, feminist commentators have noted that the result is actually murky, because the asymmetry in adultery law perpetuates sexist myths about women, who are seen as "the passive victims of aggressive male sexuality, incapable of agency in sexual relations.... The failure to interrogate the law of adultery at a deeper level leaves these assumptions in place."[17] The fact that a wife of an adulterous husband cannot prosecute him has been upheld several times, on the grounds that the chief offender is the (male) outsider who "breaks into the matrimonial home [and] occasions the violation of the sanctity of the matrimonial tie."[18] This 1988 decision seems to perpetuate the archaic notion that women are the property of men and that adultery is primarily an offense against male property rights. Thus, the Court does not attribute to the wife any rights that are threatened by a male's adultery, which is assumed to take place outside the home.

Restitution of Conjugal Rights

In the area of restitution of conjugal rights a substantive approach to equality has been influentially articulated. The issue is whether a man (or woman,

---

[14] *Dwaraka Bai v. Professor N. Mathews*, AIR 1953 Mad 792.
[15] *Swapna Ghosh v. Sadananda Ghosh*, AIR 1989 Cal 1.
[16] AIR 1954 SC 321.
[17] Kapur and Cossman, *Subversive Sites*, *supra* note 6, at 191.
[18] *Revathi v. Union of India*, AIR 1988 SC 838.

but it is almost always a man) whose spouse has left the marital home has the right to ensure a forcible return of the partner to the home (this remedy of forcible return had a long and unpleasant history in the colonial era, and was championed by the British, against the opposition of indigenous reformers). *Sareetha v. T. Venkata Subbaiah* (1983)[19] concerned a popular film actress whose husband – having been indifferent to her departure until she became rich and famous – then sued her for restitution of conjugal rights under a provision of the Hindu law of marriage that had its ultimate origins in British ecclesiastical law (as the justice notes, pointing out that forcible restitution of a woman who has left her husband to the marital home is not in line with Hindu traditions). The Andhra Pradesh High Court declared that part of the marriage law unconstitutional, on grounds of both privacy and sex equality. The privacy arm of the argument was the most stressed, and was the basis for the ultimate reversal of the decision by the Supreme Court. But in the less-noticed equality arm of the argument, Justice Choudary noted that the law was neutral on its face, applying to either a male or a female spouse. Nonetheless, he argued that it was discriminatory because of the substantive differences between the social positions of males and females in marriage. The enforcement of such a decree, especially given that it may result in the conception of a child, will alter the wife's life in a way that it could not possibly alter the husband's. It "cripples the wife's future plans of life."

Although the decision was overruled (see Section V), this arm of the argument was neither refuted nor so much as mentioned by the Supreme Court.

Property and Succession

Equal property rights are among Indian women's most persistent and urgent demands. And here even Ambedkar, the tenacious champion of substantive equality, appears to have had doubts. When the Select Committee of the Constituent Assembly suggested that daughters and sons be treated as equal with respect to an aspect of inheritance law, he characterized this proposal as an effort to render all his reform program ridiculous.

Nonetheless, the Hindu law of property and succession has been challenged on grounds of sex discrimination by both men and women. Significantly, challenges by men to asymmetries in the law that favor women have been rejected, on the grounds that these asymmetries help remedy traditional disabilities suffered by women. In both 1961 and 1985, it was held that special provisions intended to remedy traditional discrimination do not constitute hostile discrimination.[20] The justices refer to Article 15 Section 3 to uphold

---

[19] AIR 1983 A. P. 356.

[20] *Kaur Singh v. Jaggar Singh*, AIR 1961 Punj 489; and *Partap Singh v. Union of India*, AIR 1985 SC 1695. At stake was a provision of the *Hindu Succession Act* that gives a female Hindu a right of absolute ownership over her property. The courts held that this provision was an

the constitutionality of such remedies. At the same time, a patriarchal understanding of the family continues to influence some decisions in this area. The provision that when a female Hindu dies intestate any property she has inherited from her husband will pass to the husband's heirs (while no comparable rule is made for the male Hindu who dies intestate after inheriting property from his wife), challenged on grounds of sex equality, was upheld in 1984, with the argument that the intent of the law was to ensure the continuity of property in the male line.[21]

In another group of early cases, restrictions on women's ownership of land have been struck down as unconstitutional discrimination on the basis of sex in violation of Article 15;[22] by contrast, some traditional distinctions between sons and daughters were upheld.[23] Equality problems were waved away by noting that a daughter will leave to join another family after her marriage. In two more recent cases (1996 and 1999), the Supreme Court has ruled in favor of female plaintiffs in property cases by creative interpretation of the relevant discriminatory laws, without addressing constitutional issues.[24] It is difficult to discern a coherent pattern in the Court's decisions in this area.

In a comprehensive study of all property and succession cases with a gender aspect, in the nation as a whole, between the years of 1988 and 1991, Srimati Basu has concluded that women emerged victorious in 66.4 percent of the 119 cases, and were clear losers in only 29.4 percent. By contrast, a closer inspection reveals that many of these victories were only superficial: as in some of the above cases, traditional notions of the patriarchal family intervene to block some problematic aspects of the law from scrutiny. Equally problematic are the inconsistencies with which courts have treated the conditions of claiming a religious identity (in order to inherit under a given religion's laws of property – on which see Section IV). In some cases a woman's claim to be a Hindu is rejected on grounds of non-traditional behavior.

Employment

In a series of cases, restrictions on the employment of married women have been successfully challenged on sex equality grounds. But the reasoning used in the cases is not altogether unproblematic. In *Bombay Labour Union v. International Franchise* (1966),[25] a rule requiring an unmarried woman to give up her employment on marriage was successfully challenged; but the Court

---

attempt to remedy special disabilities suffered by Hindu women, and widows in particular, under traditional property law.
[21] *Sonubai Yeshwant Jadhav v. Bala Govinda Yadav*, AIR 1983 Bom 156.
[22] See, e.g., *Pritam Kaur v. State of Pepsu*, AIR 1963 Punj 9.
[23] See, e.g., *Sucha Singh Bajwa v. The State of Punjab*, AIR 1974 P & H 162.
[24] *Madhu Kishwar v. State of Bihar*, AIR 1996, 5 SCC 125; and *Geetha Hariharan*, AIR 1999, 2 SCC 228.
[25] AIR 1966 SC 942.

continued to assume that the woman is the primary caregiver for children, and simply pointed out that widows were just as likely to have such responsibilities, and so it could not be said that married women posed a greater problem of absenteeism. Maternity leave was said to be the sole significant difference between the sexes; but the employer could prevent absenteeism from being a problem by "having a few extra women on leave reserve." This opinion analyzes sex discrimination in purely formal sameness/difference terms. In *C. B. Muthamma v. Union of India* (1979),[26] a similar formal analysis was employed to strike down the Indian Foreign Service's restriction on the appointment of married women. But, in this case, the Supreme Court pointed out that "family and domestic commitments" might impede the job performance of a male employee as well as a female employee: "In these days of nuclear families, intercontinental marriages and unconventional behaviour, one fails to understand the naked bias against the gentler of the species." This opinion seems more progressive, but it still sticks to a formal model of equality, and its reference to women as "gentler" betrays a persistent tendency to view women as passive victims, a tendency repeatedly criticized by feminists.

In a complex and much-discussed 1981 case, *Air India v. Nergesh Meerza*,[27] an air hostess challenged the different rules pertaining to air hostesses and male stewards on grounds of sex discrimination. On the one hand, the Court upheld (on the basis of their reading of "only" in Article 15, see above) the basic scheme of classification by sex, holding that air hostesses were a distinct category. They also upheld the regulation that a hostess may be fired if she marries within four years after her initial employment. They reasoned that this condition was legitimate in the light of state family planning objectives: mature women would be more able to make sound decisions regarding pregnancy. On the other hand, the Court struck down as unconstitutionally unreasonable and arbitrary (thus, in violation of Article 14) a regulation requiring hostesses to terminate employment at the time of pregnancy. Here they appear to employ a substantive notion of equality: the difference between male and female with regard to pregnancy does not license a regulation that "amounts to compelling the poor air hostess not to have any children and thus interfere with and divert the ordinary course of human nature." The Court's reasoning contains a remarkable mixture of progressive and traditional elements:

It seems to us that the termination of the services of an air hostess under such circumstances is not only a callous and cruel act but an open insult to Indian womanhood – the most sacrosanct and cherished institution. We are constrained to observe that such a course of action is extremely detestable and abhorrent to the notions of a

[26] AIR 1979 SC 1868.
[27] AIR 1981, 4 SCC 335.

civilized society. Apart from being grossly unethical, it smacks of a deep rooted sense of utter selfishness at the cost of all human values.[28]

Although the woman's situation is sympathetically taken into account, and the regulation is held to violate the equal protection of the laws, woman is viewed as a fragile and sacred creature to be put on a pedestal. One might even see in the opinion the view that to be an Indian woman is to be a mother. As a result, the issue of sex discrimination does not emerge with the clarity that one might have wished.

Despite these complexities, the Court continues to overturn legislation that impedes woman's economic activity. In 1986, in *Maya Devi v. State of Maharashtra*,[29] the requirement that married women obtain their husbands' consent before applying for public employment was successfully challenged as in violation of Articles 14, 15, and 16. The Court emphasized the importance of economic independence for women, in overcoming traditional disadvantages. In these and more recent cases, a substantive understanding of equality is gradually prevailing over stereotyped visions of women's role.

We might summarize by saying that while a substantive understanding of equality is firmly entrenched in the Constitution and in the interpretive tradition, traditional ideas of woman and family repeatedly intervene to block this idea from being consistently applied. Advocates of sex equality continue to wage a determined, and reasonably productive, struggle to get the Courts to live up to the best insights of the Constitution.

III. POLITICAL PARTICIPATION: RESERVATIONS FOR WOMEN

In keeping with the generally substantive understanding of equality in the Constitution, various schemes of affirmative action on behalf of traditionally subordinated groups were contemplated at the time of the Founding. Article 46, one of the Directive Principles of State Policy, states that "The State shall promote with special care the educational and economic interests of the weaker sections of the people, and, in particular, the Scheduled Castes and the Scheduled Tribes, and shall protect them from social injustice and all forms of exploitation." As noted earlier, the bans on discrimination in Articles 15 and 16 permit the State to adopt affirmative measures to protect the interests of the lower castes, women, and children. In keeping with traditions that extend back to the 1930's, quotas or "reservations" in both employment and political representation have been generally accepted as a legitimate way of pursuing equality goals.

The Constitution explicitly provides for reserved seats for the scheduled castes and tribes. Despite controversy and many complaints, the system

---

[28] Ibid., at 1831.
[29] 1986, 1 SCR 743 (India).

seems to have worked reasonably well, effectively enfranchising these groups and promoting their economic and social well-being. By contrast, there are legitimate objections to be made. No reserved seats have ever been created or even seriously championed for Muslims, as vulnerable a minority as the Scheduled Castes and Tribes. Moreover, the practice of reservation has led over time to a situation in which castes at the very bottom of the social ladder do considerably better than those just above them. Following the 1980 report of the Mandal Commission, reservations for OBCs (Other Backward Castes) were added in civil service and employment, though not parliamentary representation. (Estimates of the proportion of India's population who belong to OBC groups range from 25 percent to 37 percent.)

Reserved seats for women have been discussed since before Independence. The All India Women's Congress opposed reservations, although strongly favoring equal civil rights for women. Feminist leaders argued that reserved seats would compromise "the universal demand of Indian women for absolute equality of political status;" their demand was for "equality and no privileges."[30] The colonial government, disregarding the prevailing attitude of women's groups, created reserved seats for women in provincial legislatures and at least some in the central legislature. At Independence, the policies of the women of the Congress Party prevailed, and reservations for women were rejected, although, as noted above, affirmative action on the basis of sex won general support in the Constitution. The *Hindu Code Bill* of 1957 made other alterations in women's civil rights.

In 1971, the Government appointed a Committee on the Status of Women in India to study the progress made by women since Independence. In its famous 1974 report *Towards Equality*, the Committee delivered a scathing critique of the political process, arguing that women's position had if anything worsened, and that women were neither able to claim their legal rights nor, in many cases, even aware of them. The majority of the Committee continued to oppose reserved seats as a remedy, but a minority report signed by the especially prominent feminists Vina Mazumdar and Lotika Sarkar argued that this remedy was necessary for women's social and political progress.

Twenty-seven years later, the representation of women in central and state government continues to be very low: 6–7 percent in the Lok Sabha, one of the lowest such figures in the world. Political parties have talked about reserving a certain proportion of candidacies for women, but have done nothing about it. At the same time, women's voter turnout has significantly increased, and is now at 55 percent, only slightly less than the national average. In this situation, it is not suprising that the idea of reserved legislative seats for women has attracted new political and constitutional attention.

---

[30] As quoted in Zoya Hasan, "Women's Reserved Seats and the 'Politics of Presence'" (December 2000) [unpublished draft].

Article 40 of the Constitution, an unenforceable Directive Principle, states that "[t]he State shall take steps to organise village panchayats and endow them with such powers and authority as may be necessary to enable them to function as units of self-government." Forty years later, national legislators successfully amended the Constitution to give formal legal status to the system of *panchayats* (councils). In 1992, the Seventy-third and Seventy-fourth Amendments established a 33 percent quota for women in the local *panchayats*. The Amendments set up a scheme of rotation that is similar to that by which reservations for lower castes have already been implemented at the national level. Initially, advocates for women were split about the merits of this scheme. Many feared that the women who would be selected would simply be proxies for male interests. But nearly ten years of experience with the scheme has shown that, on balance, its merits outweigh its drawbacks. Certainly in some cases women do initially function as proxies of men in their families. But even these women learn political skills in the process. Moreover, the extension of political power to poor and illiterate women has been dramatic. Studies show that a majority of women who serve in the *panchayats* are illiterate or barely literate. Moreover, approximately 40 percent of female representatives come from families with income below the poverty line. Women report many obstacles to their effective participation, including harassment and the threat of violence. Nonetheless, the evidence is that women are learning political skills and participating in decision making in a way that would not have been possible without the Amendments. In addition, the system has increased demands for female education.

It is in this context that one of the major constitutional conflicts of recent years has been unfolding. The proposed Eighty-fifth Amendment, which would create 33 percent reserved seats for women in the Lok Sabha, was first introduced in 1996 and has been hotly debated ever since. Women's groups overwhelmingly support the Amendment, in the light of the *panchayat* experience. And all major parties officially support it. But in fact they do not give it real support, in part because they depend on coalition partners from small caste-based parties who are its major opponents. Lower-caste men argue that reservations for women will increase the number of upper-caste people in the Lok Sabha, unless the measure is redesigned to include sub-quotas for lower-caste women, something that the Bill's supporters have not accepted.

The Amendment has been introduced several times, most recently in December 2000, when it was derailed by a riotous protest from the caste-based parties, who stood in the well of the Lok Sabha and tore up copies of the bill. Parliamentary leaders did nothing to intervene. The most consistent support for the Amendment at present comes from women's groups and, within the party system, from Left parties, who do not wield much power at the national level except through coalitions. A possible compromise outcome

is that parties may agree to reserve a certain proportion of their tickets for
female candidates.

IV. SEX EQUALITY AND PERSONAL LAWS

Although the Constitution protects sex equality and free choice of religion, it
also retains plural systems of religious personal law (Muslim, Hindu, Parsi,
and Christian). These systems govern property law, as well as family law
(marriage and divorce, maintenance, child custody, etc.). This decentralized
situation dates back to the Raj, when the British codified commercial and
criminal law for the nation as a whole, but, in the spirit of divide and rule,
encouraged the maintenance of separate spheres of civil law in noncommer-
cial areas, and actually codified Hindu law themselves (because it existed in
a plural decentralized condition). At Independence many Framers favored
a Uniform Civil Code, but the Muslims' fear that such a code would make
them second-class citizens led to controversy, and it was thought expedient
to shelve that proposal for the time; it was therefore placed in the nonen-
forceable Directive Principles of State Policy.[31]

For a time, support for a Uniform Code was growing, and many Muslims
supported it. The backlash occasioned by the *Shah Bano* judgment began to
reverse that trend (see later). More recently, the rise to power of the Bharatiya
Janata Party (BJP), for whom Uniform Code would surely mean Hindu Code,
has caused back-pedaling among all progressive people. There is currently
little likelihood that a Uniform Code will be achieved any time soon, unless
the BJP should win an outright majority and implement plans of declaring
India a Hindu nation. This would be an extremely unfortunate way for the
goal of a uniform code, in other ways desirable, to come about.

The systems operate in different ways. None is completely independent of
the central government, in the sense that all must gain their powers through
legislation (Parliament passes the laws creating a particular system of marriage law, or property law, for each of the various communities). But their
degrees of independence vary. For Muslim law, which was well developed,
though not uniform, from an early date, the Ulema (leading clerics) have
had considerable power in shaping the legislation that allows the *shariat* to
govern specific aspects of citizens' lives. The Muslim Personal Law Board, a
self-perpetuating and unelected body consisting of leading clerics, is the primary "representative" of the community that is always consulted when legal
change is contemplated. Its arbitrary claim to authority is a source of frus-
tration to Muslim feminists and other Muslim liberals. Because Hinduism is
the majority religion, Hindu law is debated (and reformed) at the national
level, and legal challenges to it operate through the usual judicial channels.

---

[31] Article 44 states that "[t]he State shall endeavour to secure for the citizens a uniform civil
code throughout the territory of India."

The minority communities, Christian and Parsi, did not make their own legislation, but were legislated for by the British (presumably after consultation with at least some parts of the community). Christian law of marriage, divorce, and custody was similarly legislated at the national level, but Christian property law was allowed to remain decentralized, and to the present day there is a plurality of Christian laws of property and succession in different regions of the nation, in some cases stemming from the different national systems from which Christian missionaries came to India.

When a child is born, it is immediately classified by religion and henceforth comes under that religion's legal system. It is possible to elect a secular identity for a child, and there are secular laws of marriage and divorce. But because ancestral property is governed by the system of religious law to which one's ancestors belonged, and in the case of Hindus is held in complex family consortia or "coparcenaries" from which individual shares cannot be detached, it is actually very difficult to extricate oneself from a religious system, whether in order to change religion or in order to elect a secular identity. Thus the system creates large difficulties for the free exercise of religion, as well as for sex equality.

All the systems have gross sex inequalities. Thus, one might suppose that they would automatically be unconstitutional under the Thirteenth Amendment, which declares that all "laws in force" that contradict fundamental rights are null and void. However, in 1952, in *State of Bombay v. Narasu Appa Mali*,[32] the Bombay High Court held that the term "laws in force" in that Amendment does not include the personal laws. More recently, the Supreme Court repeated this view in *Krishna Singh v. Mathura Ahir*.[33] A pair of cases in 1996 and 1997 addressed the relationship between fundamental rights and personal laws once again, but with no clear result, since different benches of the Supreme Court came to opposite conclusions. In 1996, in *C. Masilamani Mudaliar v. Idol of Sri S. S. Thirukoil*,[34] one bench held that personal laws "must be consistent with the Constitution lest they become void if they violate fundamental rights." However, in *Ahmedabad Women's Group's Case* (1997),[35] another bench categorically stated that personal laws are beyond the reach of fundamental rights. Thus proponents of sex equality must address equality issues within each separate religious system, and feminists have persistently sought to do so, with varying success.

One relatively successful example of internal reform has been the recent history of the Christian law of marriage and divorce. Prior to 1995, Christian women in India could get a divorce only on grounds of both adultery and cruelty; for men, adultery alone was sufficient. This law was challenged

---

[32] AIR 1952 Bom 84.
[33] AIR 1980 SC 707.
[34] AIR 1996, 8 SCC 525.
[35] AIR 1997, 3 SCC 573.

before relevant state High Courts. In 1995, in *Ammini Ej v. UOI*,[36] and in the similar case of *Mary Sonia Zachariah v. UOI*,[37] the Kerala High Court declared the relevant provisions of the law unconstitutional. As a result of a lengthy reform process, the Christian Marriage Bill was passed by Parliament in 2001; the law both equalizes and liberalizes the grounds for divorce, allowing divorce by mutual consent for men and women. Problems remain, but this case shows that reform can take place within a system of personal law, especially with constitutional pressure applied by the courts.

The most famous constitutional conflict over personal laws concerns the Muslim system of maintenance. Muslim men are able to divorce their wives summarily, by simply pronouncing the triple "*talaq.*" Women are entitled to claim only the dowry, or *mehr*, that they had brought into the marriage. Because this left many Muslim women in desperate circumstances, women had found a remedy through the Criminal Code. Section 125 of the Code forbids a man "of adequate means" to permit various close relatives, including (by special amendment in 1973) an ex-wife, to remain in a state of "destitution and vagrancy." Many women divorced under Muslim law had been able to win grants of maintenance under this Section; the recognition of ex-wives as relations under the section was introduced explicitly for this purpose (and was objected to by members of the Muslim League on grounds of religious free exercise).

In Madhya Pradesh in 1978, an elderly Muslim woman named Shah Bano was thrown out of her home by her husband, a prosperous lawyer, after forty-four years of marriage (the occasion seems to have been a quarrel over inheritance between the children of Shah Bano and the children of the husband's other wife). As required by Islamic law, he returned to her her marriage portion, Rs. 3000 (about $60 by current exchange rates). Following what was by then a common practice, she applied for relief under Section 125. The case found its way to the Supreme Court, in *Mohammed Ahmed Khan v. Shah Bano Begum & Others*.[38] Deciding in Shah Bano's favor and awarding her a maintenance of Rs. 180 per month (about $4), Chief Justice Chandrachud, a Hindu, wrote a lengthy opinion, criticizing Islamic practices and interpreting Islamic texts to show that this grant of maintenance was consistent with Islamic norms (as had been denied by the husband in his appeal). The case was not decided on constitutional grounds, and the first sentence of the opinion is: "[t]his appeal does not involve any questions of constitutional importance. . . . " Nonetheless, the opinion alluded to constitutional matters, speaking pejoratively of the whole system of personal laws, regretting that Article 44 had not already led to the framing of a uniform civil code, and opining that the state should do away with personal laws even in the absence

---

[36] AIR 1995 Ker 252.
[37] 1990 (1) KLT 130.
[38] AIR 1985 SC 945.

of the consent of the minority community. The rhetoric of the opinion was unfortunate: for example, the Chief Justice cited a British commentary on the *Koran* in support of the proposition that the "fatal point in Islam is the degradation of woman."

The high publicity given to this contemptuous opinion produced an unfortunate reaction. Up to this time, there was broad support in the Muslim community for sex equality and even for the goal of a Uniform Civil Code. But now much of the Muslim community, feeling its honor slighted and its civic position threatened, rallied round the cause of denying women maintenance. Women were barely consulted when statements were made about what Indian Muslims wished and thought; an impression was created by the Ulema that all Muslims disagreed with the judgment. Shah Bano herself was ultimately led to recant her views and to state (in a statement signed with her thumbprint) that she now understands that her salvation in the next world depends on her not pressing her demand for maintenance.

Meanwhile the Muslim leadership persuaded the government of Rajiv Gandhi to pass a law, the *Muslim Women's (Protection after Divorce) Act* of 1986, which deprives all and only Muslim women of the opportunity to win maintenance under the Criminal Code. The government never consulted with other segments of the community; they treated the Ulema as the voice of the whole community. Muslim women and many Muslim men expressed outrage.

In September 2001, a major decision concerning Muslim divorce was handed down in *Danial Latifi v. Union of India.*[39] In response to a petition from Latifi (a leading Muslim liberal) and others, asking the Court to declare the *Muslim Women's Act* unconstitutional on grounds of sex equality, the Court delivered a complicated opinion whose meaning is still being debated. On the one hand, they said that if the law really did mean to give Muslim women rights on divorce that were unequal to those that other Indian women obtained under the Criminal Procedure Code, the law would be unconstitutional. On the other hand, however, citing the familiar principal that if an interpretation can be found that makes a statute constitutional, then that interpretation should be chosen, they ruled that the law is not unconstitutional, because there is a way of interpreting it that does not give Muslim women unequal rights. The details of the proposed interpretation are tortuous and more than a little strained. But two further interpretive principles of significance were introduced by the Court in the process. First, the Court holds that any judgment reached in a case involving marital relations must be made against the background of prevailing social conditions. These conditions, in India today, prominently include male domination, both economic and social. Second, decisions that touch on "basic human rights, culture, dignity and decency of life and dictates of necessity in the pursuit

[39] 72 AIR SC 945 (1985).

of social justice should be invariably left to be decided on considerations other than religion or religious faith or beliefs or national, sectarian, racial or communal constraints." The Court left the implications of these principles for other areas of inequality in the system of personal laws unclear.

The system of personal laws has many severe problems. It creates difficulties not only for sex equality but also for freedom of religion (because it makes it so difficult to change religions) and for nondiscrimination on the basis of religion. Unfortunately but predictably, male leaders in each religion tend to define their prestige in terms of how far they can resist changes in their religious traditions; the position of women has become a focal point for this resistance. Moreover, even when internal reform is successful, as in the case of the *Christian Marriage Bill*, the cumbersome nature of the arrangement creates huge delays and uncertainties for its implementation. Nonetheless, it is possible that internal reform, combined with court pressure in areas touched on by fundamental rights, is the best option for the foreseeable future. In this day of growing Hindu fundamentalism, Uniform Code really does mean Hindu Code, and the resistance of the Muslim minority to losing their legal system is comprehensible. In this situation, the state should press much harder for sex equality as a non-negotiable feature of each religious system, through consultation with the minority communities, seeking, in the process, the opinions not simply of self-appointed male leaders of communities, but of all the members and groups within each community.

One step that would greatly help in addressing both the religious freedom problem and the sex equality problem would be the creation of a genuinely comprehensive secular code, uniform for all India, and the protection of exit options from the religious systems to that code for women who want to elect a secular identity, including protection for their property rights. The combination of some such strategy with internal reform has received a good deal of support from feminist legal scholars in recent days.

V. PRIVACY AND EQUALITY

When the constitution was being written, the Framers consulted U.S. jurists, who warned them of the bad history of substantive due process in the United States, in the *Lochner* era, when progressive economic legislation was invalidated through discovering substantive rights in the due process clauses of the Fifth and Fourteenth Amendments. The Indian framers therefore tried to avoid making room for substantive due process by phrasing Article 21 in a way that suggested that all laws passed by an appropriate procedure would be upheld: instead of the U.S. phrase "due process of law," they used the phrase "procedure established by law," with the intention of suggesting that only procedural irregularities would be found unconstitutional.

The Justices of the Supreme Court, however, soon became convinced that there was an important role for substantive due process to play in the Indian constitutional tradition. The words "life and liberty" in Article 21 have accordingly been the object of a very interesting jurisprudential tradition, which has interpreted them to entail not mere life, but life with dignity (see also Section VII). In 1950, in *Gopalan v. State of Madras*,[40] a case involving allegedly unlawful police detention, two dissenting Justices already argued that preventive detention was inconsistent with the meaning of "life and liberty," as well as with the right to movement in Article 19. In 1978, this idea was recognized by the majority in *Maneka Gandhi v. Union of India and Anr*,[41] a case in which Mrs. Gandhi's daughter-in-law moved the court against the impounding of her passport. The Court held that the rights of Articles 19 and 21 involve the right to travel abroad.[42] In 1981, in *Francis Coralie Mullin v. Administrator, Union Territory of Delhi*,[43] a case involving a female prisoner who had been denied the right to see her family and her lawyer, the Supreme Court held that the right to life involves "the right to basic necessities of life and also the right to carry on such functions and activities as constitute the bare minimum expression of the human self." They linked "life" to the idea of human dignity. In *Olga Tellis v. Bombay Municipal Corporation* (1986),[44] a case involving the eviction of poor pavement dwellers, the Court extended this doctrine, stating: "'Life' means something more than mere animal existence. It does not mean merely that life cannot be extinguished or taken away, except according to procedure established by law. That is but one aspect of the right to life. An equally important aspect of that right is the right to livelihood because, no person can live without the means of living."

During this same period, the Court also held that a right to privacy, modeled on the right recognized in U.S. constitutional law, was inherent in Article 21. This right seemed to many Indian jurists an important one for Indian constitutional law to recognize, both because of its role in protecting women's bodily autonomy and integrity and because of its other potential uses, especially in plugging a gap created by the fact that the Indian Constitution has no equivalent of the U.S. Fourth Amendment, and police surveillance was proceeding unchecked by any constitutional procedure. The first cases to recognize a right to privacy in connection with Article 21 were cases involving police surveillance. In the first of these, *Kharak Singh v. State of Uttar Pradesh* (1963),[45] the dissenters recognized such a right, and in

---

[40] AIR 1950 SC 27.

[41] AIR 1978 SC 597.

[42] Meanwhile, during the Emergency, the Court also held that the right to life can never be suspended, not even when the Constitution itself is suspended: *ADM, Jahalpur v. Shivakant Shukla*, AIR 1976 SC 1207.

[43] AIR 1981, SC 746.

[44] AIR 1986 SC 180.

[45] AIR 1963 SC 1295.

the second, *Govind v. State of Madhya Pradesh* (1975),[46] the majority recognized the right, citing American privacy cases from a variety of distinct areas,
including search and seizure, but also including the Fourteenth Amendment
privacy right cases *Griswold* and *Roe*.

At issue was a state police regulation, framed in accordance with directives
provided by a national police Act, according to which people who had a
criminal record or were in other ways suspected of "a determination to lead
a life of crime" could be subject to unannounced domiciliary visits, often
in the middle of the night, and could also be followed and spied on when
outside the house. The justices opined that "liberty" in Article 21 should be
given an expansive interpretation, as incompatible with "an invasion on the
part of the police of the sanctity of a man's home and an intrusion into his
personal security and his right to sleep, which is the normal comfort and
a dire necessity for human existence even as an animal." The justices then
brought in the notion of privacy, holding that a right to privacy in one's
home is implicated in the meaning of liberty. Citing the dissent in *Kharak
Singh*, they held that "in the last resort a person's house, where he lives with
his family, is his 'castle,' that nothing is more deleterious to a man's physical
happiness and health than a calculated interference with his privacy...."

From the beginning of this privacy jurisprudence, then, the notion of
privacy has been coupled with the notion that a (male) householder has the
right to control his functioning in a protected space. And, in fact, traditional
notions of the privacy of the home, in Indian legal tradition, strongly define
the home as a patriarchal sphere of privilege, in which a man may operate as
a king, unconstrained by the reciprocity or deference he might need to exhibit
toward others outside the home. This is the very aspect of the concept of
privacy that feminists have persistently criticized, arguing that it has been
used for centuries to defend male domination over women and children in
that sphere. Even when the issue was simply surveillance, the Court felt the
need to allude to this powerful Indian (as well as Western) tradition.

Significantly enough, the Justices understood that the actions of the police
threaten important human liberties even when they are not directed at the
"sanctity of the home." And the opinion in *Govind* does call into constitutional question not only the domiciliary visits, but the whole pattern of police
spying.[47] But at this point the opinion alludes to the enumerated liberties of
Article 19, holding that the freedom of movement must also be given an expansive construction. Again citing the dissenters in *Kharak Singh*, the opinion
argues that it is not "mere freedom to move without physical obstruction
and . . . movement under the scrutinizing gaze of the policeman cannot be

[46] AIR 1975 SC 1378.
[47] The actual holding is complex: they say that it is possible that the whole pattern is unconstitutional, but for now they will simply hold that the State needs to show a compelling interest
in public safety if it is to apply these procedures to a particular individual.

free movement." Freedom of movement "must be movement in a free country, i.e., a country where he can do whatever he likes, speak to whomsoever he wants, meet people of his own choice without any apprehension, subject of course to the law of social control, and that a person under the shadow of surveillance is certainly deprived of this freedom." Given that the right to be free from surveillance is here extracted from freedom of movement, it is not clear why the privacy of the home had to be invoked earlier on. Domiciliary visits seem to be bad in just the way surveillance outside the home is bad: they deprive a person of liberty to move around, talk to people, and so on. The Justices showed their awareness that privacy is a slippery notion: "The most serious advocate of privacy must confess that there are serious problems of defining the essence and scope of the right." But nonetheless they indulged in a vague and diffuse rhetoric about the sanctity of the home, and even referred to aspects of marital sanctity that have no evident connection to the case: "Any right to privacy must encompass and protect the personal intimacies of the home, the family, marriage, motherhood, procreation, and child rearing." This has little to do with shadowing a person not suspected of any concrete crime.

In short, the privacy right carries with it some dubious baggage. It is not surprising, then, to discover that it has been a slippery notion when we approach the area of women's sexual autonomy, an area in which even more straightforward ideas of substantive equality sometimes founder. Let us now return to *Sareetha's* case (Section II). Although the equality aspect of Justice Choudary's opinion[48] was progressive and interesting in its own right, most of the attention the case attracted focused on its novel and strongly feminist reading of Article 21 in terms of a right to privacy. Drawing on the U.S. tradition of privacy-right jurisprudence and explicitly citing *Griswold* and *Roe* as precedents, he declared that Article 21 implies a right to privacy, which must be understood to be implicit in the meaning of "life and liberty," given that it had already been established (see below) that "life" means not mere (animal) life, but a properly dignified human life. The remedy of restitution is "a savage and barbarous remedy, violating the right to privacy and human dignity guaranteed by Art. 21 of the Constitution." Justice Choudary is aware that privacy is a slippery concept, with multiple definitions. By contrast, he is satisfied that "any plausible definition of right to privacy is bound to take human body as its first and most basic reference for control over personal identity. Such a definition is bound to include body's inviolability and integrity and intimacy of personal identity, including marital privacy."

The question is, however, why one should have brought the issue of bodily integrity and liberty under privacy in the first place. Surely it does not naturally belong there. Justice Choudary's reference to "marital privacy" betrays the difficulty: the traditional concept of "marital privacy" tells precisely

---

[48] The title "justice" is used in India for both Supreme Court and state High Court judges.

against women's liberty and bodily integrity. It is that very concept that makes it so difficult, even today, to get marital rape criminalized and domestic violence prosecuted. Surely if what was wanted was a right of control over one's body, that right would much more naturally have been read out of Article 19's guarantee of freedom of movement, travel, and residence (as the surveillance cases suggest), or out of the more general notions of "life and liberty" recognized in the right-to-livelihood cases.

Despite the fact that Justice Choudary clearly intends the privacy right to have progressive implications for women's liberty, the appeal to marital privacy is slippery, strongly suggesting the traditional patriarchal household, in which women have no sexual autonomy. And indeed, it was with reference to the traditional ideal of the household that the Justice was eventually overruled. At approximately the same time, a restitution case was heard in the Delhi High Court. The Court argued directly against the Choudary opinion, which had created a stir, holding that the remedy of restitution was not unconstitutional under either Article 14 or Article 21.[49] The essence of the Delhi argument is that the intimate nature of marriage makes the application of constitutional principles inappropriate:

Introduction of Constitutional Law in the home is most inappropriate. It is like introducing a bull in a china shop. It will prove to be a ruthless destroyer of the marriage institution and all that it stands for. In the privacy of the home and the married life neither Art. 21 nor Art. 14 have any place. In a sensitive sphere which is at once intimate and delicate the introduction of the cold principles of Constitutional Law will have the effect of weakening the marriage bond.[50]

In 1984, in a different case, the Supreme Court sided with the Delhi Court and against Justice Choudary.[51] Conjugal rights, held the justices, are "inherent in the very institution of marriage itself." The decree of restitution thus "serves a social purpose as an aid to the prevention of break-up of marriage." As for the claim that the law violates women's bodily integrity, the Justices opined that the law contained "sufficient safeguards . . . to prevent it from being a tyranny." In particular, a woman who does not want to obey can always pay a fine, "provided he or she has properties to be attached."

Thus the whole strategy of appeal to Article 21 was denied. But it seems clear that it was easy to deny it because of the way in which the alleged right was framed, as a right of privacy. For it was then so easy to say, look at our concept of marital privacy. It is certainly possible that the Supreme Court would have refused to recognize any liberty-right for women here, no matter how framed. By contrast, in cases dealing with the rights of the homeless and the rights of criminals they had supported a liberal reading

[49] *Harvinder Kaur v. Harmander Singh Choudhry*, AIR 1984 Delhi 667.
[50] Ibid., at 67.
[51] *Saroj Rani v. Sudarshan Kumar*, AIR 71 (1984) 1562 S.C.

of the general notion of "life and liberty." Both Choudary's sex equality argument (which was totally ignored by the Supreme Court) and the parallel tradition of interpreting Article 21 so as to require "life with dignity" hold more promise for the interests of women than does the dubious and equivocal concept of privacy.

Abortion rights have not figured in recent constitutional cases, because abortion is legal and generally uncontroversial. Until 1971, the law on abortion was rather strict, and imposed criminal penalties for inducing a "miscarriage" except to save the life of the mother. (Although the definition of "miscarriage" appeared to restrict these penalties to the time after the first trimester, there was unclarity about this and there were at least some prosecutions for first-trimester abortions.) In 1970, under pressure from population experts, the government brought forward a liberal abortion statute, the *Medical Termination of Pregnancy Act*, which passed with little opposition in 1971. The Act permits termination of pregnancy up to twenty weeks, on a variety of grounds, including the life of the mother, her physical or mental health, possible deformities in the child, and contraceptive failure. The Act was further liberalized in 1975: the revision made it easier for a woman to get an abortion, completely removed reference to husband's consent, and established procedures for keeping the woman's identity secret.

The most serious opposition to liberal abortion laws currently comes from feminists themselves, who are disturbed at the widespread use of abortion for purposes of sex selection and at the growing imbalance of numbers between women and men.

VI. THE RIGHT TO PETITION

Article 32 of the Constitution creates a remedy for non-enforcement of rights, according to which citizens may appeal directly by petition to the Supreme Court to secure their rights, and the Court may issue writs, directions, and orders designed to secure enforcement. This remedy has proven valuable to women, especially in the area of sexual harassment.

Vishaka v. State of Rajasthan[52] (1997) was brought by petition to the Supreme Court by a group of women's groups and NGOs, on the occasion of an alleged brutal gang rape of a social worker in a village in Rajasthan (this case was the subject of a separate criminal action, and it played no further role in the petition). The petitioners argued that they and other working women are unsafe and unprotected from harassment in the workplace because of the failure of both employers and the legal system to address this problem. They argued that the sexual harassment of women in the workplace violates the fundamental constitutional rights of both gender equality and "life and liberty" (under Articles 14, 15, and 21 of the Constitution). It was also argued

---

[52] AIR 1997, 6 SCC 241; SC 3011.

that these violations entailed violations of rights to "practice any occupation, trade, or business" guaranteed under Article 19. In arguing the case, the petitioners made repeated reference to the Convention on the Elimination of All Forms of Discrimination against Women (CEDAW), which has been ratified by India, arguing that the definitions of gender equality in this document "must be read into these provisions to enlarge the meaning and content thereof, to promote the object of the constitutional guarantee." They argued that this way of understanding the binding force of CEDAW is entailed by Article 51c of the Constitution (among the Directive Principles of State Policy), which holds that "[t]he State shall endeavour to... foster respect for international law and treaty obligations in the dealings of organised people with one another." Thus it was argued that the account of rights of women in the workplace described in CEDAW were binding on India through its ratification of the treaty.

The Court accepted the petitioners' argument, holding that indeed the account of sexual harassment in CEDAW is binding on the nation, and that the relevant Constitutional provisions should henceforth be read in the expanded manner suggested by petitioners, filling in the understanding of the relevant concepts described in CEDAW. As in previous jurisprudence, the Court held that right to life means "life with dignity," and that the nation has the responsibility of enforcing such "safety and dignity through suitable legislation." Following CEDAW, the Court issued guidelines to be implemented by employers. This important case shows a productive interaction between international treaties and domestic courts; CEDAW gives domestic activists a blueprint for change that they can take to their own Courts, in this case achieving the incorporation of CEDAW standards into domestic law. Legislation binding on nongovernmental actors has not yet been passed, and the current political climate does not appear favorable to it.

In the aftermath of events in Gujarat in 2002, which showed that minorities cannot rely on the equal protection of the laws, the right to petition the Supreme Court directly is of major importance for people seeking protection for their rights. In a speech delivered at the University of Chicago Law School on May 17, 2002, retired former Chief Justice Dr. A. S. Anand expressed the view that the Supreme Court was ready to deal with violations of human rights in Gujarat (prominently including mass rapes of women) through the petition route, as soon as a suitable case presents itself. Given the subsequent failure of the ordinary criminal justice system in the *Best Bakery* case, where witnesses were threatened into recanting their testimony, one may hope that the Supreme Court will address the issue soon.

VII. RAPE AS CONSTITUTIONAL VIOLATION

In recent years, the Supreme Court has shown increasing sensitivity to sexual violence against women, and has been willing to play an active role in

the campaign for law reform. In 1983, in *Bharwada Bhogibhai Hrijibhai v.
State of Gujarat*,[53] the Court held that a refusal to act on the testimony of
a victim of sexual assault in the absence of corroboration is "adding insult
to injury." Indeed, they ask: "Why should the evidence of the girls or a
woman who complains of rape or sexual molestation be viewed with the aid
of spectacles tinged with doubt or disbelief? To do so is to justify the charge
of male chauvinism in a male dominated society." They have also criticized
judgments that cast doubt on a woman's testimony on the basis of her past
sexual history.

A dramatic stride was taken in two cases in 1996 and 2000 that recognize
rape as a violation of a woman's constitutional right to life with dignity, as
guaranteed under Article 21. *Bodhisattva Gautam v. Chakraborthy*[54] concerned
a man who persuaded a woman to have intercourse with him on the basis
of a fake marriage ceremony, lived with her for a time under this pretense,
and then abandoned her. The woman successfully sued for maintenance.
Although the charge was not one of rape as such, the Court took the opportunity to expand on this theme, declaring rape a constitutional violation:

Rape is a crime not only against the person of a woman, it is a crime against the
entire society. It destroys the entire psychology of a woman and pushes her into deep
emotional crisis. Rape is therefore the most hated crime. It is a crime against basic
human rights and is violative of the victims most cherished right, namely, right to life
which includes right to live with human dignity contained in article 21.[55]

Because of the facts of the case, the precedential value of this judgment
was unclear. In 2000, however, an important case established the reach of
the constitutional principle. In *Chairman, Railway Board v. Mrs. Chandrima
Das*,[56] the Supreme Court held not only that rape is a violation of the fundamental right to life with dignity guaranteed in Article 21 but also that
the relevant portions of the Universal Declaration of Human Rights should
also be understood to be binding on India, and fundamental rights should
be interpreted with the guidance of the Universal Declaration. Moreover,
the fundamental right in question belongs not only to citizens but to all
"persons" on Indian soil.

The facts of this landmark case are as follows: Hanuffa Khatoon, a
Bangladeshi national, was at Howrah station in Calcutta awaiting the departure of the Jodhpur Express. Becoming ill, she was offered assistance by
various men, some actual railway employees, and some posing as such. They
took her to a hotel maintained by the Railways Board and there gang-raped
her. An accomplice, pretending to rescue her from the rapists, took her to

53 AIR 1983, 2 SCC 217.
54 AIR 1996, 1 SCC 490.
55 *Bodhisattva Gautan*, ibid., at para. 10.
56 AIR 2000 S.Ct. 988.

his flat, where another group of men gang-raped her. The landlord, hearing her cries, summoned the police. The case before the Supreme Court concerned her request for damages against the Railways Board for the acts of its employees and for its failure to maintain its hotel as a safe public accommodation (the plaintiff, Mrs. Das, is an advocate of the Calcutta High Court who represented Hanuffa Khatoon). The Court noted that in the 1996 case rape was already been held to be violative of the fundamental right to life with dignity guaranteed in Article 21. Moreover, the Justices argued, these rights belong not only to citizens, but to all "persons" within the territory of India. This is not true of all the fundamental rights, they argued in a close textual discussion; but it is true of Article 21.

Then, in a most interesting discussion, the Courts pointed out that the fundamental rights are closely modeled on the list of rights in the Universal Declaration; they argue that the purpose of this section of the Constitution was to enact the Universal Declaration and "to safeguard the basic human rights from the vicissitudes of political controversy. . . . " This being so, the meaning of the word "life" can be further interpreted with reference to the Declaration, and has been so in earlier Supreme Court decisions, which give "life" a broad construction, including the idea of life with human dignity. On the grounds that gang rape is obviously inconsistent with human dignity and that the rape was committed by Government employees, the judgment of the Calcutta High Court awarding her compensation was upheld.

Violence against women remains a huge problem in India, but the Courts are becoming far more active and sympathetic. The recent constitutional strategy may energize the movement to give women more adequate protection.

VIII. EDUCATION

One of the most significant gaps between women and men in India is in the area of basic primary education. According to the data supplied by the Government to the 2000 *Human Development Report*, female literacy stands at 43.5 percent (up from 35 percent eight years ago) as contrasted with 67.1 percent for men.[57] States that make education a priority and devise imaginative ways of getting working children into school, however, do much better: the state of Kerala, though relatively poor, has an adolescent literacy rate of 99 percent in both sexes.

From the earliest days of the Republic, education has been recognized as a constitutional issue. The Directive Principles of State Policy state (in article 41) that "[t]he State shall, within the limits of its economic capacity and

---

[57] These figures, though depressing, show that India outperforms her South Asian neighbors: in Pakistan, literacy stands at 28.9 percent for women and 58 percent for men; in Bangladesh 28.6 percent for women, 51.1 percent for men.

development, make effective provision for securing the right to work, to education and to public assistance. . . . " Article 45 states that "[t]he State shall endeavor to provide, within a period of ten years from the commencement of this Constitution, for free and compulsory education for all children until they complete the age of fourteen years." And Article 46 states that "[t]he State shall promote with special care the educational and economic interests of the weaker sections of the people, and in particular, of the Scheduled Castes and Scheduled Tribes, and shall protect them from social injustice and all forms of exploitation." These goals have obviously not been realized within the time specified in Article 45. Most states have regulations making education compulsory, usually up to the age of fourteen, but these laws are not effectively enforced; in some rural areas schools exist only at a great distance and there is no effective transportation. In addition, although state schools are supposedly free of charge, they charge fees for school uniforms, for transportation, and for examinations, thus putting education out of reach of many poor parents.

In 1992, in *Mohini Jain v. State of Karnataka*,[58] the Supreme Court held that the right to education has the status of a fundamental right, and thus belongs in the enforceable Part III of the Constitution rather than in the unenforceable Part IV. In 1993, the Supreme Court took a further step. In *Unnikrishnan J. P. v. State of Andhra Pradesh*,[59] they held that the right to education means: "(a) every child/citizen of this country has a right to free education until he completes the age of 14 years; (b) after a child/citizen completes 14 years, his right to education is circumscribed by the economic capacity of the state and its development. The right to education flows directly from the right to life and is related to the dignity of the individual."

Following these decisions, in 1997, the Eighty-third Amendment to the Constitution was first introduced. Finally passed in 2002, the Amendment gives education the status of a fundamental right. (The right is attached to Article 21 as Article 21A, thus locating the right to education within the right to life, as a further specification of that right.) The Amendment provides for "free and compulsory education to all citizens of the age six to fourteen years." It is to be "enforced in such manner as the state may, by law, determine.' A financial memorandum appended to the Bill creates a fund of Rs. 40,000 for implementation over a five-year period. Subsequently, in 2003, the Court has held that the school lunch program in Kerala, which eases the burden on parents who rely on their children's labor for sustenance by providing a nutritious midday meal at state expense, is mandatory for the entire nation. Lunch programs have already been introduced in a number of other states.

[58] AIR 1992, SC 1858.
[59] AIR 1993 SC 2178.

IX. ASPIRATION AND REALITY

India's constitutional tradition embodies many high aspirations. There is no doubt that sex equality was among the central concerns of the framers, and in many respects they produced a progressive and woman-friendly document. The tradition of interpretation also manifests some fine achievements, both in specific areas relating to sex equality and in articulating the general idea of rights to life and liberty. Reserved legislative seats for women at the local level, despite the initial skepticism of many feminists about their value, are clearly bringing major progress in women's empowerment and women's education. The constitutionalization of the education right, when and if the amendment is passed, will give women new grounds to demand basic rights for themselves and their daughters. In applying the sexual harassment guidelines of CEDAW to India's situation, the Supreme Court has made a very promising move, and one may hope that other parts of CEDAW may be brought into constitutional jurisprudence in future. Violence against women is now being addressed as a constitutional violation.

One can see that much more remains to be accomplished. The debate about reserved seats at the national level has been allowed to degenerate into grotesque political in-fighting. The personal laws, which greatly impede women's full equality, are not being reformed nearly rapidly and seriously enough. Traditional ideas of women's marital role continue to crop up in Supreme Court opinions, retarding progress on issues ranging from inheritance rights to violence against women.

One thing that is badly needed, if these problems are to be solved, is reform and upgrading of the legal system. Nehru's aspirations for Indian higher education focused on the sciences and economics. To this day, the humanities are held in disregard, and fields such as women's studies have a hard time gaining adherents. Law continues to be a trade, not greatly respected. Law schools, more trade schools than academic educators, do not present students with theoretical approaches to constitutional issues. Certainly young lawyers do not learn to ponder feminist approaches. At present there is a serious effort under way to upgrade the quality of legal and judicial education in the state law schools. At the same time, feminist legal scholar Indira Jaising is attempting to start a private law school in Delhi to draw in people who think of law as a way of addressing urgent social issues (rather than as the family trade). Such efforts have to struggle uphill, because the current government, which has great power over university appointments, is not friendly to feminist concerns. Nonetheless, there are very encouraging signs of change, and it may be hoped that in future both lawyers and judges will have a higher level of awareness of issues of sex equality and of feminist criticisms of some traditional approaches. As women achieve greater parity in education, it may also be hoped that more women will choose law as a career and that the judiciary will contain more than today's few token women.

To the extent that these possibilities are realized, we can hope that the fine goals of the framers (and, indeed, goals going well beyond their vision) will be made reality. Certainly there is wide consensus in India that the empowerment of women is a key to the nation's development: India's potential will not be realized as long as it thwarts the capabilities of half of its citizens.

Suggested Readings

Bina Agarwal, *A Field of One's Own: Gender and Land Rights in South Asia* (Cambridge: Cambridge University Press, 1994).

Flavia Agnes, "Protecting Women against Violence: Review of a Decade of Legislation, 1980–89" (25 April 1992) *Economic and Political Weekly* 19–33.

Flavia Agnes, *Law and Gender Inequality: The Politics of Women's Rights in India* (Delhi: Oxford University Press, 2000).

Flavia Agnes, "Church, State and the Christian Woman" (2000) 15 *From the Lawyers Collective* 9–12.

Srimati Basu, *She Comes to Take Her Rights: Indian Women, Property, and Propriety* (Albany: State University of New York Press, 1999).

Jean Drèze and Amartya Sen, *India: Economic Development and Social Opportunity* (Delhi: Oxford, 1995).

Jean Drèze and Amartya Sen, eds., *Indian Development: Selected Regional Perspectives* (Delhi: Oxford, 1997).

Ali Asghar Engineer, ed., *The Shah Bano Controversy* (Delhi: Orient Longman, 1987).

Marc Galanter, *Competing Equalities: Law and the Backward Classes in India* (Delhi: Oxford University Press, 1984).

Marc Galanter, *Law and Society in Modern India* (Delhi: Oxford, 1989).

Marc Galanter, "The Long Half-Life of Reservations" in E. Sridharan, R. Sudarshan, and Z. Hasan, eds., *India's Living Constitution: Ideas, Practices, Controversies* (Delhi: Oxford University Press, 2002) 306–18.

K. D. Gaur, "Abortion and the Law in Countries of Indian Subcontinent, Asean Region, United Kingdom, Ireland and United States of America" (1995) 37 *Journal of the Indian Law Institute* 293–323.

Sanjoy Ghose and Kaveri Sharma, "Twenty Important Judgements of Significance" (2000) 15 *From the Lawyers Collective* 5–21.

Zoya Hasan, "Women's Reserved Seats and the 'Politics of Presence'" (December 2000) [unpublished draft].

Zoya Hasan, ed., *Forging Identities: Gender, Communities and the State in India* (Delhi and Boulder, CO: Kali for Women and Westview Press, 1994).

Indira Jaising, "Violence against Women: The Indian Perspective" in J. Peters and A. Wolper, eds., *Women's Rights, Human Rights: International Feminist Perspectives* (New York and London: Routledge, 1995), 51–56.

Indira Jaising, ed., *Justice for Women: Personal Laws, Women's Rights and Law Reform* (Mapusa, Goa: The Other India Press, 1996).

Indira Jaising, "Gender Justice and the Supreme Court" in P. N. Kripal et al., eds., *Supreme but Not Infallible: Essays in Honour of the Supreme Court of India* (Delhi: Oxford University Press, 2000) 288–320.

Niraja Jayal, *Gender and Decentralisation* [unpublished draft].

Ratna Kapur and Brenda Cossman, *Subversive Sites: Feminist Engagements with Law in India* (Delhi: Sage, 1996).

P. N. Kripal et al., eds., *Supreme but Not Infallible: Essays in Honour of the Supreme Court of India* (Delhi: Oxford University Press, 2000).

Gerald Larson, ed., *Religion and Personal Law in India: A Call to Judgment* (Bloomington: Indiana University Press, 2002).

Tahir Mahmood, *Muslim Personal Law* (Nagpur: All India Reporter, Ltd., 1983).

Archana Mehendale, "Compulsory Primary Education in India" (1998) 13 *From the Lawyers Collective* 4–12.

Martha C. Nussbaum, *Women and Human Development: The Capabilities Approach* (New York and Delhi: Cambridge University Press and Kali for Women, 2000).

Martha C. Nussbaum, "Is Privacy Bad for Women? What the Indian Constitutional Tradition Can Teach Us about Sex Equality" (2000) 25 *The Boston Review* 42–7.

Martha C. Nussbaum, "Sex Equality, Liberty, and Privacy: A Comparative Approach to the Feminist Critique" in E. Sridharan, R. Sudarshan, and Z. Hasan, eds., *India's Living Constitution: Ideas, Practices, Controversies* (Delhi: Oxford University Press, 2002) 242–83.

Martha C. Nussbaum, "Genocide in Gujarat," *Dissent* summer 2003, 15–23.

Martha C. Nussbaum, "The Modesty of Mrs. Bajaj: India's Problematic Route to Sexual Harassment Law" in C. MacKinnon and R. Siegel, eds., *Directions in Sexual Harassment Law* (New Haven, CT: Yale University Press) [forthcoming].

Archana Parashar, *Women and Family Law Reform in India: Uniform Civil Code and Gender Equality* (Delhi: Sage, 1992).

Lloyd I. Rudolph and Susanne H. Rudolph, *In Pursuit of Lakshmi: The Political Economy of the Indian State* (Chicago: University of Chicago Press, 1987).

Lloyd I. Rudolph and Susanne H. Rudolph, "Living with Difference in India: Legal Pluralism and Legal Universalism in Historical Context" in D. Marquand and R. Nettler, eds., *Religion and Democracy* (Oxford: Blackwell, 2000).

Tanika Sarkar, *Hindu Wife, Hindu Nation: Community, Religion, and Cultural Nationalism* (Bloomington: Indiana University Press, 2002).

Patricia Uberoi, ed., *Social Reform, Sexuality and the State* (Delhi: Sage, 1996).

8

Constitutional Transformation, Gender Equality, and Religious/National Conflict in Israel

Tentative Progress through the Obstacle Course

Ran Hirschl and Ayelet Shachar

Open any traveler's guidebook about Israel, and you will soon find a photo of a young woman in military uniform carrying a weapon. She is the female solider. Just like her male peers, she is subject to mandatory conscription to the defense forces when she reaches the age of eighteen. Her image is an emblem of gender equality. Unfortunately, the status of women in Israel does not match the mythology this image suggests. This gap between myth and reality makes Israel a living laboratory for the study of women's rights. As a Jewish *and* democratic state, it hosts a constant battle over its religious, national, and cultural identity, as well as engaging daily with internal and external challenges to its very existence. In each of these struggles, women's rights, among others, are tested to the limit. This chapter provides an overview of the current status of women's rights in Israel. Our intention is to analyze how, why, and under what conditions individual women and feminist organizations have been successful in advancing the gender equality agenda through constitutional rights jurisprudence and legislative initiatives. We also hope to evaluate the limits of such change by addressing the nature of the enduring inequalities that Israeli women still face in navigating the obstacles of a deeply divided society.

Our discussion is divided into three major sections. We begin with an outline of pertinent elements of Israel's unique constitutional system. Next, we analyze landmark constitutional-rights jurisprudence pertaining to the equal treatment of women in different social contexts, including the military, the home, the public sector, the private labor market, and Israel's unique system of religious councils. In this second section, we also address new legislation aimed at protecting victims of domestic violence, as well as combating sexual harassment in the military and in the workplace. In the third section of this chapter, we move on to discuss the intersection of gender, religiosity, and nationality in Israel, as well as the complex social and legal status of women as markers of identity in a multiethnic, multireligious polity.

THE RELEVANT CONSTITUTIONAL FRAMEWORK

Like several other formerly British-ruled territories, Israel inherited the British Common Law tradition with its strong emphasis on parliamentary supremacy; it thus remains without a written Constitution or entrenched bill of rights contained in one document. Instead, a web of eleven Basic Laws serves as the formal core of Israeli constitutional law. Until 1992, the *Knesset* (Israel's parliament) passed Basic Laws primarily concerned with the powers vested in the various branches of the government. However, none of these laws provided any entrenched constitutional protection of basic rights and liberties, just as none formally established any form of judicial review. The long-standing legacy of the pre-1992 constitutional stalemate impacted the Israeli definition of constitutional rights jurisprudence, which at least until 1992 involved primarily judicial review of administrative actions rather than on a full-scale U.S.-style judicial review of primary legislation. In the absence of a civil rights tradition and the necessary constitutional framework for actively reviewing primary legislation, the Supreme Court was limited in the era before 1992 to judicial review of administrative acts, informed by an "implied bill of rights" doctrine.[1] Despite this fact, over its first four decades (1948–1992), the Supreme Court of Israel (SCI) developed a fairly extensive jurisprudence dealing with gender equality. Indeed, as will be shown in the second section of this chapter, most landmark cases that advanced women's rights in the pre-1992 period were based on the "implied bill of rights" doctrine.

The constitutional landscape in Israel changed dramatically in 1992 with the enactment of two partly entrenched fundamental rights laws – *Basic Law: Human Dignity and Liberty*, and *Basic Law: Freedom of Occupation*.[2] Section 1 of *Basic Law: Freedom of Occupation* proclaims that "[f]undamental human rights in Israel are founded upon the recognition of the value of the human being, the sanctity of human life, and the principle that all persons are free; these rights shall be upheld in the spirit of the principles set forth in the Declaration of Independence of the State of Israel 5708 (1948)." Moreover, Section 1 of *Basic Law: Human Dignity and Liberty* states that the purpose of this Basic Law "is to protect human dignity and liberty, in order to establish in a Basic Law the values of the State of Israel as a Jewish and democratic state," thereby expanding the scope of rights protected by this new law beyond the scope of rights explicitly listed in it. It is generally agreed that the two new Basic Laws awarded the Supreme Court the authority

---

[1] The paradigm for this type of expansive administrative review was established in 1953 in the seminal case of *Kol Ha'am v. The Minister of the Interior*, H.C. 73/53, 7(2) P.D. 871.
[2] For a detailed discussion of the political circumstances that led to the pre-1992 stalemate, as well as the motivation for adopting the "constitutional revolution" of 1992, see Ran Hirschl, *Towards Juristocracy: The Origins and Consequences of the New Constitutionalism* (Harvard University Press, 2004), chs. 2–3.

to hold unconstitutional and therefore unenforceable primary legislation enacted by the *Knesset*.[3]

In 1995, the SCI drew upon the new constitutional framework adopted in 1992 to virtually invalidate – for the first time in Israel's constitutional history – a *Knesset* law.[4] The Court used this *Marbury v. Madison*–like occasion to firmly establish its power to declare unconstitutional acts and statutes that did not comply with the standards set out in the new Basic Laws. The majority of justices held that the two new Basic Laws had indeed ushered in a new era in the historic quest for a comprehensive constitutional catalogue of rights and active judicial review in Israel. It was recognized that these laws had formal constitutional status and were therefore superior to any ordinary legislation.

In numerous rulings over the past decade, the SCI has taken the view that fundamental rights not expressly mentioned in the two new basic laws – for example, equality rights – are protected under the umbrella of human dignity. This interpretation of the new basic laws proved instrumental in constitutional litigation pertaining to gender and sexual orientation.

Before we embark on an analysis of pertinent jurisprudence, it is material to say a few words about the SCI's structure and jurisdiction. Israel adheres to a centralized system of judicial review whereby the SCI is the only body that may determine the constitutionality of laws. The Court has jurisdiction as appellate court over appeals from the district courts in all matters, both civil and criminal. In addition, it is a court of first instance (sitting as a High Court of Justice) in direct actions launched by individual stakeholders against public authorities, and in matters where the Court considers it necessary to grant relief in the interests of justice, which are not normally within the jurisdiction of any other court or tribunal. As the High Court of Justice, the Court hears well over a thousand petitions each year. These cases are often high-profile ones challenging the acts of government officials. Originally, the Court demanded that a petitioner show possible harm to a direct and material personal interest. Since 1988, however, the Court has significantly liberalized its access rules, effectively recognizing standing rights of public petitioners and lowering the barrier of nonjusticiability. These procedural changes, along with the Court's occasional assertiveness and exclusive

---

[3] Significantly, both laws authorize judicial review. However, like the Canadian Charter of Rights and Freedoms, Israel's new Basic Laws contain a limitation clause forbidding infringement of the declared rights, "except by a statute that befits the values of the State of Israel, for a worthy purpose, and not exceeding what is necessary." Article 10 of *Basic Law: Human Dignity and Liberty* grants immunity from scrutiny to all previously existing legislation. Thus, the supremacy of this Basic Law pertains only to post-1992 legislation. Moreover, in 1994, *Basic Law: Freedom of Occupation* was amended by the *Knesset* in the spirit of the Canadian "notwithstanding" override clause to allow for future modifications by ordinary laws in the instance of an absolute majority of *Knesset* members declaring support for the amendment.
[4] *United Mizrahi Bank v. Migdal Cooperative Village*, C.A. 6821/93, 49(4) P.D. 195.

powers to issue orders against statutory bodies, establish the SCI's fairly extensive jurisdiction over, and impact upon, key policy-making processes that define the scope of women's rights in Israel.

CONSTITUTING GENDER EQUALITY: PRE- AND POST-1992

Rights and Realities

A strong symbolic manifestation of the formal commitment to gender equality is found in Israel's Declaration of Independence (1948), which pledges to "uphold the full social and political equality of all its citizens, without distinction of race, creed or sex."[5] Building on this commitment, Section 1 of the 1951 *Equal Rights for Women Law* explicitly states that "one law shall apply to a woman and to a man in every legal action; ... any legislative order that discriminates against a woman because she is a woman – is void." Unlike their counterparts in most Western democracies, Israeli women were granted universal suffrage immediately upon the establishment of the state. In the same egalitarian vein, the 1953 *Defense Service Law* imposes mandatory military service on *all* Israeli citizens, men and women alike. Similarly, the 1949 *Compulsory Education Law* mandates free schooling for all children, boys and girls, from the ages of five to fourteen. These laws, adopted at the "nation-building" stage in Israel's history, clearly reflect an unequivocal commitment to gender equality. Israel also adopted a comprehensive set of labor laws forbidding discrimination in the workplace. These laws were updated in the 1980s and 1990s to prohibit discrimination on the basis of parenthood, gender, and sexual orientation, as well as to hold sexual harassers (and their employers) accountable in criminal and civil proceedings. Israel's labor laws also prevent the dismissal from work of pregnant women and provide twelve weeks of statutory paid maternity leave to biological and adoptive mothers (the law permits fathers to take paid paternity leave for up to half of that time). In addition, incremental social security allowances were designed to encourage women with young children to reenter the workplace.

In practice, however, women in Israel have never achieved full equality. Even today, at the dawn of the third millennium, an Israeli woman earns on average only 83 percent of the earnings of an equally qualified man. Moreover, this gap *increases* with education. Thus, a woman with more than sixteen years of education (the highest bracket of education recorded for statistical purposes) earns on average 76 percent of the salary of a man

---

[5] The Declaration of Independence is not an entrenched source of operative rights. However, it serves as a "normative umbrella" that provides interpretative guidelines according to which specific laws must be read.

with the same educational qualifications.[6] Women are overrepresented in low-paying, part-time menial jobs, while remaining significantly underrepresented at the higher levels of the managerial sector, the government, the civil service, and the business community.[7] They also are underrepresented in the *Knesset* as well as in the elected bodies of the municipal government.[8] Yet socioeconomic inequality and political underrepresentation are only part of the problem.

Women's inclusion in the military, while symbolically a sign of their full inclusion in the "womb of citizenship" – especially in a country like Israel, where taking up arms is still a basic duty and rite of passage for anyone seeking full membership in its civilian society – has not always benefited women.[9] Most women who serve in the military are still relegated to low-prestige clerical functions during their mandatory service. Until the mid-1990s, they were formally blocked from acquiring high-profile instructional, technological, or combat roles.[10] Such marginalization into second-class "assistance" positions also has exposed women to potential discrimination by their male supervisors on the basis of gender, and to the troubling risk of sexual harassment in a hierarchical and often subordinating setting. Contrary to the common myth of gender equality, although Israeli women serve in the military, they do so on unequal terms with men. Indeed, if the army is the "womb of citizenship," it is a womb that nurtures gender division and inequality.

Finally, and perhaps most profoundly, women's status in Israel is significantly affected by the deep religious and national fissures that are undermining the Israeli polity from within. The most persistent impediment to the advancement of women's rights in Israel is the perception that the equality principle may contradict other fundamental values of the state, such as the preservation of its Jewish nature, or the political conception of Israel's Jewish population as a "nation in arms." The preoccupation with national security and collective identity (seen, for example, in the mandatory conscription requirement or in the debate over "who is a Jew" and who qualifies for the

---

[6] Israel Central Bureau of Statistics, *Women and Men: Major Statistical Parameters (Special Report)* (March 2000) at 8 [Hebrew].

[7] Ibid, at 6–7.

[8] The *Knesset* (the Israeli parliament) consists of 120 members (MKs) elected in a proportional representation, single-district electoral system at least once every five years. Notably, the percentage of women (52 percent of Israel's population) in the *Knesset* has remained almost unchanged over the last three decades – 10 percent in 1973; 12.5 percent as of June 2002.

[9] Sections 13 and 16 of the 1986 *Defense Service Law* require that all Israeli women serve in the Israeli Defense Force (IDF). In practice, however, religious Jewish women may seek exemption from such service based on their religious beliefs. Moreover, Arab-Israelis, regardless of gender, are not conscripted to the military as a matter of administrative practice.

[10] This situation has changed in recent years. Women can now acquire instructional and technical roles in the military, and have gradually been introduced to service in roles that bear the "direct combat" label. See our discussion of the 1995 *Miller* case below.

right to return to Israel[11]) often relegates other important problems, such as socioeconomic, ethnic, and gender inequality, to the sidelines of public debate. Significantly, in almost all legal cases where the gender equality principle has directly challenged accepted norms of collective identity – such as questioning *Halakhic* (Orthodox Jewish) rules regulating marriage and divorce, women's prayer rights, or the debate surrounding religious conversion to Judaism in Israel – women's rights have been compromised. We discuss these important issues of intersectionality in the third and final section of this chapter. But first we wish to explore the various ways in which constitutional litigation and progressive legislation have been used to advance gender equality in Israel.

Gender Equality and the Sameness Principle

As we mentioned earlier, the absence of a formal Bill of Rights did not mean that there was no protection of formal equality prior to the enactment of the two new basic laws in 1992. In a series of rulings the Supreme Court held that fundamental principles of individual freedom and equality were indeed embedded in and even integral to the Israeli legal system. These values, the Court held, were declared as guiding principles in the Declaration of Independence of 1948. Furthermore, they reflect the democratic nature of the Israeli polity. Accordingly, the state and its organs should take into account principles of formal equality and individual freedom when exercising their administrative powers.

Three clear illustrations of the application of this implied bill of rights doctrine in the realm of gender equality in the pre-1992 era are found in the *Poraz, Shakdiel*, and *Nevo* cases. The 1987 *Poraz* affair involved a challenge to a practice of the Municipality of Tel Aviv in which the municipality refrained from appointing women to the committee that selected the city's Chief Rabbis. By doing so, the municipality avoided a confrontation with the ultra-Orthodox representatives who constituted roughly two thirds of the appointment committee.[12] The Court held such exclusion of women from a publicly appointed body to be unacceptable and discriminatory, as it disregarded the principle of gender equality as a fundamental principle of Israel's legal system.

Or consider the Court's ruling in the *Shakdiel* case, which was determined in the same year as *Poraz*.[13] Leah Shakdiel, an ultra-Orthodox woman, was

---

[11] The Law of Return provides Jews with the right to "return" to Israel to take up citizenship even if they have had no previous contact with the state. Since being Jewish is sufficient to qualify for citizenship, the state's self-definition is inextricably caught up with defining "who is a Jew." For further discussion, see Ayelet Shachar, "Whose Republic? Citizenship and Membership in the Israeli Polity" (1999) 13 *Georgetown Immigration Law Journal* 233–72.

[12] *Poraz v. Municipality of Tel Aviv*, H.C. 953/87, 42(2) P.D. 309.

[13] *Shakdiel v. Minister of Religious Affairs*, H.C. 153/87, 42(2) P.D. 221.

elected by the municipal council of a small town in southern Israel to the town's religious council.[14] The town's Chief Rabbi and religious leadership refused to summon the religious council, arguing, *inter alia*, that according to Torah laws, women are not permitted to take up any public positions or political representation responsibilities. The "rebellious" Ms. Shakdiel petitioned the Supreme Court against the town's religious authorities, challenging the constitutionality of their refusal to accept her (legally obtained) membership in the Council. Drawing upon fundamental principles of formal equality and the "implied bill of rights" doctrine, the Supreme Court held that as public bodies that provide public services, religious councils are subject to the "general fundamental norms of Israel's legal system." Accordingly, the Court ordered the Council to accept Ms. Shakdiel's membership and to resume its operation without any further delay.

The *Nevo* affair, the third component in the trilogy of women's rights decisions made in 1987, involved a challenge to the legality of a Jewish Agency practice that imposed different mandatory retirement-age rules on the basis of gender. Mandatory retirement age for men was set at sixty-five, whereas women were obliged to retire at the age of sixty. In a landmark ruling, the Court accepted the claim of Dr. Naomi Nevo – a sociologist who had been employed by the Agency on a permanent basis for over three decades – that the Jewish Agency's practice in imposing differential, gender-based, mandatory retirement rules was unjustifiably discriminatory, and should therefore be rescinded.[15] In accepting Nevo's "sameness" claim, the Supreme Court overruled an earlier decision by the National Labor Court. The Court's decision in the *Nevo* affair marked a high point in the fight for eliminating explicitly gender-based discrimination in the employment arena. The *Knesset* reacted promptly to the Court's ruling in *Nevo* by enacting a law that equalized the retirement age for men and women workers while preserving women's right to early retirement.

In another landmark ruling in the early 1980s (preceding the Supreme Court's decision in *Nevo*), the National Labor Court drew upon embedded principles of equality as well as on the U.S. Supreme Court's famous decision in *Brown v. Board of Education* (1954) to declare void a gender-based, "separate but equal," employee promotion policy set by a collective labor agreement between El Al (Israel's national air carrier) and its flight attendants association:[16] "Just as there is no place for the 'separate but equal' doctrine in the realm of education because separate educational paths are unequal by definition," held the Court, "so there is no place for this doctrine in the

---

[14] Local and municipal religious councils are publicly funded statutory bodies supervising most religious affairs and services at the community level (e.g., the operation of synagogues and religious ceremonies, the enforcement of Sabbath closing laws, *Kashrut* laws, etc.).

[15] *Nevo v. The National Labor Court*, H.C. 104/87, 44(4) P.D. 749.

[16] *El Al's Flight Attendants Association v. Edna Hazon*, N.L.C. 3–25/33, 4 P.D.A. 365.

labor realm." It further held that "by their very nature, separate promotion tracks infringe upon the principle of equal opportunity."[17]

The appearance of the new Basic Laws on the SCI's post-1992 agenda advanced gender equality in at least two distinct ways: it entrenched the principle of equal treatment irrespective of sex and sexuality (i.e., formal equality), and heightened the principle of human dignity, as manifested, for example, in the right to protection from domestic violence and sexual harassment. At the same time, the Court's equality jurisprudence over the past decade has been generally noncommittal about "anti-subordination" (or substantive equality) as means for overcoming discrimination on the basis of sex or sexual orientation.

In the post-1992 era, then, the Court has proved vigilant in revoking practices and policies that have violated the sameness principle. This is best illustrated in the *Miller* decision.[18] Until the mid-1990s, the Israel Air Force (IAF) had never admitted a woman to its combat-pilot course. The IAF justified its male-only admission policy on grounds of pertinent physical differences and the risk of inefficiency involved in lengthy and expensive training of female pilots, given that women had the right to terminate their reserve service upon childbirth. This long-standing practice was challenged by Alice Miller – a young woman who held a civil aviation certificate and volunteered for the course, but was rejected in spite of the fact that she fulfilled the basic criteria for admission. Ms. Miller then turned to the Court, claiming that the IAF's decision not to admit her to the pilot-combat course infringed upon her equality rights, as it discriminated against her on the basis of her gender. In its landmark 1995 ruling, the Court held that the IAF's policy of denying qualified women admission to its combat-pilot course was unjustifiably discriminatory, as it failed to treat women in the same manner as men. The Court further ordered the IAF to eliminate the gender criterion (one among many admission parameters) from its selection criteria.[19] This decision was regarded as an important victory by those women's rights activists who adhere strictly to the sameness principle, and who believe that increasing female participation in elite combat units is the best route to advance women's status in a militaristic society such as Israel.

Interestingly, while gender still plays a role in shaping (and often limiting) the jobs and opportunities open to women in the military, similar debates

---

[17] Ibid., at 374.

[18] *Alice Miller v. Minister of Defense*, H.C. 4541/94, 49(4) P.D. 94.

[19] It is important to note that the *Miller* decision refers only to women who wish to enrol in a *voluntary* course of combat training. It says nothing about the broader, and potentially more controversial, question of the integration of women into combat roles under the terms of their *mandatory* conscription. In January 2000, the *Defense Service Law* was amended to guarantee women an equal right to serve in any role in the military. However, this general commitment may be curtailed when gender-based differentiation is justified due to the nature of a specific military occupation.

have rarely emerged in the context of drafting gay men to combat service. In contrast to the American "don't ask, don't tell" policy, the Israeli army does not dismiss any soldier on the basis of his or her sexual orientation. In the post-1992 era, gay partners of deceased military officers have won the right to receive state-funded monetary compensation similar to that provided to opposite-sex partners, and to be formally invited as family members to official commemoration ceremonies for those who died while taking up arms for the nation. It is also important to note that a year prior to the *Miller* decision, the Court held in the 1994 *Danilowitch* case that El Al, the national airline, had to provide same-sex employees (and their partners) the same benefits it provided to opposite-sex employees (and their partners).[20] Any other treatment, the Court ruled, would fail to respect the meaningful relationships of trust, support, and human dignity that individuals create in the domestic sphere. As in the *Miller* case, in *Danilowitch* the Court interpreted equality as sameness: same-sex couples must be treated in the *same* way as opposite-sex couples. In both cases, the Court ruled that similarly situated individuals could not be treated differently due to their gender or sexual orientation (the formal equality principle).[21]

In another high-profile decision released in the spring of 2000, the Court (with Madam Justice Dorner and Madam Justice Beinish sitting on a three-judge panel) drew upon this rationale in ruling that the sameness principle holds not only in the military and employment arenas, but also in other social settings, including the family.[22] Here, the Court ordered the Population Administration to register a lesbian woman as the adoptive mother of her same-sex common-law spouse's son. Although this decision was determined on the basis of a technical argument (the couple already held a valid adoption order issued by a California court), it implicitly expanded the sameness argument to include recognition of same-sex couples' family-related rights.[23]

---

[20] *El Al Airlines Ltd. v. Danilowitch et al.*, H.C. 721/94, 48(5) P.D. 749.

[21] Nor could they be treated differently due to their marital status; in the *Efrat* case, the Supreme Court declared the right of a woman to carry her common law spouse's surname in addition to her surname, and to permit the couple's children to legally bear the surname of both their common law mother and father (*Dr. Michal Efrat v. The Population Registrar*, H.C. 693/91, 47(1) P.D. 749). More than a decade later (in 2003), the European Court of Justice similarly ruled in favor of permitting a dual-nationality (Belgo-Spanish) couple to assign their children the surnames of both parents. Following the ISC ruling, the *Knesset* amended the 1958 Names Law so as to permit a married woman to keep her birth name instead of, or in addition to, her husband's surname.

[22] As of October 2003, five of the fourteen SCI Justices were women.

[23] *Brener-Kadish v. Ministry of Interior*, H.C. 1779/99, 52(2) P.D. 368. See also our discussion of *Plonit ("Jane Doe") v. Great Rabbinical Court*, H.C. 293/00, *infra* note 48, and the accompanying text. In 1999, however, a district court in Tel Aviv held that two women who lived together could not register each other's biological children as their adoptive children, because, unlike the *Brener-Kadish* case, they had no foreign court order that established the

Women's Rights as Members of Non-Orthodox Branches of Judaism

One of the symbolic pinnacles of advancing equal treatment claims in the realm of gender equality is the recent High Court of Justice jurisprudence pertaining to women's status as representatives of non-Orthodox (i.e., Reform or Conservative) branches of Judaism. The fierce struggles among Orthodox, non-Orthodox, and secular Jews have reached the Supreme Court on numerous occasions over the past decade, leading to landmark judgments pertaining to reallocation of funds to religious movements and their educational institutions; recognition of non-Orthodox conversions to Judaism; and the constitutional scrutiny of a benchmark administrative arrangement under which Orthodox yeshiva students had received draft deferments from military service.

This recent spate of jurisprudence revisiting the historic monopoly of the Orthodox branch of Judaism over (Jewish) religious matters in Israel has also addressed women's claims for equal treatment in the public sphere. In 1996, for example, the Court drew upon the sameness principle to rule that the exclusion of women and non-Orthodox representatives from Jewish municipal religious councils, and from the electoral groups that selected candidates for these councils, contravened the constitutional principle of equality.[24] Two years later, the Court reaffirmed its 1996 ruling, ordering the immediate inclusion of representatives of Reform and Conservative Jewish communities in regional religious councils; it also instructed the Minister of Religious Affairs to allow a woman to be a member of a local religious council.

The relationship between gender equality and traditional religiosity is at the heart of three recent rulings concerning the *Women of the Wall* affair. The *Women of the Wall* organization represents a group of observant Jewish women who pray together in a *minyan* – a religious quorum traditionally reserved for men. This form of collective worship is not acceptable to ultra-Orthodox Jews when practiced by women. It was therefore prohibited by the "Rabbi of the Wall," a state-nominated official authorized to regulate the prayer arrangements concerning Jews at the Western Wall. In 1994, after several years of political deliberation failed to yield a solution to the problem of women's collective "prayer rights," the Court was called upon to resolve the dispute. In its first ruling on this matter, the Court held that when the principle of gender equality came into direct conflict with the religious beliefs of some groups (as in this case), preference should be given to the religious groups in an effort to avoid scenes of confrontation at the Western Wall, a holy site and a highly volatile political area.[25] However, the Court

legality of the adoption. See (Tel Aviv District Court) 10/99 *Plonit and Palmonit ("Jane Doe" and "Jane Roe") v. Attorney General* (decision released on May 10, 2001, not yet published).

[24] *Meretz Movement et. al v. Municipality of Jerusalem,* H.C. 2463/96, 50(4) P.D. 837.

[25] *Hofmann v. Custodian of the Western Wall,* H.C. 257/89, 48(2) P.D. 265.

also urged the government to find a fair solution to the problem that would balance religious-based accommodations with women's rights to equality. A government committee was set up to find such a solution, but it failed to reach an agreement that was acceptable to the involved parties.[26] The petitioners returned to the Court to reassert their prayer rights based on the equality principle. This time around, given the failure to achieve a negotiated settlement in good faith, the Court reversed its original decision and ruled in favor of the *Women of the Wall* organization. The government was ordered to make the technical arrangements that would enable the women to pray as they wished, while minimizing the disturbance to other worshippers. Following a government appeal, an extended panel of nine judges revised the ruling in early 2003, and instructed the government to designate the adjacent Robinson's Arch area (rather than the main plaza that fronts the Wall) for the group's prayers.

Gender Equality and Preferential Treatment

While the Court has been relatively generous in its interpretation of the sameness principle in the context of gender equality, it has been less enthusiastic in dealing with preferential treatment of women – an area in which the *Knesset* has taken the lead. In two significant cases during the past decade, the Court addressed the argument that advancing a progressive notion of equality might require that qualified women benefit from affirmative action in certain social arenas. In the *Women's Network I* and *II* cases, the Court upheld *Knesset* legislation that specifically required that preference be given to women until there is "adequate" representation of both sexes in the public sector.[27] In the 1994 *Women's Network I* decision, the Court ruled that any nomination for the board of directors of governmental companies must be considered in light of the 1993 legislative amendment to the *Government Companies Law*, which required adequate representation of both sexes on the board of directors of such companies. The Court further held that according to the guiding constitutional principle of equality between the sexes, affirmative action was a legitimate means of achieving such representation.

In 1998, the *Women's Network* once again turned to the Court. This time, the issue raised was the unsatisfactory implementation of a 1995 legislative amendment of the *Civil Service Law*, which introduced affirmative action for women in the civil service (along the model of 1993 amendment of the *Government Companies Law*). The legislation imposed an obligation on the

---

[26] For an account of changes in women's domestic and public roles within the ultra-Orthodox Jewish community itself, see Tamar El-Or, *Educated and Ignorant: Ultraorthodox Women and Their World* (Boulder, CO: Lynne Rienner Publishers, 1994).

[27] *Women's Network v. Minister of Transportation*, H.C. 453/94, 48(5) P.D. 501; *Women's Network v. Minister of Labor and Welfare*, H.C. 2671/98, 52(3) P.D. 630.

Civil Service Commissioner to proactively advance adequate representation of women in the senior ranks of the civil service. In *Women's Network II*, the petitioners asked the Court to order that all government agencies enforce the statutory obligation to promote women's equality in the civil service through measures of preferential treatment aimed at achieving an adequate standard of representation.

The Court's decision in *Women's Network II* formally affirmed the 1994 judgment. It further stated that all hiring procedures for senior-level positions in the civil service were to become subject to the "adequate representation" standard. However, the Court also narrowed its reading of this standard, by holding that it did not necessarily imply that a female candidate would be chosen where the candidates possessed similar qualifications. Rather, according to this later judgment, the adequate representation standard would be met when the employer could prove that an open job search for the senior managerial position was conducted, and that women were adequately represented among the final candidates for the position. This interpretation of the adequate representation standard thus focuses on equality of opportunity – rather than equality of outcome.[28] Accordingly, the constitutional principle of equality *permits* preferential treatment when such a standard is defined in primary legislation, but it does not establish an *obligation* to promote or hire members of the underrepresented group.[29]

Domestic Violence, Sexual Harassment, and Heightened Protection for Women

The guiding principle of equality, read together with the guarantee of human dignity, has enabled the Court to interpret the new Basic Laws as promoting heightened protection for women against violence in the home and sexual harassment outside the home. For example, in 1991 the *Knesset* passed a law that enabled victims of domestic violence to obtain an immediate restraining order and an initial injunction to expel the violent family member from the home. In this way, the focus shifted towards removing the batterer from the premises rather than forcing the already beleaguered victims of abuse (usually the wife and children) to seek shelter. At the same time, additional

---

[28] In a recent decision, the Supreme Court further instructed the government to pursue affirmative action measures to increase the adequate representation of male and female members of the Arab minority (approximately 20 percent of Israel's population) in the civil service and other governmental organs.

[29] The *Women's Network I* decision is credited with the dramatic increase in the number of women represented on the boards of directors of governmental companies (7 percent in 1993; 32 percent in 2002). In the Civil Service, female representation in administrative positions rose from 17 percent in 1996 to 26 percent in 2000. In professional positions, female representation rose from 13 percent in 1996 to 20 percent in 2000.

shelter facilities have been opened since the passage of the law. These shelters are operated by nongovernmental organizations, but are supported by state and private funding. Emergency helplines have also been established to provide legal and psychological assistance to victims of domestic violence. In an attempt to reach out to women from different religious, ethnic, immigrant, and national backgrounds, these services are provided in Hebrew, Arabic, Russian, and Amharic. Women's organizations have also been granted formal standing to provide legal counseling in civil trials concerning the battering of women in the home (by their spouses, partners, or other family members), and have secured the right to assist victims of sexual assault at criminal trials. These organizations now regularly provide training for police investigators and district attorneys responsible for handling complaints of domestic abuse and sexual violence in order to ensure that victims of sexual assault are treated with dignity in the trial and pretrial proceedings. Similarly, in seeking to protect the basic rights of victims of human trafficking and sexual exploitation, the *Knesset* imposed minimum sentences – from two and a half years to four years in prison – on offenders convicted of human trafficking for prostitution. Women who were brought to Israel by traffickers are now entitled to receive legal representation by the legal aid bureau of the Justice Ministry and to testify in court without the presence of the accused.

Furthermore, in 1998 the *Knesset* passed *the Prevention of Sexual Harassment Law* – one of the most comprehensive laws against sexual harassment in the world. The constitutional principles that underlie this legislation are stated in Section 1 of the new law: to protect the human dignity, liberty, and privacy of all persons, and promote equality between the sexes by prohibiting sexual harassment. Under the new law, sexual harassment becomes both a criminal and a civil offence, making it a cause of action against both the harasser and the employer. New guidelines concerning employers' obligations to prevent sexual harassment were also introduced by the *Knesset*. These guidelines hold that the new sexual harassment law applies to a wide range of employment and professional relationships in different social settings. The regulations impose a duty on any employer of twenty-five or more employees to post the guidelines in the workplace, and to investigate complaints of harassment adequately.[30]

One of the most significant cases involving the interpretation of the new sexual harassment law involved the military. In the 1999 *Galili* case, the Court blocked the promotion of a senior Israeli Defense Force (IDF) officer who was found guilty of "inappropriate behavior" in conducting a sexual relationship

---

[30] Once a complaint is filed, it must be investigated even if the original claimant wishes to withdraw her or his claim. This provision was introduced to reduce the likelihood of pressure or punitive action being imposed on those filing complaints against co-workers or their superiors.

with a female soldier under his command.[31] The Court ruled that senior IDF military officers (Mr. Galili was about to be promoted to the rank of General) must serve as moral figures to their soldiers. Further, it was held that even fully consensual relations between an officer and a soldier should fall within the definition of sexual harassment. The Court also mentioned that this ruling should not be interpreted as stating that young female soldiers lacked individual agency, or sexual freedom. Rather, it was held that the military should provide an environment that protects the human dignity of the individual; where a soldier can be confident that her (or his) "No" is respected as a "No," regardless of the otherwise hierarchical nature of relations in the military. Here, the Court adopted its most radical reading of the equality principle, by creating a hybrid of an antisubordination approach (with its emphasis on eliminating systemic patterns of gender inequality and vulnerability) together with a strong liberal-individualistic approach (with its emphasis on respecting individuals' capacity for agency and choice).

Abortion and Reproductive Freedom

Surprisingly, unlike the United States, where abortion has become a highly divisive political and religious issue, the abortion debate in Israel has never taken a similar turn. In 1977, the *Knesset* decriminalized abortion by amending the relevant sections of the criminal law. This amendment permits the termination of pregnancy when performed in an accredited medical institution and following the approval of a medical committee.[32] The pregnant woman must be given counseling about the abortion procedure, and has to freely consent to the procedure.[33] A minor need not receive the approval of her guardians, and the male partner has no standing in the decision. While this solution subjects the pregnant woman to an often-intrusive interview by the approval committee, it at least guarantees a woman's right to a safe and publicly funded abortion. This pragmatic arrangement has mitigated

---

[31] *Plonit ("Jane Doe") v. Chief of Staff*, H.C. 1284/99, 53 (2) P.D. 62. See also *State of Israel v. Ben Asher*, SSA 6713/96, 52(1) P.D. 650 for the SCI's relatively progressive conceptualization of sexual harassment prior to the enactment of the *Sexual Harassment Prevention Law*.

[32] It is generally conceded that these committees are liberal in their approach to permitting abortion. See Frances Raday, "Israel – The Incorporation of Religious Patriarchy in a Modern State" (1992) 4 *International Review of Comparative Public Policy* 209–25 at 221.

[33] Formally, the decision of the committee is guided by considerations of age; incest; rape; extramarital relations; danger to the woman's physical or emotional health; and indications of severe genetic disorders or abnormality in the development of the fetus. In addition to setting these guidelines, the abortion law also requires that all hospitals in Israel appoint abortion-approval medical committees, which consist of two physicians and a social worker (one of whom must be a woman). This approval procedure has significantly depoliticized the issue of abortion in Israel. For an analysis of its "educational" and "control" functions, see Delila Amir and Orly Benjamin, "Defining Encounters: Who Are the Women Entitled to Join the Israeli Collective?" (1997) 20 *Women's Studies International Forum* 639–50.

much of the intense emotion that often accompanies the abortion debate in other countries. An important factor that assisted in ensuring that Israeli women could gain the right to abortion is the fact that there is no absolute prohibition against abortion in Jewish law.[34]

Women's reproductive freedom was also at the heart of the headline-grabbing *Nahmani* legal drama, involving a clash between a woman's right to motherhood and her ex-husband's right not to be forced into fatherhood. In 1984, the Nahmani couple married but remained childless. In 1987, the couple decided to attempt an in-vitro fertilization procedure, and had the wife's eggs fertilized with the husband's sperm with the intention of later finding a surrogate mother. The fertilization process was carried out in Israel, and the fertilized eggs were deposited at a medical institute in the United States, as surrogate pregnancies were forbidden in Israel at that time. The husband later withdrew his consent to use the fertilized eggs for a surrogacy procedure. His estranged wife, however, insisted on her right to become a mother by continuing the process. In 1995, a five-judge Supreme Court panel held that parenthood could not be forced on any person, male or female, and thus ruled in the husband's favor.[35] In an unprecedented second appeal before the Supreme Court, a 7–4 majority overturned the earlier decision by holding that the right to parenthood was a component of human dignity; therefore, Ms. Nahmani could attempt to become a mother by using the fertilized eggs in spite of her estranged husband's objections. The ruling in favor of Ms. Nahmani led to a lively academic debate concerning the feminist dimensions of this case; while it can be read as a victory for women's individual choice, privacy, and autonomy, it can also be seen as reifying and essentializing women's role as biological reproducers first and foremost.

Following the *Nahmani* case, Israel became the first country in the world to legalize state-supervised surrogacy. Orthodox religious parties did not oppose the *Consent to Surrogacy Motherhood Law* (passed in 1996), primarily because their major constituencies are among the law's potential beneficiaries. According to this law, a couple may enter into a surrogacy agreement with an unmarried woman. As with the abortion procedure, a committee must approve the agreement and verify that all parties have freely consented to it. Surrogate mothers may be reimbursed for legal and insurance expenses plus compensation for lost time and lost income, and are entitled to all the rights protecting a pregnant woman (such as the right to paid maternity leave). As of 2001, ninety agreements have been approved and thirty babies have been borne by surrogate mothers for twenty-two commissioning couples.[36]

---

[34] Raday, *supra* note 32, at 222.
[35] *Nahmani v. Nahmani*, A.C. 5587/93, *Nahmani v. Nahmani*, A.C.P. 2401/95, 50(4) P.D. 661.
[36] See Judy Siegel-Itzkovich, "Surrogacy: Bearing the Greatest Gift of All" *The Internet Jerusalem Post* (27 May 2001).

THE INTERSECTION OF GENDER AND
RELIGIOUS/NATIONAL IDENTITIES

A Jewish and Democratic State

Israel's constitutional system is based on two tenets: that the state is both a
Jewish and a *democratic* state. The major constitutional challenge Israel has
faced since its foundation has been the creation of an ideologically plausible
and politically feasible synthesis between these two seemingly contradictory
terms. Reaching such a synthesis is especially problematic given that approximately one fifth of Israel's citizenry consists of non-Jews (primarily Muslims,
Christians, and Druzes).[37] Even within the Jewish population itself, the exact
meaning of Israel as a Jewish state has been highly contested. Not only do
opinions differ bitterly as to whether Jews are citizens of a nation, members
of a people, participants in a culture or coreligionists, but even within the
latter – arguably the most stable of these constructions – there are widely
divergent beliefs and degrees of practice.

To complicate matters even further, state and religion are not separated
in Israel. Instead, the Orthodox stream of the Jewish religion has long enjoyed the status of being the sole branch of Judaism formally recognized
by the state.[38] In practice, this exclusive recognition means that there is an
Orthodox monopoly over the rabbinical court system, and that the least
progressive branch of Judaism has an entrenched status as the primary beneficiary of state funds allocated for Jewish religious affairs. As we have seen,
until recently, the exclusive status of the Orthodox Jews also entailed the
formal exclusion of women (Orthodox and non-Orthodox) from serving on
municipal religious councils, which are official state organs. In light of the
deep ethnic and religious cleavages embedded in the Israeli polity, it is not
surprising that some of the hardest challenges facing women in Israel have
been to advance claims that are intersectionist, or multi-faceted in nature –
that is, gender-related claims for equality that are enmeshed with religious
or national identity debates. In such cases, opponents of gender equality often present it as eroding the collective survival interests of a given religious
or national community. A major obstacle to establishing women's full participation as equals in all spheres of life in Israel thus continues to be the
intersection of gender and religious/national tensions.

Religious Courts, Legal Pluralism, and Women's Rights

The standing of marriage and divorce laws provides an ideal example of this
problem. In Israel, no unified civil law applies to all citizens in matters of

---

[37] Palestinians who reside in the occupied territories (West Bank and Gaza) are not Israeli
citizens.
[38] This is in spite of the fact that the vast majority of the world's Jews, as well as many Israeli
Jews, do not view themselves as adherents of Orthodox Judaism.

marriage and divorce. Instead, for various political and historical reasons (the roots of contemporary Israeli family law arrangements go back as far as the Ottoman empire's ancient *millet* system), the courts of the different religious communities hold exclusive jurisdiction over marriage and divorce ceremonies. As we have seen, the rabbinical (Jewish) court system is controlled by the Orthodox stream of Judaism. It has exclusive jurisdiction over matters of marriage and divorce, as well as over some other personal status matters that are directly related to the primary question of marriage or divorce. A host of other personal status matters may be adjudicated through the rabbinical court system, should the involved parties consent to such extended jurisdiction.[39] Muslim, Christian, and Druze courts also have exclusive jurisdiction over the personal status affairs of their respective communities. In fact, although Judaism has a dominant status in Israel, non-Jewish courts – *Shari'a* (Muslim) courts in particular – were until recently vested with an even wider scope of jurisdiction over the personal status affairs of their communities than rabbinical courts. This broad jurisdiction meant that prior to the introduction of a legislative amendment in 2001, Muslim women had been subject to the exclusive power of the *Shari'a* court in matters such as child custody, child support, paternity determination, and spousal maintenance.[40]

In different historical periods, the religious courts in Israel have been awarded different degrees of binding jurisdiction over matters of personal status. However, each recognized community's religious court has continuously held *exclusive* jurisdiction over matters of marriage and divorce, and has been authorized to implement religious law in resolving personal status disputes. This legal-pluralist mandate permits the religious courts to continue their practice of applying certain religious norms that treat men and women unequally, in spite of the commitment to gender equality in Israel's constitutional jurisprudence. This has led to a situation whereby religious courts expose women to systemic discrimination in matters of personal status. For example, Orthodox Jewish divorce law, which is informed by a tradition that praises women's contribution to the group as bearers of its collective identity, still permits a husband to "anchor" his wife against her will; that is, he can force her to remain legally married to him even if their relationship has ended and she wants a divorce.

---

[39] Note that Jewish couples who have their marriage ceremonies solemnized by Conservative or Reform rabbis are not considered to be married under Israeli law. See *Keren v. Minister of Religion*, H.C. 47/82, 43(2) P.D. 661. The Ministry of the Interior now recognizes certain foreign jurisdictions' marriage licenses; so Jewish couples that marry outside Israel in a civil ceremony are likely to be able to register their marriage. However, this does not release them from the jurisdiction of the rabbinical courts should they wish to divorce. A proposed bill, which would have granted valid recognition to civil marriages as well as religious marriages performed by Conservative and Reform rabbis, was defeated in the *Knesset* in March 2004.

[40] The asymmetrical powers granted to the *Shari'a* courts date back to the Ottoman Empire. Their authority was confirmed by the British Administration in the 1922 Palestine Order-in-Council, and was later adopted by the Israeli legislature.

To overcome the severe disadvantage that Jewish women may suffer due to this legal construction of divorce, contemporary Orthodox commentators have explored religiously acceptable ways to impose pressure on the recalcitrant husband to consent to the *get* (divorce decree). However, rabbinical courts in Israel have tended to reject such interpretations. Instead, they uphold a narrow reading of *Halakhic* law that often leaves women vulnerable to blackmail by their spouses who may seek material and custodial concessions in exchange for granting the *get*, or who may simply abuse their privileged status (according to religious norms) to cause injury and pain to their anchored wives. The *Knesset* also attempted to find religiously acceptable solutions to the *get* problem by enacting legislation that allows rabbinical tribunals to impose serious sanctions (including imprisonment) on husbands who refuse to divorce their wives. Yet rabbinical tribunals have generally tended to refrain from imposing these sanctions on recalcitrant husbands, even when clearly empowered to do so by the new law.

In short, in preserving religious courts' powers to adjudicate matters of personal status, the Israeli state has recognized the right of each community to demarcate its membership boundaries through its own family law codes and lineage rules. However, in doing so, the state has also granted these communities a license to maintain intragroup practices that disproportionately injure women. Under such conditions, women's equal citizenship status is impaired by a constitutional system that defers to the exclusive jurisdiction of religious communities in certain matters of personal status, including marriage and divorce, and in which the institutions of these communities systematically disadvantage women.[41]

This state of affairs is complicated by the fact that marriage and divorce affairs are immune, through explicit *Knesset* legislation, from equality challenges. This is because of the infamous Section 5 of the 1951 *Equal Rights for Women Law*, which states that "the legal norms of this law [i.e., guarantee of equality for women] have no validity over matters of prohibition and permission of marriage and divorce." Section 5 therefore creates a specific reservation, according to which the general principle of gender equality applies to all spheres of life, *except* for the family. This is very much like the pattern that emerged at the international level, where countries that signed and ratified CEDAW made explicit reservations regarding its non-applicability to certain family law matters.[42] What is unusual about the Israeli case is the fact that this reservation is not being declared against an international obligation or instrument. Rather, an earlier piece of domestic legislation now violates

[41] For detailed discussion of this problem, see Ayelet Shachar, *Multicultural Jurisdictions: Cultural Differences and Women's Rights* (Cambridge: Cambridge University Press, 2001), Ch. 3.
[42] Israel has also followed this route. While ratifying the Women's Convention in 1991, Israel added a reservation to Articles 7 and 16 (regarding the equal participation of women in public life, and equality in marriage and family law, respectively).

higher (constitutional) norms, as it shields certain state organs, namely, the religious courts, from challenges to their discriminatory practices. To date, Section 5 has not been challenged as unconstitutional *per se*.[43]

Although the basic problem of women's heightened vulnerability to gender discrimination in the religious divorce process remains unresolved, the Supreme Court, in its post-1992 Basic Law adjudication, has gradually been attempting to limit the authority exercised by the religious courts. Specifically, the Court has dealt with issues connected to marriage and divorce status, such as property allocation and child custody. The most important SCI judgment regarding these matters was promulgated in 1995 in the *Bavli* case. In this ruling, the Supreme Court held that the adjudication of *all* religious tribunals, including the Great Rabbinical Court, are in principle subject to review by the Supreme Court. While the Court recognized the special jurisdictional mandate awarded to Jewish, Muslim, Christian, and Druze courts by the legislature, it nevertheless asserted its power to impose constitutional norms upon their exercise of authority.[44] Rabbinical court officials have responded by publicly asserting their resistance to the idea that the Supreme Court, as a secular entity, possesses a mandate to review their adjudication, which rests on religious law. Some have gone so far as to declare their intention to ignore the Court's ruling in *Bavli*, which they view as an illegitimate intrusion into their protected jurisdictional sphere.

Based on its landmark decision in *Bavli*, the Court went on to rule in *Katz* (1996) that the rabbinical courts were not authorized to declare an individual who refused to have a civil matter adjudicated by the rabbinical court excommunicated or ostracized. The majority opinion stated that since the rabbinical court system is a public organ that exists by force of law and draws its authorities from the law, it could only exercise those prerogatives vested in it by law.[45] A year later, the Court overturned a rabbinical court decision that held that a divorced father who had become religious was entitled to decide where his children would be educated, even though his wife, who remained secular, had been granted custody of the children.[46] In 1998, the Court overturned another rabbinical court decision that had

[43] Although the 1992 Basic Laws are prospective in nature, a strong argument can be made about the contemporary (*post-1992*) impact of Section 5 of the 1951 law on all Israeli women, of all religious denominations, who are continuously forced by law to be subjected to the jurisdiction of the religious courts of their respective communities in matters of marriage and divorce. Arguably, Section 5 of the *Women's Equality Law* fails to comply with the limitation clause found in Section 8 of the *Basic Law: Human Dignity*, which states that "there shall be no violation of rights under this Basic Law except by a Law fitting the values of the State of Israel, designed for a proper purpose, and to an extent no greater than required."

[44] *Bavli v. The Grand Rabbinical Court*, H.C. 1000/92, 48(2) P.D. 6. On *Shari'a* court jurisdiction, see also *Plonit ("Jane Doe") v. Ploni ("John Doe")*, C.A. 3077/90, 49(2) P.D. 578.

[45] *Katz v. Jerusalem Regional Rabbinical Court*, H.C. 3269/95, 50(4) P.D. 590.

[46] *Amir v. Haifa District Court*, H.C. 5507/96, 50(3) P.D. 321.

forced a divorcee to send her son to a religious school at the demand of her ex-husband.[47] In a similar spirit, the Supreme Court ruled in March 2001 that the rabbinical courts were unauthorized to decide on a request by a man to prohibit his ex-wife from letting their children spend time with her lesbian partner.[48] While attempting to mitigate some of the inequalities that women suffer under Israel's current family law system, the Court has tended to refrain whenever possible from directly intervening against rabbinical courts on the grounds of a constitutional challenge. Instead, the more common practice is for the SCI to strike down rabbinical courts' decisions because of procedural irregularities found in the religious tribunals' exercise of power.

Group Identity versus Individual Rights

In addition to these obstacles to equal and fair treatment, women may experience a conflict between their individual rights and their group identity. As a result, at-risk women may find it difficult to turn to state officials (courts, social services, or police officers) to seek remedy when their constitutional rights have been violated by spouses, family members, or fellow group members. Women who choose to follow this path risk exposing themselves to severe intragroup pressure to withdraw their charges. This places them on the horns of a dilemma: they are asked to make a choice between their rights as citizens and their identity within the group. This amounts to a choice of penalties. *Either* they must accept the violation of their rights as citizens in intragroup situations as the precondition for retaining their religious/national loyalty, *or* they must forfeit their group identities as the price for state protection of their basic rights. Neither alternative offers women the opportunity to preserve both their cultural identities and to challenge the power relations encoded within their groups' traditions.[49]

In the Israeli situation, such pressures are often imposed upon women attempting to bring reform to the existing family law system, either by seeking more progressive readings of existing religious codes, or by lobbying for the introduction of a parallel civil system. Proposals for achieving greater gender equality through such reform have been construed as threatening the collective interest of Israel's already embattled religious and national communities. This puts pressure on all Israeli women, but especially on Muslim women. As members of a minority in the Jewish state, they run the risk of being portrayed by their own communities as cultural traitors if they air their

---

[47] *David v. Great Rabbinical Court*, H.C. 5227/97, 55(1) P.D. 453. Matters of marriage and divorce fall under the exclusive jurisdiction of rabbinical courts. Matters of children's education are not within the realm of the rabbinical courts' jurisdiction, unless they are "bound up" expressly in the suit to the rabbinical court.

[48] *Plonit ("Jane Doe") v. Great Rabbinical Court*, H.C. 293/00, 55(3) P.D. 318.

[49] For further critique of this "either/or" dilemma, see Shachar, *supra* note 41, ch. 4.

concerns publicly, or seek "outside" legal remedy to resolve problems such as domestic violence or spousal abuse within the Arab-Israeli community. One manifestation of this problem is the code of silence that surrounds instances of "honor killing" of women. Although Israeli criminal law clearly defines such killings as murders, it is generally hard to establish evidence against the perpetrator(s) when group leaders, politicians, local police officers, and relatives (male and female) refuse to cooperate with the investigation efforts. Many of these cases end up without a suspect, and without a trial.[50]

The tension between manifesting loyalty to their minority group identity and struggling against their gender-based vulnerability has long silenced Arab women. This silence has only recently been broken by female activists and academics, who have began to openly criticize the practice of honor killing, for example. Organizations such as *Al-Fanar* (the Palestinian Women's Organization), *Albadeel* (a coalition devoted to fighting the practice of honor killing), the *Working Group for Equality in Personal Status Issues*, and the *Coalition for the Advancement of Arab Women's Rights* have led the fight to challenge entrenched gender inequalities, but without compromising the Arab-Israeli community's struggle against the systemic patterns of discrimination suffered at the hands of the Jewish state. The last-mentioned coalition has advanced the passage of legislative amendments that grant Muslim women the right to settle certain matters of personal law (such as paternity, child custody, and property allocation in divorce) in secular courts, thus narrowing the jurisdictional authority of the *Shari'a* courts. This new legislative initiative has met with fierce opposition from certain quarters within the Arab community, specifically representatives of the Islamic Movement. In fact, it has caused Muslim authorities, for the first time in Israel's history, to issue a *fatwah* against supporters of the bill, branding its supporters as heretics and unbelievers.[51]

Despite this formidable opposition, the coalition's campaign proved successful in 2001, when the *Knesset* enacted the *Family Court* (Amendment No. 5) *Law*, which opened the doors of the civil courts to Muslim women. In so doing, the *Knesset* took a step to equalize the status of Muslim women and Jewish women in Israel. It also provided them access to a forum that is sensitive to power inequalities *between* men and women *within* each respective community. In practice, however, the impact of this legal change remains

---

[50] As in other countries, violence perpetuated against women by their spouses or partners is widespread in Israel. It is estimated that approximately 10 percent of the Israeli female population is subject to battering by their spouses or partners. However, Arab women are more vulnerable to domestic violence than Jewish women. It is estimated that as many as 50 percent of Arab married women are beaten at least once a year; 25 percent are beaten at least once every six months.

[51] See ICAR, "Women and Religion" online: International Coalition for Aguna Rights (ICAR) Web site <http://www.iwn.org/icar> (date accessed: February 5, 2000).

to be seen. Currently, the default rule for many couples remains the religious court. The party seeking to invoke the jurisdiction of the family court must actively turn to the secular authority. Moreover, the family court is legally prohibited from determining the core issue of marriage and divorce, which remains under the exclusive and binding jurisdiction of the religious courts. These restrictions apply equally to members of all religious communities in Israel.

Nevertheless, these legal changes triggered tenacious criticism by Muslim religious leaders, some of whom regarded this change in status quo (Muslim women were previously bound to resolve *all* matters of personal status in *Shari'a* courts) as an unjustifiable intrusion and restriction of the traditional religious autonomy held by the Muslim minority in Israel. Members of the Jewish majority also have been slow to endorse proposals that would re-form Israel's *millet*-like religious court system. This resistance can be partly attributed to the political pressure applied by religious parties in the *Knesset*, but it also seems to point to deeper problems. Even among secular Israelis, there is widespread support for preserving the mechanisms of religious mar-riage and divorce. It is commonly viewed as the price that needs to be paid to avoid internal factions within Israel's diverse Jewish community. Maintain-ing a system of religious family law not only helps to preserve the internal unity of the Jewish community; it also helps to officially delineate its exter-nal boundaries in a deeply divided society. In other words, it offers a legal tool for defining who in the Israeli polity belongs to the dominant Jewish majority (by virtue of birth and marriage) and who does not.

Viewed through this critical perspective, family law in Israel can be under-stood as a way in which individuals are allotted to prescribed groups, from which exit is rarely permitted (one cannot forgo identification as a member of a specific religious or national community for purposes of birth registration, marriage, or divorce, for example). This allows the Israeli polity to sustain and reproduce a regime of "differentiation" between formally equal citizens – although significant gender-based inequalities may also persist within each religious or national community, as our discussion has indicated. The po-tentially oppressive power of this system of legalized hierarchy is manifested on several levels. For one, it limits the freedom of choice experienced by all Israeli citizens, Jewish and non-Jewish alike. No one, under this system, can enjoy the right to freedom from religion. This is because no person perma-nently residing in Israel can "opt out" of an imposed communal identity.[52] What is more, in a divided polity like Israel, group-based demarcations of

<hr/>

[52] In a recent paper entitled "Judicial Activism of Shari'a Court of Appeals in Israel (1994–2001): Rise and Crisis" (unpublished, on file with authors), Moussa Abou Ramadan proposes a reform to the *Shari'a* court system that would strengthen the religious autonomy of the Muslim minority in Israel, but would also permit individuals a right to formally "opt out" of their religious community.

identity may quickly translate into second-class citizenship for members of minority communities.[53]

In order to maintain such a system of differentiation, there must be a legal procedure that assigns individuals into predefined categories of collective identity in the first place, that is, a mechanism that will distinguish between citizens according to their religious and national affiliation. Counter to the conventional wisdom that views the continuation of the historical arrangement of a religious family law system in Israel as a compromise between Orthodox and non-Orthodox forces within the Jewish community,[54] we suggest that an equally plausible explanation for the decision to uphold the religious family law system – in spite of the very real injuries it imposes on women and its heavy infringement of Israeli citizens' (male or female) right to freedom of conscience and belief – is to be found in the context of this broader intercommunity conflict that has been part and parcel of Israel's political reality since its inception.

CONCLUSION

This chapter has provided a brief overview of the landmark Israeli constitutional jurisprudence in matters concerning the equal treatment of women in different social contexts: the military, the home, the public sector, the private employment arena, and the family, as well as women's struggle for inclusion in state-regulated religious councils. As we have seen, the constitutional adjudication (both pre- and post-1992), along with the innovative legislation adopted by the *Knesset* in recent years, demonstrate a sincere attempt to draw upon principles of formal equality and human dignity as anchors for advancing women's rights. At the same time, the Court has been unable or

---

[53] A chilling reminder of this concern is found in the recently enacted Citizenship and Entry into Israel Law (Temporary Order), which was passed by the *Knesset* on July 31, 2003. This law is aimed at preventing the granting of citizenship to a non-Israeli spouse of an Israeli citizen (male or female), if the non-Israeli spouse is a resident of the West Bank and Gaza. The law applies equally to Israeli Jews and Arabs, though it is acknowledged that Arab-Israelis are more likely to be disproportionately affected by this law. It is estimated that the new law could affect thousands of couples and their children already living in Israel, potentially forcing them to live apart or to leave the country. Since 1967, Israelis who married residents of the occupied territories could apply for family unification to obtain legal status in Israel for their spouse. After prolonged security checks and a substantial wait, most couples were granted family unification, allowing them to live together lawfully in Israel. The new law would prohibit the granting of such status. As a Temporary Order, the new law is subject to annual renewal. The case is currently under review by the Supreme Court of Israel. See Petition and Motion for Injunction, H.C. 7052/03 *Adalah et al. v. Ministry of Interior and the Attorney General* (on file with authors). A special panel of thirteen justices will hear this case.

[54] For a clear expression of the conventional wisdom, see Phillipa Strum, "Women and the Politics of Religion in Israel" (1989) 11 *Human Rights Quarterly* 483–503.

unwilling to provide assistance to women when their rights to equality and dignity have collided with other fundamental values protected by the state.

The final section of our discussion has focused on the complexities associated with promoting women's rights at the intersection of gender and religious/national conflicts in a deeply divided society. We have shown that Israeli women living in both a Jewish and democratic state, faced with the challenge of promoting their equality in the midst of deeply felt and ongoing collective struggles, have experienced a unique mixture of progressive jurisprudence alongside enduring patterns of inequality. In this respect, the case of Israel fails to fit neatly into existing categories provided by feminist theory and liberal constitutionalism.

Having said that, we believe that a few general lessons can be drawn from the struggle for women's rights in Israel. First, the challenge of promoting women's interests through constitutionalism and rights litigation in ideologically charged polities such as Israel is no small task. Constitutional rights are never interpreted or implemented in a political or ideological vacuum. Indeed, as Robert Dahl observed, commenting some forty-five years ago on the U.S. Supreme Court, it is unrealistic to suppose that national high courts would long hold to norms of justice that are substantially at odds with the surrounding political environment, and the social and economic contexts within which these courts operate.[55] National high courts may be "the forum of principle" in public life, but the principles that their justices articulate are not likely to produce policy outcomes that are uninfluenced by national meta-narratives, prevailing ideological and cultural propensities, and the policy preferences of hegemonic elites. This sobering insight is especially relevant in assessing the potential for enhancing women's status through rights litigation in fragmented polities such as Israel, where historically entrenched legal mechanisms have maintained religious and ethnocultural divisions among different groups of formally equal citizens.

In spite of the apparently modest capacity of constitutional rights and judicial review to bring about social change, it is still important to distinguish between the impact constitutional rights jurisprudence has on formal equality and on substantive equality. By and large, as the jurisprudence surveyed above illustrates, the constitutionalization of rights has the potential to initiate a real advancement of women's rights – when it comes to the "freedom from" or "negative liberty" aspects of rights. This is especially true of those rights concerning the protection of formal equality, bodily integrity, and privacy, which all solemnize the sameness principle, as well as a "gender-free" vision of personal autonomy. However, when it comes to the positive (or "freedom to") aspect of rights, which often demands that established beneficiaries relinquish their historical advantage, the SCI, like its counterparts

---

[55] Robert Dahl, "Decision-Making in a Democracy: The Supreme Court as a National Policy-Maker" (1957) 6 *Journal of Public Law* 279–95 at 291.

in many other countries, has manifested only a limited capacity to promote progressive notions of social justice that truly allow women and other historically disadvantaged groups greater access to centers of power, influence, and status.

Finally, a major obstacle to the establishment of Israeli women's full participation as equals in all spheres of life is the (mis)perception that advancing gender equality necessarily compromises other important values of the state, such as the preservation of collective identity, national security, or religious diversity. As long as the promotion of women's rights and the promotion of other constitutive norms are seen as mutually exclusive, even the most eloquently worded rights legislation cannot guarantee women's equal treatment and human dignity. A more ambitious challenge lies in breaking down such misguided dichotomies. This entails recognizing that women citizens in ethno-religious democracies such as Israel are in fact always placed at the intersection of several larger, diverse communities of identity and interest.

Suggested Readings

Yael Azmon and Dafna N. Izraeli, eds., *Women in Israel: Studies in Israeli Society* (London: Transaction Publishers, 1993).

Sylvie Fogel-Bijaoui, "On the Way to Equality? The Struggle for Women's Suffrage in the Jewish Yishuv, 1917–1926," in Deborah S. Bernstein (ed.), *Pioneers and Homemakers: Jewish Women in Pre-State Israel* (Albany: SUNY Press, 1992).

Ran Hirschl, *Towards Juristocracy: The Origins and Consequences of the New Constitutionalism* (Cambridge, MA: Harvard University Press, 2004).

Mordechai Kremnitzer, "The High Court of Justice and the Shaping of Public Policy: Equality and Gender" (2001) 7 *Israel Affairs* 100.

David Kretzmer, "Basic Laws as a Surrogate Bill of Rights: The Case of Israel" in Philip Alston, ed., *Promoting Bills of Rights through Bills of Rights: Comparative Perspectives* (Oxford: Oxford University Press, 2000) 75.

Frances Raday, "Israel – The Incorporation of Religious Patriarchy in a Modern State" (1992) 4 *International Review of Comparative Public Policy* 209.

Moussa Abou Ramadan, "The Transition from Tradition to Reform: The Shari'a Appeals Court Ruling on Child Custody (1992–2001)" (2003) 26 *Fordham International Law Journal* 595.

Ayelet Shachar, *Multicultural Jurisdictions: Cultural Differences and Women's Rights* (Cambridge: Cambridge University Press, 2001).

Ayelet Shachar, "Whose Republic? Citizenship and Membership in the Israeli Polity" (1999) 13 *Georgetown Immigration Law Journal* 233.

Carmel Shalev, "*Halakha* and Patriarchal Motherhood – An Anatomy of the New Israeli Surrogacy Law" (1998) 32 *Israel Law Review* 51.

Philippa Strum, "Women and the Politics of Religion in Israel" (1989) 11 *Human Rights Quarterly* 483.

9

"No Nation Can Be Free When One Half of It Is Enslaved"

Constitutional Equality for Women in South Africa*

Saras Jagwanth and Christina Murray

> ...freedom cannot be achieved unless women have been emancipated from all forms of oppression...unless we see, in practical and visible terms, that the condition of the women in our country has radically changed for the better and that they have been empowered to intervene in all aspects of life as equals with any other member of society.
>
> President Mandela (1994).[1]

When, in 1993, South Africans first started drafting a constitution for a democratic dispensation, gender equality was firmly on the agenda. However, the priority it should be given and the extent to which it should determine the development of the many systems of customary law in the country were disputed.

For most of the twentieth century, politics diverged along two, separate streams. White politics developed through official political and legal channels, while black politics did so outside the official structures. In white politics, South Africa saw changes relating to women's rights that more or less matched developments in the West. White women were given the vote in 1930. Laws relating to matrimonial property for white people were gradually reformed. In the 1980s, systematic challenges to inequality in the workplace began. Grave concerns concerning the situation of women who were not classified as white were occasionally raised in official political forums but, by and large, such concerns were dismissed with the assertion that black people were "not ready" for development or, more cynically in a system

---

[1] "State of the Nation Address," Parliament, 24 May 1994, online: South African Government Information <www.polity.org.za/govdocs/speeches/1994/sp0524.html> (date accessed: 10 May 2001).

* A longer version of this chapter has appeared as "Ten Years of Transformation: How Has Gender Equality in South Africa Fared?" 2002 (14) *Canadian Journal of Women and the Law* pp. 255–99.

which gave black people no political representation, with the response "we cannot presume to tell black people how to run their affairs." Thus, a legal system that seriously disadvantaged women of color was left in place.

But women in the movement against apartheid were strong and progressive. By the early 1990s, even the governing National Party felt it necessary to pay attention to women's rights. Thus, the place of gender in the political debate was secured but not gender equality. Two major political battles needed to be fought. First, the old slogan "race first and sex equality later" needed to be laid to rest and gender equality treated as a matter of equal significance to race equality. Second, the claim of traditional leaders, the guardians of customary law, that gender equality could not extend to traditional systems needed to be rejected. This approach would have excluded the majority of South African women from the benefit of an equality clause in the crucial areas of family law, inheritance, and property ownership. The Constitution came out strongly on the side of gender equality on each of these issues. But a Constitution cannot in itself secure rights for women. At best it legitimates the demand for rights and, like the South African Constitution, may provide special forums for advancing those rights. The degree to which the gender equity promised by the Constitution has been secured is considered in Sections II to V, where we discuss legislative and policy developments that relate to gender equality and equality case law. But first, in Section I, we describe the framework provided by the Constitution.

I. THE SOUTH AFRICAN CONSTITUTION AND GENDER EQUALITY

In 1994, after its first democratic election, an interim Constitution[2] was put into effect. It governed South Africa until the elected Constitutional Assembly adopted a final Constitution.[3] The final Constitution establishes a multilevel, parliamentary system of government. In a weak form of federalism the country is divided into nine provinces and 284 municipalities. The central government retains strong powers of oversight and control. Matters relating to justice and to rights are primarily the concern of the central government. Thus, although every level of government and all government institutions must promote the Bill of Rights, provincial and local government will usually be bound to follow national policy on these issues.

The Bill of Rights is extensive, conferring first, second, and third generation rights. It demands some degree of judicial review of all these rights. In addition, Section 7(2) requires the state to "respect, protect, promote and fulfill the rights in the Bill of Rights." This means that in certain cases the

---

[2] *Constitution of the Republic of South Africa*, Act 200, 1993 (hereinafter 'the interim Constitution').

[3] *Constitution of the Republic of South Africa*, Act 108, 1996 (hereinafter 'the Constitution').

state must take proactive measures to ensure the fulfillment of it. The Bill of Rights also (although controversially) extends the protection of rights to the private sphere to some extent.[4] The extended application of the Bill of Rights to the common law governing private relations is obviously important for women, because gender inequalities and violence against women in the private sphere traditionally have been insulated from constitutional scrutiny in the name of preserving the public/private divide.

Enforcement of the Constitution, including the Bill of Rights, is finally entrusted to a Constitutional Court. Under South Africa's hybrid system, the Constitutional Court and the Supreme Court of Appeal share jurisdiction as the highest courts in constitutional and nonconstitutional matters respectively. The Constitutional Court acts largely as a court of appeal; direct access to the Court, or engaging it as a court of first instance by ordinary litigants is allowed in limited circumstances only. Although the High Courts and the Supreme Court of Appeal have the power to declare Acts of Parliament invalid, any such declaration must be confirmed by the Constitutional Court before it has any force or effect.

With the exception of the judges of the Constitutional Court, superior court judges are chosen by a judicial service commission.[5] Judges of the Constitutional Court are appointed by the President who must select the judges from a list of names supplied by the Judicial Service Commission.[6] The Commission is established by the Constitution and comprises members of the judiciary, representatives of the profession and legal academics, as well as politicians. The Commission normally holds public interviews and its proceedings receive some media coverage. Lower court judges (magistrates) are selected by the Minister of Justice.[7]

Although there is transformation in the judiciary, judges in South Africa are overwhelmingly white and male. Of the 190 judges in the superior courts in South Africa, only forty-four are black and only twenty-one women. Two of the eleven judges on the Constitutional Court are women, one black and one white.[8] They were appointed in 1994 when the Court was established

---

[4] See, in particular, Section 8(2) of the Constitution, ibid., which states that a provision in the Bill of Rights "binds a natural or a juristic person if, and to the extent that, it is applicable, taking into account the nature of the right and the nature of any duty imposed by the right." Once it has been established that a natural person is bound by a provision of the Bill of Rights, Section 8(3) requires the court to apply and if necessary develop the common law to the extent that legislation does not give effect to the right. Thus, in cases of horizontal application, the constitutional right does not apply directly to the conduct complained of but is rather mediated through the application of an existing or newly created common law rule. See *Khumalo v. Holomisa* 2002 (8) BCLR 771 (CC).

[5] The Constitution, *supra* note 3, s.174(6). The president is bound to appoint the judges selected by the Commission.

[6] The Constitution, ibid., s.174(4).

[7] There are about 2000 magistrates, all of whom are legally qualified.

[8] They are Justices Yvonne Mokgoro and Kate O'Regan.

and will serve fifteen-year terms. The Judicial Service Commission has made serious efforts to appoint women. However, women are infrequently interviewed for appointment.

Alert to the real difficulties of achieving gender equality, drafters of the Constitution sought to ensure that gender was not merely "added on" but that South Africa's new institutions were formally committed to substantial gender equality, alongside racial equality. In important ways they were successful in embedding this value in the text. Section 1 of the Constitution, which sets out the values which underpin the entire system, includes nonracialism and nonsexism alongside supremacy of the Constitution, rule of law, universal adult suffrage, and a multiparty system. According to Section 174, "[t]he need for the judiciary to reflect broadly the racial and gender composition of South Africa must be considered when judicial officers are appointed." Similarly, public administration "must be broadly representative of the South African people, with employment and personnel practices based on ability, objectivity, fairness and the need to redress the imbalances of the past to achieve broad representation."[9] These provisions are general. They are accompanied by a number of more direct ones. For instance, the Bill of Rights deals with gender issues in a number of provisions and, a special constitutional institution, the Commission for Gender Equality must promote gender equality.

The Bill of Rights

Section 9, the equality provision, is elaborate.[10] It outlaws all "unfair" discrimination, listing certain forms of discrimination that will be assumed to be unfair in Section 9(3). The list includes sex, gender, pregnancy, sexual orientation, and marital status. The section protects affirmative action programs,

---

[9] The Constitution, *supra* note 3, s.195(1)(i).
[10] The Constitution, ibid., s.9, provides:

1. Everyone is equal before the law and has the right to equal protection and benefit of the law.
2. Equality includes the full and equal enjoyment of all rights and freedoms. To promote the achievement of equality, legislative and other measures designed to protect or advance persons, or categories of persons, disadvantaged by unfair discrimination may be taken.
3. The state may not unfairly discriminate directly or indirectly against anyone on one or more grounds, including race, gender, sex, pregnancy, marital status, ethnic or social origin, colour, sexual orientation, age, disability, religion, conscience, belief, culture, language and birth.
4. No person may unfairly discriminate directly or indirectly against anyone on one or more grounds in terms of subsection 3. National legislation must be enacted to prevent or prohibit unfair discrimination.
5. Discrimination on one or more of the grounds listed in subsection 3 is unfair unless it is established that the discrimination is fair.

and it explicitly prohibits private discrimination, requiring the legislation that implements this. We discuss this legislation in Section III.

The Constitution's concern with rights for women extends beyond the equality provision. Under Section 12(1), everyone has the right to freedom from "all forms of violence from either public or private sources." The reference to private sources of violence is clearly a response to domestic violence. Section 12(2), gives everyone the right to "make decisions concerning reproduction" and "to security in and control over their body," provisions that will play a role in determining the legitimacy of legislation concerning abortion. Then, in securing the right to access to health care, Section 27 includes "reproductive health care." Finally, although the Bill of Rights protects freedom of expression, it excludes from that protection "advocacy of hatred based on . . . gender . . . that constitutes incitement to cause harm." [11]

Three sections deal directly with the tension between customary systems of law and the Bill of Rights. Section 15 provides the usual protection of freedom of "conscience, religion, thought, belief and opinion." But it also acknowledges the discrimination in South African law's recognition of Christian and Jewish marriages but not other religious forms of marriage. In response it expressly permits the recognition of marriages concluded under "any tradition, or a system of religious, personal or family law" as well as the recognition of "systems of personal and family law under any tradition, or adhered to by persons professing a particular religion." This provision immediately raises the concern that it may legitimate systems of marriage and family law that discriminate against women. Paragraph (b) prevents this, requiring the recognition of any system of marriage or family law to be consistent with the protection of freedom of religion, belief, and opinion in this section and with the other provisions of the Constitution, which, of course, includes the Bill of Rights.

Section 30 protects language and culture, giving everyone "the right to use the language and to participate in the cultural life of their choice." The section's focus on the individual and its rider, "but no one exercising these rights may do so in a manner inconsistent with any provision of the Bill of Rights," prevent cultural rights from limiting other rights. This also is the case with Section 31, which deals with "cultural, religious and linguistic communities." When read with the provisions of the Constitution that deal with the status of traditional leaders (and that subject customary law to amendment by ordinary legislation), these sections make it abundantly clear that cultural rights cannot be used to undermine other rights. The issues that arise are complicated and the challenge is to mold customary law to fit the expectations of the Constitution. Customary law should not be destroyed. What is required is a process of harmonization, which draws on the rich tradition of traditional life while setting aside unequal practices.

---

[11] The Constitution, ibid., s.16(2)(c).

Another group of constitutional rights could have a direct impact on the lives of women: the social and economic rights. These rights are justiciable and, as with the civil and political rights, a person may approach a court for relief on the basis of a violation of a socioeconomic right.[12] The Constitution secures a right to access to adequate housing, a right to access to health care, sufficient food and water, and social security, and a right to education. Women head a high proportion of families in South Africa and these households are disproportionately poor. In rural areas, for example, 37 percent of households headed by women have an income of under $100 a month.[13] If the social and economic rights promised by the Constitution were to be enforced the position of women and their families would improve considerably.

Provisions concerning the implementation and interpretation of the substantive rights (particularly the limitation clause,[14] the interpretation clause,[15] and provisions relating to standing[16]) also affect the way in which gender issues are dealt with by courts.

Commission for Gender Equality

A separate chapter of the Constitution establishes six institutions intended to "support constitutional democracy."[17] The Commission for Gender Equality is one of these. It is to "promote respect for gender equality and the protection, development and attainment of gender equality."[18] The Commission was first established under the interim Constitution and has always been controversial. As we discuss later, it has been beset by problems since its

---

[12] See *In re Certification of the Constitution of the Republic of South Africa, 1996* (1996), 10 BCLR 1253 (CC), para 77–78. Four socio-economic rights cases have been brought to the Constitutional Court: *Soobramoney v. Minister of Health, Kwa-Zulu Natal* (1997), 12 BCLR 1696 (CC) (right to access to health care); *Government of the Republic of South Africa v. Grootboom* (2000), 11 BCLR 1169 (CC); *Minister of Public Works v. Kyalami Ridge Environmental Association* (2001), 7 BCLR 652 (CC) (right to access to adequate housing) and *Minister of Health v. Treatment Action Campaign (1)* (2002), 10 BCLR 1033 (CC) (access to health care).

[13] Debbie Budlender, *Women and Men in South Africa* (Central Statistics, Pretoria: 1998) at 5.

[14] The Constitution, *supra* note 3, s.36. This provision permits governments to justify limiting rights and freedoms. It reflects the strong influence of Section 1 of the Canadian Charter and the proportionality test enunciated by the Supreme Court of Canada in *R v. Oakes*, [1986] 1 SCR 103.

[15] The Constitution, *supra* note 3, s.39. This section requires the courts to consider international law when interpreting the Bill of Rights. It also requires the courts to promote the spirit, object, and purport of the Bill of Rights when interpreting any legislation or developing the common law or customary law.

[16] Section 38 of the Constitution, ibid., has changed the traditionally restrictive common law rules of standing. Class actions and public interest litigation are now permissible.

[17] The Constitution, ibid., c.9.

[18] The Constitution, ibid., s.187.

inception but it is not clear how many are related to the wisdom of establishing such an institution and how many have other causes.

Overall, the Constitution takes a clear position on gender issues. But, as we have already remarked, a Constitution can merely provide a framework. The following sections of this chapter discuss the degree to which the promise of the Constitution has been realised.

II. INSTITUTIONS TO ADVANCE GENDER EQUALITY

Campaigns to ensure that appropriate institutions would be established to promote gender equality in a democratic South Africa started well before the first elections. By the time the new government was in place, the need for institutions dedicated to promoting gender equality in government, legislatures, and civil society was widely acknowledged. Discussions were informed by recognition of the ongoing dilemma concerning the need for special institutions and the danger that they would be marginalized. Overall, most people seemed to believe that while gender must be "mainstreamed," some institutions specifically concerned with gender were necessary.

The main government institution to promote gender equality is the Office on the Status of Women (OSW), based in the President's Office and mandated to "co-ordinate and facilitate the implementation of the national gender programme in the government."[19] However, the impact of the OSW has been limited. It drafted a national action plan but, contrary to South Africa's commitment to open, responsive government and for reasons that are unclear, the plan was embargoed for a long time. Moreover, although its position close to the President was intended to strengthen its impact, bureaucratic practices have made access by the OSW to the heads of government departments difficult. Finally, with a staff of just three members, it is difficult to see the OSW making a significant impact. Each government department is also expected to have a "gender focal point," and many do. Again, however, "gender focal points" have very small staff components and their tasks are formidable. Their personnel are expected to ensure both that departmental policies are gender sensitive and that the department itself is managed in a way that promotes gender equality. Most focus on the latter. It is hard to assess their impact but it is likely that it is uneven at best.

The most exciting new institution concerned with gender equality is probably not in government but Parliament's Joint Monitoring Committee on the Improvement of Quality of Life and Status of Women. The Committee must "monitor and oversee progress with regard to the improvement in the quality of life and status of women in South Africa with specific reference to the government's commitments to the Beijing Platform for Action, and with

---

[19] *The Beijing Platform of Action: South Africa's First Progress Report*, prepared for the technical committee meeting of 24 January 2000, final draft document (undated) at 11.

regard to the implementation of the provisions of the Convention on the Elimination of all Forms of Discrimination against Women." Initially it had some success. This may be attributed in part to the fact that it is based in a parliament in which 120 of the 400 members of the lower house are women. In addition, alert to the breadth of its mandate, the Committee has prioritized issues very carefully. Although it is not proving as effective as it would like to be in ensuring that every parliamentary committee pays attention to gender, it has been influential in a number of areas and most significantly in its "Women's Budget" project.

The Women's Budget Initiative is a project involving government, researchers, and civil society. But its most important support has come from Parliament. For five years it has analysed the budget votes of all twenty-seven government departments. The analysis highlights the extent of public spending on matters relating to women and the access of poor women to resources. It provides Parliament with data with which to assess the impact of budget proposals on women and thus has forced government to pay attention to the implications of its budgeting on women.

The Commission for Gender Equality (CGE) falls neither under the executive arm of government nor in Parliament. Instead, as mentioned above, it is an independent institution, established by the Constitution to "support constitutional democracy." It should be the most significant of all the institutions concerned with gender equality. The Constitution protects its independence strongly with provisions that echo those protecting the independence of the judiciary and, in theory, the parliamentary process through which its members are chosen[20] should mean that they have the confidence of the people. In fact, the CGE is little known and seems to have had little influence. Again poor resourcing is part of the problem. It has also been divided internally and NGOs have subjected its work to much criticism.

In South Africa, as in many other countries, institutions established to ensure that government's policy and practice promote gender equality have had limited success. And, as in other countries, it is hard to assess the causes of failure. The institutions are underresourced and lack skilled staff. Sometimes appointments have been made as political rewards. Nevertheless, the institutions are also young and participate in a very young political system. Roles and relationships are still unclear and, for many feminists, the move from activism to participation in formal structures has been difficult. As the next section shows, significant legislative initiatives that relate to women

---

[20] Persons are nominated and interviewed by a parliamentary committee for appointment as Commissioners. The short list prepared by the committee must thereafter be approved by a majority of the members of both Houses of Parliament at a joint sitting. In addition, Sections 3(3) of the Commission on Gender Equality Act 39 of 1996 provides that before the members of the Commission are appointed, the Minister of Justice must invite interested parties to propose candidates for appointment.

have been taken and, formally, the position of women in relation to the legal system is improving. It is unlikely that these changes would have taken place as quickly in the absence of formal institutions focusing on gender issues.

III. SECURING GENDER EQUALITY THROUGH LEGISLATION AND POLICY

Since the advent of democracy, the most direct way of securing change in South Africa is through legislation and policy. Unlike the situation in established democracies where much policy is fixed and legislation is difficult to amend, law and policy in South Africa are subject to massive change and revision. Moreover, South Africa's system of proportional representation for elections permitted the use of a quota to ensure the representation of women, a strategy that the governing African National Congress used. Quoting a 1999 study, a report by the Centre for Applied Legal Studies suggests that the relatively high number of women in Parliament (29.8 percent in the National Assembly in 1999) has had significant effects on the profile of gender issues in Parliament.[21] So it is in the areas of policy and legislation that one might expect most gains for gender equality. And the record of new legislation and policy development is good.

The most important Act is the *Promotion of Equality and Prevention of Unfair Discrimination Act* of 2000.[22] The Act is intended to prevent and prohibit unfair discrimination, harassment, and hate speech, and to promote equality. It has a focus on addressing past patterns of disadvantage, which is especially important for women and particularly those women who suffer from intersecting forms of discrimination.

The Act applies to both state and non-state actors, and goes beyond the requirements of the Constitution. Whereas the Constitution requires only the state to take positive measures to promote the rights in the Bill of Rights,[23] the Act places this obligation on non-state actors as well. In addition, it takes the opening provided by the Constitution's express exclusion of hate speech from freedom of expression and prohibits hate speech and harassment. Equality Courts with judicial officers are to be established to enforce the antidiscrimination provisions of the Act, while the South African Human Rights Commission is to oversee the aspects of the Act that provide for the promotion of equality.

The Act contains a general definition of discrimination but race, gender, and disability discrimination are highlighted. Gender discrimination includes violence against women, practices that prevent women from inheriting

---

[21] Hassim, "Engendering the State," citing T. Mtintso, *The contribution of women parliamentarians to gender equality* (unpublished MA thesis, University of the Witwatersrand, 1999).

[22] Act 4, 2000.

[23] See the Constitution, *supra* note 3, s.7.

property, or that unfairly limit the access to women to land rights, finances, or other resources, limiting women's access to social benefits and the denial of access to services and opportunities. The Act also specifically prohibits traditional, customary, or religious practices that undermine the dignity of women or gender equality. The Act is not yet in force, mainly because the courts necessary to implement it have yet to be established. Whether the Act will be as effective as it could be will depend on these courts and it is likely that, in the short term, implementation will be difficult: lower courts are heavily overloaded and often badly managed and the public education programs necessary to inform people of their rights under the legislation will demand resources that the Department of Justice does not have at present.

In addition to the *Promotion of Equality Act*, a number of other new laws impact directly on women, including the *Employment Equity Act*,[24] which requires certain employers to implement affirmative action programmes. The *Labour Relations Act*[25] also contains specific antidiscrimination provisions. The *Prevention of Family Violence Act*,[26] the *Choice on Termination of Pregnancy Act*,[27] the *Maintenance Act*,[28] and the *Films and Publications Act*[29] all contain provisions intended to promote equality for women. The *Prevention of Family Violence Act* provides for preventative interdicts for victims of family violence and criminalizes the rape of a woman by her husband. The *Choice on Termination of Pregnancy Act* allows a woman to terminate her pregnancy on request during the first twelve weeks and on certain prescribed conditions thereafter. The preamble to this Act places it firmly in its constitutional context by highlighting the values of human dignity, equality, security of the person and nonracialism and nonsexism, and the constitutional right of persons to make decisions concerning reproduction and to have security in and control over their bodies. The *Maintenance Act*, which, according to its preamble, attempts to establish a "sensitive and fair approach to the determination and recovery of maintenance," provides for simpler and more effective procedures for dependants to claim maintenance from their ex partners. Finally, the *Films and Publications Act*, which united women of the governing African National Congress and conservative opposition parties into a strong women's lobby in Parliament, deals fairly severely with pornography and, in particular, child pornography. The preamble to this Act again conceptualizes the Act as a means of securing gender equality – as is guaranteed in the Constitution.

[24] Act 55, 1998.
[25] Act 66, 1995.
[26] Act 133, 1993.
[27] Act 92, 1996.
[28] Act 99, 1998.
[29] Act 65, 1996.

In other parts of the world there have been many instances in which important gains made for women and other disadvantaged groups at the legislative level have been successfully challenged as violating constitutional rights such as the right to a fair trial.[30] It is thus crucial for courts to understand Acts such as those described in the light of the equality interests that they are designed to protect. The express articulation of the equality guarantee in the preamble of the new Acts is intended to remind judges to take account of South Africa's full constitutional context when they implement the Acts and not to focus myopically on a single issue. This is important both in relation to the interpretation of the ambit of an Act and during a challenge to any of its provisions.

Then, prompted by international human rights law, law-makers have paid attention to gender in other pieces of legislation. The *Prevention of Illegal Eviction from and Unlawful Occupation of Land Act*[31] is a good example. A key piece of legislation in the program to address the injustice wrought by apartheid's program of forced removals, the *Illegal Eviction Act* requires courts to consider the needs of "the elderly, children, disabled persons and households headed by women" when deciding whether or not to permit an eviction. As women bear a disproportionate responsibility for caring for the elderly, children, and disabled people, this provision will be of special significance to them.[32]

The *Recognition of Customary Marriages Act*[33] is an important development for customary law. The Act gives official recognition to customary marriages, including polygynous unions.[34] A wife of a customary marriage is given equal status and capacity to that of a wife in a civil marriage, including the previously denied capacity to acquire property and to contract.[35] Like a civil marriage, a customary marriage may be dissolved by a court on the

---

[30] The most well-known example of this phenomenon is the Canadian case of *R. v. Seaboyer* (1991), 83 DLR (4th) 193 (SCC). See J. McInnes and C. Boyle, "Judging Sexual Assault Law against a Standard of Equality" (1995) 29 *University of British Columbia Law Review* 341.

[31] Act 19, 1998.

[32] See *Illegal Eviction Act*, ibid., s.4. The provisions implement paragraph 11 of the *General Comment 7 of the UN Committee on Economic, Social and Cultural Rights (Art. 11(1) of the Covenant) forced evictions*, UN Doc. E/C.12/1997/4 (1997).

[33] Act 120, 1998.

[34] *Recognition of Customary Marriages Act*, ibid., s.2.

[35] *Recognition of Customary Marriages Act*, ibid., s.6. However, Section 7(1) provides that the "proprietary consequences of a customary marriage entered into before the commencement of this Act continues to be governed by customary law." Bronstein shows the contradictions between Section 6 of the Act, which grants full legal status to customary wives, and Section 7(1), which continues to subject the proprietary consequences of marriages entered into before the commencement of the Act to customary law – which does not allow women to own property. See V. Bronstein, "Confronting Custom in the New South African State: An Analysis of the Recognition of Customary Marriages Act 120 of 1998" (2000) 16 *South African Journal on Human Rights* 558.

ground of irretrievable breakdown.[36] The Act also abolishes the customary law practice of treating women as minors, and gives women full majority status.[37] But the Act attempts to strike a balance between gender equality and the right to culture by recognizing certain customary practices.

IV. GENDER EQUALITY IN THE COURTS

This part of this chapter examines the most important gender equality cases that have come before the courts. We focus on the jurisprudence of the Constitutional Court but we also look at selected cases in other courts. We argue that while the equality case law of the Constitutional Court contains the potential for progressive and transformative gender equality jurisprudence, there has been limited success in achieving gender equality through litigation.

In the interpretation and application of the equality guarantee, the Constitutional Court has highlighted the central place of equality in the new South African order. Early in its equality jurisprudence, the Court stressed the substantive nature of the right to equality. This was an important achievement for advocates of gender equality, since the pitfalls inherent in the formal equality approach have been a major obstacle to litigation on sex and gender discrimination in other parts of the world. The Constitutional Court has also made several significant observations directly in relation to gender equality. In *Brink v. Kitshoff*, O'Regan J held that although South Africa's history has resulted in race being the "most visible and most vicious" form of discrimination, there were other patterns of systemic discrimination which "were and are inscribed on our social fabric."[38] She observes that this accounts for the inclusion of the list of grounds in the equality provision in the Constitution, including sex, gender, and pregnancy, on which unfair discrimination is prohibited. These grounds automatically trigger a presumption that the discrimination is unfair, because, as Goldstone J observes in *Harksen v. Lane*, the specified grounds have in the past been used to "categorise, marginalize and often oppress persons who have had, or who have been associated with these characteristics."[39]

In response to another matter that has been difficult in other jurisdictions (most notably the United States), the equality provision envisages discrimination based on more than one ground. A litigant can allege discrimination "on one or more grounds" listed in Section 9 of the Constitution, meaning that she could show discrimination suffered at the intersection of

---

[36] *Recognition of Customary Marriages Act*, ibid., s.8. Traditionally, divorce under customary law was a private or community affair and had nothing to do with the courts. See Bronstein, "Confronting Custom," ibid. at 560.

[37] *Recognition of Customary Marriages Act*, ibid., s.9.

[38] (1996), 6 BCLR 752 (CC) at para. 41.

[39] (1997), 11 BCLR 1489 (CC) at para. 49.

race and gender, for instance. In *Brink*, O'Regan J observes that patterns of race and sex discrimination have resulted in "particularly acute" disadvantage in the case of black women, as race and gender overlap.[40] In *Harksen*, Goldstone J notes that there is often a complex relationship between the specified grounds, and that the temptation to force them into "neatly self-contained categories should be resisted."[41] More recently, in *National Coalition for Gay and Lesbian Equality v. Minister of Justice*, Sachs J held that an impact and context-based approach to equality must recognise that grounds of unfair discrimination may intersect, and where this is found to be the case an evaluation of the impact of the discrimination cannot be done on one ground alone. An example of people suffering multiple discrimination would be African widows, "who historically have suffered discrimination as blacks, as Africans, as women, as African women, as widows and usually, as older people, intensified by the fact that they are frequently amongst the lowest paid workers."[42]

The constitutional test for equality and the circumstances under which different treatment may constitute unfair discrimination were set out by the Constitutional Court in *Harksen v. Lane*.[43] Differentiation will amount to discrimination if it is based on one of the sixteen specified grounds in Section 9(3) of the Constitution, or if it is objectively based on a ground which has the "potential to impair the fundamental human dignity of persons as human beings or to affect them adversely in a comparably serious manner."[44] Unfairness is presumed if the discrimination is based on one or more of the listed or specified grounds in Section 9(3).[45] The effect of this is that if the differentiation is on a listed ground, it not only immediately establishes discrimination but also gives rise to a presumption of unfairness. In *Harksen* it was held that to determine whether discriminatory treatment is unfair, various factors must be considered including the position of the complainants in society and whether they have suffered from discrimination in the past; the nature of the discriminating provision or power and the purpose sought to be achieved by it; and any other relevant factors including the extent to which the discrimination has affected the rights or interests of the complainants and whether it has led to an impairment of their fundamental human dignity.[46]

---

[40] *Brink v. Kitshoff, supra* note 38 at para. 44.

[41] *Harksen v. Lane, supra* note 39 at para. 49.

[42] (1998), 12 BCLR 1517 (CC) at para. 113.

[43] *Harksen v. Lane, supra* note 39.

[44] *Harksen v. Lane, ibid.,* at para. 46.

[45] The presumption of unfairness is triggered by Section 9(5).

[46] The test for equality, and particularly the inclusion of the dignity component in both the discrimination and unfairness stages of the analysis has been severely criticized. See C. Albertyn and B. Goldblatt, "Facing the Challenges of Transformation: Difficulties in the Development of an Indigenous Jurisprudence of Equality" in (1998) 14 *South African Journal on Human Rights* 248; and Dennis Davis, "The Majesty of Legoland Jurisprudence" (1999) 116 *South*

Some of the cases discussed later show how this contextual approach has been applied in practice – the *Hugo* decision is a prime example.[47] However, there has also been much criticism of the application of the unfairness test.[48]

There have been four cases before the Constitutional Court in which the applicants have directly relied on the sex or gender equality[49] guarantee. This is a disturbingly small (but not surprising) percentage of the total number of cases heard by the Court since its inception in 1995. The few cases that have come before the Constitutional Court have not been brought by the women who have suffered the worst indignities of inequality but by members of relatively privileged groups instead. Of the four cases, two of the applicants claiming the protection of this guarantee were men. In *Fraser v. Children's Court, Pretoria North*[50] an unmarried father successfully challenged the provisions of the *Child Care Act*[51] that allowed the adoption of children born out of marriage without the consent of the father. In *President of the Republic of South Africa v. Hugo,*[52] a convicted prisoner challenged the remission of the sentence of certain women but no men prisoners. In the third case, *Brink v. Kitshoff,*[53] a woman claimed the benefits of a life insurance policy valued at approximately R2 million (U.S. $250,000). The only exception to this trend has been *S. v. Jordan,*[54] in which Section 20(1)(aA) of the *Sexual Offences Act,*[55] which penalized only the conduct of the sex worker and not the client, was unsuccessfully challenged on the grounds of gender discrimination. We discuss each of these cases later. At issue in *Brink* was the constitutionality

---

African Law Journal 398. The argument is that considering both group based systemic disadvantage and individual dignity as equal factors to be taken into account mutes the substantive nature of the equality test. Equality, it is argued, is concerned with issues related to material, economic, and social interests, and its primary purpose should be to address group based disadvantage, not individual personality issues. Thus the intention of the equality clause must be "to advance equality, not dignity, and that the dignity provisions in the Bill of Rights should take care of protecting dignity" (*National Coalition for Gay and Lesbian Equality, supra* note 42, at para. 20).

[47] *President of the Republic of South Africa v. Hugo* (1997), 6 BCLR 708 (CC). The case is discussed later.

[48] See, for example, Albertyn and Goldblatt, "Facing the Challenges of Transformation," *supra* note 46; and S. Jagwanth, "What is the Difference: Group Categorisation in *City Council of Pretoria v. Walker*" (1999) 15 *South African Journal on Human Rights* 200.

[49] The Constitutional Court has not yet pronounced on the differences between the prohibition on gender and sex discrimination (and may never need to), and has sometimes used the terms interchangeably. Both terms were included in the Constitution for inclusivity – prompted by feminist understandings of the ambit of each of them.

[50] (1997) 2 BCLR 153 (CC).

[51] Act 74, 1983.

[52] *President of the Republic of South Africa v. Hugo, supra* note 47.

[53] *Brink v. Kitshoff, supra* note 38.

[54] (2002) 11 BCLR 1117 (CC).

[55] Act 23, 1957.

of a provision of the *Insolvency Act*.[56] The effect of the provision was that where a life insurance policy had been ceded to a woman by her husband within two years of the sequestration of his estate, she would receive no benefit at all. The remaining amount would instead form part of the insolvent estate. No similar provisions limited the benefits of a life insurance policy ceded by a woman in favor of her husband. Striking the provision down as unconstitutional, the Constitutional Court held that the distinction between married men and women was not based on any cogent reasons and could not be justified.

Brink was a relatively simple case that dealt with the constitutionality of a law that was manifestly based on outdated views of gender roles and marriage. It is difficult to find legitimate justifications for a law that had different application for men and women, which had a negative impact on women, and that was based on harmful gender stereotypes. But the case was an important one in setting the stage for a substantive understanding of equality, and for its recognition of the need to understand the right in the light of South Africa's history of racial and gender discrimination. *Brink* thus provided the contextual and historical framework within which the Court was able to develop its equality jurisprudence.

The question of traditional gender roles was also raised in *Fraser v. Children's Court, Pretoria North*.[57] Here, the issue was the constitutionality of a provision of the *Child Care Act* that did not require the consent of the father to give a child up for adoption when the child was born outside of marriage. The Court held that the provision violated the right to equality. Mohamed J agreed that the equality analysis required more than a simple consideration of the fact that the legislation made a distinction based on gender. Although he chose not to tackle the allegations of the general problem of unreliability of unmarried fathers, he acknowledged that the mother has a special biological relationship with the child during and soon after pregnancy that cannot be compared to that of a father. In addition, consideration had to be given to the fact that in some circumstances, for example, in relation to a child born as a result of a rape, to require the father's consent for an adoption would lead to anomalous consequences. However, the Act went too far in its blanket exclusion of the father's consent under any circumstances regardless of the age of the child or the relationship between the father and the child. The Court's order suspending the declaration of invalidity for a period of time was intended to allow Parliament to cure the defect in a manner sensitive to these concerns.[58]

---

[56] Act 24, 1936.

[57] *Fraser v. Children's Court, Pretoria North, supra* note 50.

[58] The Act was amended in 1999 and now requires the consent of both parents in all adoptions. However, the consent of one of the parents may be dispensed with in a number of specified circumstances, for example, if that parent has deserted the child, is withholding consent unreasonably, or has failed to discharge parental duties.

The issue of the extent to which the law reflects traditional gender roles and the extent of its responsibility to avoid reflecting gendered and sometimes harmful stereotypes came up again in *President of the RSA v. Hugo.*[59] This case involved a challenge to the action of the president who, acting under his power to pardon and reprieve offenders under the interim Constitution, granted a remission of sentence to all mothers in prison on 10 May 1994 who fell into certain categories and who had children under the age of twelve years old. Hugo, a male prisoner and a single parent, challenged the constitutionality of the president's action on the ground that it discriminated against him on the basis of sex. The majority agreed that by releasing only mothers and not fathers there was discrimination on the basis of sex. As the discrimination was on a listed ground, it was presumptively unfair and the president bore the onus of rebutting this presumption. The Court accepted that by releasing mothers only, the president had relied on a generalization that women were primarily responsible for childcare in our society. The Court also accepted that:

[t]he result of being responsible for children makes it more difficult for women to compete in the labour market and is one of the causes of the deep inequalities experienced by women in employment. The generalisation on which the President relied is therefore a fact which is one of the root causes of women's inequality in our society.[60]

Nevertheless, the majority found that the discrimination was not unfair. This is because (i) fathers are not a vulnerable group adversely affected by discrimination; (ii) South Africa's high crime rate made it difficult if not impossible to release both mothers and fathers; and (iii) in any event, the release of male prisoners would not have contributed to the president's goals because fathers, as a general rule, do not play a major role in childcare. As to the last leg of the unfairness analysis, the Court held that it was not the president's decision that impacted on rights and obligations of fathers but, rather, their convictions for having committed crimes.[61]

In a strongly worded dissenting judgment, Kriegler J says that reliance on a stereotype that resulted in women's inequality could not be constitutionally permissible. He held that the limited benefit in this case – to the 440 mothers released from prison – was far outweighed by the detriment to all South African women. He summarizes his position as follows:

The limited benefit in this case cannot justify the reinforcement of a view that is a root cause of women's inequality in our society. In truth there is no advantage to women qua women in the President's conduct, merely a favour to perceived child

[59] *President of the Republic of South Africa v. Hugo, supra* note 47.
[60] *President of the Republic of South Africa v. Hugo,* ibid., at para. 38.
[61] This argument is clearly fallacious in the equality context, because equality is prima facie violated when benefits are not conferred equally on all members of a group in the same position.

minders. On the other hand there are decided disadvantages to womankind in general in perpetuating perceptions foundational to paternalistic attitudes that limit the access of women to the workplace and other sources of opportunity. There is also more diffuse disadvantage when society imposes roles on men and women, not by virtue of their individual characteristics, qualities or choices, but on the basis of predetermined, albeit time-honoured, gender scripts. I cannot agree that because a few hundred women had the advantage of being released from prison early, the Constitution permits continuation of these major societal disadvantages.[62]

In a separate concurring judgment, O'Regan J answers these concerns. She held that women's primary responsibility for childrearing was a social reality – while an egalitarian society required men and women to share the responsibilities for childrearing, the fact of the matter is that they do not. She argues that the disadvantage to women lay not in the president's action but in the social fact of the role played by mothers in child rearing, and more particularly, in the inequality that resulted from it.

The case illustrates the very real tension between a matter of important principle and the concrete lives of people in the litigation of equality issues.[63] In the application of the equality test, the majority of the Court shows a sensitivity to the social context of women, and particularly the position of mothers with young children in a society in which childrearing carries no economic value. They do this at the expense of the principle articulated by Kriegler J. They appear to be saying that concrete gain for women under these circumstances is more important than the resolute defence of principle, particularly where this would lead to no substantive transformation at all. Even though the majority judgment in this case has been criticized,[64] the approach of the Court and the outcome of the case in *Hugo* are most in line with a contextual, substantive, and group-based understanding of equality.[65] In particular, O'Regan J's approach is commendable for its recognition that an equality analysis cannot be separated from an analysis of the concrete realities of social arrangements in society. This is what is required by an impact-based and contextual understanding of equality.

In the most recent judgment dealing with gender discrimination, *Jordan*,[66] the Court was faced with the constitutionality of provisions of the *Sexual Offences Act*, which criminalized commercial sex work and the keeping of a brothel. The issue that divided the court 6 to 5 was Section 20(1)(aA) of

[62] *President of the Republic of South Africa v. Hugo*, ibid., at para. 83.
[63] See Justice A. Sachs, "Equality Jurisprudence: The Origin of the Doctrine in the Constitutional Court" (1999) 5 *Review of Constitutional Studies* 76 at 89.
[64] See, for example, Dennis Davis, *Democracy and Deliberation* (Kenwyn: Juta, 1999) especially at 74–84.
[65] See also M. Kende, "Gender Stereotypes in South African and American Constitutional Law: The Advantages of a Pragmatic Approach to Equality and Transformation" (2000) 114 *South African Law Journal* 745.
[66] *Supra* note 54.

the Act, which criminalized only the activity of the prostitute and not that of the client. Justice Ngcobo, writing for the majority, held that there was no gender discrimination. He found that "[p]enalising the recipient of the reward only does not constitute unfair discrimination on the grounds of gender" because the section is couched in gender neutral terms to cover male and female prostitutes.[67] The differentiation was thus not on the grounds of gender but simply on the basis that "the prostitute sells sex and the patron buys it."[68] He noted further that there was a "qualitative difference between the prostitute who conducts the business of prostitution and is therefore likely to be a repeat offender, on the one hand, and the customer who seeks the service of a prostitute only on occasion and thus may not be a repeat offender."[69] In any event, the reasoning went, the customer was also liable for prosecution and punishment under other legislation and the common law. Any social stigma that was attached to prostitution arose not from the law but from the nature of the conduct sex workers engaged in. Ncgobo J also rejected the argument that gender discrimination exists because there are more female prostitutes than male prostitutes, "just as I would not be persuaded if the same argument were to be advanced by males accused of certain crimes, the great majority of which are committed by men."[70]

Given the contextual nature of the equality test, the reasoning of the majority in *Jordan* is surprisingly acontextual and ignores the gendered framework within which prostitution takes place. There can be no doubt – and counsel for the state did not attempt to deny the fact – that the vast majority of sex workers are women. The economic and social reasons for this are well documented. Thus, under the equality provision, and the test laid down by the court itself, the differentiation in question clearly constitutes indirect gender discrimination. Women who are financially well off are unlikely to resort to prostitution and the qualitative difference between the sex worker and her client is more appropriately couched in economic terms rather than in the frequency of the conduct. The majority's observation that the problem lay in social attitudes towards prostitution and not in the law is also troublesome, as it reflects a lack of understanding about the way in which law reflects and reinforces social values.

The minority judgment by O'Regan and Sachs J J found that the impugned provision constituted indirect discrimination. They noted that in general prostitutes are overwhelmingly female and their patrons overwhelmingly male and that the provision reinforced patterns of sexual stereotyping by making the prostitute the primary offender. The Act reinforced the double

---

[67] Ibid. at para. 9.
[68] Ibid. at para. 15.
[69] Ibid. at para. 10.
[70] Ibid. at para. 17.

standards of sexuality, which in law and social practice are applied to men and women.

The minority observed that, while prostitutes accept the risk that their social status will be lowered, many women turn to prostitution because they have no alternatives. This situation makes them a particularly vulnerable and marginalized group, while their male customers are likely to be more economically powerful. O'Regan and Sachs J J also recognized the way in which law is "partly constitutive of invidious social standards which are in conflict with our Constitution."[71] The distinguishing feature in prostitution cases is that they are "all about regulating sex and the expression of sexuality. The element of gender is not just happenstance, but integral to the prohibited conduct and constitutive of the way [they are] treated by the law, enforcement agents and society."[72] While the minority displays an understanding of the issues underlying prostitution in a gendered society, the Court was unanimous in its finding that the prohibition on the keeping of a brothel and the criminalization of sex work passed constitutional muster under the rights to privacy, dignity, freedom, and security of the person, and the right to economic activity. The control and regulation of sex work was a complex matter, which was best left to the legislature to determine. In this regard, the deferential posture of all of the members of the court precluded a fuller and deeper analysis of some of the other rights at stake in the regulation of sex work.

The decision in *Jordan* is disappointing not only because of a lack of a gender dimension in the equality analysis but also because the court lost an opportunity to apply its substantive equality test with sensitivity to the social context of a severely disadvantaged group. As indicated earlier in this chapter, the Court has been at pains to highlight the context- and impact-based nature of its test, but *Jordan* shows that, even with the advantage of a solid, progressive jurisprudence, litigation will not always be a reliable way of effecting meaningful social change.

How has the equality guarantee been used in cases where it is not directly relied upon as a cause of action? In *S v. Baloyi*,[73] the Constitutional Court was faced with a challenge to the constitutionality of a provision in the *Prevention of Family Violence Act*,[74] which, it was contended, reversed

---

[71] Ibid. at para. 72.

[72] Ibid. at para. 73.

[73] (2000) 1 BCLR 86 (CC).

[74] The relevant provisions of the Act provided that a person who was arrested for a breach of a domestic violence interdict must be brought before a judge or magistrate as soon as possible for an enquiry. The procedure to be followed at the enquiry in terms of Section 3(5) of the Act was the same as that provided for in Section 170 of the *Criminal Procedure Act* 51, 1977. The latter provision allows a court to convict an accused person of failing to remain in attendance at court proceedings "unless the accused satisfies the court that this failure was not due to fault on his part."

the onus of proof in domestic violence matters and thus violated the right of an accused person to be presumed innocent. In rejecting this contention, Sachs J held that the distinguishing factor in domestic violence cases was its "hidden, repetitive character and its immeasurable ripple effect on our society, and, in particular, on family life. It cuts across class, race, culture and geography, and is all the more pernicious because it is so often concealed and so frequently goes unpunished."[75] Only after firmly characterising domestic violence as a matter of gender equality did Sachs J proceed with the constitutional analysis of the conflicting rights at stake. He held that because of its "systemic, pervasive and overwhelming gender specific" nature, domestic violence reflected "patriarchal domination" and gender inequality in our society. The traditional ineffectiveness of the criminal justice system in dealing with domestic violence sends the message that "[p]atterns of systemic sexist behaviour" are acceptable and the foundational values of the Constitution and gender equality are undermined when spouses can batter with impunity.[76]

This judgment is particularly important because, as we have shown, it has not been the most disadvantaged groups that have sought the protection of the equality provision in the courts. If equality is to have the prominence and status required by a primarily egalitarian Constitution, its application cannot be limited to the few cases in which relatively privileged groups bring direct equality challenges to the courts. *Baloyi* shows how the right to equality can be used as a tool to defend legislative and other benefits secured by women and other disadvantaged groups. *Bannatyne v. Bannatyne*[77] is another instance of the equality guarantee being used in the interpretation of legislation. In this case, the applicant approached the Constitutional Court for special leave to appeal against a decision of the Supreme Court of Appeal that had set aside a contempt of a maintenance order made by the High Court. Her appeal to the Constitutional Court was based on the ground that the Supreme Court of Appeal had failed to take into account children's rights enshrined in Section 28(2) of the Constitution. In considering the responsibility of the judiciary to ensure that maintenance orders are observed, Justice Mokgoro noted that the system of maintenance was inherently gendered. Thus, in addition to the rights of children, gender equality was also relevant to the analysis. She noted that it is most frequently mothers who become the custodial parent, placing an additional financial burden on them and inhibiting their ability to obtain work. She added that "[d]ivorced or separated mothers face the double disadvantage of being overburdened in terms of responsibilities and under-resourced in terms of means. Fathers, on the other hand, remain actively employed and generally become economically

---

[75] *S v. Baloyi, supra* note 73, at para. 11.
[76] *S v. Baloyi,* ibid., at para. 12.
[77] (2003), 2 BCLR 111 (CC).

enriched. Maintenance payments are therefore essential to relieve this financial burden."[78] As gender equality is one of the founding values of the Constitution, courts have a special responsibility to be aware of, and guard against, the instances of recalcitrant maintenance defaulters who use legal processes to dodge their obligations.

Finally, how have other courts interpreted and applied the equality jurisprudence developed by the Constitutional Court? Again, there have not been many cases dealing with gender equality. One decision, however, is particularly striking. It is *Woolworths (Pty) Ltd v. Whitehead*,[79] in which the Labour Appeal Court[80] dealt with the question of whether it was unfair discrimination under the *Labour Relations Act* for an employer to take into account a potential employee's pregnancy when considering her application for a permanent post. In a judgment that makes virtually no reference to the Constitution or the Constitutional Court's jurisprudence on equality, the Labour Appeal Court found that discrimination, if it existed, was not unfair because "profitability is a relevant consideration in the unfairness determination."[81] Willis J A held that taking into account pregnancy when determining suitability for a job was "perfectly rational and commercially understandable" because the employer needed someone in the position for an uninterrupted period of time.[82]

It is difficult to understand the reasoning of the Court in this case. As pointed out above, an unfairness analysis must take into account factors such as the severity of the impact of the discrimination on the complainant and whether the group to which he or she belongs has suffered from past patterns of discrimination. None of these factors appears to have been considered by Willis J A. The case was settled by the parties before it could go on appeal to the Constitutional Court.

V. GENDER AND CUSTOMARY LAW

As we noted in Section I, the South African Constitution gives effect to both the right to equality and the right to culture. However, the right to culture may not be exercised in a manner inconsistent with any provision of the Bill of Rights.[83] On a literal meaning of the text of the Constitution, it appears

---

[78] Ibid. at para. 29.

[79] (2000), 12 BCLR 1340 (LAC).

[80] The Labour Appeal Court is the final court of appeal in respect of all matters decided in the Labour Court. It is a superior court that has authority, inherent powers, and standing in relation to matters under its jurisdiction equal to that of the Supreme Court of Appeal (see S.167 of the Labour Relations Act).

[81] *Woolworths (Pty) Ltd v. Whitehead, supra* note 79 at para 134.

[82] *Woolworths (Pty) Ltd v. Whitehead*, ibid., at para. 131.

[83] See the Constitution, *supra* note 3, S.30, 31.

that where the right to culture is at odds with other rights such as equality or dignity, the latter will simply prevail. Such an interpretation, however, is an overly simple approach to the problem of the clash between the right to culture and other rights in the Bill of Rights.[84] The Constitution acknowledges the need to take into account the traditions of all sectors of South African society including, as Justice Sachs has elegantly put it, "giving long overdue recognition to African law and legal thinking as a source of legal ideas, values and practice... that have long been suppressed or marginalized."[85] But African customary law, including that part of it codified in the *Black Administration Act,*[86] is indisputably based on patriarchal values and discriminates against women. The system of African customary law includes the relegation of wives of customary marriages to the status of minors under the legal guardianship of their husbands; women may not own property or hold office in public forums; they may not negotiate or terminate their own marriages or claim custody of their children; and customary marriages require husbands to pay bridewealth and allow them to enter into polygynous unions.[87] These practices are manifestly out of step with the rights and values under the new constitutional order. How is this apparent tension to be resolved? Again, relatively few cases have made their way to the courts.

In *Mthembu v. Letsela,*[88] the Supreme Court of Appeal dealt with the question of the rights of female children to inherit under customary law. African customary law of succession is usually based on the principle of male primogeniture. In *Mthembu,* the appellant, a Zulu woman, alleged that she had entered into a customary union with the deceased and that a daughter, Tembi, had been born from the union. The deceased had died intestate; Tembi was his only child. At the time of his death, the deceased was the owner of fixed property on which he had lived with the appellant. The respondent, the father of the deceased, claimed that a customary union was not entered into between the deceased and the appellant, because certain essential elements of

---

[84] See V. Bronstein, "Reconceptualising the Customary Law Debate in South Africa" (1998) 14 *South African Journal on Human Rights* 388.

[85] Sachs J, in *S v. Makwanyane* (1995), 6 BCLR 665 (CC), at para. 365 (the death penalty case).

[86] Act 38, 1927. The Act was enacted in order to administer the affairs of black people and is a legislative example par excellence of the system of apartheid and colonialism in South Africa. In *Moseneke v. Master of the High Court,* (2001), 2 BCLR 103 (CC), Sachs J describing the Act as anachronistic, said of it as follows: "It is painful that the Act survives at all. The concepts on which it was based, the memories it evokes, the language it continues to employ, and the division it still enforces, are antithetical to the society envisaged by the Constitution" (at para. 21).

[87] TW Bennett, *Human Rights and African Customary Law under the South African Constitution* (Kenwyn: Juta, 1995) at 80–94.

[88] (2000), 3 SA 867 (SCA).

a customary union had not been met. He thus claimed that the property had devolved to him by virtue of the customary law of succession. The appellant's case was that this system of intestate succession discriminated against women and was in violation of the equality provisions in the Constitution, and that Tembi was the rightful heir to the deceased's property. In the court a quo, the factual dispute as to whether there had been a customary union between the parties could not be resolved, and the matter was decided on the basis that Tembi was an illegitimate child of the deceased. In the Supreme Court of Appeal, Mpati A J A confirmed the finding of the court a quo that "Tembi was not a victim of gender discrimination because any illegitimate child of the deceased would have been disinherited."[89] Thus, her disqualification from inheriting stemmed from her status as an illegitimate child rather than her gender. The Court also rejected a challenge to the legislative recognition of the customary law of succession. Mpati A J A held that the regulations did "not introduce something foreign to black persons … [but] merely gave legislative recognition to a principle of system which had been in existence and followed, at least, for decades."[90] The existing law allowed black people to change the way in which their estates would devolve, and if they did not do so the "consequences could not be assumed to be contrary to their wishes."[91]

Mthembu does not adequately take into account the position of black rural women in South Africa. A progressive and contextual analysis would have required the Court to balance the competing interests carefully, while showing how the right to equality could be used for the protection and benefit of the most disadvantaged groups in society. Even if the Court was reluctant to apply the equality provision directly to the dispute, it should have taken into account the constitutional injunction in Section 39(2) to promote the spirit, purport, and object of the Bill of Rights when interpreting any legislation, the common law, or customary law. This section provides a potentially useful and powerful tool where customary matters are concerned, since it allows a court to preserve many aspects of traditional practice while discarding and developing others which may be in conflict with the Bill of Rights. *Mabena v. Letsoalo,*[92] a decision of the High Court, is a good example of this. As in *Mthembu*, the deceased's father alleged that a customary union had not been entered into between a woman and his son because the mother of the woman, rather than her father, had negotiated the amount of *lobolo* (brideprice) to be paid and had consented to the marriage. It was argued that there was no proper customary union since only a male person could play the role of a guardian and negotiate the terms of a marriage. The Court rejected

---

[89] *Mthembu v. Letsela*, ibid., at para. 15.
[90] *Mthembu v. Letsela*, ibid., at para. 23.
[91] *Mthembu v. Letsela*, ibid.
[92] (1998) 2 SA 1068 (T).

this contention, and found that it was possible for mothers to negotiate the terms of and consent to the marriage of their daughters. In doing so the Court noted that customary law, like other systems of law, is in a state of continuous development. It held that customary law not only existed in the "official version" as documented by writers, but also as "living law" or that which is "actually observed by African communities" and that was the result of ongoing change and development.[93] Significantly, the Court considered the recognition of living customary law to "constitute a development in accordance with the spirit, purport and objects of chapter 3 [of the interim Constitution]."[94]

Despite *Mthembu*, the Supreme Court of Appeal has been willing to develop the common law in the light of the Bill of Rights. *Amod v. Multilateral Motor Vehicle Accidents Fund*[95] dealt with a claim by a widow of a Muslim marriage for damages for loss of support following the unlawful killing of her husband. The issue was whether the Multilateral Motor Vehicle Accidents Fund was liable to compensate the appellant for loss of support of her husband who had been killed in a motor collision. The appellant and the deceased had been married by Islamic rites. Previously, Muslim marriage contracts were not recognized by law because they were potentially polygynous and contrary to public policy.[96] This had led to particular hardships for dependent widows in Muslim marriages because they were not able to claim for loss of support.[97] In *Amod*, Mohamed C J held that to deny the appellant compensation can only be justified on the basis that the only duty of support that the law will protect in such circumstances is a duty flowing from a marriage solemnized by one faith or philosophy to the exclusion of others. This is an untenable basis for the determination of the boni mores of society. It is inconsistent with the new ethos of tolerance, pluralism, and religious freedom which had consolidated itself in the community even before the formal adoption of the interim Constitution on 22 December 1993.[98]

The *Amod* case is important because it shows how the position of widows in Muslim marriages could be improved without directly invoking the Constitution, but by developing the common law to fall in line with the spirit, purport, and objects of the Bill of Rights. It is also important because it shows – in contrast to *Mthembu* – how previously marginalized cultures and customs require recognition and protection under the new constitutional

---

[93] *Mabena v. Letsoalo*, ibid., at 1074h.
[94] *Mabena v. Letsoalo*, ibid., at 1075b.
[95] (1999), 4 SA 1319 (SCA).
[96] *Ismail v. Ismail* (1983), 1 SA 1006 (A).
[97] Ironically, the court in *Ismail*, ibid., held that potentially polygamous marriages were contrary to public policy because, in part, they discriminated against women. A more contextual and nuanced approach to equality and culture would have given protection both to the institution of Islamic marriage as well as the right of a widow to claim damages for loss of support.
[98] *Amod v. Multilateral Motor Vehicle Accidents Fund*, *supra* note 95, at para. 20.

dispensation, particularly where failure to do so would result in anomalous consequences.[99]

VI. CONCLUSION

South African feminists put enormous effort into securing a strong right to gender equality in the Constitution and, in important ways, it has borne fruit. The language of the Constitution demands more than formal equality and recognises that the struggle for equality cannot be relegated to the court-room. In the nine years since democratic government was introduced, both state and private institutions have paid unprecedented attention to gender equality and women's rights. However, as *Jordan, Woolworths,* and *Mthembu* show, our practice is still far from satisfactory. It is still too early to assess whether these cases are the exception rather than the rule; however, in the light of the substantive equality jurisprudence developed by the constitu-tional court, it is more likely that they do not presage the trend for equality case law in the future. But – at least partly – for this to occur, women and other disadvantaged groups must make it to the courts. Most cases on be-half of disadvantaged groups have been brought before the Constitutional Court by public interest law firms or NGOs which in turn rely heavily on foreign donors. However, there are few of these institutions in South Africa and the number of cases that they are able to take on is very limited. The Human Rights and Gender Commissions have the responsibility of teaching the public about their rights under the Constitution as well as assisting lit-igants to bring matters before the courts but again a lack of resources has meant that they are not able to fulfil these tasks adequately. The institu-tional and resource constraints which prevent full access to the courts must be urgently addressed if the human rights jurisprudence being developed by the Constitutional Court is to be the powerful tool for the advancement of disadvantage groups, including black women, that it should be.

The South African experience of gender equality litigation shows that ac-cessible forums are needed to give effect to an equality right, and that judicial training on equality and other human rights issues is essential. It indicates the importance of encouraging public interest litigation and ensuring that assistance is provided to litigants who may not be able to do so otherwise. But it also requires recognition of the multi-pronged approach that is needed to give effect to the equality right. The courts and litigation do play a role but it

---

[99] See B. Goldblatt, "Comment on *Amod v. Multilateral Motor Vehicle Accidents Fund*" (2000) 16 *South African Journal on Human Rights* 138. See also *Ryland v. Edros* (1997) 1 BCLR 77 (C), where the Cape High Court was also asked to give effect to a Muslim marriage contract. Farlam J held that our new constitutional order required an understanding of the values of equality, tolerance of diversity, and the recognition of pluralism, and that it was no longer contrary to public policy to give effect to the marriage contract.

is a limited one. Constitutional rights and values of equality and nondiscrimination are not within the exclusive realm of enforcement by the judiciary and other legislative and policy initiatives are important as well. Nevertheless, problems with the implementation of the legislation and the weakness of state institutions intended to promote gender equality within government, demand that we ask how long change is to remain at a rhetorical level.

Suggested Readings

P. Andrews, "The Constitutional Court Provides Succour for Victims of Domestic Violence: *S v Baloyi*" (2000) 16 *South African Journal on Human Rights* 337.

B. Clarke and L. Meintjies-Van der Walt, "The new South African Domestic Violence Bill – Rhetoric or Reality?" (1998) 115 *South African Law Journal* 760.

Convention for the Elimination of all Forms of Discrimination against Women: First South African Report (1997), online: South African Government Information <http://www.polity.org.za/govdocs/reports/cedaw1.html> (date accessed: 13 June 2002).

C. Himonga, "Law and Gender in Southern Africa: Human Rights and Family Law" in York Bradshaw and Stephen Ndegwa, eds., *The Uncertain Promise of Southern Africa* (Bloomington: Indiana University Press, 2001) 275.

S. Jagwanth and P. J. Schwikkard, "An Unconstitutional Cautionary Rule" (1998) 11 *South African Journal on Criminal Justice* 87.

J. T. R. Jones, "Battered Spouses' Actions for Damages against Unresponsive South African Police" (1997) 114 *South African Law Journal* 356.

F. Kaganas and C. Murray, "The Contest between Culture and Gender Equality under South Africa's Interim Constitution" (1994) 21 *Journal of Law and Society* 409.

S. Liebenberg, ed., *The Constitution of South African from a Gender Perspective* (Cape Town: David Philip, 1995).

T. Loenen, "The Equality Clause in the South African Constitution: Some Remarks from a Comparative Perspective" (1997) 13 *South African Journal on Human Rights* 401.

D. Meyerson, "Abortion: The Constitutional Issues" (1999) 116 *South African Law Journal* 50.

J. Milton, "Redefining Rape: the Law Commission's Proposals" (1999) 12 *South African Journal on Criminal Justice* 364.

C. Murray, ed., *Gender and the New Legal Order* (Kenwyn: Juta, 1998).

C. Murray, "Is Polygyny Wrong?" (1994) 22 *Agenda: A Journal about Women and Gender* 37.

W. Van der Meide, "Gender Equality v the Right to Culture: Debunking the Perceived Conflicts Preventing the Reform of the Marital Property Regime of the 'Official Version' of Customary Law" (1999) 116 *South African Law Journal* 100.

10

Engendering the Constitution

The Spanish Experience

Ruth Rubio-Marin

The current Spanish Constitution was enacted in December 1978, marking Spain's transition to democracy after Franco's death. The Constitution expresses its commitment with a territorially decentralized rule of law-based state inspired in democratic and welfare-state principles and establishes a parliamentary monarchy. It recognizes the separation of powers and a list of fundamental rights, which, according to an explicit interpretive rule (Art. 10.2) are to be read in conformity with the Universal Declaration of Human Rights and other relevant international treaties and agreements that Spain has ratified.[1]

The Constitution also foresees the creation of a new organ, the Constitutional Court, which is the ultimate guardian of the Constitution, and is not conceived as part of the ordinary judiciary. This Court has been functioning since 1981. The twelve justices that comprise it are elected for a nine-year term and are appointed by the different branches of government. Among its main attributes for our purposes are those of exercising judicial review of statutes (the ordinary judiciary is not entitled to review laws)[2] and the protection of constitutional rights through *amparo*. Individuals can bring an

---

[1] Constitución Española de 1978, Boletin Oficial del Estado núm. 311.1, de 29 de diciembre. The rights included in Chapter II, Title I, basically correspond to those of other European postwar Constitutions including the right to equal protection (Article 14); the right to life and physical and moral integrity (Article 15); ideological and religious freedom (Article 16); due process guarantees (Article 17 and Article 24); right to honor, privacy, and one's image (Article 18); freedom of speech and of the press (Article 20); freedom of assembly and association (Article 22); right to private property (Article 33); freedom of enterprise (Article 38); and also the right to publicly funded education (Article 27), the freedom to unionize and to strike (Article 28).

[2] Review of legislation can be triggered by either ordinary judges who can place a question before the Constitutional Court when they have to apply a statute which they consider of doubtful constitutionality to decide on a case or by certain political actors such as the *Defensor del Pueblo* (Ombudsman), the General Prosecutor, the President of the Government or fifty senators or deputies.

action known as an *amparo* before the Constitutional Court when public authorities have violated their most fundamental rights and the ordinary judiciary has failed to redress their claims.[3]

In few areas can we observe the transformation that Spain has undergone since 1978 better than in the changes women have experienced under the new constitutional order. Under Franco, women were relegated to the private realm and oppressed in a patriarchal family structure which was conceived as the main unit of civil society. The husband was legally the head of the family and divorce was not an option. Only he was entitled to dispose of and manage joint assets and he also was recognized as the main holder of the *patria potestas* over the children. Women were either obliged or actively encouraged to take indefinite leaves of absence from their jobs at marriage. Twenty-five years after the Constitution came into force the situation has dramatically changed. In most areas, formal equality between men and women is now ensured and new legislation has been enacted to protect women in virtually every sphere. The civil, criminal, and labor codes have all been changed to accommodate women's needs and views.

In this chapter, I review the constitutional tools and doctrine that have set the framework for such transformations. I will examine the gender of the Spanish Constitution, asking who created it, who interprets it, and what does it say about women, summarizing the main elements of the constitutional doctrine on gender discrimination as formulated by the Constitutional Court mostly in the field of employment discrimination. Then I will focus on the most relevant scenarios of gender struggles at the constitutional level to show the achievements, the potential, and the shortcomings of the notion of sex equality that is embodied in the constitutional doctrine.

THE GENDER OF THE CONSTITUTION AND ITS ACTORS

A commission consisting exclusively of male members of the Congress and Senate drafted the Spanish Constitution of 1978. Both Houses acting as a constituent assembly then ratified it in plenary sessions. At that time women constituted 5.5 percent of the members of Congress and 2.5 percent of the Senate membership in the Parliament that had come out of the first democratic elections. Moreover, seven members were specifically commissioned with drafting the Constitution, none of whom were women. In Spain therefore, the expression "founding fathers" is not just a metaphor.

The Spanish Constitution provides that equality is a foundational value of the legal order in Article 1, together with liberty, justice, and political

---

[3] There is no *amparo* claim against statutes in the abstract, only against individual acts of application of the statute that are presumably unconstitutional. So *amparo* can be claimed only against acts of the administration, the judiciary, and the legislature as long as the latter are not statutes.

pluralism. Moreover, equality before the law is set out as a fundamental right in Article 14 (henceforth, the equality clause). The equality clause also contains a nondiscrimination mandate that specifically prohibits discrimination on the basis of sex. Thus, Article 14 reads: "Spaniards are equal before the law, without any discrimination for reasons of birth, race, sex, religion, opinion, or any other personal or social condition or circumstance." Most of the gender battles at the constitutional level thus far have centered on this clause which can be invoked in *amparo* claims.[4] The Spanish Constitution also embraces substantive equality, if not as an individual right, at least as a promotional goal to be pursued by the public authorities. Thus, Article 9.2 provides that "it is the responsibility of the public powers to promote conditions so that liberty and equality of individuals and groups will be real and effective; and to remove those obstacles which impede or make difficult the full implementation of those conditions...."[5]

Women's equality in marriage and at work is specifically, though implicitly, sanctioned as a constitutional right. Article 32.1 provides that "man and woman have the right to contract matrimony with full legal equality" and Article 35.1 provides that "all Spaniards have the duty to work and the right to work . . . while in no case can there be discrimination for reasons of sex." Finally, the protection of women as mothers appears but only indirectly in the Constitution (i.e., through the protection of the children). This protection is not phrased as an individual right, but rather as one of the enumerated guiding principles of economic and social policy included in Chapter III of Title I. Indeed, Article 39.2 provides that "the public authorities shall assure the complete protection of children, who are equal before the law regardless of their parentage and regardless of the marital status of their mothers. The law shall make it possible to investigate paternity."[6] Finally, the Constitution sanctions the *inequality* of women in the order of succession to the Spanish Crown in its Article 57.1: "Succession to the throne will follow the regular order of primogeniture and representation, the first line always having preference over subsequent lines; within the same line, the close grade over the more remote; in the same grade, the male over the female; and in the same sex, the elder over the younger."

The Constitutional Court has operated within this normative framework that has Article 14's prohibition of sex discrimination at its center. Unfortunately, women have only sat on the Court on three occasions. The first was

---

[4] Notice that only some of the rights in the Spanish Constitution can be relied upon in an *amparo* action. Thus, not every constitutional right enjoys the same level of protection.

[5] Although Article 9.2 contains no specific reference to women, by interpretation women have been included as one of the protected groups.

[6] These principles are not subjective rights but mandates to inspire the action of the public authorities, and they refer to things such as the fair distribution of resources (Article 41), a healthy environment (Article 45), or people's access to culture (Article 44) and housing (Article 47).

when the Court was initially appointed in 1981. The second appointment did not occur until 1998 and today there are two women judges, *magistradas* María Emilia Casas Baamonde and Elisa Pérez Vera. Hence, most of the time twelve male justices have formed the Court. The best representation women have experienced is two out of ten. Moreover, it is far from clear that these precedents have created a presumption in favor of a certain number of women's seats on the Court.

THE SPANISH CONSTITUTIONAL COURT'S DOCTRINE ON GENDER DISCRIMINATION

Initially, the Court started out building its sex discrimination doctrine on the traditional liberal aspiration of a gender-neutral legal order. The Spanish Constitution's equality mandate, the Court held, implied the need to treat *similarly situated* individuals equally unless there was an *objective and reasonable justification* for doing otherwise.[7] Moreover, the inclusion of sex as one of the proscribed discrimination grounds implied the *ex Constitutione* denial of the reasonableness of distinctions and classifications based on sex that therefore could only be accepted exceptionally and after a strict test of proportionality.[8]

Although never quite abandoning the concern with *similarities and differences*, which was especially useful to analyze the claims brought forward by male plaintiffs, the Court soon took a step further, to embrace concerns with group oppression. In doing so, the Court recognized that the constitutional prohibition of sex discrimination was intended "to put an end to the traditional disadvantage of women and to remove those differences that had historically placed women in an inferior legal and social position both as a result of the action of public powers and social practices."[9] In the view of the Court, disregarding women's historical experience of legal and social discrimination would be tantamount to depriving the constitutional antidiscrimination clause of any real meaning.[10]

This emancipating role, which is assigned to Article 14's antidiscrimination clause, is often linked with Article 9.2's commitment to substantive as opposed to merely formal equality. Consistent with it is the Court's acceptance of the constitutional validity of *affirmative actions* which are conceived as actions of a transitory nature; they imply differential treatment between

---

[7] See, for all, STC 22/1981 (2 July); 20/1991 (31 January) and 117/1998 (2 June).

[8] See, e.g., STC 103/1983 (22 November); STC 229/1992 (14 December) and STC 126/1997 (3 July). Spanish Constitutional Court decisions are cited with the abbreviation STC (*Sentencia del Tribunal Constitucional* – decision of the Constitutional Court) followed by the number of reference of the case and the year of the case and date of the decision.

[9] STC 241/1988 (19 December). This translation, as well as all the others contained in the text, is attributable to the author.

[10] See STC 229/1992 (14 December); 128/1987 (16 July); 5/1992 (16 January).

men and women (as they expressly favor women over men), but are legitimate because they aim at ensuring effective equality between men and women, as groups.[11] Thus, the exceptions of public actions taken to compensate for women's disadvantaged status are viewed as legitimate substantive equality notions, but not as constitutionally mandatory or, in other words, as a matter of right. In principle, neither the right to equality nor the antidiscrimination provision can ground claims to such differential treatment.[12]

It is important to note that, before upholding protective or female-only measures, the Court has declared the need to ensure that irrespective of whether they favor women, they do not have the effect of curtailing women's equal opportunities.[13] Also, according to the Court, it is necessary to make sure that the measures at stake have not lost their meaning in the sense that, at the time when they are applied, they actually help to perpetuate cultural stereotypes that would contribute to consolidating discriminatory practices. Among those stereotypes, the Court has said, are those that assume either a greater vocation or obligation of women toward family roles.[14]

The Constitutional Court has also embraced a generous concept of "sex" when interpreting what discrimination on the basis of "sex" means. Thus it has held that the ban on sex discrimination must be conceived as pertaining not only to sex in a biological sense but also to circumstances that have a direct connection with the sex of the person, such as *pregnancy*. Dividing the world into pregnant and nonpregnant "people" on the basis that not every woman is pregnant is hardly a convincing approach, the Court has said, as it hides the fact that only women can be pregnant.[15] There are several cases declaring that using pregnancy to justify employment dismissal does not conform to the Constitution.

Pregnancy still refers to a biological reality for women. The more interesting question is whether women are or should also be protected because of the social disadvantages that they face, whether or not these are connected to their biology. In other words, to what extent can we embrace a perception of gender discrimination that accounts for women's experience of oppression instead of focusing on their biological existence? A recent case, STC 240/1999 of December 20 opens up this vision of gender as social and not merely biological. In this decision, the Court granted *amparo* to a woman who asked for an unpaid three-year maternity leave from her public employment, an option the pertinent statute recognized only for personnel who enjoyed

---

[11] See STC 28/1992 (9 March); 128/1987 (16 July); and 109/1993 (25 March), all of them referring to employment related benefits or conditions.

[12] See, for all, STC 216/1991 (14 November) and 86/1985 (10 July).

[13] See STC 28/1992 (9 March); 109/1993 (25 March); and 317/1994 (28 November, declaring the unconstitutionality of a norm that allowed only women to take indefinite employment leaves at marriage).

[14] See STC 7/1983 (14 February); and STC 128/1987 (16 July).

[15] See STC 136/1996 (23 July); and STC 173/1994 (7 June).

the status of civil servants but not for workers hired on a temporary basis. To do so, the Court took into account the statistical evidence that most of the workers, whether civil servants or those hired temporarily, who asked for maternity leave were women. Thus, although a neutral action on its face, denying this option to hired workers actually had a clearly disparate impact on women, as opposed to men, severely affecting their chances to preserve their jobs. In doing so the Court noticed that the notion of sex discrimination "does not necessarily have to refer to biological reasons or conditions, there will also be discrimination if a norm or its application has a negative and disparate impact with regard to the enjoyment of constitutionally relevant interests by a group which is formed mainly, if not exclusively, by women." In spite of the revolutionary potential of this case, it is probably too soon to assess its precedential value, although there has been another one along the same lines.[16]

WOMEN IN THE WORKPLACE

Women have won quite a few constitutional battles with regard to access and stability in the labor market. The same is true about the recognition of their right to equal pay. Let us pause to see which constitutional tools have enabled this.

Discrimination in the Workplace

As always, the easier cases have been those of direct discrimination as those are often hard to justify even under a formal equality approach. Thus, there is case law declaring women's exclusion from the professional air force or employment in the mines unconstitutional.[17] Moreover, the Court has made it clear that for an employer to discriminate unconstitutionally on the basis of sex, it is not even necessary that an actual legal relationship binding worker and employer exists. It suffices if women's legitimate expectations are affected. This is why not renewing a contract to a pregnant woman when there are reasons to believe that her pregnancy was the determining factor of the employer's decision constitutes sex discrimination.[18]

Maybe more interesting than these cases of direct discrimination, are those of indirect or *impact discrimination*, which the Court also has considered constitutionally forbidden. The Court has referred to this form of discrimination as comprising "treatments that are formally nondiscriminatory but have a negative impact on women because of the actual differences

---

[16] See STC 203/2000 (24 July). On a related topic, see also STC 20/2001 (29 January).
[17] See STC 216/1991 (14 November); and STC 229/1992 (14 December).
[18] See STC 173/1994 (7 July).

between men and women."[19] To be considered discriminatory, the treatment or practice has to lack a justification, may not be related to an indispensable and objective demand of the work itself, or, where a justification is claimed, must not adequately serve the alleged purpose.[20] This doctrine has proven essential to battles concerning women's working conditions and work stability. Based on the doctrine of indirect discrimination, the Constitutional Court has granted many *amparo* claims to women requesting equal pay for equal work, or for work of equal value. In solving them, the Court has held that in order to justify different pay for men and women, employers can't simply segregate their employees sexually where the functions performed are substantially the same or of equal value. Nor is it acceptable to justify men's better pay by calling on the larger degree of physical effort and strenuousness that the tasks performed by men entail. Taking into account only these considerations will have a disparate and negative impact on women. Rather, employers must consider other "more neutral" qualities and skills, qualities that are less prevailingly masculine – such as responsibility, care, concentration, and persistence – and thus, are more likely to have less of a disparate impact on men and women. In other words, discrimination can't be hidden by using criteria that suit men best and then applying those criteria in a purportedly gender neutral way.[21] By contrast, the doctrine of indirect discrimination has not always been consistently applied and there have been some significant exceptions as regards access to certain forms of employment.[22]

Regarding the burden of proof in employment discrimination cases, the Court's doctrine has in general been quite progressive. Basically, it suffices for a woman employee to show that there have been some indicia on which to ground a reasonable suspicion that there has been sex discrimination. After that, the burden of the proof falls on the employer who will not only have to show that the unfavorable treatment granted to a woman is not just because of her sex or to a related condition, such as pregnancy but completely unrelated to either.[23]

In spite of the progressive nature of much of this antidiscrimination doctrine the Constitutional Court has not been willing to make the connection

---

[19] See STC 145/1991 (1 July); and 147/1995 (16 October).

[20] See STC 198/1996 (3 December), citing *Bilka-Kaufhaus*, C-170/84, [1986] E.C.R. I-1607 (European Court of Justice).

[21] See STC 147/1995 (10 November), STC 145/1991 (13 October); and STC 58/1994 (28 February).

[22] See STC 198/1996, *supra* note 20, where the Court rejected the claim that the public administration's failure to specify the concrete tasks to be performed under the list of available positions from which the chosen candidates could pick did not amount to indirect discrimination even though, for their adequate performance, some of the jobs but not others required more physical strength than the average strength women have.

[23] See STC 136/1996 (23 July); STC 17/2003 (30 January) and STC 98/2003 (14 October).

between the discrimination women encounter in the homes and the difficulties they face in the labor market. In other words, the Court has been more likely to protect women from unscrupulous employers than to protect them from unfair and exploitative husbands even though the existence of the latter also has a clear impact on women's professional opportunities.

Consider, for example, the decisions STC 109/1993 of March 25 and 187/1993 of June 16. In both cases, male workers claimed sex discrimination because the labor code (which was subsequently reformed to include men) allowed women but not men to adjust their working schedule to feed a newborn, be it naturally or artificially. In both cases, the Court denied the plaintiffs' claims on the ground that the norm had been adopted to compensate for women's unfavorable situation in the labor market, in view of statistics that showed that women have more difficulty working after children arrive than men do. However sound the intentions of the legislature, there is no doubt that there are also negative consequences for women deriving from that kind of legislation. For one thing, it fails to protect them against employers who may decide not to hire women to avoid costs associated with maternity. Also, as the dissent of Justice Gimeno Sendra noted, the measure has the clear effect of perpetuating stereotypes regarding the sharing of domestic tasks. The majority decision was not completely impervious to this but claimed that the statute dealt with labor relations and was not concerned about the organization of the family or the sharing of responsibilities between the mother and the father. By tacitly embracing this separation between the public and the private spheres, the Court appears insensitive to the manifold ways in which family structure affects women's personal, social, political, and professional development.

Privacy in the Workplace: Conceptualizing Sexual Harassment

Very recently the Constitutional Court has decided that sexual harassment by private employers constitutes a constitutional violation.[24] Interestingly enough, the Court resisted conceptualizing sexual harassment as sex-based discrimination in spite of its embrace of effects-based discrimination. Instead, it saw sexual harassment as a violation of privacy.

The plaintiff was a woman who had been subjected to verbal and physical molestation by her employer, and had become depressed as a result. She claimed compensation for moral, physical, and material damages. The decision of the labor lower court rejected the claims of sexual harassment arguing that her response to the employer's advances had been hesitant, and she appealed in *amparo* grounding her claim in the constitutional provisions on human dignity (Article 10) and sex discrimination (Article 14).

[24] See STC 224/1999 (13 December).

The Court ultimately granted the *amparo*. It held that the Constitution proscribed sexual harassment, both of the *quid pro quo* and hostile environment type.[25] The requirements for the constitutional infringement were stipulated as follows: there has to be an offending conduct that takes the form of a physical or verbal behavior and is serious enough to create a radically hateful and unpleasant atmosphere, taking into account the victim's sensitivity but also objective circumstances. The conduct must be unwanted and there must be a sign of nonconsent, but the lower court's requirement of an immediate and blunt refusal is not acceptable.

It is interesting to note that the Court built this doctrine on the grounds of the right to privacy sanctioned in Article 18, instead of equality (Article 14) or the right to moral integrity (Article 15). The reason given was that sexual harassment implies an interference in a very personal sphere such as that of sexuality. But the idea fits oddly with the Court's prior doctrine. As framed by prior case law, the constitutional right to privacy is said to protect against the gathering and/or disclosure of information regarding people's private life or sphere. A narrower concept of bodily privacy has also been defined, to protect citizens from searches or inquiries concerning one's body and against one's will, as long as what are affected are the "private parts" of the body, taking into account that the body is not only a physical element but also a cultural construct.[26]

In the case at stake, it is clearly not the notion of bodily privacy that is pivotal, at least as defined in its prior doctrine. Rather, the Court seems to call on the broader notion of privacy on premises that have long been questioned by feminist thinking, namely that because of its the sexual connotations, the conduct is sex, and as sex is something private, the imposition of "sex" violates privacy. And yet it seems that "imposed sex" is not sex, at least for the person upon whom it is imposed, and does not allow for the establishment of intimacy of the kind that would deserve constitutional protection. It comes closer to violence or humiliation, and therefore in my view constitutes a violation of Article 15's right to moral integrity and Article 14's right to nondiscrimination in relation to Article 35's right to employment without discrimination on the basis of sex. The Court actually left open the theoretical possibility of conceptualizing sexual harassment as indirect sex discrimination noting that the conduct affects women more than it does men, given women's greater vulnerability in the labor market. Why, in spite of this statement, the Court still preferred to ground its

---

[25] In building this concept of the constitutionally proscribed notion of sexual harassment, the Court relies expressly on a Resolution by the Council of the European Communities of 29 May 1990 and on a Recommendation of the European Commission of 27 November 1991 (for the protection of the dignity of men and women at work).

[26] See STC 57/1994 (28 February); and STC 37/1989 (15 February).

decision exclusively on the right to privacy is not obvious, and, in my view regrettable.[27]

Whatever its shortcomings, it is clear that the application of constitutional rights to the workplace has allowed for significant progress. Stepping back, we can identify two major factors that have furthered this rather progressive doctrine. First, we have to acknowledge the relevance of the incorporation of international and European law, for the interpretation of the constitutional provisions and, more than anything, of Article 14. More specifically, some of the Covenants of the International Labor Organization ratified by Spain, and the European Social Charter of 1961, have been called on in the elaboration of the doctrine of equal pay and discrimination in employment.[28] The Convention on the Elimination of Discrimination against Women also has been invoked occasionally.[29] But more than anything it is incorporation of European Law and of the large amount of case law of the European Court of Justice, that has made a concrete impact on the constitutional interpretation. Thus, in defining the concept of equal pay and pay of equal value, the notion of indirect discrimination and the types of discrimination related to pregnancy that are constitutionally proscribed, the Constitutional Court's doctrine has practically incorporated European law.[30]

Second, another decisive factor has been the fact that the Constitutional Court has interpreted the antidiscrimination clause as having horizontal effect, that is, as binding not only state powers but also private individuals in their relationships. The Constitution contains a generic clause providing that both citizens and public powers are subject to the Constitution and the legal order (Article 9.1). However, the boundaries of the new Court's doctrine on the horizontal effects of fundamental rights is far from clear. To date, what

---

[27] It is interesting to notice that the recently approved European Directive 2002/73 of the European Parliament and of the Council of 23 September 2002 amending Council Directive 76/207/EEC on the implementation of the principle of equal treatment for men and women as regards access to employment, vocational training, promotion, and working conditions (Official Journal L 269, of 5 October 2002, pp. 15–20) does define sexual harassment as sex discrimination and might therefore encourage the Spanish Constitutional Court to follow this path as well.

[28] Some of the most cited Conventions of the ILO are Conventions numbers 100; 103; 158; 111; and three that elaborate the concept of work discrimination and specify practices related to pregnancy that are to be seen as discriminatory. See, for instance, STC 136/1996 (23 July); and STC 173/1994 (7 June).

[29] See, for instance, STC 173/1994 (7 June), referring to Article 11 of CEDAW stating the need for member states to establish mechanisms against women's employment discrimination; and STC 317/1994 (28 November 28), relying partly on Article 5 of CEDAW to distinguish, as measures that cannot validly qualify as affirmative actions, those that actually have a negative impact on women as a whole because they tend to perpetuate rather than overcome cultural prejudices and stereotypes.

[30] See, e.g., STC 58/1994, *supra* note 21; STC 145/1991 (1 July); STC 244/1999, *supra* note 24; and STC 136/ 1996 (23 July).

we have is a piecemeal construction whereby some constitutional rights limit some forms of expression of individual autonomy otherwise constitutionally protected. Thus, although the Court has been rather erratic in the application of the general equality clause to limit private action, it has accepted the limitations that derive from the recognition of the specific antidiscrimination mandates including sex discrimination.[31]

The realms in which the Court has been more sympathetic to the horizontal effect of constitutional rights have been those which imply ordinary citizens' subjection to structurally organized private powers. The employer/employee relationship has qualified among them and as we saw, not just with respect to the nondiscrimination provision but also with respect to the right to privacy. It is therefore not surprising that as the legal order has eliminated most instances of open and direct discrimination for the sake of formal equality, women have used this path to fight against some of the most common forms of injustice that they encounter in the private sector and, more specifically, in employment practices which threaten substantive equality.[32]

How much potential the doctrine has to expand so as to apply to some other areas of private discrimination in civil society is still to be seen and depends also on whether cases are brought forward to push the current boundaries of the doctrine. One could think of the possibility of constitutionally limiting associations or foundations which discriminate against women, especially if their actions affect women's access to otherwise constitutionally protected goods, such as education, employment, or social respectability. Be it as it may, the family is likely to be one of the last resorts of resistance against the constitutionalization of interpersonal ethos. Going down that path would require the explicit recognition by the Court that the family itself, as a social institution, is largely a hierarchical structure in which relations of power between men and women are exercised. There is nothing that indicates that this may happen any time soon.

---

[31] See STC 241/1988 (9 December); STC 129/1989 (17 July); STC 126/1990 (5 July); and STC 184/1991 (30 September). Compare STC 103/1987 (17 June); STC 127/1987 (16 July); STC 166/1988 (26 September); and STC 28/1992 (9 March).

[32] Procedurally, the issue poses interesting questions, as whatever the reach of the binding force of the constitutional rights and freedoms, the Constitution and the Statute that rules the functioning of the Constitutional Court (*Ley Orgánica del Tribunal Constitucional*) of 1979 provide that *amparo* can only be claimed to react against state action (Article 41.2). However, the provision that refers to the violation of rights and freedoms by the judiciary contemplates the fact that the infringement of the right or liberty has to be attributed to an action or *omission* of the judiciary (Article 44.b LOTC). It is this possibility of reacting against judicial omissions that has opened the path to the Constitutional Court in the case of private action. Since individuals must exhaust the ordinary judiciary before reaching the Constitutional Court, the last judicial decision that does not restore the violation of the right is taken to be the "state action," in this case the "state omission," against which *amparo* is claimed before the Constitutional Court.

WOMEN AND THE ORDER OF SUCCESSION TO NOBILITY TITLES: THE VALUE OF SYMBOLS

In spite of the broad notion of sexual discrimination that the Constitutional Court has articulated in the employment area, in one of its most controversial decisions about gender the Court upheld the constitutional validity of a direct and overt discriminatory practice, namely male preference rules for the inheritance of nobility titles.[33] Although the Constitution makes no mention of nobility titles, there is a general understanding that one of the prerogatives of the king contemplated under the Constitution, that of granting honors and distinctions according to the law (Article 62.f), entitles him to rehabilitate and grant new titles. Indeed, the king has exercised this prerogative together with other public authorities that are involved in the required authentication of such acts.

In 1989, the Supreme Court declared the male preference rule of transmission unconstitutional in a series of decisions because of its discriminatory nature.[34] However, in 1997, answering a constitutional consultation put by a lower judge who presumably disapproved of the doctrine set by the Supreme Court and was trying to bypass it, the Constitutional Court overruled such doctrine in a 9 to 3 decision, declaring the preference of men over women in accordance with the Constitution.[35]

According to the Court, unlike in the past, nobility titles nowadays do not assign people a truly privileged citizenship status. They merely entail a "prerogative of honor" and only have the meaning and significance that society decides to grant them. More than anything, nobility titles have a symbolic meaning. Moreover, they have a very limited social reach as they affect a very limited number of people, namely, those belonging to the lineage of the original title holder. To the extent that they have survived after the Constitution and hence are not unconstitutional in and of themselves, it is futile to try to assimilate nobility titles to a constitutional logic. Rather, they have their own logic, which is foreign to the Constitution, a logic that needs to be respected, an inherent element of which being the legally preestablished and historically consolidated order of succession. According to the Court, amending the rules governing the transmission of the titles so as to comply with the principle of the equality of the sexes would amount to introducing anachronistic requirements into a practice molded by history.

---

[33] See STC 126/1997 (3 July).

[34] The Supreme Court or *Tribunal Supremo* is the highest court within the judiciary. It can control the constitutionality of public acts as long as they are not statutes. It can also control the constitutionality of statutes if they were passed before the Constitution came into force. Only the Constitutional Court has the power of judicial review of statutes passed after the Constitution.

[35] See STC 126/1997 (3 July).

However, anyone who is minimally familiar with the issue knows that these titles attach a social status, and that economic transactions around nobility titles are not uncommon (think, for example, of the practice of renting out the use of the title's name for the denomination of wines). As some of the dissenting voices in the decision recognize, if nothing was really at stake there would not be so much litigation around the issue. But even if it were the case that only symbolic interests were in question, we lack an explanation as to why symbols should not matter. Indeed, the symbolic message that the decision sends out to society is that the medieval conception of women that the transmission order reflects can survive with no harm being done to anyone.

Deep down, the majority decision reflects an attitude of general contempt for nobility titles. The Court sees them as doomed to natural extinction because of their practical meaninglessness. From the way the decision is constructed, it is clear that the real concern in the minds of the twelve male justices who decided on the case was whether the existence of nobility titles *as such* could be reconciled with the constitutional order. In fact, by reading the decision it appears that the types of discrimination that are at stake which could affect men (men born noble vs. men not born noble, or primogenitor men vs. nonprimogenitor men) left no space in the minds of the male judges for addressing the sex discrimination question. Thus, the Court elaborates extensively on the former and only dedicates a few sentences to the latter. There is practically no mention of the prior and well-elaborated doctrine of sexual discrimination. The Court seems deeply troubled by the idea of "modernizing" the titles. And yet the issue is much simpler. To the extent that they are allowed to survive in a constitutional democracy (and granted that this should be at least questionable), such titles ought to conform to the Constitution's most basic mandates. Women should not be denied benefits, whether symbolic or material, because they are women.

The case was subsequently brought to the European Court of Human Rights for abridgment of both Article 14's nondiscrimination principle of the European Convention of Human Rights in relation to Article 8 of the Convention, which sanctions the protection of family life, and also of Article 1 of Protocol No. 1 of the Convention, which refers to the protection of possessions. In a decision of October 28, 1999, the Court declared that the case was inadmissible *ratione materiae*. Unlike surnames and forenames, the Court held that noble titles do not fall within the scope of protection that the Convention grants to family life. Neither can a noble title be considered a possession within the meaning of Article 1 of Protocol No. 1. The possibility that a title be commercially exploited is not sufficient for that purpose. And because under Article 14 of the European Convention the discriminatory treatment necessarily has to be put in relation to some other right or freedom recognized in the Convention, the Court found the appeal inadmissible.[36]

WOMEN AS MOTHERS AND SPOUSES

Constitutional litigation has played some role in bringing about necessary changes in family law. One of the most interesting victories from the woman's point of view has been in the field of recognition of paternity and in that of child support, though interestingly, both cases were articulated almost exclusively around children's needs leaving aside women's concerns. Let us take a look.

STC 7/1994 of January 15 was the landmark decision on recognition of paternity against the father's will. At stake was the evidentiary value of the unjustified refusal of the man to have a DNA paternity test done precisely in those cases where no other conclusive proof of paternity exists. The Supreme Court had invalidated a lower Court's decision for relying too heavily on the evidentiary value of the man's refusal to have the test done, holding that even a stubborn and unjustified resistance could not be considered a tacit confession (*ficta confessio*) and that additional *conclusive* evidence was required.

The woman had then challenged the Supreme Court's decision in an *amparo* before the Constitutional Court, claiming that it violated her daughter's right not to be discriminated against, because of her out-of-wedlock status, calling on Article 14's antidiscrimination provision. Nothing was said about the disparate impact of the issue on women in general. The defendant also brought his defense on constitutional grounds, claiming that the judicial order to undergo a paternity blood test against his will was an infringement of his right to privacy and physical integrity, under Articles 18 and 15 of the Constitution.

In overturning the Supreme Court's decision, the Constitutional Court reasoned that this kind of test is precisely most needed in the absence of other conclusive evidence. Far from implying an infringement on the man's right to privacy and physical integrity, as the defendant claimed, the test serves the constitutional purpose of protecting children regardless of whether they are born in or out of wedlock in accordance with Article 14's antidiscrimination clause and Article 39.3's constitutional mandate on parents to assist their children. Moreover, proportionality had been safeguarded as the test could not be said to seriously endanger the person's health.

---

[36] In this respect it is interesting to notice that the new Protocol 12 to the Convention contemplates an independent mandate of nondiscrimination, which does not require the denounced discriminatory treatment to be put in connection with the abridgment of any of the other rights of the Convention.

On these bases, the Constitutional Court reasoned that the Supreme Court's acceptance of the defendant's unwillingness to collaborate in the determination of paternity and the Court's unwillingness to deem such behavior to be conclusive evidence when there were also some other serious indicia about his paternity, implied a violation of the plaintiff's due process rights of Article 24, as the whole burden of proof was put on her while at the same time she was being deprived of the most important means of such proof.

Another battle won by women in the constitutional arena concerns child support.[37] The criminal code of the time contemplated a specific crime for the systematic disregard of the duty to pay child support. However, the statute referred only to children conceived within a marriage, and not out of wedlock. In solving the *amparo*, the Constitutional Court granted the mother's claim of discrimination against her child because of his being born out of wedlock. According to the Court, although the legislature was free to decide whether to grant criminal protection to the children against the nonfulfillment of judicially declared parental duties, such as the duty to pay for child support, once it does so, it is no longer free to exclude children born out of wedlock, as that implies discrimination on the basis of the children's status, which, again, is proscribed by Article 14 of the Constitution.

Although both these were women's victories and were largely celebrated by the feminist communities in Spain, in neither of these cases did the women's interests as such get articulated. Both cases were argued and decided in the view of the children's interests only. But what about women's right not to be discriminated against? Isn't it discrimination to punish women because of their biology, forcing them to face the psychological strains and material efforts entailed by bringing up children as single mothers? Can men be allowed to fully disregard their share of duties? It is interesting that in both cases the plaintiffs themselves acted as representatives of their children's interests and did not articulate their own interests, in spite of the obvious disparate impact on women of both the challenged norm on child support and the judicial doctrine on the value of proof to be given to a person's refusal to undergo a paternity test. To some extent, the split between public and private spheres may once again explain why claims about sex discrimination have thus far only been articulated clearly in the former, even though as we saw, the notion of the public has been expanded to include discrimination by employers. These cases however also show that women still have to appropriate to themselves the principles of equality and nondiscrimination by advancing claims that expand their realms of application in every sphere of their lives.

---

[37] See STC 67/1998 (18 March); and STC 84/1998 (20 April).

WOMEN'S REPRODUCTIVE FREEDOM

Far from being a constitutional right, abortion in Spain is still a crime.[38] There are three circumstances, however, in which by statute a woman's abortion will not trigger punishment for either the woman or the practitioner. These are the so-called tolerated abortions. These are first of all, the case in which an abortion is required to avoid a serious danger to the life or health of the women (the so-called therapeutic abortion), second, that in which the pregnancy is the result of rape (the so-called ethical abortion), and third, the case in which the fetus is likely to have serious physical or mental disabilities (the so-called eugenic abortion).

In 1985, as it was being passed, this legislation was constitutionally challenged during a short-lived phase in which a priori judicial review was statuto-Break;rily sanctioned.[39] The challenge was brought by fifty deputies of the Popular Party, which was the right-wing party in opposition to the socialist government of the time. The claim was that the regulation did not sufficiently protect the right to life of the fetus under Article 15 of the Constitution. In the end, the Constitutional Court upheld the statute in what has since been criticized as an usurpation of legislative powers, since it accepted the exemptions but suggested specific guarantees that should be added to the legislation regarding mostly the medical centers where abortion could be practiced, and the medical certifications of the prerequisites.

Following Germany's doctrine, the Court recognized that the *nasciturus* (the unborn conceived life) could not be considered a legitimate right-holder in the strict sense, given that only *persons* can be holders of constitutional rights. However, relying on the constitutional doctrine of the so-called double nature of constitutional rights, inherited from the German scholarship, the Court interpreted Article 15's right to life as sanctioning not only a subjective individual right to life but the value of life, so that unborn life could still be considered a "constitutionally protected good" calling for the protection of criminal legislation. However, such a protection could not be absolute in nature as women's constitutional rights and freedoms had to be balanced against the protection of the *nasciturus*. Calling on notions of individual autonomy as spelled out by the constitutional right to human dignity and the related right to the free development of one's personality (Article 10), the right to physical and moral integrity (Article 15), the right to honor, to privacy, and to one's own image (Article 18.1), and the freedom of thought and belief (Article 16), the Court upheld the exemptions contained in the criminal statute, subject to some additional procedural constraints.[40]

---

[38] See Article 145 of the *Criminal Code* (Organic Statute 10/1995, of November 23rd, *BOE* num. 291, of November 24th) and Article 417 bis of the 1985 *Organic Statute* 9/1985 (still in force in virtue of the Derogatory Disposition 1a) of the 1995 *Criminal Code*).

[39] See STC 53/1985 (11 April).

[40] See STC 53/1985, ibid., fj.8.

Note that neither the Court, nor those who put forth the defense of the challenged law, nor the dissenting voices in the Court that were more empathic toward women's concerns, brought Article 14's equality clause into the discussion, even though the Court in passing showed itself not to be completely insensitive to the differential itself impact of the norm on women's lives, given the specificity of the female condition. Clearly, calling on the right to equality might have implied that anything short of a constitutional right to abortion (maybe only subject to time constraints), would stand as the right answer to the question of abortion. And the Court was clearly unwilling to imply this. Granted, the constitutional question had not been framed in these terms. But from the way the opinion is constructed it is clear the Court was not ready to let women's interests in abortion take such a leading role. All its efforts to justify the need to offer constitutional protection for the life of the *nasciturus* in spite of it not being a constitutional right–holder would have made little sense otherwise.

SEXISM IN THE MEDIA AND COMMERCIALIZATION OF THE FEMALE BODY

As we mentioned before, the Constitutional Court has been most sympathetic to the horizontal effect of constitutional rights in those arenas which imply ordinary citizens' subjection to structurally organized private powers. Together with the employers/employees, the media-press/ordinary citizens relationship is probably the other area where such doctrine has best shown its potential. In fact, in sanctioning the freedom of speech and of the press, Article 20 of the Constitution recognizes as inherent limitations the necessary respect for all the rights included in Title I. In particular, it recognizes the right to privacy and honor, with special reference to the need to protect youth and children.[41]

Indeed we find some instances in which Article 18's right to honor has lent itself to the protection of women from sexist speech. This is what happened in STC 170/1994 of June 6, a case which came to be popularly known by the unfortunate name of *"the case of the seal."* To put it in context, it is necessary to elaborate briefly on the constitutional doctrine concerning the right to honor. To define such a concept the Constitutional Court has ultimately relied on the Dictionary of the Spanish Academy, which refers to honor as "people's reputation . . . or the opinion that others have about oneself." This, the Court acknowledged, "puts us in the terrain of the others, of people, whose collective option marks for each time and place the level of tolerance and rejection. The content of the right to honor is thus fluid and changing and depends on the values and the prevailing social norms in

---

[41] Spanish Constitution, Article 20.4.

each moment."[42] Briefly, the notion refers to people's social respectability, reputation, and related dignity.

The case which in popular jargon came to be known as the *case of the seal* refers to a newspaper article which describes the collapse of a public building on a couple who happened to be sitting underneath it. The woman's legs were broken. In a failed attempt of ingenious irony, the article presents the event as a humorous story turning tragedy into comedy. It literally refers to the accident as a "blessing for the mutilated woman who now, and because of her new condition, will probably not lose her boyfriend who, presumably, was about to dump her for another woman. More likely, he will now be forced to remain at her side out of pity and soothe her with sweets that will fatten her to the point of making her look like a crippled seal."

In *amparo*, the woman reacted against the decision of the lower court which had empathized with the journalist's claim that the ultimate goal of the article had not been to insult the woman but simply to call people's attention on the deplorable state of public buildings. The constitutional claim was built on her right to human dignity (Article 10) and to honor (Article 18). The Court granted the requested *amparo* in view of the fact that "making offensive and insulting comments which are completely irrelevant to the exercise of freedom of speech, or of the press, infringes unnecessarily against people's dignity"[43] and violates the individual's right to honor.

The Court was not oblivious to the sexist connotations of the message. Citing literally, "the text portrays an attitude of general contempt against women and clearly expresses a sexist stand."[44] By contrast, no appeal was made by the Court or the plaintiff to sex equality notions under Article 14. Had the Court done so, it would have underscored the collective nature of the harm done by sexist speech and maybe left the door open for the fight on constitutional grounds against the harms of other kinds of speech, which affect not only individuals' social respectability but other constitutionally protected goods such as physical or moral integrity, especially when they have a clearly differential impact on women, as is arguably the case with some forms of pornography that eroticize violence toward women. In any event, it would not have been the first case in which the Court favored some restrictions of the freedom of speech for the sake of equality values.[45]

The danger of relying exclusively on notions such as the right to honor, which, as the Court recognizes, depend so much on changing social standards that define what has the potential to harm people's "social respectability" and what does not, is that generalized sexist prejudices, from which judges

---

[42] STC 223/1992 (14 December).
[43] See STC 170/1994 (7 June), fj.2, quoting STC 105/1990 (6 June).
[44] STC 170/1994, ibid.
[45] See STC 214/1991 (11 November), interpreting the publication of an article that denied the historical truth of the Holocaust as a violation of constitutional equality and dignity values.

are not exempt, can get in the way and render the perception of the harm being done rather difficult. Instead, introducing an egalitarian perspective would encourage the use of statistics and studies showing the specific harm done to women by the ways in which the media portray them.

Maybe the *Playboy* case is best to show this.[46] At stake here were both the right to honor and the right to one's image (which is also covered by Article 18). The plaintiff, the rather popular show artist, Ana Obregón, had had some intimate pictures taken, and had consented, through a private and nonremunerated contract, to the photographer using them for journalistic purposes. Indeed, the pictures had been published in *Interview*, a businessmen's magazine that traditionally combines business and politics with pictures of nude women. *Playboy*, a clearly less "sophisticated" magazine, had then bought the publishing rights and intended to publish the pictures with some added text. Twenty days before the magazine was supposed to come out, Obregón expressly revoked her consent because of the offensive nature of the intended publication. *Playboy* went ahead with the publication and was later confirmed in its right to do so in the lower courts. In *amparo*, Obregón claimed that her constitutional rights to her image and honor had been infringed.

The decision started by laying out the fundamentals of the doctrine on the right to one's image. As a right that safeguards an individual sphere of freedom regarding one of the most personal and immediate features of the person, the right to one's image, the Court said, enjoys the highest degree of constitutional protection. Although with the authorization of the rightholder the image becomes an autonomous asset of economic value subject to the rules of commerce, because of the inalienable nature of the right, the consent is always revocable. It is the task of ordinary civil courts to decide then, in case of dispute, on the economic effects of the withdrawal of consent in terms of a preexisting contractual relationship.[47]

In spite of this, the Court denied the requested *amparo*. In doing so it took into account the contractual nature of the consent originally expressed; the right of the publisher not to suffer economic damages; the fact that the plaintiff had not offered economic compensation for the last-minute cancellation, and the fact that the most important phases of the publication process had already taken place at the time the consent was withdrawn.

In my view, whatever the amount of due economic compensation, something that, in case of disagreement, should have been resolved in the civil courts by taking the above mentioned facts into account, nothing, as a matter of principle, justifies the departure from the constitutional doctrine that consent can be withdrawn at any time. Indeed, only a final set of considerations help us understand what was really in the Court's mind. As far as the

---

[46] See STC 117/1994 (25 April).
[47] STC 117/1994, ibid., fj.3.

plaintiff's right to her own image, the Court argued, no further interference could be drawn from the second publication once the first had already taken place. As for the added comments in the text in relation with the plaintiff's right to honor, Ms Obregón, the Court said, had expressed implicit consent for, given the nature of the pictures, she should have imagined the kinds of magazines in which they were most likely to be published, and the kinds of text that were most likely to go with them. Moreover, the comments included in the text, however rude in their nature, were intended as a compliment to the physical attributes and virtues that the pictures themselves revealed.

Underlying the Court's reasoning is clearly the perception that when a woman uses her body in the pursuit of economic or professional interests, it then becomes an *intra comercium* good that ceases to deserve a zealous protection. It is as if what was really at stake was the loss of the social respectability incurred by the public disclosure of intimate body parts. Once lost through the first publication, the revocation of consent does not make sense, especially when it goes to the detriment of legitimate contractual expectations, as there is "nothing left" to protect. The same attitude underlies the Court's response to the Obregón's objection to the offensive text added in the second publication. "What else could she expect?!? Aren't those the kinds of compliments that she was asking for, after all?" But, clearly, Ms Obregón did not need anyone to be second-guessing her. Indeed, she proved quite capable of saying Yes when she meant Yes, and No when she meant No. Turning what the plaintiff takes as an insult into an "objective compliment," ignores the fact that reducing a woman to a sexual object is an insult however much one is willing to pay compliments to the "qualities" of such object. It is not the quality of the sexual attributes but reducing the person to them that is truly offensive.

CONCLUSION

Despite the underrepresentation of women both in the constituent assembly that approved the 1978 Spanish Constitution and in the Constitutional Court, the Constitution has proven to be a powerful weapon in the fight against the gender discrimination which was socially entrenched and legally sanctioned under Franco's regime. Not only the individual right not to be discriminated against on the basis of sex but, more important, the mandate requiring public authorities to take measures to ensure substantive equality, have enabled the recognition of a collective dimension, which underscores the need to see women as the main historical beneficiaries of the nondiscrimination clause. The legitimacy of affirmative action aimed at overcoming patterns of exclusion has thus been widely accepted.

In this framework, the Constitutional Court has elaborated a notion of gender discrimination that encompasses both direct and indirect or effects-based discrimination. This notion embraces a view of gender that refers not only to the biological conditions but also to the social disadvantages of women. This doctrine has facilitated the banning of discriminatory practices, especially in the workplace. Both the incorporation of the case law of the European Court of Justice and the acceptance of the horizontal effect of fundamental rights as limiting employers' autonomy have proven essential to this effect. By contrast, the Court has not always been willing to make the connection between unfair distribution of tasks in the family and women's occupational options. Even this far-reaching doctrine on sex discrimination has not outlawed the overt and direct discrimination that women encounter in some symbolically and culturally charged fields such as the access to noble titles. Maybe not completely unrelated to this is the fact that, under the Spanish Constitution, the order of succession to the Spanish Crown gives precedence to the male over the female heir.

Although some important battles have been won in the constitutional arena in the realm of motherhood, thus far the changes have been mostly achieved in the name of children's rather than women's interests. It is also interesting that the changes have taken place outside of the conventional family setting, dealing with single mothers. Nothing in the case law points to the Court's willingness to unsettle the divide between the public and the private spheres by applying the doctrine of horizontal effect of the nondiscrimination mandate to intrude upon adult family arrangements. However the Court can't be fully blamed for this. Women have not really appropriated the powerful formula of the Court's accepting of the horizontal effect of the nondiscrimination mandate, effects-based discrimination, and the view of sex as social condition, to initiate new constitutional battles against the systematic disadvantage in terms of the enjoyment of most constitutional rights and freedoms (not only in the labor market).

An obvious candidate seems the possibility to draw some constitutional protection for women against discrimination in the media. To some extent the right to one's honor and to one's image, both of which the Constitution sanctions as setting limits to the freedom of speech and of the press, have already shown some potential in this respect. Nevertheless, constraining the protected constitutional good to the honor of the person leaves out of the picture many of the important harms and the specific ways in which women are affected. Also, the right to honor cannot be the most efficient tool to fight against sexist stereotypes that are deeply entrenched into the culture, as it is this very culture which provides the parameters to define notions as fluid as that of social respectability.

Finally, in the constitutional sphere no connection is generally made between equality values and abortion. But even in terms of individual freedom and reproductive autonomy the battle for a constitutional right to abortion has not been fought yet. This may be because of the generalized belief that, in a society with an overwhelming Catholic ethos, the Court would be unwilling or, in any event, should be unwilling to take on such responsibility and because of the fact that abortions are commonly practiced and the restrictive legislation far from strictly enforced. More than by women's interest in reproductive freedom and equality, as of today, the constitutional doctrine on abortion has been shaped by the concerns of those sectors in the Spanish society that consider the current exemptions of punishment for certain types of abortion to be unacceptable encroachments on the fetus's right to life. Turning such a right into a value that objectively requires constitutional protection, as the Court did in 1985, says nothing as to how such a protection should be weighted against women's constitutional rights. But this, in the Spanish scenario, will most likely be for the legislators to decide.

Suggested Readings

A. C. Azkárate Askasua Albéniz, *Mujer y discriminación: del Tribunal de Justicia de las Comunidades al Tribunal Constitucional* (Vitoria: Instituto Vasco de la Administración Pública, 1998).

M. A. Barrete Unzueta, *Discriminación, derecho antidiscriminatorio y acción positiva en favor de las mujeres* (Madrid, 1997).

J. M. Bilbao Ubillos, *La eficacia horizontal de los derechos fundamentales* (Madrid: Centro de Estudios Constitucionales, 2000).

J. M. Bilbao Ubillos and F. Rey Martínez, *Veinte años de jurisprudencia sobre igualdad constitucional en la Constitución y la práctica del Derecho*, in M. Aragón Reyes and J. Martínez-Simancas Sánchez, eds. (Madrid: Sopec, 1998) 243–339.

J. García Torres, *"Sint ut fuerun aut non sint"* Pequeña contribución jurídico-constitucional al novísimo derecho nobiliario de creación judicial (1998) 22 *Revista Española de Derecho Constitucional* 243–289.

J. M. Martínez Pereda Rodríguez, "La inconstitucionalidad de la preferencia masculina en la sucesión de los títulos nobiliarios" (1991) III-41 545–564 and-42 565–589.

Mujer y Constitución en España (Madrid: Centro de Estudios Políticos y Constitucionales, 2000).

A. Ollero, *Discriminación por razón de sexo: valores, principios y normas en la jurisprudencia constitucional española* (Madrid: Centro de Estudios Políticos y Constitucionales, 1999).

M. Rodríguez Piñero and M. F. Fernández López, *Igualdad y Discriminación* (Madrid: Tecnos, 1986).

M. F. Fernández López, "Igualdad y no discriminación por razón de sexo. Planteamiento constitucional" in J. Aparicio and A. Baylos, eds., *Autoridad y democracia en la empresa* (Madrid: Trotta, 1992).

F. Rey Martínez, *El derecho fundamental a no ser discriminado por razón de sexo* (Madrid: McGraw-Hill, 1995).

R. Rubio Marín, *Mujer e Igualdad: La norma y su aplicación (tomo I: El ordenamiento constitucional; logros y posibilidades)* (Sevilla: Instituto Andaluz de la Mujer, 1999).

A. Ruiz Miguel, *Aborto: Problemas constitucionales* (Madrid: Centro de Estudios Constitucionales, 1990).

11

Gender Equality from a Constitutional Perspective

The Case of Turkey

Hilal Elver

POINT OF DEPARTURE

**The Modernization Project of Turkey and the Identity
of Women as Political Agents**

Turkey, a bridge connecting Asia and Europe, occupies the geographic border
zone between two vastly different regions of the world: the East and the
West. This gives Turkey a unique position, as it has cultural, social, and
legal characteristics of both regions and tries to achieve the values of both in
its current search for identity. This makes it difficult and puzzling to evaluate
the status of women in Turkey.

Although 98 percent of its population is Muslim, Turkey has had no state
religion since 1924, when the Constitution defined the country as "secular."
Indeed, Turkey's commitment to Western values was so widely accepted
that, after September 11, many mainstream Western media reports did not
even include Turkey on their lists of Muslim countries. Many journalistic
articles in the United States and elsewhere advance the view that Turkey is
the only modern, democratic Muslim society, a model for the rest of the
Islamic world. This interpretation is quite understandable, considering that
in the early 1920s, among other reforms, Turkey changed its entire legal
system from the Islamic *Shari-a* to the Continental European system, in effect
adopting a Western secular order.

This abrupt transition had a strong impact on the status of Turkish women. Since the creation of the modern Turkish Republic in 1923, the ultimate aim of the founders has been to gain acceptance among the European
states.[1] They perceived the process of modernization as a process of Europeanization: the adoption of European norms, attitudes, and the expectation

---

[1] Serif Mardin, *Turkish Modernization* [Turkish] (Istanbul: Iletisim, 1991); Bernard Lewis, *The Emergence of Modern Turkey* (London: Oxford University Press, 1961).

of European standards of living.[2] Within this context of modernization and Europeanization, Turkish women were granted certain rights; this was atypical for an Islamic country. Indeed, this enhanced status of women was considered a decisive criterion of Muslim modernity and compatibility with Western values.

For the founders of the Turkish state, improving women's status meant formalizing gender equality irrespective of religious tradition. These initiatives were inconsistent with the Islamic practice as enacted by the Ottomans, which had excluded women from participation in the public realm. The primary political concern of Turkish state-builders was to equalize women to men in the public domain, while overlooking inequalities in the private domain. Thus, the Turkish promotion of gender equality remained a limited undertaking related to their preoccupation with achieving modernity "for the good of the country."[3]

However, laws and changes in the public sphere do not necessarily control life experiences and behavioral practices. The *de facto* situation of women, a combination of domestic responsibilities and economic hardship, has made it very difficult for most women to become informed citizens, let alone socially and politically active ones. Today, while the enrollment rate of boys and girls in elementary education is equal, almost one third of adult Turkish women remain illiterate. Power and wealth (almost 75 percent of household property belongs to men) is so unequal that constitutional equality, legal rights conferred by various laws, and political rights that were given to Turkish women sometimes earlier than in many European countries, often have very little positive impact on the quality and quantity of the economic, social, and political participation of women in Turkey.

Turkish women, despite religious and cultural differences, share a similar experience of patriarchal domination with women elsewhere. This domination exists in almost every country, from the most modern to the most traditional, although to varying degrees and with differing intensities. Moreover, in Turkey, strong family ties influence the formation of values, attitudes, aspirations, and goals that have tended to weaken the position of women both inside and outside of family structure.

The legal and social norms that the founders of the Turkish state applied to women in the 1920s were considered liberal on gender equality. However, they have become controversial in the 1970s and 1980s. Women's rights organizations demanded improvements in existing domestic laws in accordance with the changing standards of "women's human rights" at the global level. After two decades of public debate about the outdated legal principles on

[2] Niyazi Berkes, *The Development of Secularism in Turkey* (Montreal: McGill University Press, 1964).

[3] Yesim Arat, *The Patriarchal Paradox: Women Politicians in Turkey* (London: Associated University Press, 1989).

women's status, in 2002 the Turkish government complied with specific demands of the European Union by enacting a major constitutional amendment
and a new Turkish Civil Code. As discussed later, these recent legal developments have provided significant changes in women's status, especially in
family law. Nevertheless, it is too soon to assess if these legal improvements
will actually enhance women's status, particularly in the areas of economic
freedom and self determination.

Given the dramatic changes in Turkey in the early twentieth century, the
major focus of this chapter will be the dilemma confronting Turkish women
who are caught between Western secular and traditional Islamic identities.
Turkish women suffer most from being "the focal point of intense debate between the two groups with conflicting political interests."[4] This dilemma of
identity is generated by clashing political and social forces. Inquiry here will
stress the consequences of this clash in the context of constitutional jurisprudence. After a short historical background, the status of Turkish women will
be examined from the perspective of the current constitutional order. The
chapter will conclude with some recent developments that illustrate the crucial role being played by international law and international institutions in
promoting gender equality on the domestic level.

Historical Background of the Constitutional Order

A constitutional movement was initiated during the last period of the
Ottoman Empire, toward the end of the eighteenth century, as a result of
Western influence when the fortunes of the Ottoman Empire began to decline.
During this early period, Turkish women were neglected entirely in constitutional law. People were segregated into groups according to religious or
ethnic affiliation, and within each group according to gender. Muslim women
were under the domain of *Shari'a* law. Polygamy was an accepted practice in
which men were permitted four wives; divorce was extremely easy for men
and very difficult for women. Rural and urban women alike were subjected
to the absolute authority of men by way of the state, religion, and family.

The emancipation of Turkish women began during the second half of
the nineteenth century with the late Ottoman Westernization project, which
led to the introduction of monogamy, free choice of female dress codes,
noninterference by the police in the private lives of women, freedom of choice
in matters of marriage, the admission of women to medical school, and the
launching of women's magazines.

In the early 1920s, a war of independence resulted in the dissolution of the
Ottoman Empire and the founding of the Turkish state. The original Constitution was announced in 1924 and remained in place until 1961. The major
significance of this first period was the emphasis given to Turkish women

---

[4] Sirin Tekeli, ed., *Women in Modern Turkish Society* (London: Zed Books, 1995).

as a principal means of signaling the changing values of Turkish society, essentially the shift from those of Islam to those of a Western-oriented secular state. The Turkish woman became a central agent in the changing image of the new Turkish state, epitomizing the embrace of modernity and secularism. These changes affecting the status of women were achieved only by legislation, not by providing any constitutional foundation other than the very general principle of equality before law that made no reference to either group or gender equality.[5]

During this period, the most important advance for Turkish women arose from the Turkish Civil Code of 1926, which adopted the Swiss Civil Code. An entire body of Turkish secular law replaced *Shari'a* law in one year. For its time in history, Turkish legislation concerning gender roles seemed egalitarian, especially for an Islamic country. In reality, the legislation reflected conventional gender ideology in Europe in the late nineteenth century, when gender roles were constructed around "male breadwinner – female homemaker" roles.[6]

The second Constitution of 1961 was enacted after the intervention of the Turkish armed forces overthrew a civilian government. Nevertheless, liberal and plural democracy was carefully entrenched in the new Constitution which also established the Constitutional Court in Turkey. Towards the end of the 1970s, the Turkish political system faced an increasingly serious crisis brought about by political polarization, violence, and terrorism. This instability again led to a military takeover on September 12, 1980. In 1982, the military government promulgated the present Constitution, which was subsequently amended October 3, 2001.

THE EQUALITY PRINCIPLE AND CONSTITUTIONAL LAW

In General

The Constitution of 1982 contains the standard principles found in other democratic constitutions. It defines Turkey as a unified state with a parliamentary regime that strictly adheres to secularism. The 1982 Constitution includes: the separation of powers among the legislative, executive, and judiciary; definition of the power structure; the duties and responsibilities of the three branches and other governmental institutions, including the Constitutional Court.[7]

---

[5] The concept of "gender" is unknown in the Turkish language. In the Turkish context, "sex equality" or "equality between man and woman" are the options to express gender equality.

[6] Simon Duncan, "Obstacles to a successful equal opportunities policy in the European Union" (1996) 3 *European Journal of Women's Studies* 399–423, cited in Meltem Muftuler-Bac, "Turkish Women Predicament" (1999) 22 *Women's Studies International Forum* 303–15.

[7] For the full text of the Constitution, see *Constitution of the Republic of Turkey, 1982*, online: Republic of Turkey, Ministry of Foreign Affairs <www.mfa.gov.tr.grupc/ca/cag/I142> (date accessed: September 10, 2001) (hereinafter *1982 Constitution*).

With regard to constitutional review, Turkey relies on a centralized model, sometimes called the "European" model, which is characterized by the existence of a special court with exclusive jurisdiction over constitutional rulings. The basic function of the Constitutional Court is to ensure that legislative power is exercised in conformity with the Constitution. If the Court declares that a law is unconstitutional, that law is annulled. Therefore, the review exercised by the Constitutional Court is a "correcting" review. The Turkish Constitution gives dissenting rights to members of the national legislature: the right to challenge the constitutional validity of laws on an "abstract" basis. In Turkey, constitutional issues are generally raised by a public authority like the executive branch, a major political party, a parliamentary majority, or a lower court (lower courts are not empowered to decide constitutional issues). Individuals cannot challenge the constitutionality of laws. These procedural features remain basically the same in the Constitutions of 1961 and 1982.

According to Article 146 of the Constitution, the Constitutional Court is composed of eleven regular and four substitute members appointed by the President of the Republic for a time-limited term. Currently, one of the eleven regular members and two of the four substitutes are female.

The Constitution of 1982 has a significant democratic deficit, arising from the intervention of the military in the democratic process. The rationale for this intervention was to strengthen the political power of the state rather than to promote liberty and safeguard democracy.[8] The Constitution of 1982 failed to establish satisfactory democratic protections for the exercise of human rights. During the European Union (EU) membership negotiations, therefore, the major issues included the improvement of human rights protection and the inclusion of democratic institutions in the Constitution. The resulting amendments to the Constitution provide comprehensive protection of individual human rights, particularly in the areas of civil and political rights.

Gender Equality in the Constitution of 1982, and the New Constitutional Amendment of 2001

Article 10 of the 1982 Constitution, entitled "equality before law," is similar to its predecessor the Constitution of 1961, granting a nongender specific, abstract, and formal notion of equality: "All individuals are equal without any discrimination before the law, irrespective of language, race, color, sex, political opinion, philosophical belief, religion and sect, or any such consideration."[9]

Besides the general equality principle of Article 10 and the protection of the family contained in Article 41, there are some provisions on rights

---

[8] Tahsin Fendoglu, "Liberty and Turkish Constitution of 1982," online: University of Dicle <www.dicle.edu/tr> (date accessed: September 10, 2001).

[9] *1982 Constitution, supra* note 7.

and responsibility of individuals which can be used to support women's rights. These include: Article 12, entitled "on the nature of fundamental rights"; Article 17, on personal inviolability, material, and spiritual integrity; Articles 49 and 50, on the right and responsibility to work; Article 55, on the minimum wage; and other provisions, such as Articles 60 and 70, related to working conditions.

The recent constitutional amendment was adopted in response to the Council of Europe's suggestions to the Turkish government in December 1999. The major aim is to reform the Turkish constitutional order and related legislation to the extent that they are not compatible with the established democratic principles of the European Community. One of the specific demands of the Council of Europe was to change the existing equality principle of the Constitution so as to give more leverage to gender specific claims. The new amendment, however, instead of changing the text of Article 10 in the direction of gender specific language, added a sentence to Article 41 dealing with the protection of the family: "The family is the foundation of Turkish society and is based on equality between wife and husband. The State shall take the necessary measures and establish the necessary organization to ensure the peace and welfare of the family, especially the protection of the mother and the children, and family planning education."[10] The new amendment did not affect other above mentioned constitutional provisions indirectly relating to women's rights.

The new amendment's cosmetic change was a big disappointment for women's organizations and civil society at large. According to their argument, this version of equality does not treat a woman as an independent individual but seems to support the patriarchal philosophy of traditional Turkey. It considers equality between men and women only in marriage. Thus, the new amendment fails to provide gender equality compatible with international standards. The success or failure of the new version of equality, what can be called "conditional gender equality," very much depends on future Constitutional jurisprudence. If the Constitutional Court were to take a progressive attitude when interpreting the new version of equality, it could be transformed into a wider gender specific equality not limited to implementation in the family environment. It is too soon to make a judgment about how this new constitutional provision will be shaped and interpreted by the Court.

Gender Equality in Constitutional Jurisprudence

Since the establishment of the Court in 1961, its jurisprudence has followed the mainstream political and social view in Turkey, which is based on the

---

[10] *The Amendment of the Constitution of the Republic of Turkey*, Nr 4709, 3 October 2001, art. 17.

principles of Ataturk, which favor a nationalist, secularist, and Western-oriented structure. The Court's view on women's issues is similar, with one exception.[11] The Court acts as protectively as possible of women if the issue fits within the traditional understanding of patriarchal Turkish society, yet acts as conservatively as possible if the issue is related to women's status as an individual and if the identity of women threatens family values. Nevertheless, during the last decade, the Court has gradually softened its approach by moving toward a more egalitarian approach. It seems to have been influenced by the feminist movement in Turkey, and by women's rights principles of a universalist nature present in international agreements. However, the Court's egalitarian approach has not been consistent.

According to the Constitutional Court, "the principle of equality in art. 10 provides equal treatment to people who are of legally equal status and allows differential treatment of those who are in different statuses."[12] Equality before the law thus does not mean that every person will be treated equally if they have a different status. This view can be expressed as: "equals be treated equally and nonequals be treated according to their differences." The Court interprets the equality principle in an absolute manner such that:

Rules cannot be implemented differently for people because of their differences of language, ethnicity, color, sex, political, philosophical, and religious belief. The Constitution will not allow privileges and discrimination among people who belong to equal status. Therefore, lawful discrimination will not be considered as a violation of the equality principle. The aim of the Constitution is to provide legal equality but not operational equality.[13]

In relation to gender equality, the Constitutional Court affirms that the principle of equal rights before law must be interpreted as conferring gender equality while seeking to "respect women's objective biological and functional differences from men."[14] This view leads the Constitutional Court to the conclusion that if biological and functional differences create a differentiated behavior or privilege for one party only, such an interpretation is not constitutionally acceptable. Nevertheless, many of the Constitutional Court decisions on gender equality interpret this principle in such a way as to limit women's rights rather than to affirm them.

[11] Even though the members of the Court are new, the gender provisions remained the same in the 1961 and 1982 Constitutions. In principle, the Court is bound by previous decisions; thus the cases decided under the 1961 Constitution are still considered relevant under the 1982 Constitution. Nevertheless, as will be discussed further, in the late 1990s judicial interpretation became more progressive and egalitarian with the influence of new international commitments, such as the ratification of CEDAW.
[12] E. 1995/22, K. 1995/37, T. 15. 8. 1995, T. 15.8.1995, *Journal of the Constitutional Court* (hereinafter JCC) 1996 at 54–55.
[13] E. 1996/10, K.1996/40, T. 22.10.1996, *Official Gazette* 23147 at 20.
[14] E. 1996/10, ibid., at 24.

The Court's interpretation of the equality principle has been criticized by women's rights scholars, especially from the perspective of the European Convention on Human Rights, to which Turkey has been a party since 1949. According to their argument, the "absolute implementation of equality principle" works only among equals; in the case of gender equality, only among individuals of the same gender.[15] The classical interpretation of the equality principle does not always maintain equal status between biologically different groups. Although an absolute or mechanical interpretation of the equality principle would maintain equal opportunity and rights and equal freedoms for men and women, issues specifically related to women such as abortion, sexual harassment, rape, domestic violence, pregnancy, birth control, and motherhood, require a different approach than one based on the absolute interpretation of the equality principle. To maintain equality for these issues, it is necessary to pursue either the relative interpretation of equality or to have a gender-specific equality principle. According to the one female member of the Constitutional Court, however, not having a specific gender equality principle in the Constitution should not be a barrier to a gender specific interpretation.[16]

Accepting this general view, several decisions of the court relating to the status of women in the family environment, the status of women in the work place, civic duties, religious freedom, and women's sexuality will be discussed in the next section.

Women in the Family. In the early 1960s, the Court's jurisprudence was mainly devoted to reviewing several discriminatory provisions in the Turkish Civil Code of 1926, the Criminal Code, and several other legal codes. Even though the former Turkish Civil Code seemed radically progressive in 1926, by the end of the 1980s there were articles (declaring the husband the head of the family, obliging him to be a provider for the family, expecting the wife to be his helper) that needed to be revised to reflect more modern attitudes.[17]

The Court has decreed an affirmative treatment for protected categories in several of its decisions relating to women's status in the family, stating that "positive discrimination or affirmative action for women is not a violation of the equality principle due to her special position in the family as a wife, and

[15] "Sexual Equality in the European Convention of Human Rights, A Survey of Case-Law," Council of Europe, EF (89) 3, cited in Aysel Celikel, "Interpretation of Equality Principle" [Turkish] (1989) 19 *Bulletin of International Law* 92–9.
[16] Fulya Kantarcioglu, "Gender Equality from the Perspective of Constitutional Court Decisions" [Turkish] in *Symposium on Gender Equality*, (Izmir: Adalet Press, May, 1998), at 55.
[17] For discussion of the old version of the Turkish Civil Code and its discriminatory provisions, see Hilal Elver, "Women Issues in Turkey" (1997) 1 *Mediterranean Journal of Human Rights* 185–202.

especially as a mother."[18] A decision dealing with the *Retirement Fund Law* is an example of the legal protection afforded to female children. Article 74 of this law distinguishes male and female children in identifying the principal beneficiary of their parents' retirement salary. Female children are eligible unless they are married, but male children must be disabled or under the age of twenty-one in order to qualify as the principal beneficiary. The lower court applied to the Constitutional Court to abolish this provision, contending that it violated the equality principle of the Constitution. The Constitutional Court, however, stated that:

art. 74 did not discriminate against male children by not giving them equal financial support unconditionally, as it did for female children. Despite equality before the law being a fundamental principle of our constitutional order, due to economic disempowerment, lack of education and traditional values, it is necessary to support women's status in society through affirmative jurisprudence and legislation. Such protective measures do not create discriminatory rules in favor of women; on the contrary, they overcome long time inequality.[19]

The decision was not unanimous, and several members of the court took the view that the provision of the *Retirement Fund Law* did violate Article 10 of the Constitution.

Although the Constitutional Court is willing to protect women in the traditional family environment, it does not find any violation to the equality principle in relation to the Civil Code's provision dealing with a husband's leadership role in the family. For many years, the Constitutional Court supported this provision of the Turkish Civil Code of 1926, arguing that: "the family as a small social group needs a leader to maintain sustainable order. The husband acts cooperatively with the wife to establish order over children. This is a suitable social standard based on Turkish tradition and does not violate the equality principle."[20] The new Constitutional amendment to Article 41 denies the husband's leadership in the family circle, but confirms at the same time that Turkish society is still willing to affirm women's rights in an equal manner only in the family environment as a "wife" or "mother," not as an individual person.

Women in the Family. Adultery. The most significant instances of discrimination against women in family settings involve adultery. Until very recently, adultery was a criminal offense in the Turkish Criminal Code, because it was considered a threat against family unity. Article 440 of the Criminal Code defines adultery by women as sexual relations between a married woman and a man other than her husband. Under Article 441, in contrast, adultery

---

[18] Zafer Goren, "Equal Rights for Different Sexes in Turkish-German – Swiss Laws" [Turkish] (Izmir: D.E.U. Law School Press, 1998) at 9.
[19] E. 1996/10, *supra* note 13 at. 22.
[20] E. 1989/7 K.1989/23, JCC 1991 55–73.

by men requires the additional proof that a married man is not only having sexual relations, but is openly living with another woman.

Lower courts applied several times to the Constitutional Court to equalize male and female adultery, arguing that the provisions of the Criminal Code violate the country's constitutional principle of equality before law.[21] The way in which adultery was treated in the Criminal Code appeared to be a clear violation of gender equality, if not violation of freedom and right to privacy. The time, though, was not ripe in 1960s and 1970s for such an assessment. It took quite a long time to put the adultery discussion on the public agenda, and even longer to persuade the Constitutional Court to conclude that the provisions of Criminal Code were a major violation of gender equality. In late 1980s and 1990s, liberal women's organizations called attention to this issue and seized every possible opportunity to raise it in the public arena. Several bills were proposed in Parliament, not to eliminate adultery entirely as a crime but to define adultery the same way for women and men. None of these efforts at reform succeeded.

Finally, and not surprisingly, it was the male provision rather than the female one that the Constitutional Court declared unconstitutional in 1996. It was not very difficult for the court to find gender discrimination, stating that:

The equality principle means that woman and man in similar status have the same rights before the law. Sex cannot be used as a tool of inequality before law, and sexual differences cannot give any privilege over the other gender.... Providing different conditionality between husband and wife relating to the same crime gives the husband a privileged position over his wife before the law. There is no difference between wife and husband with regard to loyalty in marriage. Not to punish husband because of his simple adultery (it is considered one time sexual intercourse), creates a privilege that is not acceptable according to a civilized understanding of gender equality. Of course, legislators might consider abolishing rules that make adultery a criminal activity or might change conditions to adjust to new developments in the society. However, legislators cannot violate the principle of equality that gives equal status to the wife and husband in marriage.[22]

Since this decision, male adulterers have faced no legal punishment. The legislators had a year to replace the annulled article with a new one. During this period, they were expected to enact a new law for male adulterers that imitated the definition of adultery for women. However, a new debate arose on the proposed changes. Feminist organizations and liberals advocated the abolition of Article 440, or equalization of the conditions for women and men. Conservatives and Islamists insisted that adultery should be a criminal offense for both women and men, arguing that adultery was a threat to the family. At the time, the Islamist Welfare Party of Turkey was in control

---

[21] E. 1967/12, K. 1967/52; JCC 1968 at 46; E. 1968/13, K.1968/56, JCC 1969 at 34.
[22] E. 1996/15, K. 1996/34 (1996), 7.12 *Official Gazette* No.22860 at 249–51.

of the government and the issue of family values had acquired increased importance. Some women also were in favor of a stricter punishment for men making it equal to the punishment for adultery imposed on women, rather than abolishing both articles.

However, no law was passed that made adultery a crime only for women. Finally, on 23 June 2000, the Constitutional Court annulled Article 440, under which women found guilty of committing adultery faced a prison sentence of up to three years. The decision was supported by a vote of nine to two. Most women's groups welcomed the Court ruling as long overdue.

Women's Professional Development. Despite the fact that gender equality in the workplace is affirmed as a general principle of constitutional order, there are provisions in various laws that violate this principle, such as Article 6 of the Turkish Civil Service Code. In 1963, the Constitutional Court was asked to decide whether this provision violated the equality principle. Article 6 provides that "women might be hired in government offices as civil servants. The condition of jobs and positions available for women may be regulated by each Ministry's specific legislation."[23] The lower court found that Article 6 violated the constitutional equality principle. The Constitutional Court disagreed, stating:

Due to biological differences between men and women, a specific government body might consider that some jobs are unsuitable for women. To maintain a proper and consistent public service, the government should be free to make the necessary evaluations when considering hiring women for certain types of jobs, if these jobs are not suitable for women's bodies. Therefore art. 6 cannot be considered as a violation of the equality principle.[24]

The Court in this decision clearly exhibited its view that equality between women and men is not based on gender but on biological differences. This view can be challenged on the grounds that the Constitutional Court gives government bodies the power to interpret the provision in a discriminatory manner against women in specific cases and to implement it inconsistently. Moreover, the decision also supports the traditional societal understanding that certain types of jobs are unsuitable for women. This decision was a prototype for several other rulings on this issue, and fully expressive of the Court's view in the 1960s. Nevertheless, the decision was not unanimous. The dissenting opinion took the position that Article 6 of the Turkish Civil Service Code was discriminatory against women and therefore unconstitutional.

As manifested in several decisions of the Constitutional Court, the conservative understanding of "women's role in the society" creates an opportunity

---

[23] *The Turkish Civil Service Law*, Nr. 788, 18 March 1926.
[24] E. 1963/148, K. 1963/256, T. 25. 10. 1963, JCC 1963 at 459.

to exclude women from nontraditional job sectors. According to Article 50 of the Constitution, "no one can be employed in jobs that are unsuitable, given her or his age, sex and physical capacity."[25] The interpretation of this language not only compares women's status to that of minors and physically and mentally challenged people; it discriminates against women by effectively limiting them to "traditional female jobs," excluding them from jobs that "traditionally belong to men," such as bus or truck drivers, or heavy factory jobs. Surprisingly, such discrimination has been celebrated by the female member of the Constitutional Court.[26]

The Constitutional Court adopted a more egalitarian outlook in response to the 1980s feminist movement in Turkey. In the 1990s, the first female judge had been appointed to the Court. One of the most celebrated judgments of the Court was decided in this period. For a long time, women's organizations had lobbied against the discriminatory provisions of the Turkish Civil Code, especially Article 159, which grants the husband the right to exercise control over the wife's professional or artistic activities. The Court voided this outdated provision in a decision concluding that "art. 159 of the Civil Code is not compatible with the equality principle of the Constitution that provides equal rights between man and women."[27] Besides the equality principle, the Court also referred to the right and responsibility to work in Article 49, stating that "Women, like men, have the right to choose freely their own profession and work place. There is no difference between men and women in terms of the right and responsibility to work freely." Moreover, in this decision, the Constitutional Court referred to major international law documents, the Universal Declaration of Human Rights, the European Human Rights Convention, and the Convention on Elimination of All Forms of Discrimination against Women (CEDAW). Furthermore, the Court declared:

The Court does not rely on international law principles as a major source in evaluating the compatibility of the particular legislation to the Constitution in domestic law. However, these international law principles that reject sex discrimination and inequality between men and women, are not different from the equality principle in art. 10 of the Constitution. The equality principle is the major foundation of universally accepted human rights. It must be interpreted in each human rights case as an implementation of abstract equality in concrete circumstances. The list of human rights and responsibilities has expanded over the years depending on the development of human values. Therefore, each of these particular rights will involve the concrete implementation of abstract equality principles.[28]

---

[25] *1982 Constitution, supra* note 7, art. 50, "Working Conditions and Right to Rest and Leisure: Minors, women, and persons with physical or mental disabilities shall enjoy special protection with regard to working conditions."

[26] Kantarcioglu, "Gender Equality," *supra* note 16, at 55.

[27] E. 1990/30, K. 1990/31, T. 29. 11. 1990, JCC 1991 27/1 249–271.

[28] E. 1996/15, K.1996/34, T. 23. 9. 1996, *Official Gazette* 1996 27.12. Nr. 22860 at 250–251.

With this decision, the Court actually encourages legislators to adopt and adjust the domestic legal order so that it becomes harmonious with universally accepted international human rights principles.

Women's Civic Duties. Participation in the military service is a civic duty imposed by the state. It has been expressed in Article 72 of the Turkish Constitution in nondiscriminatory language. In reality, women have only very limited access to the military, which is traditionally considered a domain reserved for men. There are only a few professional women such as doctors and engineers who work as military officers in the Turkish military. The Constitutional Court's decision on the duty to serve in the military illustrates this limited access approach. According to the Court:

art. 72 (formerly art. 60 of the constitution of 1961) of the Constitution after saying that the military service is a right and duty for all Turks, states that the duty of military service will be regulated by specific law. This duty might be different for men and women, due to the special needs and nature of military service. Therefore, regulations that give a different right and responsibility to men and women can not be considered as violation of art. 60 specifically, and of art. 10's equality principle generally.[29]

However, in 1965, the Constitutional Court had rejected the demand from the lower court to void Article 15 of the *Village Code* that obliges all village inhabitants to engage in mandatory public service.[30] The lower court argued that mandatory service for villagers violates the Constitution, which protects children, youth, and women from any duty to take on nonsuitable jobs. The Constitutional Court took a different view, concluding that:

According to the Constitution, nobody can be forced to work if it is not suitable given her/his age, physical capacity, and sex. However, this article has to be interpreted rather narrowly such that it is applicable only to labor law, in other words, contractual private works, but not to the obligations of public service such as it is defined in Village Law.[31]

The court did not follow its traditional protective approach to women and children, but took a position in favor of public service at the expense of them. The Court was again not unanimous. The dissenting opinion pointed out that the Constitution protects youth, children, and women against all forms of exploitation.

Also, one of the earlier decisions of the Court in 1963 involved art. 165 of the *Procedural Rules of Military Tribunal Act*. This article concerned the possibility of prohibiting "women" from appearing in open court hearings

---

[29] E. 1966/181, K. 1966/3, T. 3.1.1966, JCC 1997 at 131–153.
[30] Mandatory service under the *Village Law* includes basically all infrastructural jobs for village common property, such as building roads and water systems.
[31] E. 1963/198, K.1965/1, T. 5. 1. 1965, JCC 1966 at 10.

before military tribunals. The Constitutional Court decided to delete the word "women" from the provision, stating that:

art. 135 of the Constitution provides for open court hearings unless entire or partial openness violates the general ethic and public order. An open court hearing is one of the fundamental rights of due process of individuals. Moreover, this due process right is protected by art. 10 of the Universal Declaration of Human Rights. Women and men have equal rights according to the Constitution. The Court did not find any justification to deny such rights to women.[32]

This decision is an important one, because it shows the Court's commitment not only to the equality principle, but also to universal human rights principles as early as the 1960s.

Gender Equality and Religious Struggles. The battle over the headscarf worn by religiously devout women provides a symbolic and illustrative basis for evaluating the religious freedom, secularism, gender equality, and identity of women in Turkish society. Therefore, it will be discussed in a more detailed manner than other constitutional debates. In the 1980s, starting with the Iranian Revolution, when political Islam gained influence in the Middle East and Turkey, Turkish women became the victim of an image war between Islamic fundamentalists and secular fundamentalists that revolved around the issue of the headscarf. Female students have been expelled from universities. As well, professional women have lost their jobs because of the state's rather inconsistent policy toward dress-code regulation.

The revival of Islam, including in Turkey, gave rise to a new feminist movement during the course of last two decades.[33] Most Muslim feminists took the path of criticizing some Western feminist views, particularly the idea of rescuing women from the Islamic world, and searched for an alternative approach to women's issues that would fit within the realm of Islam. In the 1980s, the military regime in Turkey was determined to "sterilize" society and eliminate the polarized ideologies of the pre-coup period. In an effort to restrain radical leftist ideologies, the state relied on religion and adopted certain education policies that increased the time and resources spent on religious education in public schools. In this political environment, the Islamist

---

[32] E. 1963/143, K. 1963/167, T. 26. 6. 1963, JCC 1964 I at 347.
[33] Publications on this issue include: Chandra Talpeda Mohanty, "Under Western Eyes: Feminist Scholarship and Colonial Discourses" in Chandra Talpeda Mohanty, ed., *Third World Woman and the Politics of Feminism* (Bloomington: Indiana University Press, 1991) 51–81; Azizah al-Hibri; "Islam, Law and Custom: Redefining Muslim Women's Rights" (1997) 12:1 *American University Journal of International Law & Policy* at 11. Haifa A. Jawad, *The Rights of Women in Islam; An Authentic Approach* (New York: St. Martin Press, 1998). For a more general view, see Ruth Roded, ed., *Women in Islam and Middle East: A Reader* (London: I. B. Tauris Publishers, 1999); Herbert L. Bodman and Nayereh Tohidi, eds. *Women in Muslim Societies: Diversity within Unity* (Boulder, CO: Lynne Rienner Publishers, 1998).

groups distanced themselves from right-wing political parties and developed their own autonomous discourse.[34]

The discussion of headscarves in Turkey created a heated political debate not only between secularists and Islamists, but also among all other social and political groups. It is a rather tricky issue from the legal point of view, and it is a very important debate from a political perspective. It bears directly on democracy, human rights, religious freedom, and women's rights. Religious groups, a minority of liberals, and some feminists argued that female students should be allowed into universities with their headscarves contending that this was a matter of civil rights. Denying the right to wear headscarves in universities was seen as antidemocratic, authoritarian, and unjust. Those against the headscarf argued the contrary. If headscarves were allowed, their status as an Islamic symbol would make it impossible to reconcile with the secular identity of Turkey.[35]

Besides public debates among various groups of intellectuals, the headscarf issue has become a major official undertaking in Turkey. The government adopted an ambivalent approach to the issue, depending on which way the political winds were blowing. Sometimes it followed a strict secular view, punishing students and professionals, and even expelling them from universities and public jobs. At other times, depending on the political power of Islamic parties, enforcement mechanisms were flexibly interpreted, allowing women to wear headscarves.[36]

During the military regime (between 1980 and 1983) the notoriously secular Turkish military issued a series of regulations to prohibit headscarves in schools and public institutions. Nevertheless, even the secular military sent mixed messages to the Turkish people by making religious education mandatory in the new Constitution of 1982, with the rationale of protecting

---

[34] Aynur Ilyasoglu, "Islamist Women in Turkey: Their Identity and Self-Image" in Zehra Arat, ed., *Deconstructing Images of the Turkish Women* (New York: St. Martin Press, 1997) at 243–50.

[35] Yesim Arat, "Islamist Women, Their Headscarves and Democracy in Turkey" 2 *International Social Science Review* (2001) at 34. The compatibility between Islam and the secular democratic regime in Turkey has created a popular discussion among intellectuals as a very vexing question. While some have argued that the rise of Islamist activism is not a threat to secularism in Turkey (see Binnaz Toprak, "Islam and the State in Turkey" in *Turkey: Political, Social and Economic Challenges in the 1990's* [Leiden: E. J. Brill, 1995]); others have seen it differently (see Haldun Gülalp, "The Powerty of Democracy in Turkey: The Refah Party Episode" [Fall 1999] *New Perspective on Turkey* 35–59). Much engaging work has been done on how Islam can offer an alternative modernity in Turkey (see Nilufer Göle, *The Forbidden Modern* [Ann Arbor: University of Michigan Press, 1996]; "Snapshots of Islamic Modernities" [Winter 2000] *Daedalus*; Aynur Ilyasoðlu, *Covered Identity*, [Turkish] (Istanbul: Metis Press, 1994]).

[36] For instance, the Islamist Welfare Party received a majority (21.4 percent) of the vote in December 1995, and for the first time in Republican history, held power from July 1996 to June 1997. During this period, the government did not implement strict regulations at universities. The party was abolished with the Constitutional Court's ruling in January 1998.

the Turkish society from the influence of leftist ideologies in a cold war setting. Against mounting pressure from Islamist groups and women with headscarves who protested the decision, in 1984 the Council of Higher Education allowed women at universities to cover their hair with a "turban" that the authorities deemed to be more in line with contemporary dress codes than the larger headscarf.[37] This regulation was challenged by the opposition parties, the secularists, and the judiciary.

The headscarf was declared unlawful in the universities by the Higher Court of the Administration (Council of State), despite some earlier, more favorable, lower court decisions. The government then issued an additional regulation in favor of the headscarf. In 1987, the Council of State again rejected the particular article of the Council of Higher Education Law, and the banning of the turban was upheld. Finally, the Constitutional Court found the article that allowed use of the turban in universities to be unconstitutional and annulled it in 7 March 1989.[38] In the face of strong hostility toward Islamic parties in 1998, the Constitutional Court considered the constitutionality of the Islamist Welfare Party. In this ruling, which abolished the Welfare Party, the ban on the turban was once again reviewed, and the decision concluded that the wearing of a turban was unconstitutional.[39]

In 1999, a headscarf confrontation took place in the Turkish Parliament. Even elected representatives are subject to the ban. When Merve Kavakçi, elected as a new Islamic party deputy (Virtue Party), entered the Grand National Assembly wearing a headscarf, there was pandemonium as other deputies beat on desktops and called for her to get out. The Prime Minister denounced Ms. Kavakçi in very strong terms and called a recess. Media close to the state interpreted Ms. Kavakçi's act as a political attack on democracy and secularism. The incident triggered a move for abolition of the Virtue Party by the Constitutional Court.[40] The Turkish Council of Ministers took away her citizenship because she had breached the *Turkish Citizenship Law*, and she is no longer able to represent her constituency in Parliament.

Following the Court's decision, in 2000, more than three-hundred primary and secondary school teachers were dismissed by the Ministry of Education for defying the dress code by wearing a headscarf.[41]

---

[37] Arat, "Islamist Women," *supra* note 35.
[38] Only one member dissented from the opinion. See the Constitutional Court Decision: E. 1989/1, K. 1989/12, T. 7. 3. 1989, JCC 1991 at 25.
[39] E. 1997/1, K 1998/1, T. 1.16, 1998, JCC 1999 at 31.
[40] Nr. 1999/2, 2001/2 K., T. 22.6.2001.
[41] Regarding the dismissals, the Minister declared, "This is a crime, the punishment of which is dismissal from the civil service. Everybody must comply with this rule. If they don't they have no place among us": *Turkish Daily News*, Feb. 11, 2000. On May 31, 2000, the Istanbul Faith Primary Court sentenced Nuray Canan Bezirgan to six months' imprisonment for "obstructing the education of others" because she wore a headscarf during an examination at the Health Services Vocational Institute of Istanbul University. The sentence was later

During the headscarf battle, both sides of the conflict defended their arguments from their own perspectives. The women who demanded to be allowed to wear their headscarves at universities argued that any prohibition violated both their freedom of religious expression, as guaranteed in Article 24 of the 1982 Constitution, and the prohibition of discrimination before the law based on religious belief or differences in language, ethnicity, and sex, found in Article 10. The prohibition of headscarves, it was further claimed, obstructed their right to education as protected in Article 42.

Against these arguments, the state has made its own case, both through the decisions of the Council of State and the Constitutional Court. The Council of State has supported the prohibition of headscarves by stating that a "headscarf rather than being an innocent custom, has become a symbol of a world view opposed to the fundamental principles of the Republic and opposed to women's liberation."[42] The decisions, both of the Council of State and the Constitutional Court, mainly focused on four arguments: (1) headscarves restrict women's liberties; (2) headscarves in universities create an impression of unequal treatment before law; (3) headscarves are a symbol of opposition to the fundamental principles of the Republic (namely secularism); and (4) it is necessary to limit religious freedoms because a threat exists that the state would become organized according to the dictates of Islam.

From the perspective of women's rights and gender equality, the first two arguments have to be elaborated further. With regard to the first argument, Yesim Arat writes that:

Women who cover their heads do not share the individualistic perceptions of liberty that liberal women or men share. Their personal or individual perceptions of liberty are predicated upon the communitarian Islamic norms which dictate, they argue, women to cover their heads. They exercise their free choice if they can cover their heads in universities. By banning the headscarf, the state is authoritatively imposing its own understanding of women's liberties on a group who does not share the same understanding.[43]

The Constitutional Court in its decision does not even address this argument properly. It rejects such liberty entirely, due to its alleged incompatibility with the principles of Ataturk and the Turkish revolution, which was based on the aim of "reaching [a] contemporary level of civilization."[44] Using a headscarf is not considered as part of the dress-style that "civilized countries follow." Thus, it cannot be considered either as a matter of civil liberty or rights. Moreover, the Court argues that the headscarf is a symbol of particular religious view that supports *Shari'a* law, which is a danger

---

converted to a fine, but she faces several similar charges that will result in her imprisonment if convicted: Milliyet, *Turkish Daily News*, July 15, 2000.

[42] *The Decision of the Council of State*, 8th Session, E. 1984/636, K. 1984/1574, Dec.13, 1984.

[43] Arat, "Islamist Women," *supra* note 35.

[44] E. 1990/ 36, K. 1991/8 in JCC (1993) at 285.

for the generality of women rights, thus suggesting that women have to be protected against their free will for the sake of state official ideology.[45]

The Court has decided that demands relating to the headscarf were against the principle of equal treatment before the law as well as the principle of religious freedom. Allowing the headscarf to be worn would be a privilege given only to Islamist students, but it also would produce unequal treatment by differentiating them from others:

Religion is not a condition to have privileges before the law. To give permission to the headscarf, which is considered as religious dress, goes against the principle of equality, because it goes against secularism. Even if other religious dress is permitted it is still a violation of the principle of secularism. Allowing students to wear headscarves is a forced action rather than giving a freedom. Forcing people to dress in a specific way will result in an unequal position among people who belong to the same or different religions.[46]

The Court argues that wearing a headscarf goes against secularism, which prevails over civil liberties. Moreover, the equality principle is not considered prior to the secularism principle in the Constitution. The Court failed to address any of the arguments related to sex discrimination in the headscarf case, ignoring the fact that religious men and women were treated unequally in universities. Men who share the same beliefs with women and think that women's headscarves are a dictate of religion are admitted to universities and public offices since they have no specific religious dress code, and their heads are uncovered. Consequently women are treated unequally before law, not only because they give expression to their religious beliefs or act by them, but because they are women. In other words, despite the Court's argument that the use of the headscarf actually restricts women's rights, the Court's decision to expel female students from universities limits their professional and educational opportunities, creating unequal treatment between male and female believers. Religious discrimination is confounded with gender discrimination.

The headscarf issue brings religious belief out of the private sphere, where it belongs in a secular state, into the public sphere. In other words, the religious duty of Muslim women challenges their public participation in ways that religious men have never had to face. Moreover, the practices of the state and the Constitutional Court pit religious women against secular women and religious men. First of all, it is necessary to define "Islamist women," a category that is far from being homogenous in Turkey. The majority of traditional Turkish women are devout Muslims, but without any involvement in

---

[45] In Yesim Arat's interview with Islamist women, those who believed there was nothing wrong with Islamic law actually thought that when that law was implemented as it should be, many *Shari'a* Law principles, including polygamy, would not violate universal women's rights. Arat, "Islamist Women," *supra* note 35.

[46] E. 1997/1, *supra* note 39.

political Islam. According to recent surveys, about 15.7 percent of women in Turkey cover their heads with Islamic headscarves, and 53.4 percent cover their heads in a more traditional style. Only 27.3 percent say that they do not cover their heads.[47] Many women with headscarves do not seem to have thought through the implications of Islamic law which dictate them to cover their heads. If they have, they have thought of it only in very liberal terms.[48]

Given the results of these surveys – that the majority of Muslim women in Turkey wear a headscarf for purely traditional and religious reasons without any political agenda – it is difficult to approve of the Constitutional Court's decision, which essentializes female students by regarding them all as political followers of Islam. Beyond this, Islamist women should be given a legitimate right to pursue their own political agenda, as men do, as this would be respectful of the democratic and legal order.

The headscarf dispute also reached the European Human Rights Commission (EHRC) when one of the Turkish universities refused to give diplomas to female students who were wearing headscarves. In 1993, two female students applied to the EHRC as a last resort, claiming violations of the right to education and of the equality principle.[49] The decision of the EHRC simply followed the decision of the Turkish Constitutional Court, to the extent that it maintained the right of a secular state to restrict religious practices if consistent with citizens' right to equal treatment and religious freedom. According to the decision of the EHRC:

A student who chooses to attend a secular university, should accept the regulations of the university. These regulations provide a system to allow for students from different beliefs to coexist. Particularly in countries where the vast majority of the population belongs to a particular religion, exhibition of the rituals and symbols of this religion without regard to any restrictions of place and form can cause pressure on students who do not practice this religion or instead, belong to other religions.[50]

It was further argued that being a student in a secular university involved, by its nature, the acceptance of certain behavioral rules instituted to establish

---

[47] Ilyas Çarkoðlu and Zerrin Toprak, *Religion, Society and Politics in Turkey* (Istanbul: TESAV, 2000) at 22.

[48] Public opinion surveys also point to this contradiction of defending the Islamic Law and opposing its traditional readings regarding individual dictates. In a survey conducted in 1999 with a representative sample of the Turkish electorate, 21.2 percent responded positively to a question which asked if they want to have religious state based on the *Shari'a*. Further probes showed that this understanding of *Shari'a* was very liberal, if not idiosyncratic or Turkish. On the issue of adultery, for example, only 1.4 percent thought that the guilty should be punished according to the Koranic dictates of the death penalty. Carkoglu and Toprak, *Religion*, ibid., at 16–17.

[49] *Lamia Karabulut and Senay Karaduman* v. *Turkish Government*, Admissibility decision on application No. 18783/91, May 3, 1993 (3. 5. 1993), cited in *Cumhuriyet*, September 15, 1994.

[50] EHRC Admissibility Decision on application No. 18783/91, May 3, 1993.

respect for the rights and freedoms of others. On this basis, the Commission decided that:

Secular universities while they issue regulations on dress codes, they might consider to protect public order at universities against fundamentalist interventions. Therefore, there is no illegality of having dress-code regulations at secular universities, implementing and enforcing it. The plaintiff's argument on violation of the Human Rights Convention art. 27, paragraph 2 has been rejected.[51]

The Turkish educational establishment used the admissibility decision of EHRC, given the considerable prestige and authority of the Council of Europe, to justify the ban. An evaluation of legal issues relating to the ban, believed to have been prepared by the Council for Higher Education (YOK) and circulated to university rectors, as well as a statement by the Turkish Prime Minister's Office High Coordinating Council for Human Rights, refer to and summarize the admissibility decision in this case.[52]

The Commission's admissibility decision might be criticized on several grounds. First of all, the decision relies on "the student's choice of a secular institution" in Turkey but there are no religious schools offering professional eduction. Second, the argument that "using religious symbols by some students jeopardizes other students' position if they do not follow the same symbols" is unconvincing with respect to Turkey. There is not a single instance in which students who wear headscarves act to make other Muslim students uncomfortable due to their nonobservance of religious dress. At present, the opposite is true in Turkey. Third, the EHRC, instead of dealing with the issues of religious freedom, secularism, and gender equality, simply followed the decision of Turkish Constitutional Court. This was a disappointment for feminists, Islamists, and liberals, all of whom felt that the Commission failed to deal correctly with gender perspectives. There was no argument in the decision about unequal treatment between male and female students in terms of representing their religious beliefs or practicing their religion. The decision, however, was consistent with the Commission's other decision on the abolition of the Islamic party, supporting the actions of the Turkish government and the Constitutional Court.

These developments convinced a large portion of the Turkish public opinion that the EHRC's decision was biased against Islamist values in Europe and in Turkey, and that it had acted politically, rather than legally. In many other cases however, especially on minority rights and due process principles, the EHRC has taken a very strong position against the Turkish government. It is possible to conclude that the Commission acted on its view of Islam and

---

[51] Ibid.

[52] Human Rights Watch, "Combatting Restrictions on the Headscarf" online: Human Rights Watch Web site <http://www.hrw/org/reports/2000/turkey2> (date accessed: April 12, 2002).

secularism rather than evaluating the issue from the perspective of gender equality.[53]

Women's Sexual Indemnity and Sexual and Marital Autonomy. One of the major structural defects of the Turkish Criminal Code related to gender equality is the way in which sexual crimes are situated in the Code. Such crimes are considered "crimes against public order, and family structure" instead of "crimes against individuals."[54] This shows all too clearly how the Turkish Criminal Code treats women. The legal reasoning used reflects partly the Code's Italian origin and partly the patriarchal structure of Turkish society.[55]

The designation of sex crimes as violations of community or family morality has two consequences. First, it identifies the community and "not the individual woman" as the party that suffers the consequent harm. Second, the investigation and prosecution of sex crimes stress not the physical harm to the woman but rather her honor and thus the public decency and family order that may have been compromised. The law even provides a remedy for the perceived harm of lost honor by creating an incentive – suspension of criminal prosecution – for a man charged with certain crimes who marries his "victim" and thus supposedly minimizes her loss of honor. By giving this opportunity to perpetrators of sexual crimes, the Turkish Criminal Code punishes the "victim" by obliging her to marry him, rather than apprehending him as a "criminal." The Criminal Code differentiates criminality according to the victim's biological and legal status. For instance, sex crimes committed against nonvirgins are perceived as less serious offenses than those committed against virgins because the potential damage to family order is regarded as less grave. By the same logic, Article 430 of the Criminal Code imposes a reduced penalty on men who kidnap a girl or woman for the purpose of marriage (even if the marriage is done without the victim's

---

[53] The admissibility decision was made 10 years ago by the European Commission of Human Rights, which has now been effectively replaced by the full-time European Court of Human Rights. At least two new applications have been made to the ECHR by women excluded from their studies, including the wife of the current Minister of Foreign Affairs, but no decisions have yet been reached in these cases: *Tekin v. Turkey* No. 41556/98 (the first hearing was in November 2002).

[54] Articles 414–470 of the Turkish *Criminal Code* are not compatible with the equality principle of the Turkish Constitution.

[55] The Italian Government changed the *Criminal Code* in 1996, replacing rape crimes from the Chapter on "Crimes against Public Order," to the one on "Crimes against Individuals." The joint campaign has been organized by Italian feminists and conservative politicians, including the grandson of Benito Mussolini, Alessandro Mussolini. For the Turkish case, see: Y. Unver, "Changing Structure of the Criminal Law related to Sex Crimes against Women and the Case of Turkey" [Turkish] in *Adalet Yuksek Okulu 20.Yil Armagani* (Istanbul: Adalet Press, 2001) 293–324; Bertil Cetinkaya-Oder, "A Case Study on Protection of Human Dignity and Violation against Women" [Turkish] in *Bulletin of International Law* (2001) 19–20 577–602.

consent).[56] Article 429 of the Code applies double standards according to the victim's marital status in cases of kidnapping. As such, basic principles of human rights are violated. These provisions have never been challenged by the Constitutional Court, despite endless discussions organized by women's rights groups.

Similar discriminatory rules also can be found in the treatment of rape crimes. Article 438 provided reduced penalties for a man convicted of rape and abduction whenever the victim was shown to be a prostitute.[57] This article was challenged in the Constitutional Court, but the Court rejected the claim on the grounds that "dishonest women, i.e., a prostitute, should not be treated the same as honest women."[58] After much public debate, the Turkish Parliament in 1989 repealed the provision.[59] As this shows, the Constitutional Court's interpretation of the equality principle is extremely conservative with respect to women's sexuality. None of these criminal provisions that directly and strongly challenge the equality principle specifically, and fundamental principles of human rights generally, have ever been placed in jeopardy by the Constitutional Court.

Finally, there is no prohibition of intramarital rape in the Turkish Criminal Code. The law distinguishes between rape inside and outside of marriage. A woman can file for divorce if she is compelled to engage in sexual relations by the use of physical force; she can also claim compensation. However, the courts regard marriage as an institution that provides people with a means to fulfill their sexual needs within the law. The law enforcement mechanism and judicial authorities do not accept the idea that rape can occur in marriage, so the criminal law is not applied in such cases.[60] It is strongly argued by

---

[56] In traditional Turkish rural life, kidnapping is a social phenomenon against "arranged marriage," and an escape from the paying of a "dowry." As a general practice in Turkey, kidnapping a girl is a way of getting forced permission from the family for marriage by reason of protecting its "family honor."

[57] *Turkish Criminal Code*, No. 713 (1926), online: webpage of the Turkish Grand National Assembly Web site <www.tbmm.gove.tr/kanunlar/k713.html>.

[58] E. 1988/4, K.1989/3, T. 12.1.1989.

[59] The Turkish National Assembly banned this article in *The Amendment of Articles of Turkish Criminal Code*, nr. 3670, art. 28.

[60] A recent book on modern Turkey includes a commentary on sexual violence as part of an interview with the public prosecutor of a rural town:

90% of the sex crimes are between men and women; 10% percent may be men and men. But I've only heard of only one incident where a man has raped another man. The aim of our rapists is to marry, you see.... There are times when people just want to satisfy their sexual desire, but more that 60 percent of the rape cases have the aim of marrying. For instance, a man took a woman, and the woman wanted it a bit, but she is too young, the man has to go to prison. That's the law: You go to prison for under-age sex.... If a man has kidnapped a woman, and then he marries her, and that is approved of by the parents, then it's OK. But if they divorce within five years then he is arrested for kidnapping. I think it's unfair. Of course, I could not say such things in court or I would be considered biased ... There

women's rights organizations that excluding intra-marital rape from criminal responsibility is against the Constitutional principle of "protection of
material and spiritual wellbeing of individuals."[61] The same silence of the
Turkish legal system also exists with respect to sexual harassment in the work
place. There has been no constitutional challenge related to sexual harassment or rape in marriage simply because there is a legal gap in the system,
and the legislature has no desire to deal with issues that directly relate to
women's sexuality.

CONCLUSION

The role of the Constitutional Court in gender issues has an interesting pattern in Turkey. Artificial legal rights conferred on women as part of the
modernization project are in tension with the patriarchal values of Turkish
society and women's very limited role in public life, which reflects the traditional beliefs and practices of Islam. These mixed messages given to the
Constitutional Court have allowed it to produce an inconsistent jurisprudence. For a long time, the Constitutional Court adhered to a conservative
jurisprudence, the *status quo* interpretation of the equality principle of reluc-
tantly giving women an equal position that was more advanced than in the
existing legal system. In this period, the outdated status of Turkish women,
especially in the family environment as provided by the Civil Code of 1926,
was interpreted by the Court as "being in harmony with the fundamental
values of Turkish society and tradition."[62] Legislative bodies, however, appeared to be more forthcoming, changing outdated norms in the legal system
and influencing the political environment at the domestic and international
levels.[63]

    However, in the early 1990s, when Muslim women mounted challenges
in court by asserting their right to wear headscarves, the Court did not

---

is, of course, wife beating, but this doesn't get reported, because women tend to accept it
in families of lower culture. Tim Kelsey Dervish, *The Invention of Modern Turkey* (London:
Hamis' Hamilton, 1996) at 187.
    As illustrated in this interview, the attitude of the public prosecutor represents the main-
stream understanding of the educated male in Turkey. Many unjust consequences of the legal
system towards men are well-accepted, but women's suffering as victims of horrible crimes
are never mentioned.

[61] 1982 *Constitution, supra* note 7, art.17: "Everyone has the right to life and the right to protect
      and develop his material and spiritual integrity."
[62] Goren, "Equal Rights for Different Sexes," *supra* note 18, at 83.
[63] *Civil Code,* art. 153/1, which states that a woman must assume her husband's name upon
      marriage. Legal activists have been trying unsuccessfully to get the Constitutional Court to
      annul this provision on the ground that it violates Article 10. The action came from the
      Parliament, as May of 1997. Women may retain their birth names following marriage if they
      wish to do so. Another amendment has been issued to the *Income Tax Law* in 1998. Women
      can now independently declare their income as individual taxpayers.

hesitate to abandon its established practice of supporting traditional Turkish values and excluded such female students from universities. The Court, along with the majority of the political and military leadership, adhered to a strong secular view, contending that the equality principle and the right to education do not ever take precedence over the secularist commitments of Turkey.

Turkey is considered by many commentators to be one of the few relatively democratic countries in the Islamic Middle East. However, military interventions and their impact upon the constitutional order and human rights have made it impossible for Turkish citizens to enjoy fully the universal values associated with legal protections. This "censored democracy" flourished especially in 1980s. The 1982 Constitution forbade political associations of youth, women, and other groups, reducing the relevance of citizen action in Turkey. However, women's organizations benefited from these limitations in the long run, as they were treated as "less dangerous" by the military than leftist movements. The emergence of feminist movements in this politically sterilized environment of the 1980s is a good example of the possibilities of such policy in Turkey.[64]

On an official level, the benevolent attitude of the Turkish government to women's issues is also expressed in foreign policy. Turkey actively participated during 1979 in the drafting of CEDAW, signing and later ratifying the treaty in 1985 (although with reservations).[65] CEDAW was regarded as 'compatible' with Turkey's existing commitment to gender equality, reflecting the Republic's secular and modernist orientation. Considering that Turkey has not ratified some of the most important international human rights treaties (e.g., the Racial Discrimination Convention, the two International Covenants on Civil and Political Rights and Economic and Social Rights, respectively, and more recently the International Criminal Court), its willingness to support CEDAW can be interpreted as Turkey's pride in its record on women's rights. This support for CEDAW could be attributed to the state's strong commitment to, as well as greater confidence in, its record in the area of women's rights.[66]

In the Turkish context, the use of CEDAW by state forces, including legal-judicial bodies, has been particularly significant. Since ratification, several legislative and judicial actions have made use of the Convention by referring

---

[64] In this period, women's NGOs attempted to get the military government to legalize abortion, which it did in 1983, and to ratify CEDAW, which it did not do until a few years later.

[65] The delay of ratification has been largely attributed to the presence of military rule during this period. The civil Government's interest in ratifying CEDAW in 1984, which occurred during a period in which Turkey ratified several international and regional human rights instruments and pursued a clear policy of political and economic integration with the West, can be seen as part of the government's overall strategy of liberalization.

[66] Feride Acar, "Turkey: the First CEDAW Impact Study 2001," online: CEDAW Web site <http: www.cedaw.org> (date accessed: May 16, 2002).

to it in legal texts of a critical nature.[67] Among these, several can be noted. The *Domestic Violence Act*[68] promulgated in 1998 was influenced by CEDAW. In addition, the Parliamentary Commission, which was convened in December 1997 to inquire into women's status and determine the measures needed to ensure the full implementation of CEDAW in Turkey, was explicitly directed toward investigating what should be done to make it possible to withdraw the outstanding reservations. Finally, the Constitutional Court has, in recent years, made four very salient decisions pertaining to legal equality of men and women. As discussed earlier, in two of these decisions, the Court has specifically and extensively referred to CEDAW.[69]

Parallel to its international commitment within the UN frame, during the late 1990s, Turkey made a vigorous effort to reform its domestic legal system in every area, especially regarding human rights, so that it might qualify for membership in the EU. The Turkish experience illustrates the crucial role played by international law and international institutions in promoting human rights, including gender equality, on a domestic level. From the earliest stages of the EU, Turkey has sought to become a member, regarding EU membership as a confirmation of its contemporary values and consistent with the founding philosophy of Turkish state.

As is generally known, the relationship between the EU and Turkey has been a long roller coaster ride because of various EU concerns relating to economic, political, social, cultural, religious, and legal matters. Turkey's application for membership in the European Union is being evaluated on the basis of a series of conditions that seek Turkish compliance with well-established international human rights norms, alongside an insistence on Turkish harmonization with EU economic and monetary policies. Because the economic harmonization requirements are rarely invoked as the main stumbling block to Turkish accession, and have been treated flexibly in the cases of other states, human rights conditions would seem to pose the main obstacle to Turkish membership. In recent months, the Turkish parliament has engaged in a feverish pace of legislative activity to make the necessary changes in the Constitution and other legislation to follow specific suggestions given by the European Council in Helsinki on December 1999. In 2000,

---

[67] Ibid.

[68] *Family Protection Act*, no. 4320.

[69] One of these decisions pertained to Article 159 of the Civil Code, which had required a husband's permission for his wife's professional activity. See: Constitutional Court Decision E. 1990/30, K.1990/31, T. 29. 11. 1990, JCC 1992 2701 249–271. Also, Articles 441 and 440 of the Turkish Penal Code defined adultery of husbands and wives on different grounds; this was annulled by the Constitutional Court in December 27, 1996. This decision made extensive reference to CEDAW as a ratified international treaty which national legislation should adopt. See the Constitutional Court Decision E.1996/15, K.1996/34, T. 23.9.1996, *Official Gazette* 7.12. 1996 No.22860 at 249–51.

Turkey received another inquiry from the EU, known as "*Copenhagen acquis communautaire*," that basically demanded that the whole body of EU legislation be introduced into the Turkish legislative and constitutional order or that the latter be harmonized with the former.

During the last two years, a fast-track effort of the Turkish Parliament, especially on gender equality concerns, became one of the most discussed areas of human rights, with substantive progress being made. Some areas of human rights remain problematic in Turkey, including the cultural rights of ethnic minorities, prison conditions, military courts, law enforcement abuses, and due process principles. At the same time, the Parliament did not hesitate to change the entire Turkish Civil Code, giving Turkish women a more equal status that seems comparable with European standards. In family law, for instance, women's status was significantly improved by amendments including a progressive and egalitarian joint property regime in marriage.[70] In furtherance of the harmonization project with the EU, the Turkish Government in 2000 withdrew many of its reservations to CEDAW.[71] Finally, as part of the legal reform package, the outrageous and outdated criminal law provisions are being discussed in the Turkish Parliament.

As discussed earlier, the Constitutional amendment of 2001 reformulated the equality principle as suggested by the EU, but with a Turkish touch. Article 41 of the Constitution has been amended to establish the principle of equality between spouses as a basis for the family.[72] Feminist organizations have now started a campaign to have Turkey adopt a gender specific equality principle. The political atmosphere is very receptive to such a demand, given the combination of EU pressure on the Turkish legislature and global fears of political Islam after September 11.

It can be concluded that in the Turkish case, state agencies and the upper court have been more sensitive to international commitments than to domestic politics. This pattern can be explained partly by the general ineffectiveness of the Turkish civil society movement, which is itself explained by the depolitization efforts of military governments, dysfunctional

---

[70] The new regime gives women property rights equal to those of their husbands on divorce. However, at the last minute, the Turkish parliament limited the implementation of this new property regime with the nonretroactive interim provision that excluded seventeen million Turkish women who are already married. Women's NGOs in Turkey are now mobilizing ordinary courts to apply to the constitutional court in any divorce case to abolish the interim provision on the ground of inequality.

[71] Turkey's reservations to Article 15(2) and (4), 16(c), (d), (f), and (g) of CEDAW have been lifted. Turkey has not withdrawn its reservation to Article 29, and the declaration on Article 9 also remains.

[72] With this new amendment, another long time discriminatory provision has been abandoned. Article 66 of the Constitution no longer discriminates on the basis of gender in the case of a foreign parent with respect to Turkish citizenship.

political parties, and the limited human rights protection provided by the Constitution. Until now, the official commitments to women's rights have resulted in a dual status for Turkish women. Urban, well-educated, middle-class women in Turkey are not treated very differently than Western women both legally and factually. However, women in Anatolia, in small towns, and in rural areas continue to suffer under a patriarchal order, internal ethnic and religious pressures, traditional family structure, and most importantly, economic hardships. During the last several years, Turkey has been victimized overall by its neoliberal commitment to the global economy. The negative effects of globalization on Turkey have become unbearable for such vulnerable groups as minorities, the poor, women, and children. The majority of women in Turkey are indifferent about equal rights, while urban feminists stress equality. Domestic violence, honor killings, polygamy in rural areas, unpaid agricultural work, illiteracy, patriarchal domination, and a voiceless presence in extended family structure have generated a new social phenomenon in Turkey: a rising tide of suicide by women. Given this negative picture of the conditions affecting the majority of Turkish women, it is unclear whether recent international commitments and changes in the legal order will be able to produce hope and progress as a whole in the years ahead.

Suggested Readings

Books

Feride Acar and Ayse Gunes Ayata, eds., *Gender and Identity Construction: Women of Central Asia, Caucasus, and Turkey* (Boston: Brill, 2000).

Canan Arin, *The Legal Status of Women in Turkey* (Istanbul: Women for Women's Human Rights, 1996).

Pinar Ilkkaracan, *A Brief Overview of Women's Movements in Turkey* (Istanbul: Women for Women's Rights, 1996).

Pinar Ilkkaracan, ed., *Women and Sexuality in Muslim Societies* (Istanbul: Women for Women's Rights, 2000).

Julie Marcus, *A Word of Difference: Islam and Gender Hierarchy in Turkey* (London: Zed, 1992).

Ergun Ozbudun, *Contemporary Turkish Politics: Challenges to Democratic Consolidation* (Boulder, CO: Lynee Rienner Publishers, 2000).

Elisabeth Ozdalga, *The Veiling Issue: Official Secularism and Popular Islam in Modern Turkey* (Richmond: Curzon, 1998).

Atilla Ozer, *Comparative Study on Two Constitutions: 1961 and 1982* [Turkish] (Istanbul: Bilim Yayinlari, 1984).

Ayse Saktanber, *Living Islam: Women and Islamic Politics in Turkey* (London: I. B. Tauris, 2000).

Mumtaz Soysal, *Salient Points of the Turkish Constitution* [Turkish] (Ankara: Bilgi Yayinevi, 1995).

Online Resources

The Commission of the EC. Brussels, "2001 Regular Report on Turkey's Progress toward Accession of the EC," online: The Commission of the EU <www.deltur. cec.eu.int> (date accessed: February 11, 2002)

UNDP and The General Directorate on the Status and Problems of Women, "Women in Turkey: 1999, online: Website of the General Directorate on the Status and Problems of Women, <www.kssgm.gov.tr> (date accessed: February 10, 2002).

"Iwraw Country Report on Turkey" online: IWRAW Publications: Country Reports: Turkey <www.igc.org/iwraw/publications/countries/turkey.html> (date accessed: April 16, 2002).

Zeynep Zilelioglu, "Can Woman in Islamic Society Reclaim Their Sexuality?" (Istanbul: Turkish Daily News, August 27, 2000), online: Turkish Daily News <www.turkishdailynews.com> (date accessed September 2000).

Gender and the United States Constitution

Equal Protection, Privacy, and Federalism

Reva B. Siegel

There are no doubt thousands of pathways, direct and indirect, by which constitutions work to enforce and to unsettle the institutions, practices, and understandings that regulate social status of men and women. In this chapter, I consider a few of the more prominent ways that the United States Constitution has served to legitimate and to dismantle social arrangements that sustain inequalities between the sexes.

The U.S. Constitution prohibits government from acting in ways that deny persons within its jurisdiction the equal protection of the laws.[1] This chapter begins with a brief account of how the Supreme Court came to read this clause of the Fourteenth Amendment as a guarantee of equal citizenship for women, over a century after it was first included in the Constitution. It surveys the basic contours of equal protection doctrine, and then considers in more detail how the United States Supreme Court has applied the Equal Protection Clause to questions of sex discrimination in a variety of different practical contexts. The remainder of the essay considers two other bodies of constitutional doctrine that play an especially prominent role in shaping women's lives: privacy doctrines that protect individual decision making about reproduction from state interference, and federalism doctrines that determine the circumstances in which the United States Congress can enact laws that affect family relations.

In general, my account emphasizes description, rather than critical evaluation, of American constitutional law. In a concluding section, however, I identify one practical framework in which we might assess the American constitutional tradition. In this concluding section, I consider some of the ways that American constitutional law has served to legitimate and to undermine traditional forms of gender inequality in the family.

[1] U.S. Const. amend. XIV.

THE EQUAL CITIZENSHIP GUARANTEE: HOW STRUGGLES
OVER RACE EQUALITY HAVE SHAPED AMERICAN
CONSTITUTIONAL LAW GOVERNING SEX EQUALITY

In the United States, social movements for women's emancipation have grown out of social movements for racial emancipation, first in the nineteenth century and then in the twentieth century. This relationship has in turn shaped constitutional law. If one considers how the body of constitutional law governing questions of equal citizenship for women emerged from the body of constitutional law governing equal citizenship for racial minorities, one can better appreciate its distinctive strengths, weaknesses, and confusions.

The United States Constitution did not contain an express commitment to the equality of its citizens until sectional conflict over slavery culminated in a civil war and major constitutional reform. As part of "Reconstruction" of the United States in the aftermath of the war, its constitution was amended (1) to prohibit slavery (the Thirteenth Amendment); (2) to guarantee that all persons born or naturalized in the United States would be citizens who were entitled "the equal protection of the laws" and who could not be denied life, liberty, or property without due process of law (the Fourteenth Amendment); and (3) to provide that the right to vote would not be denied on account of race or previous condition of servitude (the Fifteenth Amendment).[2]

In the decade after ratification of the Fourteenth Amendment, the Court repudiated the constitutional claims of woman suffragists in the abolitionist movement and ruled that the Fourteenth Amendment did not protect women's right to practice law, or to vote, on the same terms as men.[3] It took another half century of political agitation before the women's movement was able to secure a constitutional amendment guaranteeing women the franchise. The Nineteenth Amendment to the U.S. Constitution, ratified in 1920, provides that the right to suffrage cannot be denied on the basis of sex.[4] In this period, a group of suffrage activists attempted to secure a

---

[2] U.S. Const. amend. XIII, s.1: "Neither slavery nor involuntary servitude, except as a punishment for crime whereof the party shall have been duly convicted, shall exist within the United States, or any place subject to their jurisdiction." U.S. Const. amend. XIV, s.1: "No State shall make or enforce any law which shall abridge the privileges or immunities of citizens of the United States; nor shall any State deprive any person of life, liberty, or property, without due process of law; nor deny to any person within its jurisdiction the equal protection of the laws." U.S. Const. amend. XV, s.1: "The right of citizens of the United States to vote shall not be denied or abridged by the United States or by any State on account of race, color, or previous condition of servitude."

[3] See *Bradwell v. State of Illinois*, 16 Wall. 130 at 141, 21 L.Ed.2d 442 (1873), upholding gender restrictions on the practice of law; *Minor v. Happersett*, 21 Wall. 162 at 178, 22 L.Ed. 627 (1875), upholding gender restrictions on the franchise.

[4] U.S. Const. amend. XIX: "The right of citizens of the United States to vote shall not be denied or abridged by the United States or by any State on account of sex."

second, more wide-reaching constitutional amendment guaranteeing equal rights for women, but the campaign failed to secure broad-based support.[5]

A mass movement for women's rights did not coalesce again for another half century – once again arising out of a movement for racial equality. By the 1960s, the United States Congress had begun to enact legislation prohibiting race discrimination in various spheres of social life; Title VII of the *Civil Rights Act* of 1964 prohibited employment discrimination on the basis of *sex*, as well as race and national origin.[6] By some accounts, the prohibition on sex discrimination in employment was added to the federal civil rights statute to ensure its defeat, but instead the *Civil Rights Act* of 1964 was enacted with the sex discrimination provision included.[7]

The National Organization of Women (NOW) was founded during this period in order to pressure the federal government into enforcing the law against sex discrimination in employment that had been included in the *Civil Rights Act* of 1964.[8] At the same time, women organized to secure legislative protections against sex discrimination from Congress, and to seek an amendment to the federal Constitution securing women equal rights at law. The text of the constitutional amendment proposed by Congress in 1972 read: "Equality of rights under the law shall not be denied or abridged by the United States or by any State on account of sex."[9] The campaign for an Equal Rights Amendment (ERA) started with energy, but expired in the 1980s without obtaining the approval of the number of states needed for ratification.[10]

This campaign for constitutional reform nevertheless had major consequences. In 1971, the Supreme Court for the first time interpreted the Equal Protection Clause of the Fourteenth Amendment to invalidate a statute that discriminated on the basis of sex.[11] In justifying this new approach to interpreting the Equal Protection Clause, a plurality of the Court, led by Justice

[5] See Joan G. Zimmerman, "The Jurisprudence of Equality: The Women's Minimum Wage, the First Equal Rights Amendment, and Adkins v. Children's Hospital, 1905–1923" (1991) 78:1 *Journal of American History* 188.

[6] *Civil Rights Act of 1964*, tit. VII, 42 U.S.C. ss.2000e-2000e-17 (1994).

[7] See Jo Freeman, "How 'Sex' Got into Title VII: Persistent Opportunism as a Maker of Public Policy" (1991) 9 *Law & Inequality* 163 at 164; see also Serena Mayeri, " 'A Common Fate of Discrimination': Race-Gender Analogies in Legal and Historical Perspective" (2001) 110 *Yale Law Journal* 1045 at 1063–6.

[8] On the founding and early development of NOW, see Jo Freeman, *The Politics of Women's Liberation* (New York: David McKay, 1975) at 71–102; Cynthia Harrison, *On Account of Sex: The Politics of Women's Issues, 1945–1968* (Berkeley: University of California Press, 1988) at 192–209.

[9] H.R.J. Res. 208, 92d Cong. s.1, 86 Stat. 1523 (1972).

[10] See Mary Frances Berry, *Why ERA Failed* (Bloomington: Indiana University Press, 1986); Jane J. Mansbridge, *Why We Lost the ERA* (Chicago: University of Chicago Press, 1986).

[11] See *Reed v. Reed*, 404 U.S. 71 (1971), striking down a state statute that preferred males over females in appointing the administrator of a deceased's estate.

Brennan, emphasized that sex discrimination resembled race discrimination and called for a similar judicial response.[12] Since that time, the Court has interpreted the Equal Protection Clause of the Fourteenth Amendment to prohibit many forms of state action that discriminate on the basis of sex.

In summary, then, today the only textual provision of the United States Constitution that expressly prohibits sex discrimination is the Nineteenth Amendment, and it is generally understood to concern voting only.[13] But the campaign for constitutional reform during the 1960s and 1970s did move the Court to change its interpretation of the Equal Protection Clause of the Fourteenth Amendment to afford rights against sex discrimination.[14] To understand these rights, it is necessary, first, to consider the basic framework of equal protection law elaborated in the Court's race discrimination cases, and then consider how this doctrine has been extended, via the race-gender analogy, to guarantee equal citizenship rights for women.

THE BASIC STRUCTURE OF MODERN EQUAL PROTECTION DOCTRINE UNDER THE FOURTEENTH AMENDMENT

The following discussion sets out the basic framework of equal protection doctrine in matters of race discrimination, and then examines in more detail the body of sex discrimination case law the Court has developed in this framework. It should be noted, at the outset of this discussion, that the Court has interpreted the Fourteenth Amendment's guarantee of "the equal protection of the laws" to protect persons against "state action" only.[15] While federal laws, such as the *Civil Rights Act* of 1964, protect persons against discrimination inflicted by "private" persons, plaintiffs advancing equal protection claims under the Constitution must show that they have suffered an injury inflicted by the state, or some person or entity formally connected to the state.[16]

---

[12] See *Frontiero v. Richardson*, 411 U.S. 677, 684, 686 & n.17 (1973) (plurality opinion), striking down a federal statute that allowed men, but not women, to claim their spouses as dependents without regard to whether the spouses were in fact dependent.

[13] For an account of the struggles that culminated in ratification of the Nineteenth Amendment that emphasizes the continuing relevance of this constitutional history for sex equality law today, see Reva B. Siegel, "She, the People: The Nineteenth Amendment, Sex Equality, Federalism, and the Family" (2002) 115 *Harvard Law Review* 947.

[14] On the interaction of the women's movement, Congress, and the Court in this period, see Robert C. Post and Reva B. Siegel, "Legislative Constitutionalism and Section Five Power: Policentric Interpretation of the Family and Medical Leave Act," 112 *Yale Law Journal* (2003) 1943, 1980–2020.

[15] *Civil Rights Cases*, 109 U.S. 3 (1883).

[16] See, e.g., *Burton v. Wilmington Parking Auth.*, 365 U.S. 715 (1961), enjoining a coffee shop from refusing to serve African Americans because the building was owned by a state agency. But see *Jackson v. Metropolitan Edison Co.*, 419 U.S. 345 (1974), holding that the acts of a privately owned, but heavily regulated, utility did not constitute state action; *Moose Lodge*

Equal Treatment Principle

The Equal Protection Clause protects persons against certain forms of discriminatory state action only. In a few discrete areas, the Court has ruled that the Clause protects certain fundamental rights that the state cannot burden.[17] But in general, the Court has not interpreted the Equal Protection Clause to guarantee minimal or "baseline" entitlements. Instead, plaintiffs can make equal protection claims on the state only insofar as they can prove that the state has treated them differently than other "similarly situated" persons.

As the Court sees it, legislatures should be free to discriminate amongst groups of citizens when fashioning social policy; that is the essence of legislative decision making in representative government. On this view, because the Court is an unelected or "countermajoritarian" institution, it should generally defer to the judgments of the legislative branches. But under modern interpretations of the Equal Protection Clause, beginning with the invalidation of racially segregated schooling in *Brown v. Board of Education*,[18] the Court reviews state action that discriminates on the basis of race differently, on the premise that courts should intervene in the political process in order to ensure that minority groups can fully and fairly participate. It calls the more rigorous standard of review that it applies to race-based state action "strict scrutiny."

Strict Scrutiny for Race-Based State Action

In the decades after World War II, as the Court moved to dismantle entrenched practices of racial apartheid, it ruled that that the state cannot regulate on the basis of race unless it can demonstrate that racially discriminatory state action is necessary to achieve a compelling governmental purpose.[19] The case law deems any form of openly race-based state action "suspect," and is hostile to almost any generalization about members of

No. 107 v. Irvis, 407 U.S. 163 (1972), holding that a state could grant a liquor license to a private club that refused to serve African Americans; and *United States v. Morrison*, 529 U.S. 528 (2000) (discussed below).

[17] There is one strand of equal protection jurisprudence that is less clearly comparative, the so-called fundamental rights strand. Regulation that burden rights the Court deems "fundamental," such as the right to travel (see *Shapiro v. Thompson*, 394 U.S. 618 [1969]), equal voting opportunities (see *Harper v. Virginia Bd. of Elections*, 383 U.S. 663, 670 [1966]), or sexual autonomy (see *Skinner v. Oklahoma* ex rel. *Williamson*, 316 U.S. 535 [1942]) may be closely scrutinized. See generally Laurence H. Tribe, *American Constitutional Law* s.s. 16–7 to – 12, 2nd ed., (Mineola, NY: Foundation Press, 1988) at 1454–65, describing the fundamental rights strand of equal protection law.

[18] 347 U.S. 483 (1954).

[19] See, e.g., *Loving v. Virginia*, 388 U.S. 1 (1967), striking down Virginia's antimiscegenation law.

racial groups that might justify such legislation. This commitment to "color blind" state action is central to modern equal protection law.

During the 1970s, the era that sex discrimination doctrine was born, the Court began to construe this commitment to colorblind state action restrictively, in ways that might preserve as well as undermine social arrangements supporting racial stratification. It was in this period that the Supreme Court began to interpret the commitment to "color blindness" as a constraint on so-called "benign discrimination": the use of group-conscious admissions criteria to integrate institutions that had once been openly segregated. As majority groups objected to "affirmative action" programs that considered race for the purpose of increasing minority representation in education or employment, the Supreme Court held that it would apply strict scrutiny to such programs, and impose substantial constitutional restrictions on their design and legitimate use.[20] (Lower courts have adopted a similar framework to determine the constitutionality of sex-based affirmative action programs.[21]) Thus, the Equal Protection Clause now constrains government when it employs group conscious measures designed to include minorities and women in activities from which they have historically been excluded and in which they are currently underrepresented.

Such affirmative action programs are, however, still permissible if implemented under tight constitutional constraints.[22] The governmental entity adopting the affirmative action program must demonstrate that it has a factual basis for believing that underrepresentation of women or minorities is likely the result of discrimination in its own prior decision-making processes or those of private actors with whom it is in close association.[23] In educational settings, the Court has adopted a somewhat more flexible framework. It allows affirmative action in admissions for the purposes of increasing the

---

[20] See *Adarand Constructors v. Pena*, 515 U.S. 200 (1995), striking down a federal program for affirmative action in highway construction; and *City of Richmond v. J.A. Croson Co.*, 488 U.S. 469 (1989), striking down a city program for affirmative action in construction projects.

[21] Federal courts are split as to the level of scrutiny to apply to sex-based affirmative action programs. Compare *Engineering Contractors Ass'n v. Metropolitan Dade County*, 122 F.3d 895 at 908 (11th Cir. 1997), using intermediate scrutiny to strike down a sex-based affirmative action program for construction projects, and *Coral Construction Co. v. King County*, 941 F.2d 910, 931 (9th Cir. 1991), applying intermediate scrutiny to uphold a sex-based set-aside program for public contract awards, with *Brunet v. City of Columbus*, 1 F.3d 390 at 403–404 (6th Cir. 1993), applying strict scrutiny to strike down a sex-based hiring program in a fire department.

[22] See John Cocchi Day, "Retelling the Story of Affirmative Action: Reflections on a Decade of Federal Jurisprudence in the Public Workplace" (2001) 89 *California Law Review* 59, surveying the constitutional challenges of forty-nine remedial workplace affirmative action plans, finding over 40 percent (twenty-one) survived the application of strict scrutiny by the federal courts.

[23] See Ian Ayres and Fredrick E. Vars, "When Does Private Discrimination Justify Public Affirmative Action?" (1998) 98 *Columbia Law Review* 1577 at 1586–7.

"diversity" of the institution.[24] Yet it has emphasized that affirmative action in admissions may not function as a quota system.[25] Instead, educational institutions may consider race as a "plus" factor in making admissions decisions, so long as the institution has considered and deemed ineffective race-neutral alternatives. An institution may consider race in admissions only if it is only one of many enhancing factors the institution considers; and if the institution considers all candidates in an individualized and flexible assessment process.[26]

During this same period, the Court also adopted a quite restrictive interpretation of the constitutional prohibition against state action that discriminates on the basis of race. Although in 1971 the Court interpreted the employment discrimination provisions of the *Civil Rights Act* of 1964 to cover "facially neutral" practices that had a disparate impact on minorities or women,[27] it declined to apply a similar framework in interpreting the Constitution. Instead, in the 1976 case of *Washington v. Davis*,[28] the Court held that facially neutral state action that has a disparate impact on racial minorities does not violate the Equal Protection Clause unless the state acted for the purpose of discriminating against minorities. Constitutional standards for proof of race and sex discrimination are the same in this regard.

To prove discriminatory purpose, the Court has ruled, it is not enough to show that the adverse racial impact was foreseeable; something more is required. In some of its cases, the Court has held that the plaintiff must prove something like malice: that the challenged action was undertaken "at least in part 'because of,' rather than 'in spite of,' its adverse effects upon an identifiable group."[29] The Court adopted this definition of "discriminatory purpose" in a sex discrimination case in which the Court upheld a state law that gave military veterans a substantial preference in hiring for government positions, even though the foreseeable effect of the preference was to give most of the government jobs in question to men.

---

[24] This rationale was first articulated in an opinion by Justice Powell in *Regents of California v. Bakke*, 438 U.S. 265 at 311–5 (1978). It has since been affirmed in *Grutter v. Bollinger*, 123 S.Ct. 2325, 2338–41 (2003).

[25] In *Grutter v. Bollinger*, *supra* note 24 at 2342, the Court affirmed its language in *Regents of California v. Bakke*, *supra* note 24 at 315–6, asserting, "universities cannot establish quotas for members of certain racial groups or put members of those groups on separate admissions tracks. Nor can universities insulate applicants who belong to certain racial or ethnic groups from the competition for admission."

[26] *Grutter v. Bollinger*, *supra* note 24 at 2342–7. In *Gratz v. Bollinger*, 123 S.Ct. 2411 (2003), the Court struck down a policy that granted twenty points to all underrepresented minority applicants, an amount equal to one-fifth of the points necessary for admission.

[27] See *Griggs v. Duke Power Co.*, 401 U.S. 424 (1971).

[28] 426 U.S. 229 at 239 (1976).

[29] *Personnel Adm'r v. Feeney*, 442 U.S. 256, 279 (1979). The Court in fact applies the intent requirement in different ways in different contexts, see Daniel R. Ortiz, "The Myth of Intent in Equal Protection" (1989) 41 *Stanford Law Review* 1105.

SEX DISCRIMINATION DOCTRINE UNDER THE EQUAL PROTECTION CLAUSE OF THE FOURTEENTH AMENDMENT

"Intermediate" not "Strict" Scrutiny

The framework for analyzing sex discrimination claims under the Equal Protection Clause of the Fourteenth Amendment emerged in the 1970s as the women's movement renewed its campaign for equal-citizenship rights. A litigation campaign building on these developments persuaded a plurality of the Court to join an opinion that would have extended the strict scrutiny framework generally applied to race discrimination claims to sex discrimination claims as well.[30] Soon thereafter a majority of the Court embraced a somewhat different standard of review that is now generally referred to as "intermediate scrutiny."

In *Craig v. Boren*, the Court adopted this intermediate scrutiny framework when it held that the state cannot regulate on the basis of sex, unless it can show that its sexually discriminatory means are "substantially related" to an "important" government purpose.[31] (Modern equal protection doctrine holds that the state cannot regulate on the basis of race unless the state can show that its racially discriminatory means are "necessary" to achieve a "compelling" government purpose.") The more permissive standard the Court articulated in *Craig* gives government more latitude to consider sex than race in the ways it designs and administers social policy.

Two reasons are most commonly given for the difference in equal protection standards. First, the more permissive standard for sex discrimination expresses the understanding that concerns about sex discrimination are not central to the original purpose of the Fourteenth Amendment in the way that concerns about race discrimination are. Second, the more permissive standard is said to express the judgment that sex differentiation is not always invidious in the way that racial differentiation is generally assumed to be.

Comparing Equal Protection Cases Concerning Race and Sex Discrimination

Yet, since the 1970s, the Court, with some hesitation and some very important exceptions, has applied the Equal Protection Clause to sex-based state action in terms that often seem to approach the rigor of its race discrimination cases. The Court is suspicious of claims that the state should take the sex of citizens into account in fashioning social policy – whether such claims are rooted in empirical generalizations about differences between men and

---

[30] See *Frontiero v. Richardson supra* note 12.
[31] *Craig v. Boren*, 429 U.S. 190, 197 (1976), striking down a state law that established a drinking age of twenty-one for men and eighteen for women for low-alcohol beer.

women, or normative claims about appropriate roles for men and women. Since the 1970s, the Court's equal protection cases have rejected "'archaic and overbroad' generalizations" about differences between the sexes and "increasingly outdated misconceptions concerning the role of females in the home rather than in the 'marketplace and the world of ideas'... as loose-fitting characterizations incapable of supporting state statutory schemes that were premised on their accuracy."[32]

Modern equal protection law thus views sex distinctions in public law as presumptively unconstitutional. In numerous cases – many of them brought by *male* plaintiffs complaining of sex discrimination – the Court has invalidated a variety of laws that drew distinctions on the basis of sex. Many of these statutes employed sex-specific rules to regulate aspects of marriage and family life, including control over marital property,[33] duty to pay alimony,[34] the administration of estates,[35] the duration of a parent's obligation to support children,[36] as well as a variety of laws distributing welfare, pension, and survivor benefits.[37] The Court also has struck down sex-based restrictions on jury service,[38] employment,[39] and education. Note that, in all these cases, the Court required only that the state eliminate sex-distinctions from the law, leaving to the state's discretion all other aspects of the policy in question. Because of these constitutional rulings, most law regulating family relationships is now written in gender-neutral language[40] – with the exceedingly

---

[32] Ibid., at 198–9.

[33] See *Kirchberg v. Feenstra*, 450 U.S. 455 (1981), striking down a state statute that gave the husband, as "head and master" of marital property, the right to dispose of it unilaterally.

[34] See *Orr v. Orr*, 440 U.S. 268 (1979), invalidating a state statute that required husbands, but not wives, to pay alimony upon divorce.

[35] See *Reed v. Reed*, 404 U.S. 71 (1971), striking down a state statute that preferred males over females in appointing the administrator of a deceased's estate.

[36] See *Stanton v. Stanton*, 421 U.S. 7 (1975), striking down a state statute that defined the age of majority as twenty-one for males but eighteen for females.

[37] See, e.g., *Heckler v. Mathews*, 465 U.S. 728 (1984), upholding a federal law that allowed the beneficiaries of an invalidated sex-based retirement program to continue to receive benefits; *Califano v. Westcott*, 443 U.S. 76 (1979), striking down a federal law that provided welfare benefits to families with unemployed fathers, but not to those with unemployed mothers; and *Weinberger v. Wiesenfeld*, 420 U.S. 636 (1975), striking down a federal law that allowed widows, but not widowers, to collect certain Social Security benefits.

[38] See *J.E.B. v. Alabama* ex rel. *T.B.*, 511 U.S. 127 (1994), holding that the state may not use its peremptory challenges to juror selections in a sexually discriminatory manner; and *Taylor v. Louisiana*, 419 U.S. 522 (1975), striking down a state statute that excluded women from jury service unless they filed a written declaration seeking to serve.

[39] See *Davis v. Passman*, 442 U.S. 228 (1979), holding that an administrative assistant to a federal official, fired because she was female, had a cause of action against her employer.

[40] See Reva B. Siegel, "'The Rule of Love': Wife Beating as Prerogative and Privacy" (1996) 105 *Yale Law Journal* 2117 at 2188–96, tracing this shift in the language of family law, with special attention to questions concerning the regulation of domestic violence; see also Herma Hill Kay, "From the Second Sex to the Joint Venture: An Overview of Rights and Family Law in the United States during the Twentieth Century" (2000) 88 *California Law*

important exception of laws defining marriage as a relation between a man and a woman.[41]

We might pause and consider the education cases for a moment, as they demonstrate similarities and differences in the Court's approach to matters of race and sex discrimination.

Modern equal protection doctrine originates in cases prohibiting racial segregation in public education, and the first equal protection cases striking down sex-based state action grew out of an analogy between race and sex discrimination. One would therefore assume that the Court would have prohibited sex segregation in education as it has prohibited racial segregation in education. But the Court has not dealt with the question in such straightforward terms.

In the 1970s, the Court affirmed without opinion a lower court decision that allowed a public high school, which prepared students for college, to operate on a sex segregated basis, so long as the two schools offered equal educational benefits and opportunities to girls and boys.[42] A dissenting judge questioned how "separate but equal" could be unconstitutional in matters of race, but constitutional in matters of sex.[43] While the *Vorcheimer* case has been questioned, it has never been overruled, and continues to provide some authority allowing the state to segregate the sexes in certain social settings so long as it provides equal resources to the segregated institutions. For

Review 2017, surveying legislative and constitutional reforms affecting family law during the twentieth century.

[41] To date, no federal court, at any level, has ruled that the Equal Protection Clause prohibits the state from taking sex into account in the way it defines the marriage relationship. However, a few state courts have edged toward recognizing a right to marry a partner of the same sex as a matter of state constitutional law, and Vermont law mandates recognition of same-sex civil unions. See William N. Eskridge, Jr., "Equality Practice: Liberal Reflections on the Jurisprudence of Civil Unions" (2001) 64 *Albany Law Review* 853 at 874, discussing Hawaii, Alaska, and Vermont rulings, and the forms of backlash they precipitated. Reacting to the possibility that a state court might declare, under its own state constitution, that the use of sex to define, and restrict access to, the marriage relation, was unconstitutional, the U.S. Congress recently adopted a law defining marriage as a union between a man and a woman for purposes of all federal laws and programs. See, e.g., *Defense of Marriage Act*, Pub. L. No. 104–199, 110 Stat. 2419 (codified as amended at 1 U.S.C. s. 7, 28 U.S.C. s. 1738C (1996)). Many states have now enacted similar laws.

For more information regarding gay civil rights in the marriage context, see Lambda Legal Defense Fund, *The Marriage Project*, online: Lambda Legal Defense Fund <lambdalegal.org/cgi-bin/iowa/issues/> (date accessed July 28, 2003), providing links to information on all state marriage initiatives, legislation, constitutional amendments, and pro-gay initiatives.

[42] See *Vorchheimer v. School District*, 532 F.2d 880 (3d Cir. 1976), *aff'd by an equally divided court*, 430 U.S. 703 (1977).

[43] Ibid., at 888–889 (Gibbons, J., dissenting). "Separate but equal" was the framework in which the Court upheld racial segregation under the Fourteenth Amendment's equal protection clause in the decades after the Civil War, until repudiating the doctrine in *Brown v. Board of Education, supra* note 18.

example, lower courts seem to have accepted application of the "separate but equal" principle to school sponsored sports,[44] – and, outside the educational setting, in certain contexts, such as the administration of prisons.[45]

But sex-segregated arrangements, even when there are parallel institutions with nominally equal resources, remain suspect for this Court. The Supreme Court has twice now declared sex-segregated admissions policies in public universities to be unconstitutional, most recently in 1996, in the case of *United States v. Virginia*.[46]

In *United States v. Virginia*, the Court required a state military academy that for several hundred years had only enrolled men to admit women. While a lower federal court had allowed the school to admit women to a new "sister" school that would have trained women for leadership in a style suited to women's distinctive needs and temperament, the Supreme Court ruled that this remedy was constitutionally inadequate. It held that state's offer to admit women to a separate military academy for women would deny women applicants equal access to the distinctive learning experience and alumni network of the state's premier military academy.[47] Instead, the Court ordered the state to make minor accommodations in the school's housing and physical training programs so that women could participate in the military academy on substantially the same terms as men.[48]

In the *Virginia* case, the Court thus rejected a separate-but-equal framework in a setting where it had been elaborated in terms that emphasized

---

[44] See, e.g., *O'Connor v. Board of Education*, 645 F.2d 578, 581 (7th Cir. 1981): "'Separate but equal' teams have received endorsement in many circuits, including this one." Federal civil rights law has extended the application of equality norms to private as well as public institutions through *Title IX of the Education Amendments of 1972*, 20 U.S.C. s. 1681 (1994), which requires gender equity in educational programs and activities that receive federal funding. Title IX, rather than equal protection law, has provided the major impetus for change in educational sports programming. See generally Deborah Brake, "The Struggle for Sex Equality in Sport and the Theory Behind Title IX" (2000–2001) 34 *University of Michigan Journal of Law Reform* 13 at 15–16.

[45] Courts have allowed sex segregation of prisons to persist under modern interpretations of the Equal Protection Clause, so long as the state provides prisoners substantially equivalent conditions and resources – a flexible standard that in fact allows for considerable variance in treatment. See, e.g., *Batton v. North Carolina*, 501 F. Supp. 1173, 1176 (E.D.N.C. 1980), discussing the "parity of treatment" standard that courts have applied to prisons and observing that it is difficult to reconcile with sex discrimination law in other constitutional contexts.

[46] 518 U.S. 515 (1996), holding that the state could not exclude women from its citizen-soldier program at the Virginia Military Institute; see also *Mississippi Univ. for Women v. Hogan*, 458 U.S. 718 (1982), holding that the state could not exclude men from a nursing school.

[47] *United States v. Virginia*, supra note 46 at 547–1, finding the proposed sister school inferior in terms of faculty, course offerings, facilities, and prestige.

[48] Ibid., at 550: "Admitting women to VMI would undoubtedly require alterations necessary to afford members of each sex privacy from the other sex in living arrangements, and to adjust aspects of the physical training programs."

differences between men and women,[49] and instead endorsed the goal of integrating women into the formerly all-male institution, in terms that assumed that women would assimilate to the norms and practices of that institution, in most if not all respects.

The Court's opinion in the *Virginia* case is widely regarded as signaling the Court's commitment to a more rigorous standard of scrutiny in sex discrimination cases. The opinion was authored by Justice Ruth Bader Ginsburg, who was appointed to serve as the second woman on the United States Supreme Court after a career that included litigating the first constitutional sex discrimination cases.[50] But if the *Virginia* case approaches sex segregation with a deep, historically informed skepticism, it does not take the stance that all sex segregation in education is constitutionally impermissible.

Instead, in a remarkable passage, the *Virginia* opinion restates the framework for evaluating the constitutionality of sex-based state action: "Sex classifications may be used to compensate women 'for particular economic disabilities [they have] suffered,' to 'promote equal employment opportunity,' to advance full development of the talent and capacities of our Nation's people. But such classifications may not be used, as they once were, to create or perpetuate the legal, social, and economic inferiority of women."[51] As *Virginia* explains the "intermediate scrutiny" standard (which allows the state to employ sex-based modes of regulation when the discrimination is "substantially related to an important governmental end"), the opinion is not merely interested in discrimination as a problem concerning means-ends rationality (are the state's discriminatory means sufficiently related to the achievement of some important governmental end?). Instead, this passage suggests that intermediate scrutiny is fundamentally concerned with questions of subordination: Sex-based state action offends the Equal Protection Clause in those circumstances where it perpetuates the status inferiority of women.

---

[49] In rejecting Virginia's proposal to create a separate school for women, the Court observed, ibid.: "Generalizations about 'the way women are,' estimates of what is appropriate for most women, no longer justify denying opportunity to women whose talent and capacity place them outside the average description. Notably, Virginia never asserted that VMI's method of education suits most men."

[50] The president with the advice and consent of the Senate appoints federal judges. At present, two of the nine Supreme Court Justices are women: Sandra Day O'Connor, the first appointee in 1981, and Ruth Bader Ginsburg appointed in 1993. Excluding the Supreme Court there are 1,612 Federal judges; 332 (20.6 percent) are women, up from 154 (9.5 percent) in 1997. For further detail, including race and ethnicity, see Gender Gap in Government, online: GenderGap.com<http://www.gendergap.com/governme.htm> (date accessed: July 28, 2003), citing Employee Relations Office, U.S. Courts, "The Judiciary Fair Employment Practices Report, Fiscal [sic] Year 1999 and the Federal Judicial Center, History Office, as of Feb. 24, 1997."

[51] "The Judiciary Fair Employment Practices Report," ibid., at 533–4.

This new expression of the intermediate scrutiny standard represents a potentially important shift of emphasis in the sex discrimination case law, although it by no means promises greater clarity in the standard's application. In education and many other social spheres, there is, of course, much disagreement about the kinds of institutions and practices that perpetuate the status inferiority of women. Presumably for this reason, the Court's opinion in *United States v. Virginia* postpones addressing in any detail the question of when sex segregation in education offends the Constitution. The opinion acknowledges that some forms of sex-segregated education might actually break down traditional forms of status inequality between the sexes.[52] And the opinion suggests that the Court might find such sex-specific educational programming constitutional, if it were offered on an equal basis to men and women.[53] To summarize, the Virginia Military Institute case does not repudiate sex segregation in public education, but expresses the understanding that the practice can only be constitutional if it does not perpetuate historic forms of status inequality between men and women, and if the program is designed in such a way as to provide equality of opportunity to members of both sexes.[54]

Cases Where the Court Allows Sex-Differentiated Regulation

The Court's most recent education decision thus offers a forceful expression of the view that the primary question for equal protection law is determining whether sex-based state action perpetuates historic forms of status inequality between the sexes. But it is unclear how far the Court's restatement of the intermediate scrutiny standard in *Virginia* will guide the application of equal protection doctrine outside the education context. I now consider several areas where the Court has protected sex-based regulation from constitutional reform in the last several decades.

Despite the Court's genuine skepticism about the rationality or fairness of openly sex-based rules in most areas of social life, there are certain domains where the Court simply reverts to the understanding that informed constitutional law before the 1970s. In matters concerning conscription for military service,[55] certain aspects of rape law,[56] and matters concerning pregnancy

---

[52] See *United States v. Virginia*, *supra* note 46 at 533–4, acknowledging that "it is the mission of some single-sex schools 'to dissipate,' rather than perpetuate, traditional gender classifications."

[53] Ibid.: "We do not question the State's prerogative evenhandedly to support diverse educational opportunities."

[54] See Tod Christopher Gurney, "Comment: The Aftermath of the Virginia Military Institute Decision: Will Single-Gender Education Survive?" (1998) 38 *Santa Clara Law Review* 1183.

[55] See *Rostker v. Goldberg*, 453 U.S. 57 (1981), upholding a federal statute that registered only men for the military draft.

[56] *Michael M. v. Superior Court*, 450 U.S. 464, 471 (1981).

and reproduction,[57] the Court continues to treat sex as a "real" and "relevant" difference that the state may constitutionally consider in making social policy.[58]

Military Service. Although the U.S. military has dramatically altered the ways in which it allows women to serve in the armed forces over the last several decades, constitutional law has played no direct role in bringing about these changes. In *Rostker v. Goldberg*,[59] decided in 1981, the Court allowed the U.S. Congress to require that only men must register for military draft or conscription purposes. The Court's decision assumed, without discussion, that women could be constitutionally excluded from serving in combat positions in the armed services, and then reasoned that Congress could limit conscription for military service to those who would be eligible to serve in combat.[60]

The U.S. military has not yet allowed women to serve in combat, but, since the time of the *Rostker* decision, it has opened up a vast array of positions to women which were once closed to them, and has spent considerable resources recruiting women to serve in a "volunteer" army. Beginning in the 1990s, Congress repealed several statutes that restricted women's service in the Air Force and Navy, and the Secretary of Defense modified the rules governing women's eligibility to serve in a variety of combat-related positions.[61] Given women's growing eligibility to serve in military roles in and outside of the zone of combat, the reasoning of the *Rostker* opinion no longer seems credible as a justification for restricting conscription for military service to men. At the same time, it is entirely unclear how the Court would handle questions concerning the constitutionality of sex distinctions in military policy today. The Court has thus far refused to take a leadership role in integrating the military, leaving it to the political branches to experiment with how far women's participation in the military might be integrated with men's. Nor is it clear that judicial intervention in this process would accelerate the rate of change.

Public acceptance of women's participation in military life has in fact changed greatly over the last decade, but these changes have emerged from a

---

[57] See *Geduldig v. Aiello*, 417 U.S. 484 (1974,) upholding a state insurance program that did not cover pregnancy.

[58] See generally Wendy W. Williams, "The Equality Crisis: Some Reflections on Culture, Courts, and Feminism" (1992) 14 *Women's Rights Law Reporter* 151.

[59] *Rostker v. Goldberg, supra* note 55.

[60] Ibid. at 79: "The fact that Congress and the Executive have decided that women should not serve in combat fully justifies Congress in not authorizing their registration, since the purpose of the registration is to develop a pool of potential combat troops."

[61] See Leslie Ann Rowley, "Comment: Gender Discrimination and the Military Selective Service Act: Would the MSSA Pass Constitutional Muster Today?" (1997) 36 *Duquesne Law Review* 171.

cautiously conducted public experiment in which women volunteers have undertaken roles formally restricted to men, allowing women who are averse – for all manner of reasons – to military service to avoid it. If the Court were to rule that Congress could no longer exempt women from a draft, a much larger group of women would potentially be obliged to serve in newly opened military positions, and public support for eliminating gender-restrictions on military service might potentially diminish. In recent decades, while the government allowed women to perform an increasing number of military roles, no one initiated litigation challenging the gendered terms of this public experiment – even though the recent changes in military policy have completely undermined the premises of the Court's original decision in *Rostker*. This changed in 2003, when a group of men and women filed suit challenging the constitutionality of a male-only registration requirement for a male-only draft.[62] (The government continues to require draft registration, even though the military is presently organized on an all-volunteer basis.)

Military policy is one area where the Supreme Court has openly tolerated sex-based regulation; matters concerning childbearing are another. Currently, equal protection law is riddled with contradictions in its approach to pregnancy.

State Regulation of Pregnancy. Early on, in the notorious case of *Geduldig v. Aiello*,[63] the Court simply declared that, for equal protection purposes, state action which distinguishes persons on the basis of pregnancy does not classify on the basis of sex. To justify this somewhat startling claim, the Court reasoned that laws regulating pregnancy divide the world into two groups: pregnant women and nonpregnant persons. Because the latter group includes women as well as men, the Court concluded that state policies regulating pregnancy are not sex-based and should not receive heightened scrutiny under the equal protection clause, however unequally such policies may distribute opportunities between women and men.[64] As a practical matter, *Geduldig* frees state regulation of the pregnant woman's conduct – in matters of abortion or maternity leave – from equal protection scrutiny. Although *Geduldig* was decided early in the development of constitutional sex discrimination doctrine, in 1993 the Court reaffirmed its reasoning in

---

[62] See 265 F. Supp. 2d 130 (2003).

[63] *Geduldig v. Aiello, supra* note 57.

[64] Ibid., at 496: "The lack of identity between the excluded disability [pregnancy] and gender as such under this insurance becomes clear upon the most cursory analysis. The program divides potential recipients into two groups – pregnant women and nonpregnant persons. While the first group is exclusively female, the second includes members of both sexes."

the course of interpreting a civil rights statute that had been invoked in a dispute arising out of protests at an abortion clinic.[65]

It is worth noting, however, that Congress has rejected the Court's reasoning about pregnancy outside the context of constitutional law, in the federal statute governing employment discrimination. That statute applies the equal treatment model to pregnancy by treating pregnancy as a potential work disability. It provides that distinctions on the basis of pregnancy are distinctions on the basis of sex, and requires an employer to treat pregnant employees the same as the employer treats other employees who are similar in their ability or inability to work.[66] Under the federal employment discrimination statute employers cannot single out pregnant workers for adverse treatment, but they are generally not required to accommodate pregnant employees more than they accommodate other workers suffering temporary disabilities.[67]

Reproductive Difference as a Justification for Other Forms of Sex-Specific Regulation: the Case of Rape Law. As we have seen, the Court has refused to treat regulation directed at pregnant women as sex-based state action that should trigger heightened equal protection scrutiny. The Court can thus declare that women are protected against sex discrimination by the state while reasoning in a legal framework that does not constrain state action directed at women who are pregnant. The formal logic the Court has invoked to justify this restriction on antidiscrimination law is not terribly persuasive; but the restrictions do seem to conform with the widespread intuition that pregnancy is an important sex difference that can justify differential treatment of the sexes.

From time to time, the Court has openly voiced this view of the matter. While the Court has rejected most justifications for state policies that

---

[65] See *Bray v. Alexandria Women's Health*, 506 U.S. 263, 270–71 (1993), reaffirming *Geduldig*, and holding that abortion protesters obstructing access to a clinic were not targeting women as a class.

[66] See 42 U.S.C. s. 2000e(k) (1994):

The terms "because of sex" or "on the basis of sex" include, but are not limited to, because of or on the basis of pregnancy, childbirth, or related medical conditions; and women affected by pregnancy, childbirth, or related medical conditions shall be treated the same for all employment-related purposes . . . as other persons not so affected but similar in their ability or inability to work. . . .

[67] See *International Union, United Automobile Workers of Am. v. Johnson Controls*, 499 U.S. 187 (1991), prohibiting a company from excluding all potentially fertile women from jobs involving lead exposure; and *California Fed. Sav. & Loan Ass'n v. Guerra*, 479 U.S. 272 (1987), holding that federal law does not prohibit the state from enacting *greater* protections for pregnant women than for other disabled workers. A more recent federal law allows some employees to take up to 12 weeks of unpaid leave to care for a newborn child, after adopting a child, or to care for an ill family member. See *Family and Medical Leave Act of 1993*, 29 U.S.C. s.s. 2601–2654 (1994).

distinguish between men and women, in several of its cases the Court has accepted the argument that the state can treat men and women (who are not pregnant) differently because the sexes are differently situated with respect to matters of reproduction. In a body of case law that rejects most justifications for openly sex-based modes of regulation, pregnancy still counts as a "real" difference between the sexes that can justify state action that openly discriminates between the sexes.

For example, during the 1980s, when the Court upheld a sex-based "statutory rape" law under the Equal Protection Clause, it reasoned that the state could punish men for engaging in sex with women who were under the legal age of consent, as a reasonable means of preventing teen pregnancy.[68] The pregnancy-prevention rationale seems to have been invented to supply a constitutional basis for upholding a sex-based criminal law that had long been justified in terms of conventional sexual morality (protecting female virginity). Lower courts have invoked the pregnancy-prevention rationale to uphold against equal protection challenge laws that define and criminalize rape on a sex-specific basis.[69]

More recently, the Court has invoked the fact of reproductive difference between the sexes to uphold against equal protection challenge laws that impose different rules for determining the citizenship status of children born abroad and out of wedlock to American men and women. The Court reasoned that the government could legitimately require children born abroad and out of wedlock to American men to go through more steps to establish citizenship than it imposed on children born abroad and out of wedlock to American women, on the grounds that "fathers and mothers are not similarly situated with regard to the proof of biological parenthood" or even awareness of the parental relationship.[70] Critics of the statutory scheme argued that the gender-differentiated rules for determining citizenship status reflected historically entrenched "double standards" in gender roles concerning parental responsibility for out of wedlock births.[71] But the Court insisted that the gender-differentiated standard reflected facts of nature that the government could legitimately take into account:

To fail to acknowledge even our most basic biological differences – such as the fact that the mother must be present at birth but the father need not be – risks making the guarantee of equal protection superficial, and so disserving it. Mechanistic

---

[68] *Michael M. v. Superior Court, supra* note 56 at 471.

[69] See, e.g., *Liberta v. Kelly*, 839 F.2d 77 (2d Cir. 1988), upholding a state statute that provided that only men could be convicted of rape; and *Country v. Parratt*, 684 F.2d 588 (8th Cir. 1982) (same).

[70] *Tuan Ahn Nguyen v. Immigration and Naturalization Service*, 121 S.Ct. 2053, 2055 (2001).

[71] See Kristin Collins, "Note: When Fathers' Rights are Mothers' Duties: The Failure of Equal Protection in *Miller v. Albright*" (2000) 109 *Yale Law Journal* 1669, analysis of traditional gender understandings informing the differential treatment of children born out-of-wedlock, overseas, to American mothers and fathers.

classification of all our differences as stereotypes would operate to obscure those misconceptions and prejudices that are real. The distinction embodied in the statutory scheme here is not marked by misconception and prejudice, nor does it show disrespect for either class. The difference between men and women in relation to the birth process is a real one, and the principle of equal protection does not forbid Congress to address the problem at hand in a manner specific to each gender.[72]

There is a long tradition of invoking differences in male and female reproductive physiology to justify differential treatment of the sexes,[73] and we might simply read equal protection law as carrying forward this time-honored tradition. Yet, as the above-quoted passage suggests, if this mode of justification remains persuasive, it is also highly contested. The argument has proven persuasive in only a very few of the thirty sex discrimination cases the Court has decided under the Equal Protection Clause to date. Sometimes claims about reproductive difference are powerful enough to legitimate policies that treat the sexes differently – especially when such policies perpetuate time-honored gender conventions in matters involving the regulation of sexual relations. But more often such arguments falter before the weight of the presumption that the Constitution protects a sphere of citizenship in which men and women are entitled to face each other as equal in position and prerogative.

CONSTITUTIONAL PROTECTIONS FOR ABORTION AND CONTRACEPTION AS RIGHTS OF PRIVACY

Although the Court's equal protection cases impose no significant constraints on state regulation of pregnancy,[74] there is another body of constitutional case law that does protect women's right to make decisions concerning childbearing. Under the U.S. Constitution, women have a right to make decisions about contraception and abortion without undue state interference, and this right is protected as a right of privacy. The privacy right is often criticized, not only on familiar moral and religious grounds, but for jurisprudential reasons as well. As critics of the Court's privacy decisions have repeatedly emphasized, there is no constitutionally enumerated "right to privacy." (The Court rests the privacy right on the Fourteenth Amendment's guarantee that

---

[72] *Tuan Anh Nguyen v. Immigration and Naturalization Service, supra* note 70 at 2066. See *Miller v. Albright*, 523 U.S. 420, 433–34 (1998), (plurality opinion) justifying the sex distinctions in the federal immigration statute by linking them to the different male and female roles in reproduction.

[73] See Reva B. Siegel, "Reasoning from the Body: A Historical Perspective on Abortion Regulation and Questions of Equal Protection" (1992) 44 *Stanford Law Review* 261.

[74] A small body of fundamental rights decisions under the equal protection clause provides some recognition of a right to sexual autonomy; see *Skinner v. Oklahoma* ex rel. *Williamson, supra* note 17.

no state shall "deprive any person of life, liberty, or property, without due process of law.")

The first of the modern privacy decisions that extended constitutional protection to decisions concerning reproduction is *Griswold v. Connecticut*,[75] a case in which the Court ruled that a state could not criminalize the use of contraceptive devices. The Court reasoned that while the United States Constitution did not expressly protect a right of privacy, "specific guarantees in the Bill of Rights have penumbras, formed by emanations from those guarantees that help give them life and substance," and that "[v]arious guarantees create zones of privacy."[76] The Court viewed the law criminalizing the use of contraceptives as impermissibly invading the privacy of the marriage relationship.[77] As the Court saw it, this right of privacy was older than the Constitution, and foundational to it.[78] The Court has never restricted the constitutional right of privacy to married persons.[79] For nearly two decades it endeavored to limit the right so that it protected decisions concerning heterosexual sexual and reproductive activity, while excluding same-sex relations; but recently the Court has reversed itself and ruled that the privacy right extended to same-sex intimate relations as well.[80]

Roe and the Early Abortion Decisions

In *Roe v. Wade*,[81] the Court ruled that the right of privacy "is broad enough to encompass a woman's decision whether or not to terminate her pregnancy."[82] The Court specifically rejected the claim that "the fetus is a 'person' within the language and meaning of the Fourteenth Amendment."[83] And, after surveying the long-standing theological, philosophical, and scientific debates about the question of when life begins, and observing the law's historic tendency to regulate born persons, the Court ruled that states could

[75] 381 U.S. 479 (1965).
[76] Ibid., at 484.
[77] Ibid., at 485–6.
[78] Ibid., at 486.
[79] See *Eisenstadt v. Baird*, 405 U.S. 438 (1972).
[80] *Bowers v. Hardwick*, 478 U.S. 186 (1986), holding the right of privacy does not protect an individual against criminal prosecution for engaging in sodomy with a person of the same sex, was overruled in *Lawrence v. Texas*, 123 S.Ct. 2472 (2003), a case involving a statute that criminalized same-sex sodomy only. At 2484, the Court extended constitutional protection to "two adults who, with full and mutual consent from each other, engaged in sexual practices common to a homosexual lifestyle," observing that "[t]he petitioners are entitled to respect for their private lives." The decision, while not rooted in the Equal Protection Clause of the Fourteenth Amendment, plainly drew on equality values, and was understood by many to bring the Court and the nation one step closer to confronting constitutional questions concerning same-sex marriage.
[81] 410 U.S. 113 (1973).
[82] Ibid., at 153.
[83] Ibid., at 156.

not adopt a theory of life that would "override the rights of the pregnant woman that are at stake."[84]

The Court did not, however, give women making decisions about abortion immunity from state regulation. Although the Court did extend "strict scrutiny" to state action interfering with abortion decisions, it designed the framework of review in a fashion that recognized both the pregnant woman's interest in making decisions about abortion free from state interference, and the state's interest in regulating her conduct. *Roe* balances these countervailing interests in a "trimester framework" that gives the state more freedom to regulate as the pregnancy progresses. The state is not allowed to restrict abortion in the interest of protecting "potential life" until the end of the second trimester, at the point at which the fetus is "viable" (capable of living outside the mother's womb).[85]

In the years after *Roe*, no doubt in part because of the controversy steadily gathering around *Roe*,[86] the Court ruled that government had no duty to fund abortions, even when it paid for the childbirth expenses of pregnant women.[87] As the Court saw it, if the state had not interposed the obstacle to an abortion, it was not constitutionally obliged to remove it.

By the 1980s, *Roe* was engulfed in legal and political controversy, and the decision appeared increasingly vulnerable to reversal. An administration openly hostile to *Roe* was elected, and announced its commitment to select Supreme Court justices from the growing body of jurists and scholars who questioned the constitutional basis of the privacy right on which *Roe* rested.[88] As jurisprudential criticism of the *Roe* decision mounted, legal academics began to explore alternative constitutional foundations for the abortion right. Drawing on a variety disciplinary and analytical frameworks, these scholars offered a range of reasons why the abortion right should be understood as resting on values of equality as well as privacy.[89] These impassioned arguments, for and against the *Roe* decision, left their impress on the Court.

Reframing the Abortion Right: *Casey*, Sex Equality, and Unborn Life

In 1992, in the case of *Planned Parenthood of Southeastern Pennsylvania v. Casey*,[90] the Court reaffirmed, while significantly reformulating, constitutional protections for the abortion right. Justice Sandra Day O'Connor, the

---

[84] *Roe v. Wade, supra* note 81 at 162.

[85] Ibid., at 163–4.

[86] See David, J. Garrow, "Abortion before and after Roe v. Wade: An Historical Perspective" (1999) 62 *Albany Law Review* 833.

[87] See *Maher v. Roe*, 432 U.S. 464 (1977); and *Harris v. McRae*, 448 U.S. 297 (1980).

[88] See Laurence H. Tribe, *Abortion: The Clash of Absolutes* (New York: Norton, 1992), at 17–21.

[89] For an overview of these arguments, see Reva B. Siegel, "Abortion As a Sex Equality Right: Its Basis in Feminist Theory" in Martha Fineman and Isabel Karpin, eds., *Mothers in Law: Feminist Theory and the Legal Regulation of Motherhood* (New York: Columbia University Press, 1995); see also Reva B. Siegel, "Reasoning from the Body," *supra* note 73.

[90] 505 U.S. 833 (1992).

first woman ever appointed to the United States Supreme Court and a long time critic of the *Roe* decision, played a pivotal role in this reaffirmation and reformulation of the *Roe* framework.

The *Casey* decision restates the woman's privacy interest in making decisions about whether to terminate a pregnancy and the state's interest in deterring her from doing so, and, quite arguably, gives more respectful expression to each. In *Casey*, the Court identified constitutional reasons for protecting a woman's privacy right to make decisions about childbearing that were not discussed in *Roe*. The Court observed that the state was obliged to respect a pregnant woman's decisions about abortion because her "suffering is too intimate and personal for the State to insist... upon its own vision of the woman's role, however dominant that vision has been in the course of our history and our culture. The destiny of the woman must be shaped to a large extent on her own conception of her spiritual imperatives and her place in society."[91] The Court thus announced that laws prohibiting abortion offend the Constitution because they use the power of the state to impose traditional sex roles on women.

At the same time the Court gave greater weight and regulatory ambit to the state's interest in protecting unborn life. *Roe*'s trimester framework prohibited fetal-protective restrictions on abortion prior to the point of fetal viability; *Casey* explicitly repudiates the trimester framework. The Court announced that it would allow states to regulate abortion in furtherance of protecting unborn life throughout the pregnancy, so long as such regulation did not impose undue burdens on women's constitutional right to make decisions about terminating a pregnancy prior to the point of fetal viability. As the Court reasoned, regulation that would support "thoughtful and informed" deliberation about the abortion decision was consistent with exercise of the privacy right.[92]

In the place of the trimester framework, *Casey* adopted a new framework for reconciling a woman's privacy right in making decisions about abortion and the state's interest in deterring her. Only some forms of fetal-protective regulation directed at a pregnant woman in the period before viability were unconstitutional: "The fact that a law which serves a valid purpose, one not designed to strike at the right itself, has the incidental effect of making it more difficult or more expensive to procure an abortion cannot be enough to invalidate it. Only where state regulation imposes an undue burden on a

---

[91] Ibid., at 852.
[92] Ibid., at 872–3:

> Even in the earliest stages of pregnancy, the State may enact rules and regulations designed to encourage her to know that there are philosophic and social arguments of great weight that can be brought to bear in favor of continuing the pregnancy to full term and that there are procedures and institutions to allow adoption of unwanted children as well as a certain degree of state assistance if the mother chooses to raise the child herself.

woman's ability to make this decision does the power of the State reach into the heart of the liberty protected by the Due Process Clause."[93]

The tensions in this new "undue burden" framework were immediately apparent as *Casey* applied the standard to two different provisions of the Pennsylvania statute challenged in the case.

The Court upheld a provision of the statute that required pregnant women to wait twenty-four hours before proceeding with an abortion, on the theory that the delay was reasonably calculated to prompt deliberation about the decision. It so ruled, even in the face of evidence that the statutorily imposed delay could function as a huge practical impediment to certain women who had to travel long distances to reach an abortion provider.[94] At the same time, the Court struck down a provision of the Pennsylvania statute that required a married woman to notify her husband before obtaining an abortion. Here the Court seemed to give far more weight to concerns that the statutory requirement might interact with the practical exigencies of women's lives in such a way as to deter many from obtaining abortions. Specifically, the Court was concerned that, in conflict-ridden marriages where women were subject to domestic violence, forcing women to inform their husbands about an abortion might deter them from "procuring an abortion as surely as if the Commonwealth had outlawed abortion in all cases."[95] The Court ruled that the state lacked authority to constrain women's choices this way.

The Court's differential application of the undue burden standard in *Casey* seems best explained by concerns that the standard itself does not explicitly address. For the Court, the spousal notice provision presented sex equality concerns that the twenty-four-hour waiting period did not. As the Court expressed these concerns, the notice requirement "give[s] to a man the kind of dominion over his wife that parents exercise over their children"[96] and thus reflects a "common-law understanding of a woman's role within the family," harkening back to a time when "'a woman had no legal existence separate from her husband, who was regarded as her head and representative in the social state....'"[97] "These views," the Court observed, "are no longer consistent with our understanding of the family, the individual, or the Constitution."[98] These passages of the opinion echo *Casey*'s initial articulation of the privacy right as protecting women's choices about whether to assume the maternal role.

Justice Blackmun, who authored *Roe*, endorsed the gender-conscious reasoning of the *Casey* decision, and drew upon it to develop an alternative

---

[93] Ibid., at 874.
[94] Ibid., at 885–6.
[95] Ibid., at 894.
[96] Ibid., at 898.
[97] Ibid., at 897 (quoting *Bradwell v. Illinois*, *supra* note 3, Bradley, J., concurring).
[98] Ibid.

constitutional framework for the abortion right. In his concurring opinion, Justice Blackmun reasoned that restrictions on abortion offend constitutional guarantees of *equality* as well as privacy. Justice Blackmun's opinion argues that abortion restrictions are gender-biased in impetus and impact:

> The State does not compensate women for their services; instead, it assumes that they owe this duty as a matter of course. This assumption – that women can simply be forced to accept the "natural" status and incidents of motherhood – appears to rest upon a conception of women's role that has triggered the protection of the Equal Protection Clause. The joint opinion recognizes that these assumptions about women's place in society "are no longer consistent with our understanding of the family, the individual, or the Constitution."[99]

Restrictions on abortion do not stem solely from a desire to protect the unborn; they reflect, and enforce, judgments about women's roles. The community's decision to intervene in women's lives is no longer presumptively benign; its decision to compel motherhood is presumptively suspect, one more instance of the sex-role restrictions imposed on women throughout American history.

In sum, *Casey* goes beyond *Roe* in suggesting that women's right to make decisions about childbearing has roots in constitutional values of sex equality as well as privacy. At the same time, *Casey* provides less practical protections for exercise of the abortion right than did *Roe*. The opinion recognizes that the state has an interest in protecting unborn life that it may vindicate by attempting to dissuade a pregnant woman from exercising her right to obtain an abortion. State regulation before the period of fetal viability is permissible so long as it is calculated to inform the pregnant woman's decision-making process, rather than to impede her access to abortion.

CONCLUSION: REFLECTIONS ON HOW MODERN AMERICAN
CONSTITUTIONAL LAW UNDERMINES AND PRESERVES GENDER
INEQUALITY IN THE FAMILY

Evaluating the body of law I have just described is a major undertaking, beyond the scope of this brief presentation. Still, I would like to close by inviting consideration of some of the ways that modern interpretation of the U.S. Constitution has affected family law, in order to illustrate how this body of law works simultaneously to disturb and preserve traditional gender arrangements.

There is no doubt that the body of privacy doctrine the Court developed in the last half of the twentieth century altered the climate in which women make decisions about bearing children. Of course, the Court has only given women partial protection against the variety of pressures that are commonly

[99] Ibid., at 928–9.

brought to bear on the decision to use contraception or abortion, but the Court has nonetheless altered the environment in which women make such decisions, removing a variety of regulatory impediments and, at least in part, altering the social meaning of the decision to avoid motherhood.

What of women who by circumstance or choice, find themselves assuming the role of motherhood? How has modern constitutional law affected their lives? We can begin with the observation that modern equal protection law has forced states to eliminate overt sex-based classifications from the laws that define the rights and obligations of family life. The Constitution has thus required legislatures to make the rights and obligations of marriage symmetrical, if they had not already adopted such reforms of their own accord. There is a powerful symbolic message communicated by such reforms, insofar as they express aspirational norms of reciprocity, mutuality, and equality in marriage. There is another potentially more troubling message communicated by such reforms – that, by eliminating overtly sex-based rights and obligations, the state has in fact conferred equality on women in marriage.

Under pressure of equal protection law, state legislatures have made the rights and obligations of marriage formally gender neutral, but too often this change makes little practical difference in the ways the state structures marriage.[100] Because of entrenched patterns of socialization, there are dramatic differences in the numbers of men and women who engage in violent assault or retire from the market to engage in uncompensated caretaking labor. If equal protection law enabled plaintiffs to challenge "facially neutral" laws regulating gender-salient activities that have a disparate impact on women, equal protection doctrine might prompt a more genuine break with the gender-hierarchical traditions of the Anglo-American common law. Yet for all practical purposes doctrine immunizes family law from constitutional challenge, once sex distinctions in the law are removed.

Of course, changes of this sort need not come from constitutional adjudication alone. Legislative fora may well be better suited to exploring the kinds of reforms that would make family law less onerous for women – especially given the complexity of providing for the diverse social and economic circumstances in which women negotiate their family obligations. Yet, at present, American constitutional law does not encourage legislatures to reform family law in gender-egalitarian directions or to enact legislation that would help alleviate burdens on parents who engage in family caretaking.

Perhaps even more remarkably, the Supreme Court is now interpreting the Constitution to *restrict* the power of the federal government to enact legislation that supports more gender-egalitarian relationships in family life. The Court has imposed restrictions on Congress' power to enact civil rights

[100] See Reva B. Siegel, "'The Rule of Love'," *supra* note 40.

laws, especially in matters affecting family relations,[101] for two kinds of reasons. The Court seeks to enforce constitutional limits on the powers of the federal government (in order to preserve federalism values), and to protect the prerogative of the Court to determine the Constitution's meaning (in order to preserve "separation of powers" values). Thus, when Congress enacted a statute that would give persons a right to be free from gender-motivated violence, the Supreme Court ruled that Congress lacked power to enact the contested provision of the *Violence against Women Act*, either by exercise of its power to regulate commerce or its power to enact legislation enforcing the Fourteenth Amendment.[102] The commerce portions of the decision emphasize limits on Congress' power to regulate the family[103] and the Fourteenth Amendment holding emphasizes limits on Congress' power to regulate private actors.[104] What is perhaps most remarkable about *Morrison* is the unselfconscious manner in which the Court advances traditional privacy-based rationales for limiting government's power to protect women from domestic violence. Notwithstanding the Court's experience in adjudicating sex discrimination claims under the Equal Protection Clause for three decades now, the Court was oblivious to the way that traditional gendered assumptions shaped its federalism analysis in *Morrison*.[105]

More promising was the Court's recent decision in *Nevada Department of Human Resources v. Hibbs*,[106] holding that Congress was authorized to enact a statute alleviating work/family conflicts as an exercise of its power to enforce the Equal Protection Clause of the Fourteenth Amendment. The *Family and Medical Leave Act*[107] only provides a right to twelve weeks of unpaid leave for workers with medical or family-care needs; but it goes well beyond anything the Court's cases interpreting the Equal Protection Clause require. The Court minimized this discrepancy by treating the statute as a remedy for past, judicially cognizable constitutional violations: "By setting

---

[101] See, e.g., Kenneth R. Redden, *Federal Regulation of Family Law* (Charlottesville, VA: Michie, Co., 1982), surveying areas of federal law addressing families. The tenet of federalism in the American constitutional tradition that states retain the right to regulate family life is most likely to be invoked in circumstances where federal regulation disturbs gender-conventional modes of regulation. See, e.g., Jill Elaine Hasday, "Federalism and the Family Reconstructed" (1998) 45 *UCLA Law Review* 1297.

[102] *United States v. Morrison*, 529 U.S. 598 (2000).

[103] Ibid., at 613, 615–16.

[104] Ibid., at 621–5.

[105] See, e.g., Catharine A. MacKinnon, "Disputing Male Sovereignty: On *United States v. Morrison*" (2000) 114 *Harvard Law Review* 135, 145–8; Robert C. Post and Reva B. Siegel, "Equal Protection by Law: Federal Antidiscrimination Legislation after *Morrison* and *Kimel*" (2000) 110 *Yale Law Journal* 441, 525 and n. 344; Judith Resnik, "Categorical Federalism: Jurisdiction, Gender, and the Globe" (2001) 111 *Yale Law Journal* 619 at 630–5; Reva B. Siegel, "She, the People," *supra* note 13 at 1024–30 and 1035–9.

[106] 123 S.Ct. 1972 (2003).

[107] 29 U.S.C. §2612(a)(1)(C) (2000).

a minimum standard of family leave for *all* eligible employees, irrespective of gender, the FMLA attacks the formerly state-sanctioned stereotype that only women are responsible for family caregiving, thereby reducing employers' incentives to engage in discrimination by basing hiring and promotion decisions in stereotypes."[108] The *Hibbs* decision suggests how Congress might use its powers to enact legislation that significantly expands protections afforded by judicially enforceable constitutional rights, if the Court does not constrain it on separation-of-powers or federalism grounds.

For this Court, sex discrimination would seem to be a problem involving group-based distinctions or "classifications" only. Perhaps because the constitutional law of sex discrimination was derived from the constitutional law of race discrimination, judicially crafted equality doctrine does not recognize the family as an institution of special regulatory concern to women. But the *Hibbs* decision suggests that Congress, a more politically responsive body, might once again be able to lead the nation in grappling with questions of sex equality as Americans live them today, in the institutions, practices, and understandings that define everyday life. It remains an open question whether, and in what ways, this Court will allow the Congress to so lead. In the foreseeable future, the development of sex equality law in the United States would seem to depend on it.

Suggested Readings

Books

Katharine T. Bartlett and Angela P. Harris, *Gender and Law: Theory, Doctrine, Commentary*, 2nd ed. (New York: Aspen Law & Business, 2002).

Martha Chamallas, *Introduction to Feminist Legal Theory* (Gaithersburg, MD: Aspen Law & Business, 2003).

Catharine MacKinnon, *Sex Equality* (New York: Foundation Press, 2001).

Articles

Kimberlé Crenshaw, "Demarginalizing the Intersection of Race and Sex: A Black Feminist Critique of Antidiscrimination Doctrine, Feminist Theory, and Antiracist Politics" (1989) *University of Chicago Legal Forum* 139.

David J. Garrow, "Abortion before and after Roe v. Wade: An Historical Perspective" (1999) 62 *Albany Law Review* 833.

Nan D. Hunter, "Panel VI: Fighting Gender and Sexual Orientation Harassment: The Sex Discrimination Argument in Gay Rights Cases" (2000) 9 *Journal of Law and Policy* 397.

Catharine Mackinnon, "Difference and Dominance: On Sex Discrimination" (1987) *Feminism Unmodified: Discourses on Life and Law* (Cambridge, MA: Harvard University Press, 1987) 32.

---

[108] *Nevada Department of Human Resources v. Hibbs*, *supra* note 106 at 1982–3.

Frances Olsen, "Statutory Rape: A Feminist Critique of Rights Analysis" (1984) 63
    Texas Law Review 387.
Robert C. Post & Reva B. Siegel, "Legislative Constitutionalism and Section Five
    Power: Policentric Interpretation of the Family and Medical Leave Act" (2003)
    112 *Yale Law Journal* 1943, 1980–2020.
Reva B. Siegel, "'The Rule of Love': Wife Beating as Prerogative and Privacy" (1996)
    105 *Yale Law Journal* 2117.
Wendy W. Williams, "The Equality Crisis: Some Reflections on Culture, Courts, and
    Feminism" (1992) 14 *Women's Rights Law Reporter* 151.

Index

International Labor Organization, 115,
 265
Irving, Helen, 25, 26, 28, 30–31
Islamist Welfare Party (Turkey), 292,
 293
Israel: 205; abortion, 216–219;
 affirmative action, 215–218;
 Constitution, 206–207, 220–224,
 227; CEDAW, 222; citizenship, 210,
 220, 227; constitutional
 anti-discrimination provisions, 208;
 divorce, 224; domestic violence,
 216–217, 225; education, 208;
 employment, 208–209;
 constitutional equality provisions,
 206, 212; *Equal Rights for Women
 Law*, 208, 222–223; family,
 225–226; formal equality, 209,
 210–213; homosexuality, 213; honor
 killing, 225; marriage, 220–224,
 227; military service, 208–209, 212;
 motherhood, 219; Muslim women
 in, 225–226; political participation,
 209–210; pregnancy, 208; religious
 influence on women, 209–210,
 214–215, 220–221, 224–226, 227;
 religious identity as an obstacle to
 equality, 220–227, 228–229;
 retirement, 211; sexual exploitation,
 217; sexual harassment, 217–218;
 voting rights of women, 208;
 Women's Convention; women's
 status in, 208–210, 228–229

Jaising, Indira, 174, 202

Kahana, Tsvi, 50
Kalanke case, 158
Kantarcioglu, Fulya, 285
Karitnyeri v. Commonwealth,
 42–46
Katz case, 223–224
Kerala v. N.M. Thomas, 179
Keshavanda Bharati, 176
Kharak Signh v. State of Uttar Pradesh,
 193
Kol Ha'am v The Minister of the Interior,
 206
Kome, Penny, 50

Krishna Singh v. Mathura Ahir, 189
Kruger v. Commonwealth, 33–34

L'Heureux-Dube, Claire, 57
Lake, Marlyn, 27, 30–31
Leeth v. Commonwealth, 33, 39,
 70
Lyons' Dame Enid, 27

MacKinnon, Catharine, 2
Macklem, Patrick, 38
Majury, Diane, 54
Malberg, Carre de, 125, 126
Mandela, Nelson, 230
*Maneka Gandhi v. Union of India and
 Anr*, 193
Mardin, Sarif, 278, 280
*Marri Chandra Shekar Rio v. Dean Seth
 G.S.M.*, 180
Marriage: 30, 79, 150, 153, 176, 190,
 230–231; interracial marriage, 62,
 66–67, 227; Recognition of
 Customary Marriage Act (South
 Africa), 230–231; religious
 jurisdiction, 220–224, 252–254
Martin, Sheilah, 52
Mary Sonia Zachariah v. Union of India,
*Masilamani Mudaliar v. Idol of Sri S.S.
 Thirukoil*, 189
Maternity, 256, 260–261; *also see*
 motherhood *and* pregnancy
Maya Devi v. State of Maharashtra,
 185
Mazumdar, Vina, 186
McBain, Dr. John, 39–40
McLachlin, Justice, 57
Media, women in, 272–275
Mercer, Pamela, 81–83, 85
Merve Kavakci, 293
Military: 85, 103, 131, 208–209, 212,
 290–291, 319–320; sexual
 harassment in, 217–218; *Miller*
 decision, 212; *Rostker v. Goldberg*,
 319
Miller Decision, 212
Minerva Mills case, 174
*Minister for Immigration and Ethic Affairs
 v. Teoh*, 36
Mitchell, Dame Rom, 26–27, 37